SPORTS *in* LITERATURE

Ken,
Hope you can use this book.
Best wishes with all
your "good sports"!
Sincere best wishes,

Bruce Emra

11/7/90

SPORTS *in* LITERATURE

Bruce Emra

Northern Highlands Regional High School
Allendale, New Jersey

National Textbook Company
a division of *NTC Publishing Group*

Cover credit

Night Game-'Tis a Bunt signed and dated 1981. Medium: oil on canvas. Copyright Ralph Fasanella. Collection of Eva Fasanella.

Published by National Textbook Company, a division of NTC Publishing Group.
© 1991 by NTC Publishing Group, 4255 West Touhy Avenue,
Lincolnwood (Chicago), Illinois 60646-1975 U.S.A.
Library of Congress Catalog Card Number: 90-60408
Manufactured in the United States of America.

0 1 2 3 4 5 6 7 8 9 VP 9 8 7 6 5 4 3 2 1

Acknowledgments

Interior photo credits
Wide World Photos, Inc., pages 2, 88, 160, 256, 360
Curtis Management Group, page 316

Excerpts

"The Passer" from *Collected Poems, 1932-1961,* by George Abbe, reprinted by permission of William L. Bauhan, Publisher, Dublin, New Hampshire, 1961.

"Who's on First?" © 1990 Abbott & Costello Enterprises, authorized by Curtis Management Group, Indianapolis, Indiana 46202.

"Ashe Looks Back at a Year of Troubles and Triumph," by Peter Alfano. Copyright © 1988/89 by The New York Times Company. Reprinted by permission.

"Tennis," by Roger Angell, from THE STONE ARBOR (Little Brown). © 1950, 1978 Roger Angell. Originally in *The New Yorker.*

"A Public Nuisance" from *Playing the Game* by Reginald Arkell. Herbert Jenkins Limited.

"One Down" by Richard Armour. Reprinted by permission.

"Pass, Punt, and Talk" by Russell Baker. Copyright © 1977/78 by The New York Times Company. Reprinted by permission.

"The Four-Minute Mile," reprinted by permission of Sir Roger Bannister.

"First Lesson," from RELATIONS by Philip Booth. Copyright © Philip Booth, 1986. All rights reserved. Reprinted by permission of Viking Penguin, a division of Penguin Books USA, Inc.

"The Fifty-first Dragon," from *The Collected Edition of Heywood Broun.* Permission granted by Bill Cooper Associates, Inc. Copyright by Heywood Hale Broun and Patricia Broun.

"Mary Fidrych" by Tom Clark. © Tom Clark, 1983.

"Who Killed Benny Paret?" by Norman Cousins, Adjunct Professor, School of Medicine, University of California at Los Angeles. Originally published in the *Saturday Review.*

Dedication

Not to Ted Williams nor to Bill Bradley, who need no more acknowledgment of their athletic abilities, but to Christine Lavin and Andrew Ward, who do.

For suggestions about and help with this book, I wish to thank the following:

Bruce Brackett	Sally Emra
Faye and Fred Conrad	Bob Hillenbrand
Billy Darrow	Ben Reynolds
Chris deVinck	Pat Riccobene
Andy Dunn	Fred Smith
Karin Emra	Linda L. Waddle

and finally, but clearly not least, I wish to thank my editor, Sue Schumer.

Contents

Chapter Five
The Fun Side 317

Chapter Six
A Valedictory: To Those in the Arena 361

SPORTS *in* LITERATURE

• CHAPTER ONE •

The Game of Life

*Sports is life speeded up. In an hour or two the cycle of life
is reenacted on the playing field—the beginning of the contest,
the struggle, the triumph (all too brief), and the defeat.*

*All of life's emotions appear in sports—sports is a microcosm,
a world in miniature. In sports, life is crystalized and made intense.*

*As you read and react to the selections in this chapter,
think of sports as a part of life, not an escape from it.
Whether you participate in sports or not, you are likely to find
yourself in this chapter. Give yourself wholeheartedly to these
selections, as you might give yourself to a sport, and you will find
moments here that touch your experience and values.*

Ball Game

How is wanting to steal second base—but then racing back to first—like the journey through life?

Caught off first, he leaped to run to second, but
Then struggled back to first.
He left first because of a natural desire
To leap, to get on with the game.
When you jerk to run to second   5
You do not necessarily think of a home run.
You want to go on. You want to get to the next stage,
The entire soul is bent on second base.
The fact is that the mind flashes
Faster in action than the muscles can move.   10
Dramatic! Off first, taut, heading for second,
In a split second, total realization,
Heading for first. Head first! Legs follow fast.
You struggle back to first with victor effort
As, even, after a life of effort and chill,   15
One flashes back to the safety of childhood,
To that strange place where one had first begun.

---

11. *taut:* tightly drawn.

Understanding What You Read

1. Which of the following statements best sums up the theme of this poem?
   a. Baseball is a risky game.
   b. Though sometimes unwise, it is natural to take chances.
   c. It is always better to play it safe.

2. "Ball Game" has no rhymes. Nor does it have a regular meter. Is it really a poem? How does it differ from a paragraph in a newspaper account of a game?

3. If he had chosen, the poet could have written this poem in a regular meter. He could have begun like this:
   > Caught off first base, he leaped to second,
   > But then with fear he struggled back to first.

   Is this version in a regular meter better or worse than what the poet actually wrote? Why do you think so?

4. Suppose the runner in this poem had been tagged out. Would that have made a different kind of poem? If so, what kind?

Writer's Workshop

The poet selects a moment from a game and compares it to a moment from life. Write a paragraph or a stanza of verse in which you do the same. You might think of a personal experience—one in which you "punted out of trouble" or "cleared the hurdle" or even "dropped the ball"— and use that as the basis for your writing.

First Lesson

Just a father talking his daughter through her first swimming lesson—or is it?

Lie back, daughter, let your head
be tipped back in the cup of my hand.
Gently, and I will hold you. Spread
your arms wide, lie out on the stream
and look high at the gulls. A dead-   5
man's-float is face down. You will dive
and swim soon enough where this tidewater
ebbs to the sea. Daughter, believe
me, when you tire on the long thrash
to your island, lie up, and survive.   10
As you float now, where I held you
and let go, remember when fear
cramps your heart what I told you:
lie gently and wide to the light-year
stars, lie back, and the sea will hold you.   15

Understanding What You Read

1. To what does "the long thrash to your island" refer?

2. When the poet writes "lie back, and the sea will hold you," what does he mean?

3. Is the advice given in this poem only about swimming? How do you know?

Writer's Workshop

1. Tone in writing is the attitude the author takes toward his or her subject matter. It may be described as funny or tragic, comic or sad. Mainly, tone is revealed through the author's choices of words and details. How would you describe the tone of "First Lesson"? Use words from the poem to back up your description.

2. Think back to the time you first kicked a soccer ball correctly or connected with a baseball bat. Write a short poem about how you felt. Choose your words carefully to convey a specific tone. Perhaps this was the first time you felt physically coordinated and gained a sense of self-confidence. Perhaps it was the first time you worked with others as part of a team.

Offsides

Did you ever feel out of place in gym class? Find a soul mate in Andrew Ward, who looks back on an athletic career that was never "onsides."

My height might have afforded a natural athlete some magnificent opportunities, but my growth rate always seemed to me ominous, like the overextension of a rubber band. In the mirror at night I would examine the stretch marks that crosshatched my middle like tribal tattoos, and I had a nightmare once in which I actually split apart and had to be patched together with special elastic substances. My bedroom was a half-refurbished cellar rec area in a home of niggardly[1] construction. The acoustical-tiled ceiling was six feet high, and I was always parting my hair on the halo-shaped fluorescent light fixtures in the dark.

I was nearing my present height of six feet four inches by the tenth grade, and had been plagued throughout my boyhood by middle-aged men who mistook me for basketball material. I managed to avoid actual team sign-up sheets all through junior high school, but during my first senior high school gym class Coach Odarizzi took me aside and said, "Ward, with that height you could go places. Why don't you take your glasses off and live a little?"

Somehow I found the coach's call to action irresistible. While I was not about to dispose of my glasses (which were crucial to any slim hope of athletic accomplishment I might have had), I did in fact show up for the first junior varsity practice that year.

After the usual setting-up exercises, we were informed of our first passing pattern. Three of us were to stand side by side at the starting line, the man in the middle holding the ball. When the whistle blew, each man was to weave in among the others, passing the ball to the man directly in front. I am still a little shaky on how it was supposed to work. I guess it was like braiding, or maybe square dancing. In any case, I was in one of the first trios, and when the whistle blew and I was passed the ball, I kind of zigzagged across the court in no particular pattern, throwing the ball at whoever

---

1 *niggardly*: cheap.

was handy. I think at one point I threw the ball into the air and caught it myself, but I might have imagined that.

I never could chin myself. Still can't, without taking a little leap to start with, which is cheating. Chinning was part of our high school physical fitness test, and when my turn came (we were to chin ourselves as many times as we could in thirty seconds) I would jump up, grab hold of the bar, and just hang there, for all intents and purposes, until my time was up, or my hands slipped, or Coach Odarizzi told me to give it up.

"Work on that, Ward," he'd mutter, jotting something down on his clipboard. (Perhaps "jotting" is not the word for it; the coach was a laborious penman who tended to bite down on his tongue as he wrote.)

I suppose Richard Walters, who was more than a hundred pounds overweight, had a harder time of it than I did. He would spend his thirty seconds jumping up and down beneath the bar in a vain effort to reach it, as the coach solemnly stood by with his stopwatch.

We usually kicked off gym class by climbing ropes to the gymnasium ceiling. I started on the smooth, knotless ropes, but after a few floor-bound, rope-burned days I was shown to the one knotted rope, before which I queued[2] up with the anemic, the obese, and the cowardly, who could not have made it up a ladder, let alone a rope.

I would grab hold of the rope and then try to get it tangled with my legs as I dangled. Within seconds, I would get this drained feeling in my arms and down I would slide to the floor, folding up like a spider. The coach sometimes said I wasn't trying, but he never noticed how the pits of my elbows hollowed during rope climbing—sure evidence of my exertion.

I don't think I was ever the very last to be chosen for gym class teams, but I was usually among the last four. This group also included Richard Walters, who had about as much trouble getting around as he did chinning, a nearly blind boy named Merritt Hull who was always losing school days to urinary tract complications, and an eruptive menace named Merenski, who frequently fell into rages, kicking at groins when anyone tried to tell him what to do. By the time the choice was narrowed down to this foursome, one of the captains would say, "What the hell, at least he's tall," and I'd be chosen.

I still don't know what "offsides"

---

2 *queued*: lined up.

means, and I avoid all games in which the term is used. I played soccer once in summer camp, but only because I had to, and every few days someone would shout that I was offsides. I would always apologize profusely,[3] and stomp around kicking at the turf, but I never knew what they were talking about.

Football huddles were a source of mystery and confusion for me. There would always be a short, feisty[4] character who called the plays. I rarely had a key role in these plays, and usually wound up somewhere on the line, halfheartedly shoving somebody around.

But I do remember a time when, in a desperation move, the captain selected me to go out for a long one. I guess the reasoning was that no one on the opposing team would ever suspect me of such a thing. I was told, in the redolent[5] hush of the huddle, that I was to break formation on 24, try a lateral cutback on 47, head forward on hike, and then plunket closed quarters in a weaving "T" down the straightaway. That may not have been the precise terminology, but it might as well have been.

I think I ran in place on 24, turned 360 degrees on 47, was totally ignored on hike, ran a little

ways, and then turned in time to see everybody on both teams, it seemed, piling on top of the quarterback, who was shrieking, "Where are you? Where are you?" I suppose if I had gotten hold of the ball we might have managed a first down, but I don't know what that means, either.

The first gym teacher I remember was a soft-spoken and great-jawed man named Mr. Bobbins. Mr. Bobbins took me under his wing when I showed up in the middle of the seventh grade, the new kid from India. My family had been living in India for four years, and most of us returned to find we were profoundly out of touch. It was basketball season when I arrived, and the class was already pounding up and down the court, shooting hoops. "The idea here, Andy," Mr. Bobbins said when I confessed my ignorance of the game, "is to put the ball through the basket."

I had known that much, but found Mr. Bobbins so reassuring that I asked, "From the top or from underneath?"

"Definitely from the top," Mr. Bobbins replied gravely. "You won't get anywhere the other way."

My gym suits fit me only in sports shop dressing rooms. By the time I

---

3 *profusely*: abundantly.

4 *feisty*: spunky.

5 *redolent*: suggestive.

got them to school they'd be several sizes too small. I don't think I ever passed a happy hour in a gym suit, and at no time was I unhappier than during the week we had coed gymnastics. All the equipment was set up in the girls' gym, and I guess the Phys. Ed. department figured it would be logistically too difficult to have the boys and girls trade gyms for a couple of weeks.

Nowhere was I flatter of foot, spindlier and paler of leg, more equivocal[6] of shoulder, and heavier of acned brow than in the girls' gymnasium. We would have to line up boy-girl-boy-girl in front of the parallel bars, and it was no picnic when my turn came. I could never straighten my arms on the parallel bars, and spent a lot of time swinging from my armpits and making exertive noises.

We had to jump over horses in gymnastics class. We were supposed to run up to the things, grab them by their handles, and swing our legs over them. This seemed to me to be an unreasonable expectation, and I always balked on my approach. "You're always balking on your approach," the woman gym teacher would shout at me. "Don't balk on your approach." Thus lacking momentum, I would manage to grab the bars and kind of climb over the things with my knees. My only comfort was in

watching Richard Walters try to clear the horse, which he never did, even by climbing.

The balance beam was probably the least threatening piece of equipment as far as I was concerned. I had a fair sense of balance and enormous, clutching feet, and I could make it across all right. But when the exercise called for straddling, and my flaring shorts endangered coed decorum,[7] I would pretend to slip from the balance beam and then hurry to the next piece of equipment. Coed gymnastics was in some ways a mixed bag, for while there was always the agony of failing miserably and almost nakedly before the fair sex (as it was known at the time), we were afforded chances to observe the girls exercising in their turbulent Danskins.[8] I hope I'll never forget how Janet Gibbs moved along the balance beam, how Denise Dyktor bounced upon the trampoline, how Carol Dower arched and somersaulted across the tumbling mats. Perhaps one of the true high points of my adolescence was spotting for Suzie Hawley, who had the most beautiful, academically disruptive calves in Greenwich High School, and who happened once to slip from the high bar into my startled and grate-

---

6 *equivocal*: of uncertain nature.

7 *decorum*: propriety, good taste.

8 *turbulent Danskins*: irregularly moving leotards.

ful clutches.

But that was a fleeting delight in a context of misery. Mostly I remember just standing around, or ducking from the end of one line to the end of another, evading the apparatus and mortification[9] of coed gymnastics as best I could.

Wrestling class was held in the cellar of the high school on gray, dusty plastic mats. Perhaps it was the cellar that made these classes seem clandestine, like cock fights.[10] We were all paired up according to weight. I think at one point I was six feet two inches and weighed 130 pounds, and I was usually paired up with five-feet-two-inch 130-pounders, rippling little dynamos who fought with savage intensity.

I would often start off a match by collapsing into my last-ditch defensive posture, spread-eagled on my belly, clutching at the mat. That way, no matter how much Napoleonic[11] might was brought to bear on flipping me over for a pin, one of my outstretched limbs would prevent it. I remember an opponent's actually bursting into tears, because every time he man-

aged to fold one of my limbs into an operable bundle, out would flop another, too distant to reach without letting go of the first. I may never have won a match this way, but at least I lost on points, not pins.

By my senior year I had really stopped taking sports—even their mortifications—very seriously. I still hated to be among the last chosen, but no more for gym teams than for anything else. I took to making jokes when it seemed to me that my teammates were getting all worked up over nothing. I winked at opposing linemen, I limped around with tennis balls in my socks, I did Gillette commercials between plays, I stuffed the soccer ball under my T-shirt and accused my teammates of getting me into trouble.

None of this went over well with the athletes among us, nor with Coach Odarizzi. "Knock it off, Ward," he would bellow from the sidelines, "and grow up."

Playing games still comes up from time to time, and when it does, some of the old miseries return. I pass a couple of friends who are shooting baskets on an outdoor court. "Hey, Ward," one of them shouts. "Come on, Stretch. Let's see what you can do." I have mastered the weary shrug, the scornful wave, the hurried departure. But

---

9 *mortification:* humiliation.

10 *clandestine, like cockfights:* held in secret, like the illegal sport of fighting gamecocks.

11 *Napoleonic:* like Napoleon, the ambitious French emperor who ruled in the 1800s.

the ball is tossed my way—deftly,[12] by a man who comes to my shoulders—before I can escape.

I make a pawing motion to gather it toward me, try to trap it in the hollow of my stomach. It rolls down my clamped legs, bounces upon one of my size fourteens, rolls listlessly away. I reach for it with a clapping movement, capture it between my palms, straighten up, and sigh.

"Okay, Ace," someone shouts, "swish it in there."

"It's been a while," I say, giving the ball a tentative bounce. I squint over the top of the ball, regard the distant basket, hold my breath, and at last, with a hunching lunge, throw the damn thing.

It takes a direct route to the rim of the hoop, which makes a chattering noise on contact and sends the ball back in a high arc over my head. "Man," I say, lurching after it, "am I out of practice."

---

12 *deftly*: skillfully.

Understanding What You Read

1. Andrew Ward's athletic experiences as a teenager can best be described in which of the following ways?

    a. He wasn't a great athlete, but he gave his all.

    b. His experiences were disasters because of his height and lack of athletic ability and grace.

    c. He wasn't graceful, but he enjoyed the competition.

2. In a few words, describe the tone—the author's attitude toward his subject matter—of "Offsides." Use examples from the essay to support your opinion.

3. Suppose that instead of being unusually tall, Andrew Ward had been unusually short. How might this have affected the tone of his essay? Describe the kind of essay you think he might have written then.

Writer's Workshop

Similes are comparisons between unlike objects or ideas. The items compared are usually linked by the words **like** ("O, my love's like a red, red rose") or **as.** Similes are most often associated with poetry, but prose writers use them, too. Andrew Ward is especially good at the humorous simile. He compares his growth rate to "the overextension of a rubber band." A passing pattern in basketball is "like braiding, or maybe square dancing." At one point Ward collapses on the gym floor, "folding up like a spider."

Write a few paragraphs about one of your athletic experiences. Try to picture yourself as a clumsy person, as Andrew Ward did. Use similes to capture the right tone.

Ballad of a Ballgame

A contemporary folksinger wrote this ballad about the pain and joy of playing a team sport.

Do you remember that song by Janis Ian?
The one where she complains about not getting chosen
   for the basketball team?
Remember "For those whose names were never called
   when choosing sides for basketball"?   5
I would've written about that
   except she'd done it first.
'Cause when you're five foot two—
   okay, five one-and-a-half—
And everybody else in the whole gym class   10
   is five foot three and even taller,
   it hurts.

Truth is, I hadn't thought about that for years,
   and then a recent phone call rekindled all those fears.   15
"A softball game," Robin said. "And you're invited."

Softball, great, that's my game,
   why, softball's practically my middle name.
"I'll be right over," I said, sounding excited.   20
   Even though I can't throw, I can't hit,
I can't run, I admit.
   I can't catch, I can't pitch;
In softball I haven't found my niche.

But I don't let details get in my way.   **25**
   Team sports, that's what I love to play.
So I got dressed.
   I got my sneakers tied.
Made it to the park in time for choosing sides.

   "Pick me, pick me, pick me, pick me."   30

   "Pick me, pick me, pick me, pick me."

Glove? Yeah, I own a glove, but I didn't bring it because
   it's being repaired.

But I could always borrow from the other team.   35

    "Pick me, pick me, pick me, pick me."

This part goes on for quite awhile
    because twenty people showed up to play,
They picked ten to a side.
    So the ranks of unchosen were depleted
And ranks of the chosen swelled, and I was still standing there. 40
    I tried to act really casual
You know, I looked down at the ground,
    looked up at the sky.
I noticed clouds were rolling in,
    and a wind had kicked up off the river, a bad sign.   45
Well, déjà vu, I was the last one chosen,
    even after her highness Felicity Rosen.
They put me in a field so far out and to the right,
    I was practically out of sight.
But everybody said I had a   50
    real good day.
I didn't make any errors.
    I didn't make any plays.

You see, the ball never actually came out my way, and I figured,
    the afternoon is gonna end this way.   55

Now, coming up to bat was a whole different
    kind of humbling experience.
I took one swing and missed, which was no surprise.
    I took another swing and missed; that was no surprise.
But I practiced strategy.   60
I let one go by; it was called a ball.
    And I had a proud moment which didn't last long,
'cause then the pitcher threw one,
    I just couldn't resist,
I swung and I actually hit it.   65
    But it was a pathetic little dribbler
right back to the mound,
    and the pitcher threw it over to first base
    and I was out.   70
Which again is no surprise.

But as I was walking to the bench to pick up my glove,
the captain of the other team
Said to the captain of my team,
"Hey, it's okay,
She doesn't know how to play,   75
so we won't count her outs."
And I turned to her and I said,
"No, wait a minute!
I want my outs to count, I want you to count my outs,"
which made me instantly unpopular with my whole team.   80
So I said, "Oh, I get it,
don't count my outs,
That's good strategy, too; it makes me feel so special.
Thank you very much, thank you, thank you."

Well, eventually I resumed my place in the outfield   85
and continued watching the dandelions grow
And blossom and turn into puffs and blow away
in the chilly wind.
Watch the clouds above me spelling doom in the sky.
And it wasn't long before I began to question   90
My worth as a human being.
And my reason for living.

And then top of the seventh,
two on, two out.
A crack of the bat, a mighty clout.   95
My whole team turned and cringed to see
That speeding ball heading vaguely toward me.
I ran as fast as I could.
I said a prayer.
I stuck out my glove. The ball landed in there.   100
No one could believe it on either team.
They hooped and hollered. They stomped and screamed.
And even total strangers watching clapped and cheered,
aware that God had performed a miracle here.

I was carried to the bench.   105

I was handed a beer.

And then the clouds broke apart and the sun reappeared.
I'm exaggerating about the sun coming out
    but it feels like it did in my heart
Because I wanted to live again.   110
Oh, by the way, we lost that game 17 to 3,
    but I considered it a moral victory.
And Janis Ian, wherever you might be,
    take heart:
There's hope for you 'cause there's hope for me.   115

  Oh, take me out to the ballgame.
  Take me out to the crowd.
  Buy me some peanuts, I'll buy you Crackerjacks
  As long as you count my outs when I come up to bat
  Root, root, root, root, root, root, for both teams   120
  We don't want to lose; we're all the same.
  Oh, won't you please take me out
  To the old ballgame?

Understanding What You Read

1. Which of the following statements do you feel best describes the narrator of "Ballad of a Ballgame"?

    a. She is very proud of her athletic abilities.

    b. Though she realizes she is not a great athlete, she doesn't want to be humiliated in front of everyone.

    c. She is very competitive and wants to win at any cost.

2. Which incident in "Ballad of a Ballgame" upsets the narrator most? Why?

3. An allusion is a reference to a person, a place, an event, or an idea. For the writer, using allusions can be an effective way of packing a good deal of

meaning into a few words. Christine Lavin alludes to two other songs in "Ballad of a Ballgame," and even quotes from them. What are they? What do they add to her song? If they were removed, what would the effect be?

Writer's Workshop

1. A ballad is a song that tells a story. Most ballads are divided into stanzas of four lines with the last word in every other line rhyming. Early ballads often dealt with violent events. Later ballads, particularly in America, dealt with legendary heroes, such as Casey Jones or John Henry. The language of a ballad is plain and direct. In what respects is "Ballad of a Ballgame" a true ballad? In what respects is it different?

2. Writing humor is no joke. It doesn't come easily. See if you can capture in verse a moment in sports that contains failure and, finally, some kind of triumph. Take a fresh, humorous approach to your subject. You may want to set your words to the melody of a song that you like. Try to include one or more allusions.

Ace Teenage Sportscribe

Being a sportswriter sounds exciting. Author Donald Hall recounts his high school days covering sports for a local newspaper.

When I was a freshman at Hamden High School—in a suburb of New Haven, Connecticut—back in 1942, I became aware of a rakish character, a senior who wore chic jackets and loafers, who talked fast, and who aroused interest in glamorous seventeen-year-old women clutching books to their sprouting bosoms. I *think* his name was Herbie, and I *know* that he wrote about high school sports for the *New Haven Register*. I looked on him with the envy that I usually reserved for athletes. Herbie was no more an athlete than I was; writing newspaper sports was compensation for this bitter accident of nature. Gradually I realized that next year Herbie would be gone to the war, and his employers would need a replacement. I dropped some hints—and Herbie tried me out by allowing me to cover a couple of baseball games. I was hired. I met the *Register's* sports editor—call him Ed McGuire—and signed on to cover Hamden High for ten cents a column inch. I was fifteen.

Autumn of my sophomore year was football and anguish. I rode the team bus to out-of-town games, the only ununiformed young male except for the manager who wore a leg brace from polio. I sat at the rear, behind already-shoulder-padded warriors like Batso Biscaglia the five-foot fullback, halfback Luigi Mertino, and Rafael Domartino, the center who weighed two hundred and eighty pounds. At this time, Hamden was a colony of Calabria.[1]

I sat at the rear in melancholy swooning isolation among cheerleaders in small green pleated skirts, little white socks, green sneakers—and great expanses of naked shimmering LEG. I sat in a lovesick impossible daydream, so near and yet so far—and the girls (the prettiest in school; by reputation the fastest) were pleasant and condescending. I heard them talk

---

1 *colony of Calabria:* humorously meant, having many Italian residents; Calabria was a district of ancient Italy.

about dates after the game—each with her football player, one with a backfield—as they gossiped in front of me without taking account of me as *male*. Oh, I was male—and a hopeless shy devoted tongue-tied Oedipal nympholept,[2] haggard and woe-begone, palely loitering on a bus to Ansonia. . . . The cold ride back from the game, which we usually lost, the players sat silent and hurt; the girls were quiet as they looked ahead to pleasing the sullen boys.

At home I would write a brief game story and my father would drive me down to the *Register* with it. Soon I wrote for the *Journal-Courier* as well, poorer and slimmer of the city's two newspapers, published in the morning while the *Register* came out in the afternoon. The *Journal-Courier* could not afford to pay ten cents an inch. Scottie MacDonald was Assistant Sports Editor (the entire staff) and promised me *lots* of by-lines and an occasional couple of bucks. I remember those offices in a second- or third-floor building in downtown New Haven. Scottie had a cubbyhole with a typewriter. He wore his hat all the time, set way back, above a brown suit and tie; he kept the tie pulled down and the top button of his shirt unbut-

toned; pretty Bohemian[3] for 1942. Every two or three weeks he handed me a slip of paper with which I could extract two dollars petty cash from the cashier.

I wrote my *Register* story first, then worked it a second way for the *Courier*. For the *Register* I clipped my columns, measured them with a ruler, and presented my column-inches to Ed McGuire, who wore a perpetual green eye-shade, who always looked angry, who tucked a continual cigar in the corner of his mouth. (Everybody entered the *Front Page*[4] lookalike contest in those days.) He would re-measure my clips, take his cigar out of his mouth, spit, and write me a chit for the cashier. Eight dollars, maybe. . . .

I did not get rich as a sports-writer, but I observed an amelioration[5] of my social life. To my astonishment, people like Batso began to wave at me in the cafeteria; Pongi Piscatelli, the famous tackle *six-feet-tall* smiled at me in the corridor and said, "'Hi, John.'" Maybe he thought all Protestants were named John. Well, I thought, "Don" *sounds* a lot like "John."

---

2 *Oedipal nympholept:* a young man full of sexual confusion, like the mythical hero Oedipus.

3 *Bohemian:* unconventional, radical.

4 *Front Page:* a reference to the popular play about fast-paced newspaper life, *The Front Page,* written by Ben Hecht and Charles MacArthur and first produced in 1928.

5 *amelioration:* improvement.

Baseball was always my favorite sport and I liked writing about it; but neither newspaper printed much about high school baseball. Basketball was virtually ignored at Hamden High. Sometimes I covered games at our gym and watched as our midget centers and forwards planted their feet and pushed up two-handed set shots, often in the direction of the basket. We always lost thirty-eight to nineteen. When the games were away, or when they coincided with hockey games, one of the athletes would feed me box scores over the telephone and I would fabricate a thirty-word story to go with it. The three-quarter-inch gamestory would appear in the *Journal-Courier* under a by-line. Glory.

The glory and the glamor accrued[6] to hockey. All over Hamden boys skated when they could toddle and played hockey as soon as they could lift a stick. Hamden was Ontario South. I do not know the etiology[7] of this obsession, but it was a tradition; hockey was already king when my father was a boy, before Hamden built its own high school. The best neighborhood athletes concentrated their powers on hockey—which was difficult in those days, when there were few indoor rinks and only two or three months of good ice.

Hamden's teams were good, and although the school was much smaller than its archrival Hillhouse in New Haven—Hillhouse beat us easily in other sports—in hockey we often prevailed. Hamden High's hockey players went on to play for Yale, for Harvard, for Providence College, even out west for Big Ten schools.

The biggest hockey occasions were Saturday night high school doubleheaders at the New Haven Arena, home of New Haven's minor league professional hockey team, site of Willie Pep's bouts as Featherweight Champion. West Haven, Hillhouse, Commercial, and Hamden gathered for hockey, and when the confrontation was between Hamden and Hillhouse, it was the Greeks and the Trojans. Often the crowd fights were as grand as fights on ice. Pongi Piscatelli, it was widely asserted, broke four noses one Saturday night alone.

The rule about no cheering from the press box was suspended for these games. There was a Hillhouse defense man I will call Bobby Adams who could not keep from smiling when his team was ahead. "Laughing-Boy Bobby Adams," I would write, "stopped giggling when Hamden's stalwarts forged three goals. . . ." Ed

---

6 *accrued:* came as a result of.

7 *etiology:* cause, origin.

McGuire learned (from "Letters to the Editor," I suppose) that he had to keep an eye on my copy when Hamden played Hillhouse.

The Saturday night doubleheaders were my greatest challenge as infant-journalist because the *Register* turned into a morning paper on Sunday, and it was eleven at night before the games were over. I walked the few blocks from the Arena to the *Register* in wartime darkness and ascended to the deserted sports department, everybody gone home except an exasperated Ed McGuire. There he sat, cigar in mouth, eyes hidden under green celluloid,[8] telling me I was late and everything was late . . . stop standing around get to work. . . .

The typewriter was an enormous old manual standard. I put a sheet of paper into the machine, spread out my notes, and began to type—one-finger . . . *Rapidly*, but one-finger . . . Ed McGuire sat at this desk half the room away from me and pulled from a pint bottle that he kept in a drawer. If I paused in my typing to think of a word—or to consider variant orthography,[9] I could spell nothing in those days—his head snapped quickly up and he snarled some-

thing unintelligible except in import. Every now and then he stalked from his desk to mine, ripped out whatever I had typed, and disappeared to the Linotype room—presumably taking time to remove any "Laughing-Boy Bobby" editorials. I feathered another piece of paper into the steam-locomotive typewriter and continued midsentence.

That year was my career, for after sophomore year I transferred from Hamden to Exeter, where I found it impossible to get A's by literacy alone. Symptoms of Journalist's Swelled Head disappeared when my Exeter teacher gave me C-minuses on my first English papers: "paragraphs too short"; "newspaper jargon . . ."

Earlier, the swelled head had been temporarily helpful in the struggle to grow up. I cherished the *adventure*; I daydreamed myself Ace Teenage Sportscribe, and I noticed faint signs of interest from certain young women—not, of course, the cheerleaders, but girls who wrote features for the Hamden High School *Dial*, girls who read books—girls I could *talk* to.

In the dark *Register* building I finished my last lines for Ed McGuire, who took them to the Linotype room muttering imprecations.[10] I

---

8 *celluloid:* a reference to the green plastic eyeshade often worn by newspaper editors in the past.

9 *orthography:* the study of letters and spelling.

---

10 *imprecations:* curses

put on my overcoat, mittens, and earmuffs; I stepped outside into the midnight air to wait a long time for the late-night bus that would take me four miles out Whitney Avenue and leave me at the corner of Ardmore to walk the dark block to my parents' house. I whistled white steam into the cold air of early morning, fifteen years old, thinking of *maybe* being brave enough to ask Patsy Luther to the movies—the proud author of a story right now multiplying itself into morning newsprint, ready to turn up on the doorstep in a few hours, large as life, BY DON HALL.

Understanding What You Read

1. What was one of Donald Hall's main motives in applying for the job as a local sportswriter?
    a. To get an early jump on a professional career
    b. To attend as many sports events as he could
    c. To be involved with an activity that might impress girls.

2. In this essay Hall provides vivid portraits of his bosses, Ed McGuire and Scottie MacDonald. Briefly describe McGuire and MacDonald as they are portrayed by Hall.

3. Hall's essay takes a humorous approach to sports and to writing about sports. Pick one incident in this essay and describe as precisely as you can what makes it funny. Is it Hall's use of big words where you don't expect to find them? Is it a contrast between the real and the ideal? Or is it something else?

Writer's Workshop

You may have had a part-time job, either in or out of sports. Delivering newspapers, babysitting, cutting lawns—these all count. Write a brief scene profiling a person you met on your job. Show what the person looks like, how he or she speaks, how the person acts—make the person real, vivid. Create dialogue to show how you interacted with the person.

Fishing

Life slows down when you go fishing and time seems to stop as you wait for a bite.

We were a noisy crew; the sun in heaven
Beheld not vales more beautiful than ours;
Nor saw a band in happiness and joy
Richer, or worthier of the ground they trod.
I could record with no reluctant voice   5
The woods of autumn, and their hazel bowers
With milk-white clusters hung; the rod and line,
True symbol of hope's foolishness, whose strong
And unreproved enchantment led us on
By rocks and pools shut out from every star,   10
All the green summer, to forlorn cascades
Among the windings hid of mountain brooks.

---

2. *vales:* valleys.

6. *hazel bowers:* branches of hazel trees (a type of birch), forming a kind of enclosure.

9. *unreproved:* uncensored, unchallenged.

11. *forlorn cascades:* lonely, little waterfalls.

12. *windings:* curved or sinuous courses.

Understanding What You Read

1. In a sentence, describe Wordsworth's attitude toward his summer of fishing.
2. How are the rod and line the "true symbol of hope's foolishness"?

Writer's Workshop

1. One measure of a poet's skill lies in the ability to "make phrases," to put together groups of words that catch the reader's attention, that seem just right, and that stick in the mind. In this poem, written over 150 years ago, there are several memorable phrases: "We were a noisy crew," "shut out from every star," and "all the green summer." Begin a notebook in which you create such phrases of your own that capture things you see, moods you feel. Some of the phrases might even serve as potential titles or subjects for your own writing.

2. Fishing is a sport, even though it is not one of the popular team sports that receive so much attention in the media. In a poem or piece of prose, capture a feeling you have experienced with an individual sport—fishing, swimming, riding, cycling, sailing, and so on.

Casey at the Bat

There's never been a more famous batter than the subject of this time-less poem.

The outlook wasn't brilliant for the Mudville nine that day;
The score stood four to two with but one inning more to play.
And then, when Cooney died at first, and Barrows did the same,
A sickly silence fell upon the patrons of the game.

A straggling few got up to go in deep despair. The rest   5
Clung to that hope which springs eternal in the human breast;
They thought, If only Casey could get a whack at that
We'd put up even money now, with Casey at the bat.

But Flynn preceded Casey, as did also Jimmy Blake,
And the former was a lulu and the latter was a cake;   10
So upon that stricken multitude grim melancholy sat,
For there seemed but little chance of Casey's getting to the bat.

But Flynn let drive a single, to the wonderment of all,
And Blake, the much despised, tore the cover off the ball;
And when the dust had lifted, and men saw what had occurred, 15
There was Jimmy safe at second, and Flynn a-hugging third.

Then from five thousand throats and more there rose a lusty
      yell;
It rumbled through the valley, it rattled in the dell;
It knocked upon the mountain and recoiled upon the flat,
For Casey, mighty Casey, was advancing to the bat.   20

There was ease in Casey's manner as he stepped into his place;
There was pride in Casey's bearing and a smile on Casey's face.
And when, responding to the cheers, he lightly doffed his hat,

---

23. *doffed:* took off.

No stranger in the crowd could doubt 'twas Casey at the bat.

Ten thousand eyes were on him as he rubbed his hands with
    dirt,   25
Five thousand tongues applauded when he wiped them on his
    shirt;
Then while the writhing pitcher ground the ball into his hip,
Defiance gleamed from Casey's eye, a sneer curled Casey's lip. 30

And now the leather-covered sphere came hurtling through the
    air,
And Casey stood a-watching it in haughty grandeur there.
Close by the sturdy batsman the ball unheeded sped;
"That ain't my style," said Casey. "Strike one," the umpire said. 35

From the benches, black with people, there went up a muffled
    roar,
Like the beating of the storm waves on a stern and distant
    shore.
"Kill him! Kill the umpire!" shouted someone on the stand;
And it's likely they'd have killed him had not Casey raised his
    hand.

With a smile of Christian charity great Casey's visage shone;   40
He stilled the rising tumult, he bade the game go on;
He signaled to the pitcher, and once more the spheroid flew;
But Casey still ignored it, and the umpire said, "Strike two."

"Fraud!" cried the maddened thousands, and echo answered
    "Fraud!"   45
But one scornful look from Casey and the audience was awed;
They saw his face grow stern and cold, they saw his muscles
    strain,
And they knew that Casey wouldn't let that ball go by again.

The sneer is gone from Casey's lip, his teeth are clenched in   50
    hate,

---

40. *visage:* face.

41. *tumult:* commotion; din; uproar.

. . . .

He pounds with cruel violence his bat upon the plate;
And now the pitcher holds the ball, and now he lets it go,
And now the air is shattered by the force of Casey's blow.

Oh, somewhere in this favored land the sun is shining bright.   55
The band is playing somewhere, and somewhere hearts are
    light;
And somewhere men are laughing, and somewhere children
    shout,
But there is no joy in Mudville—mighty Casey has struck out.

Understanding What You Read

1. What is the game-situation narrated in this poem?
    a. It's early in the game with the Mudville team trailing by two runs.
    b. Mudville trails and has only one more time at bat.
    c. Mudville is leading, but the opposing team is catching up.

2. When Casey has his last at bat, what is the situation?
    a. It is the last inning and two men are on base.
    b. It is the last inning and the bases are loaded.
    c. It is the last inning, the score is tied, and the bases are empty.

3. What is Casey's bearing as he takes the plate for his last at bat?
    a. He is frightened and anxious but tries not to let it show.
    b. He has great self-confidence.
    c. He is shy and modest about the important role he is playing.

4. Explain the writer's technique in the last two stanzas. How does the writer
    toy with the reader?

Writer's Workshop

1. The following excerpt is from a parody of "Casey at the Bat" called "O'Toole's Touchdown," written by Les Desmond. A **parody** imitates and sometimes makes fun of another work. For a parody to be effective, it should parallel the original work very closely, and then go off in its own direction, for comic effect. What similarities do you notice between the style of "Casey at the Bat" and these two concluding stanzas of "O'Toole's Touchdown"? What writing technique of Thayer does Desmond employ to conclude "O'Toole's Touchdown"?

> But look! It is a forward pass from quarter to O'Toole!
> The Mighty Mike has grabbed it; he has started for the
>   goal!
> With ball clutched firmly to his breast, he speeds with
>   bound on bound.
> He flies across the goal line, and then drops to the ground.
>
> Oh, somewhere men are laughing, and children shout
>   with glee;
> And somewhere bands are playing, and somewhere hearts
>   are free.
> And somewhere in this favored land the glorious sun
>   does shine,
> But there is no joy in Hokus, O'Toole crossed the wrong
>   goal line!

2. Try to write your own parody of "Casey at the Bat." It doesn't have to be thirteen stanzas—maybe just six or seven if you can tell your story in that space—but try to parallel Ernest Lawrence Thayer's rhythms, plot development, and technique for ending his piece. You can write about any sport.

The Fifty-first Dragon

Do you believe in superstitions? Will they win the game—or slay the dragon—for you?

O f all the pupils at the knight school Gawaine le Coeur-Hardy was among the least promising. He was tall and sturdy, but his instructors soon discovered that he lacked spirit. He would hide in the woods when the jousting class was called, although his companions and members of the faculty sought to appeal to his better nature by shouting to him to come out and break his neck like a man. Even when they told him that the lances were padded, the horses no more than ponies and the field unusually soft for late autumn, Gawaine refused to grow enthusiastic. The Headmaster and the Assistant Professor of Pleasaunce were discussing the case one spring afternoon and the Assistant Professor could see no remedy but expulsion.

"No," said the Headmaster, as he looked out at the purple hills which ringed the school, "I think I'll train him to slay dragons."

"He might be killed," objected the Assistant Professor.

"So he might," replied the Headmaster brightly, but he added, more soberly, "we must consider the greater good. We are responsible for the formation of this lad's character."

"Are the dragons particularly bad this year?" interrupted the Assistant Professor. This was characteristic. He always seemed restive[1] when the head of the school began to talk ethics and the ideals of the institution.

"I've never known them worse," replied the Headmaster. "Up in the hills to the south last week they killed a number of peasants, two cows and a prize pig. And if this dry spell holds there's no telling when they may start a forest fire simply by breathing around indiscriminately."

"Would any refund on the tuition fee be necessary in case of an accident to young Coeur-Hardy?"

"No," the principal answered, judicially, "that's all covered in the

---

1 *restive:* restless, fidgety.

contract. But as a matter of fact he won't be killed. Before I send him up in the hills I'm going to give him a magic word."

"That's a good idea," said the Professor. "Sometimes they work wonders."

From that day on Gawaine specialized in dragons. His course included both theory and practice. In the morning there were long lectures on the history, anatomy, manners and customs of dragons. Gawaine did not distinguish himself in these studies. He had a marvelously versatile gift for forgetting things. In the afternoon he showed to better advantage, for then he would go down to the South Meadow and practice with a battle-ax. In this exercise he was truly impressive, for he had enormous strength as well as speed and grace. He even developed a deceptive display of ferocity. Old alumni say that it was a thrilling sight to see Gawaine charging across the field toward the dummy paper dragon which had been set up for his practice. As he ran he would brandish his ax and shout, "a murrain[2] on thee!" or some other vivid bit of campus slang. It never took him more than one stroke to behead the dummy dragon.

Gradually his task was made more difficult. Paper gave way to papier-mâché and finally to wood, but even the toughest of these dummy dragons had no terrors for Gawaine. One sweep of the ax always did the business. There were those who said that when the practice was protracted[3] until dusk and the dragons threw long, fantastic shadows across the meadow, Gawaine did not charge so impetuously nor shout so loudly. It is possible there was malice in this charge. At any rate, the Headmaster decided by the end of June that it was time for the test. Only the night before a dragon had come close to the school grounds and had eaten some of the lettuce from the garden. The faculty decided that Gawaine was ready. They gave him a diploma and a new battle-ax and the Headmaster summoned him to a private conference.

"Sit down," said the Headmaster. "Have a cigarette."

Gawaine hesitated.

"Oh, I know it's against the rules," said the Headmaster. "But after all, you have received your preliminary degree. You are no longer a boy. You are a man. Tomorrow you will go out into the world, the great world of achievement."

Gawaine took a cigarette. The Headmaster offered him a match, but he produced one of his own

---

2 *murrain:* plague.

3 *protracted:* extended

. . . .

and began to puff away with a dexterity which quite amazed the principal.

"Here you have learned the theories of life," continued the Headmaster, resuming the thread of his discourse, "but after all, life is not a matter of theories. Life is a matter of facts. It calls on the young and the old alike to face these facts, even though they are hard and sometimes unpleasant. Your problem, for example, is to slay dragons."

"They say that those dragons down in the south wood are five hundred feet long," ventured Gawaine, timorously.[4]

"Stuff and nonsense!" said the Headmaster. "The curate[5] saw one last week from the top of Arthur's Hill. The dragon was sunning himself down in the valley. The curate didn't have an opportunity to look at him very long because he felt it was his duty to hurry back to make a report to me. He said the monster—or shall I say, the big lizard?—wasn't an inch over two hundred feet. But the size has nothing at all to do with it. You'll find the big ones even easier than the little ones. They're far slower on their feet and less aggressive, I'm told. Besides, before you go I'm going to equip you in such fashion that you need have no fear of all the dragons in the world."

"I'd like an enchanted cap," said Gawaine.

"What's that?" asked the Headmaster, testily.[6]

"A cap to make me disappear," explained Gawaine.

The Headmaster laughed indulgently. "You mustn't believe all those old wives' stories," he said. "There isn't any such thing. A cap to make you disappear, indeed! What would you do with it? You haven't even appeared yet. Why, my boy, you could walk from here to London, and nobody would so much as look at you. You're nobody. You couldn't be more invisible than that."

Gawaine seemed dangerously close to a relapse into his old habit of whimpering. The Headmaster reassured him: "Don't worry; I'll give you something much better than an enchanted cap. I'm going to give you a magic word. All you have to do is to repeat this magic charm once and no dragon can possibly harm a hair of your head. You can cut off his head at your leisure."

He took a heavy book from the shelf behind his desk and began to run through it. "Sometimes," he said, "the charm is a whole phrase or even a sentence. I might, for instance, give you 'To make the'—no, that might not do. I think

---

4 *timorously:* timidly, fearfully.

5 *curate:* clergyman.

---

6 *testily:* irritably.

a single word would be best for dragons."

"A short word," suggested Gawaine.

"It can't be too short or it wouldn't be potent. There isn't so much hurry as all that. Here's a splendid magic word: 'Rumplesnitz.' Do you think you can learn that?"

Gawaine tried and in an hour or so he seemed to have the word well in hand. Again and again he interrupted the lesson to inquire, "And if I say 'Rumplesnitz' the dragon can't possibly hurt me?" And always the Headmaster replied, "If you only say 'Rumplesnitz,' you are perfectly safe."

Toward morning Gawaine seemed resigned to his career. At daybreak the Headmaster saw him to the edge of the forest and pointed him to the direction in which he should proceed. About a mile away to the southwest a cloud of steam hovered over an open meadow in the woods and the Headmaster assured Gawaine that under the steam he would find a dragon. Gawaine went forward slowly. He wondered whether it would be best to approach the dragon on the run as he did in his practice in the South Meadow or to walk slowly toward him, shouting "Rumplesnitz" all the way.

The problem was decided for him. No sooner had he come to the fringe of the meadow than the dragon spied him and began to charge. It was a large dragon and yet it seemed decidedly aggressive in spite of the Headmaster's statement to the contrary. As the dragon charged it released huge clouds of hissing steam through its nostrils. It was almost as if a gigantic teapot had gone mad. The dragon came forward so fast and Gawaine was so frightened that he had time to say "Rumplesnitz" only once. As he said it, he swung his battle-ax and off popped the head of the dragon. Gawaine had to admit that it was even easier to kill a real dragon than a wooden one if only you said "Rumplesnitz."

Gawaine brought the ears home and a small section of the tail. His school mates and the faculty made much of him, but the Headmaster wisely kept him from being spoiled by insisting that he go on with his work. Every clear day Gawaine rose at dawn and went out to kill dragons. The Headmaster kept him at home when it rained, because he said the woods were damp and unhealthy at such times and that he didn't want the boy to run needless risks. Few good days passed in which Gawaine failed to get a dragon. On one particularly fortunate day he killed three, a husband and wife and a visiting relative. Gradually he developed a technique. Pupils who sometimes watched him from the hill-tops a long way off said that he often allowed the dragon to come within a few feet before he said "Rumplesnitz." He came to say it with a mocking sneer. Occasionally he did stunts. Once when an excursion party from London was watching him he went into action with his right hand tied behind his back. The dragon's head came off just as easily.

As Gawaine's record of killings mounted higher the Headmaster found it impossible to keep him completely in hand. He fell into the habit of stealing out at night and engaging in long drinking bouts at the village tavern. It was after such a debauch[7] that he rose a little before dawn one fine August morning and started out after his fiftieth dragon. His head was heavy and his mind sluggish. He was heavy in other respects as well, for he had adopted the somewhat vulgar practice of wearing his medals, ribbons and all, when he went out dragon hunting. The decorations began on his chest and ran all the way down to his abdomen. They must have weighed at least eight pounds.

Gawaine found a dragon in the same meadow where he had killed the first one. It was a fair-sized dragon, but evidently an old one.

Its face was wrinkled and Gawaine thought he had never seen so hideous a countenance. Much to the lad's disgust, the monster refused to charge and Gawaine was obliged to walk toward him. He whistled as he went. The dragon regarded him hopelessly, but craftily. Of course it had heard of Gawaine. Even when the lad raised his battle-ax the dragon made no move. It knew that there was no salvation in the quickest thrust of the head, for it had been informed that this hunter was protected by an enchantment. It merely waited, hoping something would turn up.

Gawaine raised the battle-ax and suddenly lowered it again. He had grown very pale and he trembled violently.

The dragon suspected a trick. "What's the matter?" it asked, with false solicitude.[8]

"I've forgotten the magic word," stammered Gawaine.

"What a pity," said the dragon. "So that was the secret. It doesn't seem quite sporting to me, all this magic stuff, you know. Not cricket,[9] as we used to say when I was a little dragon; but after all, that's a matter of opinion."

Gawaine was so helpless with terror that the dragon's confidence rose immeasurably and it could not

---

7 *debauch:* an occasion of drunkenness.

8 *solicitude:* concern or care.

9 *cricket:* a British term for fair or honorable behavior.

resist the temptation to show off a bit.

"Could I possibly be of any assistance?" it asked. "What's the first letter of the magic word?"

"It begins with an 'r,'" said Gawaine weakly.

"Let's see," mused the dragon, "that doesn't tell us much, does it? What sort of a word is this? Is it an epithet,[10] do you think?"

Gawaine could do no more than nod.

"Why, of course," exclaimed the dragon, "reactionary Republican."

Gawaine shook his head.

"Well, then," said the dragon, "we'd better get down to business. Will you surrender?"

With the suggestion of a compromise Gawaine mustered up enough courage to speak.

"What will you do if I surrender?" he asked.

"Why, I'll eat you," said the dragon.

"And if I don't surrender?"

"I'll eat you just the same."

"Then it doesn't make any difference, does it?" moaned Gawaine.

"It does to me," said the dragon with a smile. "I'd rather you didn't surrender. You'd taste much better if you didn't."

The dragon waited for a long time for Gawaine to ask "Why?" but the boy was too frightened to speak. At last the dragon had to give the explanation without his cue line. "You see," he said, "if you don't surrender you'll taste better because you'll die game."[11]

This was an old and ancient trick of the dragon's. By means of some such quip he was accustomed to paralyze his victims with laughter and then to destroy them. Gawaine was sufficiently paralyzed as it was, but laughter had no part in his helplessness. With the last word of the joke the dragon drew back his head and struck. In that second there flashed into the mind of Gawaine the magic word "Rumplesnitz," but there was no time to say it. There was time only to strike and, without a word, Gawaine met the onrush of the dragon with a full swing. He put all his back and shoulders into it. The impact was terrific and the head of the dragon flew almost a hundred yards and landed in a thicket.

Gawaine did not remain frightened very long after the death of the dragon. His mood was one of wonder. He was enormously puzzled. He cut off the ears of the monster almost in a trance. Again and again he thought to himself, "I didn't say 'Rumplesnitz'!" He was

---

10 *epithet:* a characterizing word or phrase used in place of a name.

11 *game:* having an unyielding spirit; pun on wild animals hunted for sport.

sure of that and yet there was no question that he had killed the dragon. In fact, he had never killed one so utterly. Never before had he driven a head for anything like the same distance. Twenty-five yards was perhaps his best previous record. All the way back to the knight school he kept rumbling about in his mind seeking an explanation for what had occurred. He went to the Headmaster immediately and after closing the door told him what had happened. "I didn't say 'Rumplesnitz,'" he explained with great earnestness.

The Headmaster laughed. "I'm glad you've found out," he said. "It makes you ever so much more of a hero. Don't you see that? Now you know that it was you who killed all these dragons and not that foolish little word 'Rumplesnitz.'"

Gawaine frowned. "Then it wasn't a magic word after all?" he asked.

"Of course not," said the Headmaster, "you ought to be too old for such foolishness. There isn't any such thing as a magic word."

"But you told me it was magic," protested Gawaine. "You said it was magic and now you say it isn't."

"It wasn't magic in a literal sense," answered the Headmaster, "but it was much more wonderful than that. The word gave you confidence. It took away your fears. If

I hadn't told you that, you might have been killed the very first time. It was your battle-ax did the trick."

Gawaine surprised the Headmaster by his attitude. He was obviously distressed by the explanation. He interrupted a long philosophic and ethical discourse by the Headmaster with "If I hadn't of hit 'em all mighty hard and fast any one of 'em might have crushed me like a, like a—" He fumbled for a word.

"Egg shell," suggested theHeadmaster.

"Like a egg shell," assented Gawaine, and he said it many times. All through the evening meal people who sat near him heard him muttering, "Like a egg shell, like a egg shell."

The next day was clear, but Gawaine did not get up at dawn. Indeed, it was almost noon when the Headmaster found him cowering in bed, with the clothes pulled over his head. The principal called the Assistant Professor of Pleasaunce, and together they dragged the boy toward the forest.

"He'll be all right as soon as he gets a couple more dragons under his belt," explained the Headmaster.

The Assistant Professor of Pleasaunce agreed. It would be a shame to stop such a fine run," he said. "Why, counting that one yesterday, he's killed fifty dragons."

They pushed the boy into a thicket above which hung a meager cloud of steam. It was obviously quite a small dragon. But Gawaine did not come back that night or the next. In fact, he never came back. Some weeks afterward brave spirits from the school explored the thicket, but they could find nothing to remind them of Gawaine except the metal parts of his medals. Even the ribbons had been devoured.

The Headmaster and the Assistant Professor of Pleasaunce agreed that it would be just as well not to tell the school how Gawaine had achieved his record and still less how he came to die. They held that it might have a bad effect on school spirit. Accordingly, Gawaine has lived in the memory of the school as its greatest hero. No visitor succeeds in leaving the building today without seeing a great shield which hangs on the wall of the dining hall. Fifty pairs of dragons' ears are mounted upon the shield and underneath in gilt letters is "Gawaine le Coeur-Hardy," followed by the simple inscription, "He killed fifty dragons." The record has never been equaled.

Understanding What You Read

1. Dragon-slaying probably isn't a big sport in your school. And "Wide World of Sports" never seems to feature "The International Dragon-Slaying Playoffs." Then why should "The Fifty-first Dragon" appear in a book of literature about sports? There are several reasons. This is a story about competition, skill, self-confidence, and superstition—the fundamentals of any sport. What's more, it was written by a famous sportswriter and columnist.

   "The Fifty-first Dragon" is a **parable**. It is a story that illustrates a moral. It's similar to a fable, except the characters are not animals and the moral is not stated at the end. The story of the Good Samaritan is one of the most famous parables, illustrating the moral that everyone has an obligation to help others. Which of the following statements do you feel best illustrates the moral of "The Fifty-first Dragon"?
   a. Slaying dragons isn't as easy as it used to be.
   b. One must rely on oneself, not on a magic word or trick, to accomplish things in life.
   c. Even great tasks become routine and boring.

2. Why was the slaying of the fiftieth dragon a different experience—and such an important one—for Gawaine?

3. Why was Gawaine so gloomy and depressed after his last talk with the Head-master?

4. Consider the moral of this parable. How might it apply in today's society?

Writer's Workshop

1. A famous baseball player ate only chicken before a game. Many people carry good-luck charms. In a few paragraphs, explain your attitude toward super-stitions. Are superstitions always bad?

2. Write your own parable with a sport as its main focus. It doesn't have to be a serious, big-time sport—it could be tiddlywinks or shuffleboard, if you like. You might start by thinking of the moral you wish to illustrate. Do not state your moral in the story; it should be implied. Make your characters seem real and human.

Just Because We're Female

In this essay an incident at a high school soccer practice prompts a team member to think about what it means to be female in today's world.

I used to listen to my grandmother's stories of how difficult things were in her time, how hard it was to be an independent woman when she was young. She told of being called an "upstart" and a "trouble maker," a woman who "didn't know her place" in "this man's world" whenever she refused to sit nicely and quietly, whenever she tried to express her views. I listened to her tales of encounters with men who refused to recognize a woman as a person, as an intelligent, socially-aware human being rather than a docile domestic machine. I heard her stories and thought how fortunate I was to be living in such enlightened times, where men recognized women as equals and not just child-bearing maids. Attitudes towards women had certainly come full circle, I believed; nobody thought like that anymore.

My shoelaces flapped around my ankles as I jogged out to the field. I didn't have time to bend down and tie them now; I was already late for practice. My cleats almost fell off as I ran the last fifty yards to the bleachers. There were only a few girls on the bench when I got there; they were all the "walking wounded," according to Coach Guilford—those injured players who hobbled through practice, trying to convince themselves and the coaches that they could play in the next day's game. Merri was lacing up her ankle brace as I arrived; Jody was icing her pulled quadricep, and Lauren was patching up her blisters caused by her new cleats. Mink wasn't injured; she was just too lazy to run perimeters with the rest of the team. I sat down on the second bleacher and began lacing up my cleats. Mike, our head coach, talked to us about tomorrow's game as he juggled a soccer ball on his knees, and we waited for everyone else to finish running.

The athletic director walked up to the field just then and came over to the bleachers where we sat. It was still just the five of us and Mike; the rest of the team was still doing perimeters. The athletic director propped one foot up on the bottom bleacher and began talking to Mike. We didn't pay much attention to their discussion at first, but we became more interested as the conversation wore on.

Apparently, the athletic director was canceling one of the extra games that Mike had scheduled for us, a non-league contest with Bayonne to be played toward the end of the season. He just had too many other things to schedule—y'know, football games, and buses, and everything, he told Mike, and besides it was just an extra game anyway. Mike tried to explain why he had set up the game in the first place.

"Well, Frank, it'll give some of these kids a chance to pad their statistics a little. I'm gonna be putting them up for All-County, All-State—kids like Merri and Debbie and Mink—and the stats will really give them a stronger case. And the honors and stuff can really help them get into college."

The athletic director smiled and laughed, not a mean laugh, or a sarcastic laugh—a genuine laugh. "Oh, come on, Mike—these girls don't need that for college."

"No, really, it can be a big help—"

He laughed again, "Hey, Mike, these girls aren't going to college. They all want to go to beauty school anyway." He winked as he said it; c'mon girls, can't you take a

joke? We didn't take it as a joke; it seemed to us that that's what he really believed. Mike just pushed his hair back with his hand and looked at the ground, then tugged at his beard. We sat on the bench, openly eavesdropping now, not pretending to be attending to our shoes or our injuries.

"They'll go until they find a husband at least."

Mike asked, still looking downward, "So that's it? No game?"

The athletic director smiled, "Well, we'll see what we can do, okay?" He waved in our general direction as he turned to walk back to the school. "See ya later, girls."

The rest of the team had come back from perimeters, and they were standing around, panting and sweating, recovering from the run. Mike slammed three soccer balls into mid-field with his foot and barked, "Go warm up!" and turned away from the field again. Merri, Mink and I trotted out to the center circle, with Lauren and Jody close behind, leaving Mike sitting on the bench, his elbows propped on his knees and holding his head in his hands. Merri twisted her ankle and cursed loudly, while the rest of us were silent, absorbing what we'd just heard. And so practice began.

Some of my stories to my grandchildren might sound suspiciously like those of my grandmother.

Understanding What You Read

1. What type of person was the grandmother described in the essay?
   a. An independent person who was ahead of her time in terms of feminism
   b. A loveable grandmother who cared for nothing more than being a good wife, mother, and grandmother
   c. A difficult person for everyone to get along with as she got older

2. In one sentence, what is the main idea—or theme, or thesis—of Christine Meding's essay?

3. Why does the author include the first and last paragraph about her grandmother and then never mention her in other paragraphs?

4. How do the athletic director's final words, "See ya later, girls," contribute to the essay's overall effect?

Writer's Workshop

Write a short essay in which you imply—as Christine Meding did—a critical comment about some aspect of sports. It could be over-competitiveness in sports or the imbalance of certain sports in your own school. Or, of course, you could find your own topic. As always, choose something you care about—that makes the best writing. Use Christine Meding's unifying device of opening and closing paragraphs that, while not directly about the main idea, parallel it and tie the essay together.

Pitcher

A poet looks at what being a pitcher is all about.

His art is eccentricity, his aim
How not to hit the mark he seems to aim at,

His passion how to avoid the obvious,
His technique how to vary the avoidance.

The others throw to be comprehended. He   5
Throws to be a moment misunderstood.

Yet not too much. Not errant, arrant, wild,
But every seeming aberration willed.

Not to, yet still, still to communicate
Making the batter understand too late.   10

---

1. *eccentricity:* a deviation from an accepted or established pattern.
7. *errant:* traveling outside the proper path; moving about aimlessly.
   arrant: without moderation, extreme.
8. *aberration:* a departure from standard behavior.

Understanding What You Read

1. Think about the poet's choice of words, such as **eccentricity** and **aberration,** and the meanings his words convey. What does a pitcher have to do to be successful, according to this poem?

2. One of the techniques used in this poem is **alliteration,** the repetition of initial consonant sounds, for example, in line 2, "**H**ow not to **h**it the mark **h**e seems to aim at." Used subtly, alliteration can bind key words together and give them emphasis. Find one or more additional examples of alliteration in the poem.

3. Who are the "others" in line 5? How is the way they throw different from the way a pitcher throws?

4. This poem is about being a baseball pitcher. But it might also be about the act of writing a poem. Explain.

Writer's Workshop

Choose a specific position of a sport—an end in football, a guard in basketball, a second baseman in baseball, or a goalie in hockey or soccer. In a stanza or a paragraph, sketch exactly what a player in that position does that is unique. Try to describe the position in an original and creative way, as Robert Francis does with "Pitcher."

Jump Shot

Here is a critical moment in a basketball game, slowed down, so that you can see what it is made of.

Lithe, quicker than the ball itself;
Spinning through the blocking forearms,
Hands like stars, spread to suspend
The ball from five, and only five,
Magic fingerprints.   5

The rebound resounding down the pole
And into asphalt, pounded hard by sneakers
Raggedier than the missing-tooth grimaces.

Grimaces. No smiles here. Concentration.
Movement. The calculation.   10
The arch-back leap. And off the rim again.
Once in ten the satisfying swoosh.

And no time wasted to enjoy it.
Grasp that globe and keep it dribbling:
Elbows were meant for eyesockets;   15
Work it up higher than hands,
Higher than the grab of gravity.

Working, each man for himself,
Yet neatly, neatly weaving in the pattern.

---

1. *lithe:* flexible and graceful.

Understanding What You Read

1. What message about sports is Richard Peck communicating?
   a. It's every athlete for himself or herself.
   b. Players are individuals but they need to work together.
   c. Glory and fame are fleeting.

2. A simile makes a comparison between two dissimilar things and joins them with the words **like**, **as**, or **than**. A **metaphor** makes a similar comparison but doesn't use any linking word. "Magic fingerprints" is a metaphor. What are the two things being compared in that metaphor? Can you find another metaphor in Richard Peck's poem?

3. Is this a professional game? How do you know?

Writer's Workshop

Write a free-verse poem (no rhyme, no regular rhythm or meter) in which you capture one aspect—like the jump shot—of one sport. Zero in on one part of a larger game. In your writing, create at least two striking comparisons between dissimilar things, using either similes or metaphors.

from **The Chosen**

Winning takes on a new meaning in this intense softball game.

Danny and I probably would never have met—or we would have met under altogether different circumstances—had it not been for America's entry into the Second World War and the desire this bred on the part of some English teachers in the Jewish parochial schools to show the gentile world that yeshiva[1] students were as physically fit, despite their long hours of study, as any other American student. They went about proving this by organizing the Jewish parochial schools in and around our area into competitive leagues, and once every two weeks the schools would compete against one another in a variety of sports. I became a member of my school's varsity softball team.

On a Sunday afternoon in early June, the fifteen members of my team met with our gym instructor in the play yard of our school. It was a warm day, and the sun was bright on the asphalt floor of the yard. The gym instructor was a short, chunky man in his early thirties who taught in the mornings in

a nearby public high school and supplemented his income by teaching in our yeshiva during the afternoons. He wore a white polo shirt, white pants, and white sweater, and from the awkward way the little black skullcap sat perched on his round, balding head, it was clearly apparent that he was not accustomed to wearing it with any sort of regularity. When he talked he frequently thumped his right fist into his left palm to emphasize a point. He walked on the balls of his feet, almost in imitation of a boxer's ring stance, and he was fanatically addicted to professional baseball. He had nursed our softball team along for two years, and by a mixture of patience, luck, shrewd manipulations during some tight ball games, and hard, fist-thumping harangues[2] calculated to shove us into a patriotic awareness of the importance of athletics and physical fitness for the war effort, he was able to mold our original team of fifteen awkward fumblers into the top team of our league. His name was Mr. Galanter, and all

---

1 *yeshiva:* a Jewish day school.

2 *harangues:* ranting lectures.

of us wondered why he was not off somewhere fighting in the war.

During my two years with the team, I had become quite adept at second base and had also developed a swift underhand pitch that would tempt a batter into a swing but would drop into a curve at the last moment and slide just below the flaying bat for a strike. Mr. Galanter always began a ball game by putting me at second base and would use me as a pitcher only in very tight moments, because, as he put it once, "My baseball philosophy is grounded on the defensive solidarity of the infield."

That afternoon we were scheduled to play the winning team of another neighborhood league, a team with a reputation for wild, offensive slugging and poor fielding. Mr. Galanter said he was counting upon our infield to act as a solid defensive front. Throughout the warm-up period, with only our team in the yard, he kept thumping his right fist into his left palm and shouting at us to be a solid defensive front.

"No holes," he shouted from near home plate. "No holes, you hear? Goldberg, what kind of solid defensive front is that? Close in. A battleship could get between you and Malter. That's it. Schwartz, what are you doing, looking for paratroops? This is a ball game.

The enemy's on the ground. That throw was wide, Goldberg. Throw it like a sharpshooter. Give him the ball again. Throw it. Good. Like a sharpshooter. Very good. Keep the infield solid. No defensive holes in this war."

We batted and threw the ball around, and it was warm and sunny, and there was the smooth, happy feeling of the summer soon to come, and the tight excitement of the ball game. We wanted very much to win, both for ourselves and, more especially, for Mr. Galanter, for we had all come to like his fist-thumping sincerity. To the rabbis[3] who taught in the Jewish parochial schools, baseball was an evil waste of time, a spawn of the potentially assimilationist English portion of the yeshiva day. But to the students of most of the parochial schools, an inter-league baseball victory had come to take on only a shade less significance than a top grade in Talmud,[4] for it was an unquestioned mark of one's Americanism, and to be counted a loyal American had become increasingly important to us during these last years of the war.

So Mr. Galanter stood near

3 *rabbis:* spiritual leaders of the Jewish community.

4 *Talmud:* the body of knowledge and tradition upon which the Jewish faith is based.

home plate, shouting instructions and words of encouragement, and we batted and tossed the ball around. I walked off the field for a moment to set up my eyeglasses for the game. I wore shell-rimmed glasses, and before every game I would bend the earpieces in so the glasses would stay tight on my head and not slip down the bridge of my nose when I began to sweat. I always waited until just before a game to bend down the earpieces, because, bent, they would cut into the skin over my ears, and I did not want to feel the pain a moment longer than I had to. The tops of my ears would be sore for days after every game, but better that, I thought, than the need to keep pushing my glasses up the bridge of my nose or the possibility of having them fall off suddenly during an important play.

Davey Cantor, one of the boys who acted as a replacement if a first-stringer had to leave the game, was standing near the wire screen behind home plate. He was a short boy, with a round face, dark hair, owlish glasses, and a very Semitic[5] nose. He watched me fix my glasses.

"You're looking good out there, Reuven," he told me.

"Thanks," I said.

"Everyone is looking real good."

---

5 *Semitic:* Jewish.

"It'll be a good game."

He stared at me through his glasses. "You think so?" he asked.

"Sure, why not?"

"You ever seen them play, Reuven?"

"No."

"They're murderers."

"Sure," I said.

"No, really. They're wild."

"You saw them play?"

"Twice. They're murderers."

"Everyone plays to win, Davey."

"They don't only play to win. They play like it's the first of the Ten Commandments."

I laughed. "That yeshiva?" I said. "Oh, come on, Davey."

"It's the truth."

"Sure," I said.

"Reb Saunders ordered them never to lose because it would shame their yeshiva or something. I don't know. You'll see."

"Hey, Malter!" Mr. Galanter shouted. "What are you doing, sitting this one out?"

"You'll see," Davey Cantor said.

"Sure." I grinned at him. "A holy war."

He looked at me.

"Are you playing?" I asked him.

"Mr. Galanter said I might take second base if you have to pitch."

"Well, good luck."

"Hey, Malter!" Mr. Galanter shouted. "There's a war on, remember?"

"Yes, sir!" I said, and ran back

out to my position at second base.

We threw the ball around a few more minutes, and then I went up to home plate for some batting practice. I hit a long one out to left field, and then a fast one to the shortstop, who fielded it neatly and whipped it to first. I had the bat ready for another swing when someone said, "Here they are," and I rested the bat on my shoulder and saw the team we were going to play turn up our block and come into the yard. I saw Davey Cantor kick nervously at the wire screen behind home plate, then put his hands into the pockets of his dungarees.[6] His eyes were wide and gloomy behind his owlish glasses.

I watched them come into the yard.

There were fifteen of them, and they were dressed alike in white shirts, dark pants, white sweaters, and small black skullcaps. In the fashion of the very Orthodox,[7] their hair was closely cropped, except for the area near their ears from which mushroomed the untouched hair that tumbled down into the long side curls. Some of them had the beginnings of beards, straggly tufts of hair that stood in isolated clumps on their chins, jawbones,

and upper lips. They all wore the traditional undergarment beneath their shirts, and the tzitzit, the long fringes appended to the four corners of the garment, came out above their belts and swung against their pants as they walked. These were the very Orthodox, and they obeyed literally the Biblical commandment *And ye shall look upon it*, which pertains to the fringes.

In contrast, our team had no particular uniform, and each of us wore whatever he wished: dungarees, shorts, pants, polo shirts, sweat shirts, even undershirts. Some of us wore the garment, others did not. None of us wore the fringes outside his trousers. The only element of uniform that we had in common was the small, black skullcap which we, too, wore.

They came up to the first-base side of the wire screen behind home plate and stood there in a silent black-and-white mass, holding bats and balls and gloves in their hands. I looked at them. They did not seem to me to present any picture of ferocity. I saw Davey Cantor kick again at the wire screen, then walk away from them to the third-base line, his hands moving nervously against his dungarees.

Mr. Galanter smiled and started toward them, moving quickly on

---

6 *dungarees:* denim pants, jeans.

7 *Orthodox:* a reference to those Jews who adhere strictly to Jewish law and apply it to everyday life.

the balls of his feet, his skullcap perched precariously on the top of his balding head.

A man disentangled himself from the black-and-white mass of players and took a step forward. He looked to be in his late twenties and wore a black suit, black shoes, and a black hat. He had a black beard, and he carried a book under one arm. He was obviously a rabbi, and I marveled that the yeshiva had placed a rabbi instead of an athletic coach over its team.

Mr. Galanter came up to him and offered his hand.

"We are ready to play," the rabbi said in Yiddish,[8] shaking Mr. Galanter's hand with obvious uninterest.

"Fine," Mr. Galanter said in English, smiling.

"The rabbi looked out at the field. "You played already?" he asked.

"How's that?" Mr. Galanter said.

"You had practice?"

"Well, sure—"

"We want to practice."

"How's that?" Mr. Galanter said again, looking surprised.

"You practiced, now we practice."

"You didn't practice in your own yard?"

---

8 *Yiddish:* a Jewish language derived from the German, Hebrew, and Slavic languages that originated in Middle and Eastern Europe.

"We practiced."

"Well, then—"

"But we have never played in your yard before. We want a few minutes."

"Well, now," Mr. Galanter said, "there isn't much time. The rules are each team practices in its own yard."

"We want five minutes," the rabbi insisted.

"Well—" Mr. Galanter said. He was no longer smiling. He always liked to go right into a game when we played in our own yard. It kept us from cooling off, he said.

"Five minutes," the rabbi said. "Tell your people to leave the field."

"How's that?" Mr. Galanter said.

"We cannot practice with your people on the field. Tell them to leave the field."

"Well, now," Mr. Galanter said, then stopped. He thought for a long moment. The black-and-white mass of players behind the rabbi stood very still, waiting. I saw Davey Cantor kick at the asphalt floor of the yard. "Well, all right. Five minutes. Just five minutes, now."

"Tell your people to leave the field," the rabbi said.

Mr. Galanter stared gloomily out at the field, looking a little deflated. "Everybody off!" he shouted, not very loudly. "They want a five-minute warm-up. Hustle, hustle. Keep those arms going. Keep it hot. Toss some balls around behind home. Let's go!"

The players scrambled off the field.

The black-and-white mass near the wire screen remained intact. The young rabbi turned and faced his team.

He talked in Yiddish. "We have the field for five minutes," he said. "Remember why and for whom we play."

Then he stepped aside, and the black-and-white mass dissolved into fifteen individual players who came quickly onto the field. One of them, a tall boy with sand-colored hair and long arms and legs that seemed all bones and angles, stood at home plate and commenced hitting balls out to the players. He hit a few easy grounders and pop-ups, and the fielders shouted encouragement to one another in Yiddish. They handled themselves awkwardly, dropping easy grounders, throwing wild, fumbling fly balls. I looked over at the young rabbi. He had sat down on the bench near the wire screen and was reading his book.

Behind the wire screen was a wide area, and Mr. Galanter kept us busy there throwing balls around.

"Keep those balls going!" he fist-thumped at us. "No one sits out this fire fight! Never underestimate the enemy!"

But there was a broad smile on his face. Now that he was actually seeing the other team, he seemed not at all concerned about the outcome of the game. In the interim between throwing a ball and having it thrown back to me, I told myself that I liked Mr. Galanter, and I wondered about his constant use of war expressions and why he wasn't in the army.

Davey Cantor came past me, chasing a ball that had gone between his legs.

"Some murderers," I grinned at him.

"You'll see," he said as he bent to retrieve the ball.

"Sure," I said.

"Especially the one batting. You'll see."

The ball was coming back to me, and I caught it neatly and flipped it back.

"Who's the one batting?" I asked.

"Danny Saunders."

"Pardon my ignorance, but who is Danny Saunders?"

"Reb Saunders' son," Davey Cantor said, blinking his eyes.

"I'm impressed."

"You'll see," Davey Cantor said, and ran off with his ball.

My father, who had no love at all for Hasidic[9] communities and their rabbinical overlords, had told

---

9 *Hasidic:* a reference to those Jews who are Hasidim, members of a sect

me about Rabbi Isaac Saunders and the zealousness with which he ruled his people and settled questions of Jewish law.

I saw Mr. Galanter look at his wristwatch, then stare out at the team on the field. The five minutes were apparently over, but the players were making no move to abandon the field. Danny Saunders was now at first base, and I noticed that his long arms and legs were being used to good advantage, for by stretching and jumping he was able to catch most of the wild throws that came his way.

Mr. Galanter went over to the young rabbi who was still sitting on the bench and reading.

"It's five minutes," he said.

The rabbi looked up from his book. "Ah?" he said.

"The five minutes are up," Mr. Galanter said.

The rabbi stared out at the field. "Enough!" he shouted in Yiddish. "It's time to play!" Then he looked down at the book and resumed his reading.

The players threw the ball around for another minute or two, and then slowly came off the field. Danny Saunders walked past me, still wearing his first baseman's glove. He was a good deal taller than I, and in contrast to my somewhat ordinary but decently propor-

tioned features and dark hair, his face seemed to have been cut from stone. His chin, jaw and cheekbones were made up of jutting hard lines, his nose was straight and pointed, his lips full, rising to a steep angle from the center point beneath his nose and then slanting off to form a too-wide mouth. His eyes were deep blue, and the sparse tufts of hair on his chin, jawbones, and upper lip, the close-cropped hair on his head, and the flow of side curls along his ears were the color of sand. He moved in a loose-jointed, disheveled sort of way, all arms and legs, talking in Yiddish to one of his teammates and ignoring me completely as he passed by. I told myself that I did not like his Hasidic-bred sense of superiority and that it would be a great pleasure to defeat him and his team in this afternoon's game.

The umpire, a gym instructor from a parochial school two blocks away, called the teams together to determine who would bat first. I saw him throw a bat into the air. It was caught and almost dropped by a member of the other team.

During the brief hand-over-hand choosing, Davey Cantor came over and stood next to me.

"What do you think?" he asked.

"They're a snooty bunch," I told him.

"What do you think about their playing?"

---

that originated in Poland and demands strict obedience of religious law.

"They're lousy."

"They're murderers."

"Oh, come on, Davey."

"You'll see, " Davey Cantor said, looking at me gloomily.

"I just did see."

"You didn't see anything."

"Sure," I said. "Elijah the prophet comes in to pitch for them in tight spots."

"I'm not being funny," he said, looking hurt.

"Some murderers," I told him, and laughed.

The teams began to disperse. We had lost the choosing, and they had decided to bat first. We scampered onto the field. I took up my position at second base. I saw the young rabbi sitting on the bench near the wire fence and reading. We threw a ball around for a minute. Mr. Galanter stood alongside third base, shouting his words of encouragement at us. It was warm, and I was sweating a little and feeling very good. Then the umpire, who had taken up his position behind the pitcher, called for the ball and someone tossed it to him. He handed it to the pitcher and shouted, "Here we go! Play ball!" We settled into our positions.

Mr. Galanter shouted, "Goldberg, move in!" and Sidney Goldberg, our shortstop, took two steps forward and moved a little closer to third base. "Okay, fine," Mr. Galanter said. "Keep that infield

solid!"

A short, thin boy came up to the plate and stood there with his feet together, holding the bat awkwardly over his head. He wore steel-rimmed glasses that gave his face a pinched, old man's look. He swung wildly at the first pitch, and the force of the swing spun him completely around. His earlocks lifted off the sides of his head and followed him around in an almost horizontal circle. Then he steadied himself and resumed his position near the plate, short, thin, his feet together, holding his bat over his head in an awkward grip.

The umpire called the strike in a loud, clear voice, and I saw Sidney Goldberg look over at me and grin broadly.

"If he studies Talmud like that, he's dead," Sidney Goldberg said.

I grinned back at him.

"Keep that infield solid!" Mr. Galanter shouted from third base. "Malter, a little to your left! Good!"

The next pitch was too high, and the boy chopped at it, lost his bat and fell forward on his hands. Sidney Goldberg and I looked at each other again. Sidney was in my class. We were similar in build, tall and lithe, with somewhat spindly arms and legs. He was not a very good student, but he was an excellent shortstop. We lived on the same block and were good but not close friends. He was dressed in an undershirt and dungarees and was not wearing the four-cornered garment. I had on a light-blue shirt and dark-blue work pants, and I wore the four-cornered garment under the shirt.

The short, thin boy was back at the plate, standing with his feet together and holding the bat in his awkward grip. He let the next pitch go by, and the umpire called it a strike. I saw the young rabbi look up a moment from his book, then resume reading.

"Two more just like that!" I shouted encouragingly to the pitcher. "Two more, Schwartzie!" And I thought to myself, Some murderers.

I saw Danny Saunders go over to the boy who had just struck out and talk to him. The boy looked down and seemed to shrivel with hurt. He hung his head and walked away behind the wire screen. Another short, thin boy took his place at the plate. I looked around for Davey Cantor but could not see him.

The boy at bat swung wildly at the first two pitches and missed them both. He swung again at the third pitch, and I heard the loud *thwack* of the bat as it connected with the ball, and saw the ball move in a swift, straight line toward Sidney Goldberg, who caught it, bobbled it for a moment, and finally got it into his glove. He

tossed the ball to me, and we threw it around. I saw him take off his glove and shake his left hand.

"That hurt," he said, grinning at me.

"Good catch," I told him.

"That hurt like hell," he said, and put his glove back on his hand.

The batter who stood now at the plate was broad-shouldered and built like a bear. He swung at the first pitch, missed, then swung again at the second pitch and sent the ball in a straight line over the head of the third baseman into left field. I scrambled to second, stood on the base and shouted for the ball. I saw the left fielder pick it up on the second bounce and relay it to me. It was coming in a little high, and I had my glove raised for it. I felt more than saw the batter charging toward second, and as I was getting my glove on the ball he smashed into me like a truck. The ball went over my head, and I fell forward heavily onto the asphalt floor of the yard, and he passed me, going toward third, his fringes flying out behind him, holding his skullcap to his head with his right hand so it would not fall off. Abe Goodstein, our first baseman, retrieved the ball and whipped it home, and the batter stood at third, a wide grin on his face.

The yeshiva team exploded into

wild cheers and shouted loud words of congratulations in Yiddish to the batter.

Sidney Goldberg helped me get to my feet.

"That momzer!"[10] he said. "You weren't in his way!"

"Wow!" I said, taking a few deep breaths. I had scraped the palm of my right hand.

"What a momzer!" Sidney Goldberg said.

I saw Mr. Galanter come storming onto the field to talk to the umpire. "What kind of play was that?" he asked heatedly. "How are you going to rule that?"

"Safe at third," the umpire said. "Your boy was in the way."

Mr. Galanter's mouth fell open. "How's that again?"

"Safe at third," the umpire repeated.

Mr. Galanter looked ready to argue, thought better of it, then stared over at me. "Are you all right, Malter?"

"I'm okay," I said, taking another deep breath.

Mr. Galanter walked angrily off the field.

"Play ball!" the umpire shouted.

The yeshiva team quieted down. I saw that the young rabbi was now looking up from his book and smiling faintly.

A tall, thin player came up to the plate, set his feet in correct position, swung his bat a few times, then crouched into a waiting stance. I saw it was Danny Saunders. I opened and closed my right hand, which was still sore from the fall.

"Move back! Move back!" Mr. Galanter was shouting from alongside third base, and I took two steps back.

I crouched, waiting.

The first pitch was wild, and the yeshiva team burst into loud laughter. The young rabbi was sitting on the bench, watching Danny Saunders intently.

"Take it easy, Schwartzie!" I shouted encouragingly to the pitcher. "There's only one more to go!"

The next pitch was about a foot over Danny Saunders' head, and the yeshiva team howled with laughter. Sidney Goldberg and I looked at each other. I saw Mr. Galanter standing very still alongside third, staring at the pitcher. The rabbi was still watching Danny Saunders.

The next pitch left Schwartzie's hand in a long, slow line, and before it was halfway to the plate I knew Danny Saunders would try for it. I knew it from the way his left foot came forward and the bat snapped back and his long, thin body began its swift pivot. I tensed, waiting for the sound of the bat against the ball, and when it came

---

10 *momzer:* a Yiddish term of abuse, usually directed to one who is nasty or devious.

it sounded like a gunshot. For a wild fraction of a second I lost sight of the ball. Then I saw Schwartzie dive to the ground, and there was the ball coming through the air where his head had been, and I tried for it but it was moving too fast, and I barely had my glove raised before it was in center field. It was caught on a bounce and thrown to Sidney Goldberg, but by that time Danny Saunders was standing solidly on my base and the yeshiva team was screaming with joy.

Mr. Galanter called for time and walked over to talk to Schwartzie. Sidney Goldberg nodded to me, and the two of us went over to them.

"That ball could've killed me!" Schwartzie was saying. He was of medium size, with a long face and a bad case of acne. He wiped sweat from his face. "My God, did you see that ball?"

"I saw it," Mr. Galanter said grimly.

"That was too fast to stop, Mr. Galanter," I said in Schwartzie's defense.

"I heard about that Danny Saunders," Sidney Goldberg said. "He always hits the pitcher."

"You could've told me," Schwartzie lamented. "I could've been ready."

"I only *heard* about it," Sidney Goldberg said. "You always believe

everything you hear?"

"God, that ball could've killed me!" Schwartzie said again.

"You want to go on pitching?" Mr. Galanter said. A thin sheen of sweat covered his forehead, and he looked very grim.

"Sure, Mr. Galanter," Schwartzie said. "I'm okay."

"You're sure?"

"Sure I'm sure."

"No heroes in this war, now," Mr. Galanter said. "I want live soldiers, not dead heroes."

"I'm no hero," Schwartzie muttered lamely. "I can still get it over, Mr. Galanter. God, it's only the first inning."

"Okay, soldier," Mr. Galanter said, not very enthusiastically. "Just keep our side of this war fighting."

"I'm trying my best, Mr. Galanter," Schwartzie said.

Mr. Galanter nodded, still looking grim, and started off the field. I saw him take a handkerchief out of his pocket and wipe his forehead.

• • • • •

The umpire came over to us. "You boys planning to chat here all afternoon?" he asked. He was a squat man in his late forties, and he looked impatient.

"No, sir," I said very politely, and Sidney and I ran back to our places.

Danny Saunders was standing

on my base. His white shirt was pasted to his arms and back with sweat.

"That was a nice shot," I offered.

He looked at me curiously and said nothing.

"You always hit it like that to the pitcher?" I asked.

He smiled faintly. "You're Reuven Malter," he said in perfect English. He had a low, nasal voice.

"That's right," I said, wondering where he had heard my name.

"You're father is David Malter, the one who writes articles on the Talmud?"

"Yes."

"I told my team we're going to kill you apikorsim[11] this afternoon." He said it flatly, without a trace of expression in his voice.

I stared at him and hoped the sudden tight coldness I felt wasn't showing on my face. "Sure," I said. "Rub your tzitzit for good luck."

I walked away from him and took up my position near the base. I looked toward the wire screen and saw Davey Cantor standing there, staring out at the field, his hands in his pockets. I crouched down quickly, because Schwartzie was going into his pitch.

The batter swung wildly at the first two pitches and missed each time. The next one was low, and he let it go by, then hit a grounder to the first baseman, who dropped it, flailed about for it wildly, and recovered it in time to see Danny Saunders cross the plate. The first baseman stood there for a moment, drenched in shame, then tossed the ball to Schwartzie. I saw Mr. Galanter standing near third base, wiping his forehead. The yeshiva team had gone wild again, and they were all trying to get to Danny Saunders and shake his hand. I saw the rabbi smile broadly, then look down at his book and resume reading.

Sidney Goldberg came over to me. "What did Saunders tell you?" he asked.

"He said they were going to kill us apikorsim this afternoon."

He stared at me. "Those are nice people, those yeshiva people," he said, and walked slowly back to his position.

The next batter hit a long fly ball to right field. It was caught on the run.

"Hooray for us," Sidney Goldberg said grimly as we headed off the field. "Any longer and they'd ask us to join them for the Mincha Service."[12]

"Not us," I said. "We're not holy enough."

"Where did they learn to hit like that?"

"Who knows?" I said.

---

11 *apikorsim: Gr.,* those who lack religious conviction.

12 *Mincha Service:* an afternoon prayer service held daily in a synagogue.

We were standing near the wire screen, forming a tight circle around Mr. Galanter.

"Only two runs," Mr. Galanter said, smashing his right fist into his left hand. "And they hit us with all they had. Now we give them *our* heavy artillery. Now *we* barrage *them*!" I saw that he looked relieved but that he was still sweating. His skullcap seemed pasted to his head with sweat. "Okay!" he said. "Fire away!"

The circle broke up, and Sidney Goldberg walked to the plate, carrying a bat. I saw the rabbi was still sitting on the bench, reading. I started to walk around behind him to see what book it was, when Davey Cantor came over, his hands in his pockets, his eyes still gloomy.

"Well?" he asked.

"Well what?" I said.

"I told you they could hit."

"So you told me. So what?" I was in no mood for his feelings of doom, and I let my voice show it.

He sensed my annoyance. "I wasn't bragging or anything," he said, looking hurt. "I just wanted to know what you thought."

"They can hit," I said.

"They're murderers," he said.

I watched Sidney Goldberg let a strike go by and said nothing.

"How's your hand?" Davey Cantor asked.

"I scraped it."

"He ran into you real hard."

"Who is he?"

"Dov Shlomowitz," Davey Cantor said. "Like his name, that's what he is," he added in Hebrew. "Dov" is the Hebrew word for bear.

"Was I blocking him?"

Davey Cantor shrugged. "You were and you weren't. The ump could've called it either way."

"He felt like a truck," I said, watching Sidney Goldberg step back from a close pitch.

"You should see his father. He's one of Reb Saunders' shamashim. Some bodyguard he makes."

"Reb Saunders has bodyguards?"

"Sure he has bodyguards," Davey Cantor said. "They protect him from his own popularity. Where're you been living all these years?"

"I don't have anything to do with them."

"You're not missing a thing, Reuven."

"How do you know so much about Reb Saunders?"

"My father gives him contributions."

"Well, good for your father," I said.

"He doesn't pray there or anything. He just gives him contributions."

"You're on the wrong team."

"No, I'm not, Reuven. Don't be like that." He was looking very hurt. "My father isn't a Hasid or anything. He just gives them some money a couple times a year."

"I was only kidding, Davey." I grinned at him. "Don't be so serious about everything."

I saw his face break into a happy smile, and just then Sidney Goldberg hit a fast, low grounder and raced off to first. The ball went right through the legs of the shortstop and into center field.

"Hold it at first!" Mr. Galanter screamed at him, and Sidney stopped at first and stood on the base.

The ball had been tossed quickly to second base. The second baseman looked over toward first, then threw the ball to the pitcher. The rabbi glanced up from the book for a moment, then went back to his reading.

"Malter, coach him at first!" Mr. Galanter shouted, and I ran up the base line.

"They can hit, but they can't field," Sidney Goldberg said, grinning at me as I came to a stop alongside the base.

"Davey Cantor says they're murderers," I said.

"Old gloom-and-doom Davey," Sidney Goldberg said, grinning.

Danny Saunders was standing away from the base, making a point of ignoring us both.

The next batter hit a high fly to the second baseman, who caught it, dropped it, retrieved it, and made a wild attempt at tagging Sidney Goldberg as he raced past him to second.

"Safe all around!" the umpire called, and our team burst out with shouts of joy. Mr. Galanter was smiling. The rabbi continued reading, and I saw that he was now slowly moving the upper part of his body back and forth.

"Keep your eyes open, Sidney!" I shouted from alongside first base. I saw Danny Saunders look at me, then look away. Some murderers, I thought. Shleppers[13] is more like it.

"If it's on the ground run like hell," I said to the batter who had just come onto first base, and he nodded at me. He was our third baseman, and he was about my size.

"If they keep fielding like that we'll be here till tomorrow," he said, and I grinned at him.

I saw Mr. Galanter talking to the next batter, who was nodding his head vigorously. He stepped to the plate, hit a hard grounder to the pitcher, who fumbled it for a moment then threw it to first. I saw Danny Saunders stretch for it and stop it.

"Out!" the umpire called. "Safe on second and third!"

As I ran up to the plate to bat, I

---

13 *shleppers:* a Yiddish term denoting those who move slowly or awkwardly.

. . . .

almost laughed aloud at the pitcher's stupidity. He had thrown it to first rather than third, and now we had Sidney Goldberg on third, and a man on second. I hit a grounder to the shortstop and instead of throwing it to second he threw it to first, wildly, and again Danny Saunders stretched and stopped the ball. But I beat the throw and heard the umpire call out, "Safe all around! One in!" And everyone on our team was patting Sidney Goldberg on the back. Mr. Galanter smiled broadly.

"Hello again," I said to Danny Saunders, who was standing near me, guarding his base. "Been rubbing your tzitzit lately?"

He looked at me, then looked slowly away, his face expressionless.

Schwartzie was at the plate, swinging his bat.

"Keep your eyes open!" I shouted to the runner on third. He looked too eager to head for home. "It's only one out!"

He waved a hand at me.

Schwartzie took two balls and a strike, then I saw him begin to pivot on the fourth pitch. The runner on third started for home. He was almost halfway down the base line when the bat sent the ball in a hard line drive straight at the third baseman, the short, thin boy with the spectacles and the old man's face, who had stood hugging the base and who now caught the ball more with his stomach than with his glove, managed somehow to hold on to it, and stood there, looking bewildered and astonished.

I returned to first and saw our player who had been on third and who was now halfway to home plate turn sharply and start a panicky race back.

"Step on the base!" Danny Saunders screamed in Yiddish across the field, and more out of obedience than awareness the third baseman put a foot on the base.

The yeshiva team howled its happiness and raced off the field. Danny Saunders looked at me, started to say something, stopped, then walked quickly away.

I saw Mr. Galanter going back up the third-base line, his face grim. The rabbi was looking up from his book and smiling.

I took up my position near second base, and Sidney Goldberg came over to me.

"Why'd he have to take off like that?" he asked.

I glared at our third baseman, who was standing near Mr. Galanter and looking very dejected.

"He was in a hurry to win the war," I said bitterly.

"What a jerk," Sidney Goldberg said.

"Goldberg, get over to your place!" Mr. Galanter called out. There was an angry edge to his voice. "Let's keep that infield solid!"

Sidney Goldberg went quickly to his position. I stood still and waited.

It was hot, and I was sweating beneath my clothes. I felt the earpieces of my glasses cutting into the skin over my ears, and I took the glasses off for a moment and ran a finger over the pinched ridges of skin, the put them back on quickly because Schwartzie was going into a windup. I crouched down, waiting, remembering Danny Saunders' promise to his team that they would kill us apikorsim. The word had meant, originally, a Jew educated in Judaism who denied basic tenets of his faith, like the existence of God, the revelation, the resurrection of the dead. To people like Reb Saunders, it also meant any educated Jew who might be reading, say, Darwin,[14] and who was not wearing side curls and fringes outside his trousers. I was an apikoros to Danny Saunders, despite my belief in God and Torah,[15] because I did not have side curls and was attending a parochial school where too many English subjects were offered and where Jewish subjects were taught in Hebrew instead of Yiddish, both unheard-of sins, the former because it took time away from the study of Torah, the latter because Hebrew was the Holy Tongue and to use it in ordinary classroom discourse was a desecration of God's Name. I had never really had any personal contact with this kind of Jew before. My father had told me he didn't mind their beliefs. What annoyed him was their fanatic sense of righteousness, their absolute certainty that they and they alone had God's ear, and every other Jew was wrong, totally wrong, a sinner, a hypocrite, an apikoros, and doomed, therefore, to burn in hell. I found myself wondering again how they had learned to hit a ball like that if time for the study of Torah was so precious to them and why they had sent a rabbi along to waste his time sitting on a bench during a ball game.

Standing on the field and watching the boy at the plate swing at a high ball and miss, I felt myself suddenly very angry, and it was at that point for me the game stopped being merely a game and became a war. The fun and excitement was out of it now. Somehow the yeshiva team had translated this after-

---

14 *Darwin:* Charles Darwin, the scientist who originated the theory of evolution in 1860.

15 *Torah:* The law of the Jewish religion.

noon's baseball game into a conflict between what they regarded as their righteousness and our sinfulness. I found myself growing more and more angry, and I felt the anger begin to focus itself upon Danny Saunders, and suddenly it was not at all difficult for me to hate him.

Schwartzie let five of their men come up to the plate that half inning and let one of those five score. Sometime during that half inning, one of the members of the yeshiva team had shouted at us in Yiddish, "Burn in hell, you apikorsim!" and by the time that half inning was over and we were standing around Mr. Galanter near the wire screen, all of us knew that this was not just another ball game.

Mr. Galanter was sweating heavily, and his face was grim. All he said was, "We fight it careful from now on. No more mistakes." He said it very quietly, and we were all quiet, too, as the batter stepped up to the plate.

We proceeded to play a slow, careful game, bunting whenever we had to, sacrificing to move runners forward, obeying Mr. Galanter's instructions. I noticed that no matter where the runners were on the bases, the yeshiva team always threw to Danny Saunders, and I realized that they did this because he was the only

infielder who could be relied upon to stop their wild throws. Sometime during the inning, I walked over behind the rabbi and looked over his shoulder at the book he was reading. I saw the words were Yiddish. I walked back to the wire screen. Davey Cantor came over and stood next to me, but he remained silent.

We scored only one run that inning, and we walked onto the field for the first half of the third inning with a sense of doom.

Dov Shlomowitz came up to the plate. He stood there like a bear, the bat looking like a matchstick in his beefy hands. Schwartzie pitched, and he sliced one neatly over the head of the third baseman for a single. The yeshiva team howled, and again one of them called out to us in Yiddish, "Burn, you apikorsim!" and Sidney Goldberg and I looked at each other without saying a word.

Mr. Galanter was standing alongside third base, wiping his forehead. The rabbi was sitting quietly, reading his book.

I took off my glasses and rubbed the tops of my ears. I felt a sudden momentary sense of unreality, as if the play yard, with its black asphalt and its white base lines, were my entire world now, as if all the previous years of my life had led me somehow to this one ball game, and all the future years of my life would depend upon its outcome. I stood there for a moment, holding the glasses in my hand and feeling frightened. Then I took a deep breath, and the feeling passed. It's only a ball game, I told myself. What's a ball game?

Mr. Galanter was shouting at us to move back. I was standing a few feet to the left of second, and I took two steps back. I saw Danny Saunders walk up to the plate, swinging a bat. The yeshiva team was shouting at him in Yiddish to kill us apikorsim.

Schwartzie turned around to check the field. He looked nervous and was taking his time. Sidney Goldberg was standing up straight, waiting. We looked at each other, then looked away. Mr. Galanter stood very still alongside third base, looking at Schwartzie.

The first pitch was low, and Danny Saunders ignored it. The second one started to come in shoulder-high, and before it was two thirds of the way to the plate, I was already standing on second base. My glove was going up as the bat cracked against the ball, and I saw the ball move in a straight line directly over Schwartzie's head, high over his head, moving so fast he hadn't even had time to regain his balance from the pitch before it went past

him. I saw Dov Shlomowitz heading toward me and Danny Saunders racing to first, and I heard the yeshiva team shouting and Sidney Goldberg screaming, and I jumped, pushing myself upward off the ground with all the strength I had in my legs and stretching my glove hand till I thought it would pull out of my shoulder. The ball hit the pocket of my glove with an impact that numbed my hand and went through me like an electric shock, and I felt the force pull me backward and throw me off balance, and I came down hard on my left hip and elbow. I saw Dov Shlomowitz whirl and start back to first, and I pushed myself up into a sitting position and threw the ball awkwardly to Sidney Goldberg, who caught it and shipped it to first. I heard the umpire scream "Out!" and Sidney Goldberg ran over to help me to my feet, a look of disbelief and ecstatic joy on his face. Mr. Galanter shouted "Time!" and came racing onto the field. Schwartzie was standing in his pitcher's position with his mouth open. Danny Saunders stood on the base line a few feet from first, where he had stopped after I had caught the ball, staring out at me, his face frozen to stone. The rabbi was staring at me, too, and the yeshiva team was deathly silent.

"That was a great catch, Reuven!" Sidney Goldberg said,

thumping my back. "That was sensational!"

I saw the rest of our team had suddenly come back to life and was throwing the ball around and talking up the game.

Mr. Galanter came over. "You all right, Malter?" he asked. "Let me see that elbow."

I showed him the elbow. I had scraped it, but the skin had not been broken.

"That was a good play," Mr. Galanter said, beaming at me. I saw his face was still covered with sweat, but he was smiling broadly now.

"Thanks, Mr. Galanter."

"How's that hand?"

"It hurts a little."

"Let me see it."

I took off the glove, and Mr. Galanter poked and bent the wrist and fingers of the hand.

"Does that hurt?" he asked.

"No," I lied.

"You want to go on playing?"

"Sure, Mr. Galanter."

"Okay," he said, smiling at me and patting my back. "We'll put you in for a Purple Heart on that one, Malter."

I grinned at him.

"Okay," Mr. Galanter said. "Let's keep this infield solid!"

He walked away, smiling.

"I can't get over that catch," Sidney Goldberg said.

"You threw it real good to first," I told him.

"Yeah," he said. "While you were sitting on your tail."

We grinned at each other, and went to our positions.

Two more of the yeshiva team got to bat that inning. The first one hit a single, and the second one sent a high fly to short, which Sidney Goldberg caught without having to move a step. We scored two runs that inning and one run the next, and by the top half of the fifth inning we were leading five to three. Four of their men had stood up to bat during the top half of the fourth inning, and they had got only a single on an error to first. When we took to the field in the top half of the fifth inning, Mr. Galanter was walking back and forth alongside third on the balls of his feet, sweating, smiling, grinning, wiping his head nervously; the rabbi was no longer reading; the yeshiva team was silent as death. Davey Cantor was playing second, and I stood in the pitcher's position. Schwartzie had pleaded exhaustion, and since this was the final inning—our parochial school schedules only permitted us time for five-inning games—and the yeshiva team's last chance at bat, Mr. Galanter was taking no chances and told me to pitch. Davey Cantor was a poor fielder, but Mr. Galanter was counting on my pitching to finish off the game. My left hand was still sore from the catch, and the wrist hurt whenever I caught a ball, but the right hand was fine, and the pitches went in fast and dropped into the curve just when I wanted them to. Dov Shlomowitz stood at the plate, swung three times at what looked to him to be perfect pitches, and hit nothing but air. He stood there looking bewildered after the third swing, then slowly walked away. We threw the ball around the infield, and Danny Saunders came up to the plate.

The members of the yeshiva team stood near the wire fence, watching Danny Saunders. They were very quiet. The rabbi was sitting on the bench, his book closed. Mr. Galanter was shouting at everyone to move back. Danny Saunders swung his bat a few times, then fixed himself into position and looked out at me.

Here's a present from an apikoros, I thought, and let go the ball. It went in fast and straight, and I saw Danny Saunders' left foot move out and his bat go up and his body begin to pivot. He swung just as the ball slid into its curve, and the bat cut savagely through empty air, twisting him around and sending him off balance. His black skullcap fell off his head, and he regained his balance and bent quickly to retrieve it. He stood there for a moment, very still, staring out at

me. Then he resumed his position at the plate. The ball came back to me from the catcher, and my wrist hurt as I caught it.

The yeshiva team was very quiet, and the rabbi had begun to chew his lip.

I lost control of the next pitch, and it was wide. On the third pitch, I went into a long, elaborate windup and sent him a slow, curving blooper, the kind a batter always wants to hit and always misses. He ignored it completely, and the umpire called it a ball.

I felt my left wrist begin to throb as I caught the throw from the catcher. I was hot and sweaty, and the earpieces of my glasses were cutting deeply into the flesh above my ears as a result of the head movements that went with my pitching.

Danny Saunders stood very still at the plate, waiting.

Okay, I thought, hating him bitterly. Here's another present.

The ball went to the plate fast and straight, and dropped just below his swing. He checked himself with difficulty so as not to spin around, but he went off his balance again and took two or three staggering steps forward before he was able to stand up straight.

The catcher threw the ball back, and I winced at the pain in my wrist. I took the ball out of the glove, held it in my right hand and turned around for a moment to look out at the field and let the pain in my wrist subside. When I turned back I saw that Danny Saunders hadn't moved. He was holding his bat in his left hand, standing very still and staring at me. His eyes were dark, and his lips were parted in a crazy, idiot grin. I heard the umpire yell "Play ball!" but Danny Saunders stood there, staring at me and grinning. I turned and looked out at the field again, and when I turned back he was still standing there, staring at me and grinning. I could see his teeth between his parted lips. I took a deep breath and felt myself wet with sweat. I wiped my right hand on my pants and saw Danny Saunders step slowly to the plate and set his legs in position. He was no longer grinning. He stood looking at me over his left shoulder, waiting.

I wanted to finish it quickly because of the pain in my wrist, and I sent in another fast ball. I watched it head straight for the plate. I saw him go into a sudden crouch, and in the fraction of a second before he hit the ball I realized that he had anticipated the curve and was deliberately swinging low. I was still a little off balance from the pitch, but I managed to bring my glove hand up in front of my face just as he hit the ball. I saw it coming at me, and there was noth-

ing I could do. It hit the finger section of my glove, deflected off, smashed into the upper rim of the left lens of my glasses, glanced off my forehead, and knocked me down. I scrambled around for it wildly, but by the time I got my hand on it Danny Saunders was standing safely on first.

I heard Mr. Galanter call time, and everyone on the field came racing over to me. My glasses lay shattered on the asphalt floor, and I felt a sharp pain in my left eye when I blinked. My wrist throbbed, and I could feel the bump coming up on my forehead. I looked over at first, but without my glasses Danny Saunders was only a blur. I imagined I could still see him grinning.

I saw Mr. Galanter put his face next to mine. It was sweaty and full of concern. I wondered what all the fuss was about. I had only lost a pair of glasses, and we had at least two more good pitchers on the team.

"Are you all right, boy?" Mr. Galanter was saying. He looked at my face and forehead. "Somebody wet a handkerchief with cold water!" he shouted. I wondered why he was shouting. His voice hurt my head and rang in my ears. I saw Davey Cantor run off, looking frightened. I heard Sidney Goldberg say something, but I couldn't make out his words. Mr.

Galanter put his arm around my shoulders and walked me off the field. He sat me down on the bench next to the rabbi. Without my glasses everything more than about ten feet away from me was blurred. I blinked and wondered about the pain in my left eye. I heard voices and shouts, and then Mr. Galanter was putting a wet handkerchief on my head.

"You feel dizzy, boy?" he said.

I shook my head.

"You're sure now?"

"I'm all right," I said, and wondered why my voice sounded husky and why talking hurt my head.

"You sit quiet now," Mr. Galanter said. "You begin to feel dizzy, you let me know right away."

"Yes, sir," I said.

He went away. I sat on the bench next to the rabbi, who looked at me once, then looked away. I heard shouts in Yiddish. The pain in my left eye was so intense I could feel it in the base of my spine. I sat on the bench a long time, long enough to see us lose the game by a score of eight to seven, long enough to hear the yeshiva team shout with joy, long enough to begin to cry at the pain in my left eye, long enough for Mr. Galanter to come over to me at the end of the game, take one look at my face and go running out of the yard to call a cab.

Understanding What You Read

1. Why did some teachers in the Jewish schools arrange sports competition among the schools?

    a. To give the boys a chance at competing

    b. To try to determine a state champion

    c. To help the yeshiva students be physically fit for the national war effort

2. Mr. Galanter most emphasized what aspect of baseball in his coaching?

    a. defensive play

    b. teamwork

    c. hitting

3. Mr. Galanter's personality could best be characterized as
   a. relaxed and laid-back
   b. aggressive and determined
   c. inconsistent and moody

4. Why are Reuven and his teammates scorned by Danny Saunders and his father, a rabbi?
   a. They don't play baseball well
   b. They don't observe their Judaic faith fully and appropriately enough, in the Saunders' view
   c. They are not good sports

5. Mr. Galanter speaks to his team in the language of war. Why is the image of war appropriate for this story? Consider both the story's setting and what happens in the story.

Writer's Workshop

This story (part of Chapter 1 of the novel **The Chosen**) is a skillful extended narration of just one scene. Quick-moving dialogue makes up about one-half of the text. Write a scene involving one moment or aspect of some sport. Load the story with details of people doing something and of people speaking. The use of dialogue will guarantee that you "show, don't tell," a classic piece of advice for all fiction writers.

A Turn with the Sun

Think about your first year at a new school. Can an exceptional performance in a sport help you fit in?

It was dusk; the warm air of the early spring afternoon was edged with an exhilarating chill, and in the half-light the dark green turf of the playing field acquired the smooth perfection of a thick rug, spreading up to the thin woods lightly brushed with color along one sideline, and down to the river, with the stolid little bridge arching over it, along the other. Across the stream more playing fields, appearing smoother still in the distance, sloped gently up to the square gray shape of the gymnasium; and behind it the towers and turrets of the boys' school were etched against the darkening blue sky.

The lacrosse game was over, and the Red team, pleased by a three-to-two victory, but only mildly pleased since it was just an intramural game, formed a loose circle and cheered for themselves and their opponents: "Reds, Reds, Reds, Reds, Rah, Rah, Rah, Blues!" A few players tarried for some extra shots at the cage, which the second-string Blue goalie made halfhearted attempts to defend; but most of them straggled off toward the bridge, swinging their lacrosse sticks carelessly along beside them. Three boys played catch as they went; one of them missed a pass near the bridge and the ball plopped into the stream.

"Nuts!" he said. "I'm not going in after it."

"No, too cold," the others agreed.

As Lawrence stepped onto the gravel road which led over the bridge he experienced that thrill of feeling himself strong and athletic which the sound of his cleats on a hard surface always excited. His stride became more free-swinging, authoritative.

"I scored," he said simply. "D'you see that, Bead? I scored my first goal."

"Yeah," Bead's scratchy voice had an overtone of cordiality. "Good going, boy. The winning point too."

They crunched along in silence up to the bridge, and then Lawrence was emboldened to issue an invitation. "You going to the flick tonight? I mean I guess it's

Shelley Winters or someone . . . "

Bead balanced his companion's possible new status for an indecisive instant, and then elected to hedge. "Yeah, well I'll see you after dinner in the Butt Room for a smoke. I'm prob'ly going. Bruce," he added with careful casualness, "said something about it."

Bruce! Lawrence sensed once again that he was helplessly sliding back, into the foggy social bottomland where unacceptable first-year boys dwell. He had risen out of it just now: the goal he had scored, the sweaty ease of his body, the grump-grump of his shoes on the gravel had suggested something better. But here was Bead, like himself only seven months at the school, and yet going to the movies with Bruce. Lawrence marvelled at the speed with which Bead was settling into the school, and he marvelled again at his own failure, after seven months, to win a single close friend.

Not that Lawrence Stuart was a pariah;[1] the hockey captain had never invaded his room, as he had Fruitcake Putsby's next door, and festooned his clothes through the hall; he had never found a mixture of sour cream and cereal in his bed at night, no one had ever poured ink into the tub while he was bathing. The victims of such violations were genuine outcasts.

But the very fact of their persecutions had, Lawrence reflected, some kind of negative value. They were at least notable in their way. "There goes Fruitcake Putsby!" someone would should, "Hi ya, Fruitie." They had a status all their own; and a few of them, by senior year, could succeed by some miraculous alchemy[2] in becoming accepted and even respected by the whole school.

Lawrence was neither grotesque enough nor courageous enough for that. He merely inhabited the nether world of the unregarded, where no one bothered him or bothered about him. He had entered in fourth form year, when the class was already clearly stratified, knowing only one person in the school; he came from a small Virginia town which no one had ever heard of, his clothes were wrong, his vocabulary was wrong, and when he talked at all it was about the wrong things.

He had been assigned to an out-of-the-way house (instead of to one of the exuberant dormitories) with six other nebulous[3] flotsam,[4] and there on the edge of the school he had been waiting all year for something to happen to

1 *pariah:* an outcast.

2 *alchemy:* the process of transforming something common into something special.

3 *nebulous:* indistinct, vague.

4 *flotsam:* unimportant miscellaneous material.

him, living alone in a little room tucked up under the eaves.

His failure to strike out in some, in any, direction puzzled him in October, when he had been at Devon six weeks, angered him in December, made him contemptuous in February, and on this burgeoning April day when everything else stirred with life, took on the coloration of tragedy.

He crossed over the bridge with Bead, and his heart stopped for an instant as it always did on this bridge; in his imagination he again stood on the railing, with his image white and mysterious in the green-black water twenty-five feet below, and he leaped out and over, as he had done last September on his fourth day there, somersaulting twice while most of the school looked on in admiration at the new boy, and knifed cleanly into the icy water.

Last September, his fourth day at school. He hadn't been thinking of anything in particular there on the bridge; everyone was diving from it so he did too. When he plunged from the railing he had been just another of the unknown new boys, but when he broke the surface of the water in that remarkable dive, one that he had never attempted before and was never to repeat, he became for his schoolmates a boy to be considered. That is why Ging Powers, a senior from

his own town who had seemed these first days to be decisively avoiding him, came over in the shower room afterwards and dropped an invitation to dinner like a negligible piece of soap. "Come over to the Inn for dinner tonight. Got a couple of friends I want you to meet."

There is a trophy room in the Devon School gymnasium much visited by returning alumni; during June reunions they wander whispering past its softly lighted cases, in which gleam the cups and medals of athletic greatness. Proud banners hang from its panelled walls, inscribed with the records of triumphant, forgotten afternoons. It is like a small, peculiarly sacred chapel in a great cathedral.

At the far end, standing long and bright in the focal niche, the alumni would admire the James Harvey Fullerton Cup, Awarded Each Year to That Member of the Sixth Form Who, in the Opinion of his Fellows and Masters, Most Closely Exemplifies the Highest Traditions of Devon. There is no mention of athletics on the inscription, but it has come to rest in the gymnasium, in the place of honor, because the highest tradition of Devon is the thinking athlete. Thirty-four names have been engraved on its burnished surface since Mr. Fullerton decided to confirm the reality of his untroubled childhood by donating it, with a small endowment, to his old school, like some symbol of royalty.

Lawrence had approached it that afternoon, his fourth day at the school, and was struck by the beauty and sacredness of the place. This surely was the heart of Devon: the chapel was like an assembly hall, the library was a clearing house, the houses were dormitories, the classrooms, classrooms; only here did he sense that behind the visible were deeper meanings, that these trophies and banners were clues to the hidden core of the school. He left the gymnasium lost in thought.

He had felt he was still in the air as he walked from the gym back to his room that afternoon, still spinning down upon his own bright image in the murky water. He dressed hurriedly for the dinner at the Inn, for this was surely the beginning of his career at Devon. He explained how wonderfully everything was going in an ardent letter to Janine, and then walked, holding himself back from running by an intoxicating exercise of will power, and arrived at last at the Inn. Everything within him was released; it was as though his dive into the river had washed away his boyhood, and he stood clean and happy, wondering dreamily what he would be like now.

The hushed dining room was pervaded[5] by the atmosphere of middle-aged gentility characteristic of Inns at boys' schools: the dull walnut woodwork, the pink and green wallpaper depicting Colonial scenes, the virginal fireplace. At the far end of the room Lawrence saw his dinner partners huddled conspiratorily at a corner table. He wheeled past other, empty tables, bright with white cloths and silver, realized dimly that there were murmuring groups here and there in the room; and then Ging, his thin frame unfolding from a chair, was muttering introductions. "This is Vinnie Ump," he seemed to say, and Lawrence recognized Vinnie James, vice-chairman of the senior council, a calm, blond Bostonian who was allowed to be as articulate as he chose because he was so unassertively sure of himself. "And this," said Ging, in a somewhat more stately cadence, "is Charles Morrell." Lawrence recognized him too, of course; this was Morrell, the fabled "Captain Marvel" of the football field, the baseball field, and the hockey rink. Lawrence had never seen him at close quarters before; he seemed more formidable[6] than ever.

Vinnie James was talking, and after pausing for a neutral, birdlike nod to Lawrence, he continued.

---

5 *pervaded:* filled throughout every part.

6 *formidable:* causing fear or dread.

"So if you want to put up with being patronized by a lot of crashing bores, then you can go to Harvard, and be Punched all sophomore year."

Captain Marvel leaned his heavily handsome face out over the table, "I don't get you, Vinnie, what's this Punching?"

"That's how you get into the clubs at Harvard, Dim One," Vinnie's eyes flickered humorously at him for an instant. "They invite you to Punch parties all sophomore year, and when they stop inviting you then you know you're not going to be asked to join the club."

"Well," Ging looked with masked apprehension from one to the other, "they've got to take *some* guys, don't they? And Devon isn't such a bad background."

"It's not Groton," said Vinnie mercilessly, "of course."

"Groton!" Ging clutched his tastefully striped tie savagely. "I wouldn't be caught dead at that snobatorium. I could 'ev' if I'd wanted to I could 'ev' gone to Groton. But mother said wild horses couldn't drag a son of hers to that snobatorium."

Lawrence felt dizzy at the barefaceness of this lie. He knew that Mrs. Powers would cheerfully have violated most of the customs of civilization to get a son of hers into Groton. Devon had been a hasty compromise after Groton had proved out of the question.

"In any case," Vinnie remarked drily, "Marvel here won't have any trouble. Personable athletes are kidnapped by the most desirable clubs the moment they appear." Vinnie made no comment on Ging's chances.

Lawrence disliked and felt superior to Ging at once. The climber! He had never realized before what a fool Ging was, it made him feel older to realize it now. It was so clear when you could see him beside Captain Marvel, cool, unconcerned Marvel, who would easily rise to the top of every group he entered, leaving Ging clawing and snarling below.

Lawrence looked away irritably, regretting that it was Ging who had introduced him to the others. At the same time he felt himself more thoroughly aware than he had ever been of how the world went, of who fitted where, of what was grand and genuine and what was shoddy and fake. Devon had posed a question to him, and demanded that he do something. This afternoon he had done a single, beautiful dive, it was just right and he knew it the moment he hit the water. And now he had come to understand Captain Marvel. The answer was athletics; not just winning a major D, but the personality of the athlete itself, the unconscious authority which his strength, his skill, his acclaim gave him. Lawrence stirred his tomato soup reflectively, and felt his diffuse[7] ambitions coming into focus, experienced a vision of himself as the Majestic Athlete; he decided instinctively and immediately to accept it, there at dinner among the walnut and silver and the polite murmurings of the other diners. He gathered about himself the mantle of the Olympiad, and lost in its folds, he burst into speech.

"I have some cousins, two cousins, you know, Ging—George and Carter—they're in clubs at Harvard, I mean a club at Harvard, one club, both of 'em are in the same club. It's the . . . the . . ." Lawrence was suddenly stricken with the thought that George and Carter might very easily not be in the best Harvard club, or even the second best; but everyone, even Marvel, was listening with interest, "It's called," he felt his color rising at the inelegance of the name, "The Gas—or something."

"Oh yes," said Vinnie crisply, "that's a very good club, for New Yorkers mostly, they have some very good men."

"Oh," Lawrence breathed with fake innocence and real relief. This success swept him spinning on. "George and Carter, they go there for dinners, but they always have lunch in the—is it the houses?" his wide, brightened blue eyes searched his listeners' faces avidly; Vinnie nodded a brief assent. "They said those clubs make you so ingrown, you just know all these fancy socialites and everything and they wanted to know, you know, everybody, they didn't want to be exclusive or anything like that. It isn't like up here, I mean there isn't, aren't all these clubs and things. They said that I'd get raided and my bed pied and all but nothing like that seems to happen up here; but they *did* say that when I went on to Harvard, if I do go there, that after being here it'll be easier and I'll know people and not have to study, but I don't really study so hard here, 'course it's only been four days, but after what everybody said about prep school I thought I'd be studying all the time, but, well, take this afternoon"—that was good, *take this afternoon* smacked of maturity; he paused an instant for the two important seniors (Ging was a bystander now) to catch the overtone of authority in it—"we went swimming off the bridge, and that flip, I thought a two-and-a-half flip might be tough, but . . ." he paused again, hoping Ging might make himself useful as a witness to this feat; nothing happened so he finished a little out of breath, "it wasn't."

---

7 *diffuse:* scattered, not concentrated.

"Yeah," Captain Marvel said, "I saw you do it."

This swept down Lawrence's last controls. His best moment had been seen, and doubtless admired, by the most important athlete in school. He rushed ahead now, eager to impress him even more; no, by golly, he was through impressing people. Now he was ready to leap, in one magnificent bound, to the very peak of his ambitions, to become Captain Marvel's protégé[8] to learn what it meant to be unconcerned, powerful, and a man. So he stuttered gaily on, snatching at everything inside him that seemed presentable—home, his family, Janine, the play he had seen in New York; he assumed every grown-up attitude he could find. All of it he brought forth, as an offering of fealty.[9]

The seniors followed this unwinding of a new boy carefully, looked where he pointed, gauging all his information and attitudes according to their own more precisely graded yardsticks, and took his measure.

"Devon is like some kind of country club-penitentiary, where the inmates don't take walks around the courtyard, they go to the private penitentiary golf course for eighteen holes. And the dean, is that who he is? That queer, stuttery old bird, you know, the one in chapel the first day, the one who looks like Hoover with an Oxford accent . . ."

"Yes, that's the dean," said Vinnie, fingering his water glass, "Dean Eleazer Markham Bings-Smith."

"No!" exploded Lawrence, "is that his name! His honest name?" He regretted the *honest*, it should have been *actual*.

"Why does he talk that way, and *look* that way! Like my beagle, that's the way he looks, like the beagle I've got at home, my beagle looks just like that right after he's had a bath."

There was something like consternation passing around the table. Lawrence felt it and looked wonderingly from one to the other. Ging was watching an elderly couple making their way toward the door. The others examined their desserts.

"Was that the dean?" Lawrence asked in a shocked whisper. "Did he hear me?"

No one really answered, but Lawrence, alive in every nerve now, responded symbolically. He slipped like a boneless organism from his chair and sank beneath the table; there he performed the appropriate expiation; he banged

---

8 *protégé:* one who is protected or trained by someone of experience or prominence.

9 *fealty:* the faithfulness of a vassal to a lord.

his head, not too hard, against the table's underside.

There was a scraping of chairs, Lawrence saw napkins flutter onto the seats, and suddenly he realized the impossibility of his position: under a table in the Anthony Wayne Dining Room of the Devon Inn, making a fool of himself.

He could not recall afterwards how he got to his feet, but he remembered very clearly what was said.

"I have an appointment," Vinnie was informing Ging, and then to Lawrence, "That was not the dean, that was Dr. Farnham, the registrar. I doubt whether he heard you. And if he did, I doubt whether he knows or cares *who* you are."

"Are you British?" demanded Captain Marvel with heavy distaste. "Is that why you talk so queer?"

Lawrence felt the exuberance within him turn over, leaving a sob pressing against his chest. He could not speak and would not cry, but drew a deep, shuddering breath.

Marvel and Vinnie strode out through the door, Ging followed, and Lawrence roamed out a few paces behind, out into the damp September night, down the deserted street to the quadrangle, where the dormitory lights streamed hospitably from cosy windows. Ging said "G'night" there as though he were saying "pass" during a dull

bridge game, and Lawrence was left to wander down the lane to the cluttered old house, to the little room stuck up under the eaves where he lived.

In the next weeks, after the first storms had subsided, Lawrence tried again and again to analyze his failure. Whom had he offended, how, why? Why was everything he had ever wanted sparkling like a trophy in his hands one minute, and smashed to bits at his feet the next?

Defeat seemed to follow upon defeat after that. Having missed the peak of his ambition, he assumed that lesser heights could be attained automatically; he felt like a veteran of violent foreign wars whose scars entitled him to homage and precedence. Instead he was battered on every occasion: one day he offered to move into the empty half of a double room down the hall and the boy living there had simply ignored him, had pretended not to hear. Then he turned wildly delinquent; he threw his small steamer trunk, filled with shoes and books, down the long flight of stairs under which the housemaster lived. It slammed against Mr. Kuzak's door at the bottom, and the resultant methodical investigation and punishment made him briefly notable to his housemates, until they concluded that he was strange.

This was the final, the unbearable affront; they thought him strange, undisciplined, an inferior little boy given to pettish[10] tantrums. He would show them. If there was one thing he was sure he possessed, it was a capacity for self-discipline. If there was one thing he would not be, it was a clown, a butt. He knew there was a certain dignity in his bearing, even though it shaded into pomposity, and he would not violate that, he would not become a Fruit-cake Putsby, even if people would like him better that way.

He decided, in the season when the last leaves were drifting down from the trees bordering the playing fields, and the sunlight cut obliquely across the town, that there remained this one quality on which he could rely: his capacity for self-discipline. He would turn his back upon the school, he would no longer be embroiled in Devon's cheap competition for importance. He would be intelligent; yes, he told himself, he would be *exceedingly* intelligent; and by God, if he only could, he would be the greatest athlete ever to electrify a crowd on the playing fields of Devon. The greatest, and the most inaccessible.

The earth was turning wintery; the season of Steam Heat arrived. It filled every inhabited room in the school, the steam hissed and clanged with power, and could not be shut off. Slowly the heat drained the the spirit from them, dried their healthy faces, seared the freshest skin. The usual number of colds appeared, the usual amount of force faded from lectures and application from homework, the usual apathy slipped into the school through the radiators. Winter was here.

Lawrence moved from one steaming box to another, crossing the sharp, drily cold outdoors in between, and felt his own inner strength grow as it waned in those about him. He had learned to study very systematically, and his responses in class were apt and laconic,[11] several of his teachers became noticeably interested in winning his good opinion; they would make remarks about Kafka[12] or Turgenev[13] and then glance at him. He would smile knowingly back, and resolve to find out who these people might be.

His free time he spent watching athletics, religiously following the major sports, football games and football drill, enjoying every moment except when Captain Mar-

---

10 *pettish:* irritable; ill tempered.

11 *laconic:* concise.

12 *Kafka:* Franz Kafka (1883–1924); Austrian writer.

13 *Turgenev:* Ivan Sergeyevich Turgenev (1818–1883); Russian novelist.

vel made a really brilliant play, which made him feel uneasy and guilty. He watched soccer and track and tennis and squash, and as winter sports replaced them, he watched basketball, wrestling, boxing, hockey, and even fencing.

In the fall he had played a little intramural football at which he was generally inept and abstracted, but once in a while he would startle everyone, including himself, with a brilliantly skillful play. But there was too much freedom on a football field, too much room to maneuver, too many possibilities; so in the winter he turned to swimming, in which the lanes were rigidly predetermined, and he had only to swim up and down, up and down. Into this he poured all the intensity he possessed, and as a result made the junior varsity squad. He was uniformly cooperative with his teammates, and the coach thought him a promising boy.

His housemates now felt disposed to revise their opinion of him; yes, Stuart was strange, but if he was going to turn out to to be not only bright but also something of an athlete, they thought they had better accept him.

The proctor[14] and the others made a few fumbling, gruff overtures. Lawrence sensed this at once

and became more thoroughly disturbed than at any time since the dinner at the Inn. He loathed them all, of course, and he felt cheated; now that his defenses were invulnerable they were calling off the assault, inviting him to talk terms, asking for a conference out in the open. The cold wind tore around the angles of the old house, and Lawrence camped in his steamy room, speaking politely to those who came to his door, doing his homework, and feeling confusedly vindicated. He had proved the strongest of all, for what was strength if not the capacity for self-denial? He had divorced himself from them so successfully that now he didn't care; *they* cared, so it seemed, now; they were seeking his friendship, therefore they were weak. Strength, Lawrence was sure, was the capacity for self-denial; life was conquered by the strong-willed, success was demonstrated by austerity; it was the bleak who would inherit the earth. Yes, that was right and he would not allow them to change the rules now that he had won; he decided to continue his triumphant game, even though he was playing it alone.

Only in his anger did he draw close to them; one dismal afternoon in February, Billy Baldwin, the boy down the hall who had refused to room with him in September, came to his door:

---

14 *proctor:* one appointed to supervise students.

"Hi, Varsity." This was the nickname Lawrence had been given by the other boys, who understood him better than he thought. "You going to Bermuda for spring vacation?" Since he was excluded from the gay round of parties which the boys from Boston and New York described as typical of their holidays, Lawrence had intimated that he was going to Bermuda with his family. This afternoon he was too depressed to lie.

"No," he parroted, "I'm not going to Bermuda for spring vacation."

Billy was a little put off, but continued with determined good humor. "Well then how about coming down, I mean if you aren't going home . . ." Billy had no champagne vacation in the offing either, but he had grown up a little during the winter and forgiven his parents for making their home in Bridgeport, Connecticut. He had also changed his mind about Lawrence, whom he now thought pleasantly temperamental and handsome. "Why don't you, if you want, you could always . . ."

"What?" interrupted Lawrence irritably. "Why don't I what?"

"All I was going to say," Billy continued on a stronger note, "what I was going to say if you didn't interrupt all the time. . ." but then he couldn't say it.

"You were going to say noth-ing," Lawrence said disgustedly, turning back to his book, "as usual."

"Just one thing," Billy exclaimed sharply, "all I was going to say was why *don't* you go to Bermuda? If you're so rich."

"Rich enough," Lawrence's voice thickening with controlled anger, "richer than some people who live in little dump towns on the New Haven Railroad."

"Yeah!" Billy shouted. "Yeah, so rich your pop couldn't pay the last bursar's bill on time!"

"What!" screamed Lawrence, tearing the book from his lap and jumping up, "Wha'd you say?" His blood was pounding because it wasn't the truth, but it was close to it. He was standing now in the middle of his little garret, his shoulders slightly forward. His voice turned coarse, "Get out." Neither of them knew his voice had a savage depth like that. "Just get out of my room." Then in a single motion, he snatched the book from the floor and hurled it at Billy's head. Billy sprang back from the doorway, deeply frightened, not so much *of* him as with him. Both of them stood panting on either side of the doorway, and then Billy went back to his own room.

Lawrence pretended to be totally unconcerned about such flare-ups, which occurred several times in the late winter. He eventually allowed Billy to reestablish a civil relationship with him; *After all,* Lawrence reasoned, *he should be the one to make up, after the way he insulted me right in my own room. I never did like him,* he reflected with strengthening satisfaction, *no I never did.* Billy didn't matter to him; in September when he was so alone, Billy could have helped. But now; what good was Billy? He was no athlete, no star, he did not possess that unconcerned majesty, he was a person of no importance. And Billy, who was just finding out about kindness, looked regretfully elsewhere for friends.

Except for these explosions, Lawrence maintained his admirable outer imperviousness throughout the winter. He spent spring vacation in Virginia with his family. It was an uneventful two weeks except for a bitter little fight with Janine. "You're changed and I hate you," she cried at the end of it, and then indignantly, "Who do you think you are anyhow? I hate you!"

He returned in the middle of April to find Devon transformed. He had forgotten that the bleak lanes and roads were beautiful when the earth turned once again toward the sun. Tiny leaves of callow[15] green sprouted from the gray branches of the skeletal trees, and the living scents of the earth hung

---

15 *callow:* immature.

in the air. Windows which had been stuck closed with winter were opened to allow the promising air to circulate; the steamy dryness of his little room drifted away; when he opened the single window and the door a tantalizing breeze whipped across his papers and notebooks, fluttered the college pennants on his wall, and danced on to the other rooms where his housemates stirred restlessly.

Then, unexpectedly, he began to slip in his studies. For two successive French classes he appeared unprepared, and when called on to discuss the lesson, he fumbled. The others snickered behind their notebooks. But the boy sitting next to him, with whom he had had a relationship consisting only of "Excuse me," and "Hard assignment, wasn't it?", nudged him in the ribs as they were going out after the second class and exclaimed robustly, "Boy, did *you* stink today!" Lawrence was about to coin some cutting rejoinder when the boy grinned broadly. "You were really lousy," he added, punching him again. Lawrence tried and failed to keep from grinning back, and then muttered that well, it was spring wasn't it.

That afternoon he went as usual to watch the varsity lacrosse team practice. His own intramural team was having a game that day and could have used even his unsteady stick, but he had wrangled a medical excuse. Varsity lacrosse was almost as meaningful for him as varsity baseball, and he didn't have to watch Captain Marvel there. So he sat alone on the empty bleachers and followed the practice shots intently, watching the careless skill of the players, marvelling at the grand unawareness with which they played. *This is the best part of the day*, he thought, *this is wonderful.* He pondered the assumptions on which these athletes operated, that they would not miss the ball, that if they did they would catch it next time, that their teammates accepted them regardless, that there was a basic peace among them taken for granted. Lawrence could take nothing for granted; *yes, this is the best part of the day*, he told himself, and as he watched the skillful, confident boys warming to the game he saw only himself, he watched the others but he was seeing himself, doing all the skillful, impossible things. He looked very pleased, *This is the best*, he thought, and despair flamed up in him.

He decided not to stay for the whole practice, and wandering back to the gym, he met his own team coming out; Hey, Lawrence, get dressed, There's a game, Lawrence, C'mon, Stuart. Whathahelleryadoin? The one thing he had wanted to avoid that day was his own team. Lately he always seemed to be stumbling into the very situations he wanted fervently to avoid.

"Yeah," he called lamely to them, "but I got a . . ." *medical excuse?* An Olympian unable to take the field because of sniffles? It wouldn't do. "Yeah, okay, I was just . . . the varsity . . . I thought maybe if I watched them . . ." Shouting complicated explanations was impossible, "you know," he yelled even though they were moving away, not listening, "I thought I might learn something."

"Forget the varsity, Varsity," one of them called over his shoulder. "The second-string Red midfield wants you."

This then was the afternoon when Lawrence scored his first goal. He felt an odd looseness playing that day, the hot rays of the sun seemed to draw the rigidity out of his body, leaving his muscles and sinews free to function as they would. Something about the way he held his stick was different, he found himself in the right place at the right time; his teammates sensed the change and passed the ball to him, and in the last minutes of the game he made a fast instinctive turn around a burly Blue defenseman and scored the winning goal with a quick, sure shot.

It was a minor triumph which calmed his spirit for approximately seven minutes, until the invitation to the movies was issued and turned aside, until he crossed over the little arching bridge, observed the water where his heroic reflection had shone, and stepped onto the turf on the other side, the varsity field. By the time they reached the gym it was Lawrence the unrecognized Olympian again, Lawrence the unknown and unloved.

After his shower he dressed and went, as he so often did, into the trophy room for a pacifying moment of dreaming. He knew the inscription and most of the names on the Fullerton Cup by heart, and in the space below 1951—Robert Graves Hartshorne, he would visualize 1952—Charles Taylor Morrell, for unquestionably the cup would be Marvel's this year. And the list should go on and on, with one celebrated name after another (even perhaps 1954—Lawrence Bates Stuart); but here reality always intervened. The fact, the shocking fact was that the front plate of the cup was almost filled, after Marvel's name had been inscribed the list would reach the little silver relief statues around the base—the old-fashioned football player looking slim and inadequate, the pompous baseball player with his squarely planted little cap, and the others—

there would be no more room. Nor was there any space to start a second list, since all the remaining circumference of the cup was devoted to an etched allegorical representation of the flame of knowledge passing from hand to hand through the ages, until it found its way into a device at the top, a coat-of-arms of birds and Latin and moons which was the seal of Devon.

Always a little amazed at the finiteness of the cup, Lawrence backed thoughtfully away from it. Wasn't this the core of everything, didn't it sum up, absorb, glorify everything at Devon? And still, the cup would be full this year. One of these days it would be moved to a case along the walls with the other old trophies which had once reigned in the niche, it would be honorably, obscurely retired. In his imagination the heroic list stretched back over cup after cup, into the past, and forward, upon cups not yet conceived, into the future. It was odd, he thought, all these great names fading into the past, getting less important every year, until finally they must just go out, like the last burned out ember in a fire. It was sad of course, but well, there was something almost *monotonous* about it.

Lawrence squirmed. He had never thought about time's passage before. It made him feel better to realize it now, to see that the circle of the years changed things; it wasn't all up to him personally.

Puzzled, he gazed around this chilly and damp chamber which had seemed so cool and serene in February, untouched by the bone-chilling winds outside or the rasping steam in the other rooms of the school.

But now it was April, and Lawrence felt and saw April everywhere. This room isn't a chapel at all, he thought with a passing wave of indignation, it's a crypt.

Then, right there in the trophy room, he yawned, comfortably. And stretching his legs, to get a feeling of cramp out of them, he strode contentedly toward the door, through which the sunlight poured, and as he stepped into it he felt its warmth on his shoulders. It was going to be a good summer.

He never knew that he was right in this, because Lawrence drowned that night, by the purest accident, in the river which winds between the playing fields. Bead and Bruce tried to save him; the water was very cold and black and the night moonless. They eventually found him, doubled over among some rushes. He had not cried out when the cramp convulsed him, so they did not know where to begin searching and after they found him, it was a hard, clumsy job getting him to shore. They tried artificial respiration at first, and then becoming very frightened, started for help. But then Bruce thought again and came back to try to revive him while Bead ran to the gym, completely disrupting the movie in his frantic search for a master.

There was a conference two days later, attended by the headmaster, the dean, Mr. Kuzak from Lawrence's house, Bruce and Bead. The boys explained that it had been just a little lark; students always swam in the river in the spring, and although they usually waited until it was warmer, they had decided in the Butt Room Saturday night to have the first swim of the season while the rest of the school was at the movie. Bruce and Bead had planned it alone, but Lawrence had been there, very enthusiastic to go to the movie. Then when he heard they were going swimming, that had become the one thing he wanted to do.

"You know, sir," Bruce explained earnestly to the dean, "he was a good swimmer, and he wanted to go so much."

"Yeah," Bead confirmed this eagerly, "we didn't ask him to go, did we, Bruce?"

"No, he just asked if he could and we said yes."

Bead set his face maturely, "He wasn't a very good friend of ours, but he just wanted to go. So we said okay, but it wasn't like we planned it together. I didn't know him very well, did you, Bruce?"

"No, I didn't either."

Mr. Kuzak studied the backs of his hands, and the headmaster asked, "Who were his close friends?"

"I don't know," Bead answered.

"The fellows in his house, I guess," said Bruce. Everyone looked at Mr. Kuzak, who thought of several perfunctory ways of confirming this but knowing it was not true, he was unable to say anything. It is easy to write, "Lawrence Stuart is beginning to find himself" on a report to the dean, when Stuart was alive and could be heard trudging up the stairs every day; undoubtedly he *would* have found himself. But now the boy was dead, Mr. Kuzak had seen his body, had telephoned his parents; he said nothing.

Irritated, the headmaster leaned out of his throne-like chair. "He *had* close friends?" he persisted.

Still Mr. Kuzak could not speak.

"Well," the dean broke the uneasy silence, his kind, mournful eyes studying the two boys, "Well how did he, was he—" his fingers searched the lines in his forehead, "He enjoyed it, did he?" The dean's face reddened, he indulged in his chronic cough for several seconds. "He seemed lively? I mean did he act . . . happy, before, before this

cramp seized him?"

"Oh, sure!" Bead exclaimed.

"Yes, yes he did," Bruce said at the same time.

"When we first got there," Bruce continued, "he got up on the bridge. Bead and I just slipped into the water from the bank, it was awfully cold."

"I never was in such cold water," Bead agreed.

"But Stuart got up on the bridge and stood there a minute."

"Then he dove," said Bead.

"Dived," someone corrected abstractly.

"It was a real dive," Bruce added thoughtfully. "He did a beautiful dive."

It had been like the free curve of powerful wings. Lawrence had cut the water almost soundlessly, and then burst up again a moment later, breaking a foaming circle on the black surface. Then he twisted over on his back and sank out of sight.

"I believe he enjoyed the water," said Mr. Kuzak quietly.

"Yeah," Bead agreed, "he liked it a lot, I think. That was the one thing he did like. He was good in the water."

"I don't think he cared," Bruce remarked suddenly.

The headmaster straightened sharply. "What do you mean?" Bruce's thoughts doubled over this instinctive statement, to censor it or deny it, but then because this was death and the first he had ever really encountered, he persisted. "I mean in the dive, he just seemed to trust everything, all of a sudden. He looked different, standing up there on the bridge."

"Happy?" asked the dean in a very low voice.

"Something like that. He wasn't scared, I know that."

The conference ended shortly afterward, with everyone agreed that it had been a wholly accidental death. A photograph of Lawrence in his swimming suit, taken when he made the junior varsity team, was enlarged, framed, and hung on the wall of the gym among pictures of athletic teams. He stood very straight in the picture and his young eyes looked directly at the camera.

But the season moved on; that summer was the most beautiful and fruitful anyone could remember at Devon. Blossoms scented the air and hung over the river winding quietly through the playing fields. And the earth, turned full toward the sun, brought forth its annual harvest.

Understanding What You Read

1. After seven months at Devon, Lawrence Stuart feels
   a. popular and in the in-group at the school.
   b. that he's hardly noticed at the school.
   c. that he successfully made the transition from his previous school.

2. in his first few days at Devon, Lawrence attracted attention by
   a. diving spectacularly from a bridge.
   b. scoring a key lacrosse goal.
   c. throwing a winning pass in an intramural football game.

3. For Lawrence, what is the most sacred place on campus?
   a. the gymnasium
   b. the chapel
   c. the library

4. Lawrence's dinner at the Inn in his first days at Devon ended
   a. in failure as he was scorned by the older classmates
   b. triumphantly as he amused his classmates
   c. early because of his not feeling well

5. How does the final dive and swim of Lawrence represent a kind of "freedom" for him?

Writer's Workshop

1. Irony has a number of meanings. When something happens that is the direct opposite of what one would have expected to happen, it is ironic. A firehouse burning or a race car driver dying in an accident backing out of his driveway would be ironic situations. Why is it ironic that Lawrence's photograph is hung in the gym?
2. Reread the last paragraph of this story. Discuss all the levels of meaning, including irony, that you can see in this paragraph. Why did the author choose to end the story here?

• CHAPTER TWO •

Moments
of Glory

*Here are the times that don't get any better—those moments of
exhilaration in which human beings give their all in an athletic
endeavor and then triumph. Journalist Gloria Emerson felt that
exhilaration at the end of a parachute, skydiving for the first time.
Roger Bannister felt it as the first person ever to run the mile in
fewer than four minutes. Bill Bradley felt it on the basketball court
in his senior year at Princeton.*

*In the poems and prose in this chapter, the high points of athletic
performance are captured. As you read, you will experience the
power of literature to take you on the search for glory. Start the
game. Take a chance. Everything's possible—as baseball immortal
Lou Gehrig said—in the world of sports.*

Take the Plunge

Why did this writer decide to try skydiving? And what happened to her?

It was usually men who asked me why I did it. Some were amused, others puzzled. I didn't mind the jokes in the newspaper office where I worked about whether I left the building by window, roof or in the elevator. The truth is that I was an unlikely person to jump out of an airplane, being neither graceful, daring nor self-possessed. I had a bad back, uncertain ankles and could not drive with competence because of deficient depth perception and a fear of all buses coming toward me. A friend joked that if I broke any bones I would have to be shot because I would never mend.

I never knew why I did it. It was in May, a bright and dull May, the last May that made me want to feel reckless. But there was nothing to do then at the beginning of a decade that changed almost everything. I could not wait that May for the Sixties to unroll. I worked in women's news; my stories came out like little cookies. I wanted to be brave about something, not just about love, or a root canal, or writing that the shoes at Arnold Constable looked strangely sad.

Once I read of men who had to run so far it burned their chests to breathe. But I could not run very far. Jumping from a plane, which required no talent or endurance, seemed perfect. I wanted to feel the big, puzzling lump on my back that they promised was a parachute, to take serious strides in the absurd black boots that I believed all generals wore.

I wanted all of it: the rising of a tiny plane with the door off, the earth rushing away, the plunge, the slap of the wind, my hands on the back straps, the huge curve of white silk above me, the drift through the space we call sky.

It looked pale green that morning I fell into it, not the baby blue I expected. I must have been crying; my cheeks were wet. Only the thumps of a wild heart made noise; I did not know how to keep it quiet.

That May, that May my mind was as clear as clay. I did not have the imagination to perceive the risks, to understand that if the wind grew nasty I might be electrocuted on high-tension wires, smashed on a roof, drowned in water, hanged in a tree. I was sure nothing would happen, because my intentions were so good, just as young soldiers start out certain of their safety because they know nothing.

Friends drove me to Orange, Massachusetts, seventy miles west of Boston, for the opening of the first U.S. sports parachuting center, where I was to perform. It was the creation, the passion, of a Princetonian and an ex-Marine named Jacques Istel, who organized the first U.S. jumping team in 1956. Parachuting was "as safe as swimming," he kept saying, calling it the "world's most stimulating and soul-satisfying sport." His center was for competitions and the teaching of skydiving. Instead of hurtling toward the earth, sky divers maintain a swan-dive position, using the air as a cushion to support them while they maneuver with leg and arm movements until the rip cord must be pulled.

None of that stuff was expected from any of us in the little beginners class. We were only to jump, after brief but intense instruction, with Istel's newly designed parachute, to show that any dope could do it. It was a parachute with a thirty-two-foot canopy; a large cutout hole funneled escaping air. You steered with two wooden knobs instead of having to pull hard on the back straps, or risers. The new parachute increased later-al speed, slowed down the rate of descent, reduced oscillation. We were told we could even land standing up but that we should bend our knees and lean to one side. The beginners jumped at eight a.m., the expert sky divers performed their dazzling tricks later when a crowd came.

Two of us boarded a Cessna 180 that lovely morning, the wind no more than a trickle. I was not myself, no longer thin and no longer fast. The jump suit, the equipment, the helmet, the boots, had made me into someone thick and clumsy, moving as strangely as if they had put me underwater and said I must walk. It was hard to bend, to sit, to stand up. I did not like the man with me; he was eager and composed. I wanted to smoke, to go to the bathroom, but there were many straps around me that I did not understand. At twenty-three hundred feet, the hateful, happy man went out, making a dumb thumbs-up sign.

When my turn came, I suddenly felt a stab of pain for all the forgotten soldiers who balked and were kicked out, perhaps shot, for their panic and for delaying the troops. I was hooked to a static line, an automatic opening device, which made it impossible to lie down or tie myself to something. The drill-master could not hear all that I shouted at him. But he knew the signs of mutiny and removed my arms from his neck. He took me to the doorway, sat me down, and yelled "Go!" or "Now!" or "Out!" There was nothing to do but be punched by the wind, which knocked the spit from my mouth, reach for the wing strut, hold on hard, kick back the feet so weighted and helpless in those boots, and let go. The parachute opened with a plop, as Istel had sworn to me that it would. When my eyelids opened as well, I saw the white gloves on my hands were old ones from Saks Fifth Avenue, gloves I wore with summer dresses. There was dribble on my chin; my eyes and nose were leaking. I wiped everything with the gloves.

There was no noise; the racket of the plane and wind had gone away. The cold and sweet stillness seemed an astonishing, un-dreamed-of gift. Then I saw what I had never seen before, will never see again; endless sky and earth in colors and textures no one had ever described. Only then did the parachute become a most lovable and docile toy: this wooden knob to go left, this wooden knob to go right. The pleasure of being there, the drifting and the calm, rose to a fever; I wanted to stay pinned in the air and stop the ground from coming closer. The target was a huge arrow in a sandpit. I was cross to see it, afraid of nothing now, for even the wind was kind and the trees looked soft. I landed on my feet in the pit with a bump, then sat down for a bit. Later that day I was taken over to meet General James Gavin, who had led the 82nd Airborne in the D-Day landing at Normandy. Perhaps it was to prove to him that the least promising pupil, the gawkiest, could jump. It did not matter that I stumbled and fell before him in those boots, which walked with a will of their own. Later, Mr. Istel's mother wrote me a charming note of congratulations. Everyone at the center was pleased; in fact, I am sure they were surprised. Perhaps this is what I had in mind all the time.

Understanding What You Read

1. Gloria Emerson's motive for skydiving was
    a. a challenge made to her by a friend
    b. a desire to take on something that required courage and that promised excitement
    c. an assignment given to her by the newspaper where she worked

2. At the moment when she had to jump, Gloria Emerson
    a. felt the exhilaration of eager anticipation
    b. was panicky
    c. prayed

3. Gloria Emerson portrays the sky dive as
    a. unique and glorious
    b. disappointing
    c. exciting but not memorable

4. Why did the author write the last two sentences of this essay? What point do they make?

Writer's Workshop

What was the most courageous physical feat that you ever attempted? Describe it following the structure Gloria Emerson used: tell how you got involved in the activity and what your thoughts were prior to the experience, then describe the actual experience and your reaction to it.

Three Cheers for My Daughter

Being a cheerleader requires athletic prowess, almost as much as the
athlete being cheered, but this mother didn't see it that way.

I screamed when my daughter told me at 16 that she was trying out to be a cheerleader; I remember the moment precisely. My daughter—strong-willed and strong-armed, critical and deep and smart—approached me with a trace of hesitation in her step. Mom, she said, I have something to tell you, and I don't think you're going to like it.

In that instant I saw her at six months, at six years, as a young teen-ager and in all the years before and after, her promise and prowess and the way she marched against hunger and held placards on highway bridges for Mondale and Ferraro. How could this child born of the Summer of Love, this darling of my countercultured eye, catapult so squarely into the conventional as to become a cheerleader! I *knew* this would happen, I wailed in wanton shame, forgetting everything I ever learned about what good mothers are supposed to say and do. I knew it 16 years ago—I knew, I knew.

Of course, she made the team. Of course, in fact, by the next year, through sheer will and desire, she became the captain of that motley squad of girls who braved ignominy[1] before the crowds with their pom-poms and their perms. I would not go to the games; I could picture them all too clearly. She would leave in her little blue skirt, her sturdy legs exposed from the tops of her panty hose down to the little white socks—sox—above the borrowed black-and-white saddle shoes. Her handed-down sweater pulled across her chest. When she opened her mouth to yell in those first games, my husband told me—for he would go to watch, out of loyalty and fascination and an attraction for basketball in any form—barely a whisper came out. My daughter was not one to shout out loud before a crowd.

Reports trickled in. They had attempted a pyramid and she had

---

1 *ignominy:* embarrassment.

fallen off. They had made up a dance in practice, to an old song by the Supremes. One girl, in the terrible face of the crowd, had turned and fled; others sulked in the girls locker room, offended by imagined slights. She came home from one game, her face distended with tears, and would not speak at all. An acquaintance remarked on her amazing pluck—she had done a back flip on the gym floor for an individual cheer routine. I cringed. The girls were athletes, I pointed out to her one night, just as much as the basketball players were. I know that, Mom, she said. That's why I do it, so everyone else will know it, too.

Finally one evening, fortified by wine at dinner, disguised in a voluminous down coat left by a house guest, carrying the baby so I might leave at the half, I showed up at the gym on a game night. From the bench, her face registered disbelief, along with an ambiguous rictus[2] that could have been effort, pain, or even pleasure. I imagine my smile looked about the same. I perched precariously on an upper bleacher's edge and held the baby's bottle with white knuckles, waiting to watch them cheer.

It wasn't so bad. The gymnasium steamed with sweat and wet wool, surged with the continuous tidal roar of hormones, adrenalin

and the public address system. The crowd leaned forward on their seats, shifted and turned and revealed themselves as only teachers, only parents, only kids. When our team would make a point, the kid who scored was cheered by name, by one of the girls in blue and white; and when there was a break, for time out or for the end of the quarter, the girls would all get up and bounce. It passed swiftly like some familiar ritual, the maidens paying homage to the warriors. Its very familiarity was alarming and comforting in like degree. No one winced but me, and I only inside, I think.

The next spring, when two full seasons had passed and my daughter was still a cheerleader, I found myself in another, large gym, an hour's drive away, speechless again in the face of these cheerleaders together. I had grown resigned and even equable[3] with time, and she more confident.

These days her cheers were audible and her smiles less forced, and I would show up at games recognizable in my own coat. The pyramids worked; the chants showed the mark of her wit. The audiences had grown to expect the girls' skills; they bellowed approval and stayed in their seats at the half. Now the squad was competing for

---

2 *rictus:* a gaping grin or grimace.

3 *equable:* marked by lack of extremes or of sudden sharp changes.

a regional cheerleading crown, and I was there, waving a little blue flag and feeling like a person from another planet and wishing her luck.

All through the long day in the echoing gym, the teams pranced forth and did their drills. Little girls from Catholic schools, silky Spandex reflecting every prepubescent curve, ground their baby hips to sexy music in front of beaming parents and nuns. Squads of young women in flouncing pleats paraded like stiff-armed robots, their girlish voices disguised and gruff, grunting drill-sergeant monosyllables that exhorted us—ordered us—to score, fight, win. At the break, rock-and-roll poured out from giant speakers and all the girls danced on the wide wooden floor, a swirling kaleidoscope of school colors. The whole event was Dionysian,[4] ritualistic, bizarre—a wild concatenation of female passions, a screaming, ritualized celebration of sex and power, under the sanction of the state.

Our girls did fine. They were awarded a trophy for "most spirit," which meant that they had cheered loud and visibly for all the other teams that won. The dance they had prepared for weeks was perfectly executed, very tight; no one knew why they were not judged the best. At the end of the day, exhausted and drooping, they took their brave blue banner and went home.

The cheerleading season was over. The girls scattered to their summer jobs before college; their trophy gathers dust on the principal's shelf. I don't see a lot of those manic smiles these days; my daughter's face has relaxed into its usual weary lines; she shouts only when the phone is for me. But once in a while some gesture or some look will flicker like summer lightning through her limbs, across her face, and I am reminded that she has seen the face of the god, drunk the wine of female power and known its rites—and I tell myself with humble awe that strange as it may seem, it was cheerleading that made it so.

---

4 *Dionysian:* being of a frenzied nature; derived from Dionysus, the god of wine in Roman mythology.

Understanding What You Read

1. Why did the narrator react so negatively to her daughter's trying out to be a cheerleader?
   a. The mother was worried about possible injury to her daughter.
   b. The mother had a negative image about cheerleading and didn't want her daughter to be a part of such "conventionality."
   c. The mother was afraid the girl would neglect her studies because of all the time involved in cheerleading.
2. The author compares the cheerleaders' performances to
   a. a kind of primitive ritual centered around sex and power
   b. a football team's well-practiced plays
   c. a ballet company's precision
3. Why do you think the mother says of the cheerleading performance, "Its very familiarity was alarming and comforting in like degree"?

Writer's Workshop

Describe a sports activity as seen from two very different points of view. For example, the daughter in "Three Cheers for My Daughter" would have described the cheerleading routines very differently from the way her mother did. Pick some activity and describe it first with a positive tone and then, as Kathleen Cushman did in her essay, with a decidedly negative tone. Use specific words and images to carry the tone; don't just label something "wonderful" or "awful."

The Four-Minute Mile

"Now bid me run,
And I will strive with things impossible."
—Shakespeare

I expected that the summer of 1954 would be my last competitive season. It was certain to be a big year in athletics. There would be the Empire Games in Vancouver, the European Games in Berne, and hopes were running high of a four-minute mile.

The great change that now came over my running was that I no longer trained and raced alone. Perhaps I had mellowed a little and was becoming more sociable. Every day between twelve-thirty and one-thirty I trained on a track in Paddington and had a quick lunch before returning to hospital.[1] We called ourselves the Paddington Lunch Time Club. We came from all parts of London and our common bond was a love of running.

I felt extremely happy in the friendships I made there, as we shared the hard work of repetitive quarter-miles and sprints. These training sessions came to mean almost as much to me as had those at the Oxford track. I could now identify myself more intimately with the failure and success of other runners.

In my hardest training Chris Brasher was with me, and he made the task very much lighter. On Friday evenings he took me along to Chelsea Barracks where his coach, Franz Stampfl, held a training session. At weekends Chris Chataway would join us, and in this friendly atmosphere the very severe training we did became most enjoyable.

In December, 1953, we started a new intensive course of training and ran several times a week a series of ten consecutive quarter-miles, each in 66 seconds. Through January and February we gradually speeded them up, keeping to an interval of two minutes between each. By April we could manage them in 61 seconds, but however hard we tried it did not seem possible to reach our target of 60 seconds. We were stuck, or as Chris Brasher expressed

---

1 *hospital:* St. Mary's Hospital Medical School, London, where Bannister was a student at the time.

it—"bogged down." The training had ceased to do us any good and we needed a change.

Chris Brasher and I drove up to Scotland overnight for a few days' climbing. We turned into the Pass of Glencoe as the sun crept above the horizon at dawn. A misty curtain drew back from the mountains and the "sun's sleepless eye" cast a fresh cold light on the world. The air was calm and fragrant, and the colors of sunrise were mirrored in peaty pools on the moor. Soon the sun was up and we were off climbing. The weekend was a complete mental and physical change. It probably did us more harm than good physically. We climbed hard for the four days we were there, using the wrong muscles in slow and jerking movements.

There was an element of danger too. I remember Chris falling a short way when leading a climb up a rock face depressingly named "Jericho's Wall." Luckily he did not hurt himself. We were both worried lest a sprained ankle might set our training back by several weeks.

After three days our minds turned to running again. We suddenly became alarmed at the thought of taking any more risks, and decided to return. We had slept little, our meals had been irregular. But when we tried to run

those quarter-miles again, the time came down to 59 seconds!

It was now less than three weeks to the Oxford University versus A.A.A.[2] race, the first opportunity of the year for us to attack the four-minute mile. Chris Chataway had decided to join Chris Brasher and myself in the A.A.A. team. He doubted his ability to run a three quarter-mile in three minutes, but he generously offered to attempt it.

I had now abandoned the severe training of the previous months and was concentrating entirely on gaining speed and freshness. I had to learn to release in four short minutes the energy I usually spent in half an hour's training. Each training session took on a special significance as the day of the Oxford race drew near. It felt a privilege and joy each time I ran a trial on the track.

There was no longer any need for my mind to force my limbs to run faster—my body became a unity in motion much greater than the sum of its component parts. I never thought of length of stride or style, or even my judgment of pace. All this had become automatically ingrained. In this way a singleness of drive could be achieved, leaving my mind free from the task of directing operations so that it could fix itself on

2 *A.A.A.:* Amateur Athletic Association.

the great objective ahead. There was more enjoyment in my running than ever before, a new health and vigor. It was as if all my muscles were a part of a perfectly tuned machine. I felt fresh now at the end of each training session.

On April 24 I ran a three-quarter-mile trial in three minutes at Motspur Park with Chataway. I led for the first two laps and we both returned exactly the same time. Four days later I ran a last solo three-quarter-mile trial at Paddington. Norris McWhirter, who had been my patient timekeeper through most of 1953, came over to hold the watch.

The energy of the twins, Norris and Ross McWhirter, was boundless. For them nothing was too much trouble, and they accepted my challenge joyfully. After running together in Oxford as sprinters they carried their partnership into journalism, keeping me posted of the performances of my overseas rivals. They often drove me to athletics meetings, so that I arrived with no fuss, never a minute too soon or too late. Sometimes I was not sure whether it was Norris or Ross who held the watch or drove the car, but I knew that either could be relied upon.

For the trial at Paddington there was as usual a high wind blowing. I would have given almost anything to be able to shirk the test that would tell me with ruthless accuracy what my chances were of achieving a four-minute mile at Oxford. I felt that 2 minutes 59.9 seconds for the three-quarter-mile in a solo training run meant 3 minutes 59.9 seconds in a mile race. A time of 3 minutes 0.1 second would mean 4 minutes 0.1 second for the mile—just the difference between success and failure. The watch recorded a time of 2 minutes 59.9 seconds! I felt a little sick afterward and had the taste of nervousness in my mouth. My speedy recovery within five minutes suggested that I had been holding something back. Two days later at Paddington I ran a 1 minute 54 second half-mile quite easily, after a late night, and then took five days' complete rest before the race.

I had been training daily since the previous November, and now that the crisis was approaching I barely knew what to do with myself. I spent most of the time imagining I was developing a cold and wondering if the gale-force winds would ever drop. The day before the race I slipped on a highly polished hospital floor and spent the rest of the day limping. Each night in the week before the race there came a moment when I saw myself at the starting line. My whole body would grow nervous and tremble. I ran the race over in my mind. Then I would calm myself and sometimes get off to sleep.

Next day was Thursday, May 6, 1954. I went into the hospital as usual, and at eleven o'clock I was sharpening my spikes on a grindstone in the laboratory. Someone passing said, "You don't really think that's going to make any difference, do you?"

I knew the weather conditions made the chances of success practically nil. Yet all day I was taking the usual precautions for the race, feeling at the same time that they would prove useless.

I decided to travel up to Oxford alone because I wanted to think quietly. I took an early train deliberately, opened a carriage door, and, quite by chance, there was Franz Stampfl inside. I was delighted to see him, as a friend with the sort of attractive cheerful personality I badly needed at that moment. Through Chris Brasher, Franz had been in touch with my training program, but my own connection with him was slight.

I would have liked his advice and help at this moment, but could not bring myself to ask him. It was as if now, at the end of my running career, I was being forced to admit that coaches were necessary after all, and that I had been wrong to think that the athlete could be suf-

ficient unto himself.

In my mind there lurked the memory of an earlier occasion when I had visited a coach. He had expounded his views on my running and suggested a whole series of changes. The following week I read a newspaper article he wrote about my plans, claiming to be my adviser for the 1952 Olympics. This experience made me inclined to move slowly.

But Franz is not like this. He has no wish to turn the athlete into a machine working at his dictation. We shared a common view of athletics as a means of "recreation" of each individual, as a result of the liberation and expression of the latent power within him. Franz is an artist who can see beauty in human struggle and achievement.

We talked, almost impersonally, about the problem I faced. In my mind I had settled this as the day when, with every ounce of strength I possessed, I would attempt to run the four-minute mile. A wind of gale force was blowing which would slow me up by a second a lap. In order to succeed I must run not merely a four-minute mile, but the equivalent of a 3 minute 56 second mile in calm weather.

I had reached my peak physically and psychologically. There would never be another day like it. I had to drive myself to the limit of my power without the stimulus of competitive opposition. This was my first race for eight months and all this time I had been storing nervous energy. If I tried and failed I should be dejected, and my chances would be less on any later attempt. Yet it seemed that the high wind was going to make it impossible.

I had almost decided when I entered the carriage at Paddington that unless the wind dropped soon I would postpone the attempt. I would just run an easy mile in Oxford and make the attempt on the next possible occasion—ten days later at the White City in London.

Franz understood my apprehension. He thought I was capable of running a mile in 3 minutes 56 seconds, or 3:57, so he could argue convincingly that it was worthwhile making the attempt. "With the proper motivation, that is, a good reason for wanting to do it," he said, "your mind can overcome any sort of adversity. In any case the wind might drop. I remember J. J. Barry in Ireland. He ran a 4 minute 8 second mile without any training or even proper food—simply because he had the will to run. Later in America, where he was given every facility and encouragement, he never ran a fast race. In any case, what if this were your only chance?"

He had won his point. Racing has always been more of a mental that a physical problem to me. He went on talking about athletes and performances, but I heard no more. The dilemma was not banished from my mind, and the idea left uppermost was that this might be my only chance. "How would you ever forgive yourself if you rejected it?" I thought, as the train arrived in Oxford. As it happened, ten days later it was just as windy!

I was met at the station by Charles Wenden, a great friend from my early days in Oxford, who drove me straight down to Iffley Road. The wind was almost gale force. Together we walked round the deserted track. The St. George's flag on a nearby church stood out from the flagpole. The attempt seemed hopeless, yet for some unknown reason I tried out both pairs of spikes. I had a new pair which were specially made for me on the instructions of a climber and fell walker,[3] Eustace Thomas of Manchester. Some weeks before he had come up to London and together we worked out modifications which would reduce the weight of each running shoe from six to four ounces. This saving in weight might well mean the difference between success and failure.

Still undecided, I drove back to Charles Wenden's home for lunch.

---

3 *fell walker:* hiker.

On this day, as on many others, I was glad of the peace which I found there. Although both he and his wife Eileen knew the importance of the decision that had to be made, and cared about it as much as I did myself, it was treated by common consent as a question to be settled later.

The immediate problem was to prepare a suitable lunch, and to see that the children, Felicity and Sally, ate theirs. Absorbed in watching the endless small routine of running a home and family, I could forget some of my apprehensions. Charles Wenden had been one of the ex-service students in Oxford after the war, and some of my earliest running had been in his company. Later his house had become a second home for me during my research studies in Oxford, and the calm efficiency of Eileen had often helped to still my own restless worries. Never was this factor so important as on this day.

In the afternoon I called on Chris Chataway. At the moment the sun was shining, and he lay stretched on the window seat. He smiled and said, just as I knew he would, "The day could be a lot worse, couldn't it? Just now it's fine. The forecast says the wind may drop toward evening. Let's not decide until five o'clock."

I spent the afternoon watching

from the window the swaying of the leaves. "The wind's hopeless," said Joe Binks on the way down to the track. At five-fifteen there was a shower of rain. The wind blew strongly, but now came in gusts, as if uncertain. As Brasher, Chataway and I warmed up, we knew the eyes of the spectators were on us; they were hoping that the wind would drop just a little—if not enough to run a four-minute mile, enough to make the attempt.

Failure is as exciting to watch as success, provided the effort is absolutely genuine and complete. But the spectators fail to understand—and how can they know—the mental agony through which an athlete must pass before he can give his maximum effort. And how rarely, if he is built as I am, he can give it.

No one tried to persuade me. The decision was mine alone, and the moment was getting closer. As we lined up for the start I glanced at the flag again. It fluttered more gently now, and the scene from Shaw's *Saint Joan* flashed through my mind, how she, at her desperate moment, waited for the wind to change. Yes, the wind was dropping slightly. This was the moment when I made my decision. The attempt was on.

There was complete silence on the ground . . . a false start . . . I felt angry that precious moments during the lull in the wind might be slipping by. The gun fired a second time. . . . . Brasher went into the lead and I slipped in effortlessly behind him, feeling tremendously full of running. My legs seemed to meet no resistance at all, as if propelled by some unknown force.

We seemed to be going so slowly! Impatiently I shouted "Faster!" But Brasher kept his head and did not change the pace. I went on worrying until I heard the first lap time, 57.5 seconds. In the excitement my knowledge of pace had deserted me. Brasher could have run the first quarter in 55 seconds without my realizing it, because I felt so full of running, but I should have had to pay for it later. Instead, he had made success possible.

At one and a half laps I was still worrying about the pace. A voice shouting "Relax" penetrated to me above the noise of the crowd. I learnt afterward it was Stampfl's. Unconsciously I obeyed. If the speed was wrong it was too late to do anything about it, so why worry? I was relaxing so much that my mind seemed almost detached from my body. There was no strain.

I barely noticed the half-mile, passed in 1 minute 58 seconds, nor when, round the next bend, Chat-away went into the lead. At three-quarters of a mile the effort was still barely perceptible; the time was 3 minutes 0.7 second, and by now the crowd was roaring. Somehow I had to run that last lap in 59 seconds. Chataway led round the next bend and then I pounced past him at the beginning of the back straight, three hundred yards from the finish.

I had a moment of mixed joy and anguish, when my mind took over. It raced well ahead of my body and drew my body compellingly forward. I felt that the moment of a lifetime had come. There was no pain, only a great unity of movement and aim. The world seemed to stand still, or did not exist. The only reality was the next two hundred yards of track under my feet. The tape meant finality—extinction perhaps.

I felt at that moment that it was my chance to do one thing supremely well. I drove on, impelled by a combination of fear and pride. The air I breathed filled me with the spirit of the track where I had run my first race. The noise in my ears was that of the faithful Oxford crowd. Their hope and encouragement gave me greater strength. I had now turned the last bend and there were only fifty yards more.

My body had long since exhausted all its energy, but it went on running just the same. The physical overdraft came only from greater willpower. This was the crucial moment when my legs were strong enough to carry me over the last few yards as they could never have done in previous years. With five yards to go the tape seemed almost to recede. Would I ever reach it?

Those last few seconds seemed never-ending. The faint line of the finishing tape stood ahead as a haven of peace, after the struggle. The arms of the world were waiting to receive me if only I reached the tape without slackening my speed. If I faltered, there would be no arms to hold me and the world would be a cold, forbidding place, because I had been so close. I leapt at the tape like a man taking his last spring to save himself from the chasm that threatens to engulf him.

My effort was over and I collapsed almost unconscious, with an arm on either side of me. It was only then that real pain overtook me. I felt like an exploded flashlight with no will to live; I just went on existing in the most passive physical state without being quite conscious. Blood surged from my muscles and seemed to fell me. It was as if all my limbs were caught in an ever-tightening vise. I knew that I had done it before I even heard the time. I was too close to have failed, unless my legs had played strange tricks at the finish by slowing me down and not telling my tiring brain that they had done so.

The stop-watches held the answer. The announcement came—"Result of one mile . . . time, three minutes"—the rest lost in the roar of excitement. I grabbed Brasher and Chataway, and together we scampered round the track in a burst of spontaneous joy. We had done it—the three of us!

We shared a place where no man had yet ventured—secured for all time, however fast men might run miles in future. We had done it where we wanted, when we wanted, how we wanted, in our first attempt of the year. In the wonderful joy my pain was forgotten and I wanted to prolong those precious moments of realization.

I felt suddenly and gloriously free of the burden of athletic ambition that I had been carrying for years. No words could be invented for such supreme happiness, eclipsing all other feelings. I thought at that moment I could never again reach such a climax of single-mindedness. I felt bewildered and overpowered. I knew it would be some time before I caught up with myself.

Understanding What You Read

1. Explain why Bannister felt that a three-quarter-mile race run in 2 minutes 59.9 seconds was vastly different from the same race run in 3 minutes 0.1 second.

2. How did Bannister and his friend Franz Stampfl define **recreation**?

3. After the record was broken, Bannister says, "We had done it—the three of us!" What do you think he means?

Writer's Workshop

1. Athletes have a reputation for being narrow and not too smart. Judging from this piece, would you say Roger Bannister deserves such a reputation? Why or why not? Write a brief essay in which you take a position on the public reputation of athletes.

2. It is difficult to read this piece and not get caught up in the excitement of Bannister's attempt. Of course, Bannister had a compelling story to tell, but he makes it truly forceful by taking the time to put in all the details. His frankness and honesty help, too.

   Write in detail about some moment in sports you experienced. Narrow your focus—a single at bat, a wrestling match, a game in a tennis match—and pack it with vivid details.

The Sprinters

In this poem runners try to beat the clock—and more.

The gun explodes them.
Pummeling, pistoning they fly
In time's face.
A go at the limit,
A terrible try   5
To smash the ticking glass,
Outpace the beat
That runs, that streaks away
Tireless, and faster than they.

Beside ourselves   10
(It is for us they run!)
We shout and pound the stands
For one to win
Loving him, whose hard
Grace-driven stride   15
Most mocks the clock
And almost breaks the bands
Which lock us in.

Understanding What You Read

1. Usually, you think of a person shooting or "exploding" a gun. How can a gun "explode" the sprinters?

2. How can a runner fly "in time's face"?

3. Name and explain several things this poem is saying about time.

Writer's Workshop

A comparison and contrast essay notes the similarities (comparisons) and differences (contrasts) between two things. Aside from the fact that "The Four-Minute Mile" is prose and "The Sprinters" is poetry, write one or two paragraphs pointing out similarities between the two pieces. Then write one or two paragraphs about the differences in the ideas contained in the two pieces of writing. You are, in essence, producing a standard piece of critical writing—the comparison and contrast essay.

Ain't God Good to Indiana!

Here's a look at high school basketball at fever pitch.

Baseball was a game that took a frankly professional road, and eventually became entertainment. Football, also a widely played sport, grew up in the schools and colleges, emerging as an industry that fools nobody by pretending it is a game. Basketball, a nationwide pastime, started from small beginnings also. Today it has developed even further along the path to a kind of submerged professionalism. For the first time we are seeing this professional approach to a sport seep down as far as the high school level. Observe how deep and pervasive is this trend from the healthy outdoor attitude that existed at the time of Theodore Roosevelt.

What is this thing called basketball? It is, first of all, a game, a sport; next, a business; finally, a disease. It is also color, drama, and excitement in the lives of millions of small-town Americans, many of whom lack art galleries, symphonies, books, and the theater in their daily lives. In these small towns in winter basketball dominates the whole place. On Friday nights, when there are games, nothing else takes place. The whole town stops.

This game of basketball, which we play so well and like so much, is suited to our temperament, *sec et nerveux.*[1] The American is apt to be suspicious of intelligence, which is one reason why games such as basketball require coordination, muscular skill, quick thinking rather than the intensive thoughtfulness of games such as cricket, billiards, and chess. (This doesn't mean they aren't played in the United States, only that they are not popular.)

Basketball was invented by a Canadian medic named Dr. James Naismith, then teaching in the Springfield, Massachusetts, Y.M.C.A. Training School, in 1891. Originally it was a sport with nine to a side, but the number of players on a team was later reduced to five. The colleges took it up about 1900. Today it is popular everywhere in

---

1 *sec et nerveux: Fr.,* high strung, nervous.

the United States, in South America, Japan, Russia, and Europe.

Moreover, basketball is the biggest single sport played and watched in the United States. More compete, more attend games. A total of 950 college teams in 1958 played before 15,000,000 spectators. The University of Kansas, one of the more famous teams, is watched annually by 350,000 fans, almost as many as see the Washington Senators of the American League in a 154-game schedule.

However, it is in the high schools and in the small towns, where more than one hundred million see teams play each year, that the fever is most virulent. During the Depression, in Muncie, Indiana, $100,000 was spent for a new high school basketball arena when all city departments suffered budget cuts, and the public library was understaffed because no assistant could be secured for less than $1,800 and only $1,500 was available. The Lynds, in their *Middletown,* a study of this city, report:

> No distinctions divide the crowds which pack the high school gymnasium for the games, and which in every kind of machine crowd the road for out-of-town games. North Side, South Side, Catholic and

2 *Kluxer:* member of the Ku Klux Klan, a white supremacist organization.

Kluxer,[2] banker and machinist— their one shout is, "Eat 'Em, Beat 'Em, Bearcats!"

Fred Russell, of the Nashville, Tennessee, *Banner,* points out one reason for its popularity. Basketball is at times played outdoors, but it is really a winter game played under cover. In summer a man may be fishing, golfing, or mowing the lawn. There isn't much lawn to mow in Kansas in winter.

Certainly nowhere in the United States is the sport devoured by players and fans alike as in the Middle West, and in no part of the Middle West more intensively than Indiana. Folks there tell you that a Hoosier talks basketball for an hour after he is dead and has stopped breathing.

Autumn in Indiana means yellow corn stacked in the fields and county fairs from north to south. As the days grow shorter, politics rears its ugly head around Courthouse Square, and a bit later comes the thing that unites everyone: basketball.

For here is the game of the people, rich, poor, young, old, town dweller and farmer, the sport that stirs every Hoosier heart, that everyone in the state understands and responds to. Unlike some of its neighbors, Indiana is full of small towns and small homes. Here in the middle land folks are, as Dreiser said, warm, generous, hospitable, the epitome of American virtues. There are more lawn mowers per capita in this state than in any other. Indiana also has basketball.

Basketball means various things to different people. To the high school principal or superintendent, the game is a big headache. Folks besiege him for seats he hasn't got. Businessmen downtown want a winning team—or else. If the school continues to lose, the principal's head rolls. Unless that of the coach rolls first. On the other hand, victory helps the principal with the school board, and to the winning coach means more money, power, and prestige.

To the boys on the high school team—in some states girls play interscholastic basketball—this is the Great Adventure, their first chance to see the big outside world. The sport can be fun and torture at the same time with its daily drudgery of practice, elation of competition, agony of losing, and ecstasy of triumph. To folks in town, Saturday night is something to look ahead to, the high point of many a drab existence. To the men shooting pool in the rear of Joe's Steak House on East Michigan, basketball is their bread and butter, a large part of their yearly take. (Nobody knows how many millions are bet on basketball; but far more than on any other game). For although some teams win and some lose, gamblers are apt to come out ahead.

Throughout the state there are hoops over every garage door and above every barn. You'll find them also inside the homes—nailed up to bedroom doors or hanging in the hall. There are grade schools with no other recreational equipment; but a basketball court is a must. Not long ago a high school in a fair-sized Indiana town burned to the ground. The gymnasium was rebuilt immediately; the school not for several years. In one south-central town of 23,000, a new school, the first for thirty years, was built at a cost of $375,000. The hat was then passed around among the townspeople for a gymnasium, and more than one million dollars was raised for a magnificent structure of stone, brick, and glass, the fourth largest in the state. The high school gymnasium today in the Midwest has the role of the playhouse of the Elizabethans, the bull ring of Sevilla, the theater of the ancient Greeks. Indeed the Greeks would have been entirely at home watching a basketball game in Kokomo, Indiana.

Kids throughout the state play alley basketball all summer and even go to bed with a basketball. Dad gives his youngster a regulation ball as soon as he can toddle, and teaches him to toss it through his elder brother's outstretched arms. And each year comes the biggest event of all, the Tournament, usually called "The State." Eight hundred teams from high school compete each winter, with 4,500 boys from fourteen to eighteen in action. This event has been held regularly without interruption since 1911. About a million and a half admissions, costing almost nine hundred thousand dollars, are sold every winter.

In this game, in this region, no coach ever has to worry about material. His problem is to assimilate it, to pick out the five best youngsters for the team, and get them out on that hardwood. Businessmen, housewives, kids, the president of the Merchants National Bank, the chief of police, that loafer in the booth at Hank's Bar and Grill, the farmers turning on their television sets out on the National Road, and Doc Showalter, the local osteopath, all know basketball. They know it, love it, live it.

And every single one of them could coach a team better'n that fella down to the high school, too!

Going to the game tonight, Mac?
Silly question. Of course we're going.

For this is *our* team, not just the high school's team. It's Muncie, Marion, Logansport, Jeffersonville, East Chicago, or Vincennes. We know these boys. That six-foot-four-inch center lives two doors down the street. We remember the cold January day he was born, and that hot summer he was so sick with polio; we recall the first day he went to kindergarten, and when he got well and made his grade school team. That blond guard with the crew haircut tosses the *Sentinel* up to our front porch each evening. Joe, one of the forwards, carries our groceries out from Kroger's on Fridays. Chester, the other guard, cuts our lawn each summer. We've watched these youngsters all their lives, know them and their parents.

Going to the game tonight, Mac?
Don't be silly. Of course we're going.

Who watches basketball in an Indiana town? Everyone. That means everyone who can hobble to the Gymnasium, the Field House, the Auditorium, or the Coliseum. Men, women, kids, young, old, and middle-aged, business leaders, doctors and lawyers, factory workers, machinists from the Chrysler plant, storekeepers, and the lady who runs the best beauty parlor in town on West Walnut. Everybody is there save the blind, the crippled, and the town drunk. And, of course, those unfortunates who didn't apply for a seat in time and must watch the game over television, or, worse, listen to it on the radio.

I stepped off the train at the Monon Depot that rainy February night to find my friend waiting. To him it was very meet[3] and right that if anybody wanted to understand basketball he should come to Indiana. Across the wide Mississippi and over the wide Missouri they're nuts about basketball, too. Granted. But not the way Hoosiers are. And if a seeker for truth comes to Indiana, naturally he should first visit Springfield.

Listen to the pride in his voice. "Why, man, there's no town in Indiana for basketball like Springfield. Hurry up! First game's almost over." He chucks my bag onto the rear seat and jumps quickly in behind the wheel. "Wildcats were behind, 36 to 38, end of the third quarter."

Through the icy, slithery streets at a fast pace, too fast, and so to the Gymnasium, and into that hot, fetid smell of popcorn and 6,000 people cooped up together. He led me up to the balcony where a seat had been reserved in the front row. The electric scoreboard at the end showed fifty-six seconds to play and the Wildcats behind by a single point. The entire crowd was on its feet shrieking, yelling to the ten sweat-stained youngsters on the floor below.

Beside me was a little old lady in gray. She wore a faded gray dress, an especially ancient gray hat, and held in her right hand an umbrella. Down on the floor cheerleaders leaped and turned handsprings, people in the stands thumped each other's backs and screamed. An orgy of emotion gripped the place and everyone in it.

Suddenly a towhead on the floor below stole the ball. Now the noise overwhelmed us all; you found yourself on your feet yelling in that Niagara of sound. Although insulated, indifferent to the two teams you never saw five minutes ago, this fever was contagious. It conquered you until you were one with the screaming mob as the little towhead dribbled the ball down the floor, passed to a teammate, took it back again.

The tension tightened, became taut, unendurable. There was no world but this. Reality was the heated enclosure below. Space was the confines of these four walls. Time was the electric clock beating out these final seconds. Life was this thrusting surge beneath.

The boy swung the ball around adroitly, passed and received it

---

3 *meet:* proper.

back, zigzagging nearer the goal, pivoting, turning, twisting. The little old lady in gray beside me could stand it no longer. Leaning over the balcony rail, she waved her umbrella. . . .

This is the Finals of the State in the Butler Field House in Indianapolis. We are in the dressing room of the Springfield Wildcats, favorites to win the title, just as the first half is ending. Now comes the last act of this drama which started four weeks ago when 832 teams hopefully began the long, hard road through the Sectionals (64 teams left), to the Regionals (32 teams left), to the Semi-finals (16 left), to the Finals (4 left). Only the Wildcats and Tigers remain to fight it out this evening.

The dressing room, like all dressing rooms, is spare, square, humid, with steam pipes crossing the ceiling, and over everything that dressing room odor of sweaty flesh, the smell of Doc Showalter's liniment mingled with that of a pile of dirty towels in one corner. Lockers stretch along the side. Opposite is a bank of showers. The walls are a dingy concrete, the floor the same. Two long benches form a kind of V. A blackboard leans against a side wall, a clothes rack with plaid shirts, windbreakers, and slacks stands near the lockers. Two wooden chairs and a table complete the furnishings, save for a large sign hung on the wall.

EVERY DAY THINGS ARE BEING DONE WHICH COULDN'T BE DONE

The only person in the room is Tommy Kates, the assistant manager, a chubby, bespectacled boy of fifteen in a red-and-blue Wildcat sweater. He is placing clean towels along the benches, moving the blackboard up against one locker where it will be accessible. From outside come bursts of noise. Listen! You can distinguish the hoarse, tense shouts of the players, the cheers from both sides of the arena. Then there is a sudden roar, a cry of piercing elation that penetrates the room, seems to possess the whole building.

Tommy stops, a pile of towels in his arms. He knows the first half is dying in that frenzy of exultation. He also knows what he hears isn't good for the Wildcats.

The door bangs open and a man rushes in. It's Doc Showalter, followed by Russ Davis, the assistant coach, and a couple of subs in satin jackets with WILDCATS and their numbers on them. Then a hot, dejected boy in shorts and a red jersey, a big 34 on front, stumbles in. Another enters, another, and another, all tall, for this team averages six feet two. They tromp into the room, fall slumping and sprawling onto the benches.

Behind them is Jack Stevens, the manager, with the score book in one hand, and last of all Art Benson, the coach.

Art, which is what everyone in town calls him, is a youngish man with an oldish look. Gray hair is traced over his ears, there is a deep furrow above his eyes, he is tight-lipped and tense. He steps to the center of the V made by the two benches, facing the exhausted team. The assistant manager walks silently past, handing out two vitamin pills to each player. Heads come up, heads drop again. The Doc goes along the row, kneeling to adjust an ankle brace on one player, tightening a knee supporter on the next man.

The coach's voice is hoarse after all the shouting at them he has done from the bench. "Lemme see the score book." Notice how his hand trembles as the manager hands him the book, and says in low tones, "Two on Spike. One on Jerry. Three on Tom."

Now the room is silent. Not a sound, not a movement, save for the everlasting panting from the benches. No friends, no parents or school officials, no reporters fight their way past the guard at the door. They are all in the dressing room of the other team. The dressing room of a losing team is usually empty. We are not interested in losers in the United States.

"Nice boys? Oh, sure, too bad they couldn't make it. But d'ja see that Tiger forward, that boy Karson? He's fast, he's sneaky, he's shifty, all right . . . ."

The coach stands engrossed, reading the score book in agony. There in black and white is the story of disaster. All the time the boys sit, heads down, not even using the towels in their fists; necks, backs, shoulders, and shirts soaked with sweat.

At last he reaches down, picks up a basketball from the floor, slapping it back and forth in his hands, the only outward and visible sight of the nerves he tries to suppress. He looks at each boy carefully. Their heads are still down, their eyes avoid his, they gaze at the dingy concrete, miserable, panting. Suddenly he screams at them, at the lowered heads along the bench:

"Well! You got anything to say?" No response. He shrieks at them. "Have ya?"

Nobody answers. Although each man is dying of thirst, not one ventures as far as the water cooler, or even looks at him. Heads remain down.

The manager, who has been walking around handing out towels, stands immobile. Even the Doc, his arms full of bottles and adhesive tape, is motionless.

"You patted yerselves on the

back too soon." Half-crazed with the agony of it, he stalks back and forth, turning the ball around and around in his palms. "Thought you'd get by the easy way, on your reputation. Won the State last year, so you were the champs, you were the best. Then you met this gutsy gang of kids from a school of ninety students, a gang that wasn't scared of you. Didn't you? Hey?"

Still no sound or movement from the benches save that everlasting panting. No heads rise. Just an awful silence over the room. "Now mebbe you realize in Indiana a team . . . cannot . . . get by . . . on its reputation. That's something. If you guys will stop reading your clippings . . . we might get back to basketball."

Heads down, they listen as they never listened before. A bench creaks ominously. The coach's tone burns them, sears everyone in the room, the subs in the background, the two managers.

Slap-slap, slap-slap, the ball goes from one hand to the other. "Got anything to say? If you have, please say it. You figgered you were safe because you had an eight-point lead at the quarter, 'cause you were the great Wildcats you thought they'd fold. You fell asleep out there, didn't you. Hey?

"Is there anything I can do'll wake you up?"

Still they sit panting, not even using the towels, in a state of shock. With a quick gesture the coach tosses away the basketball and grabs a wooden chair beside him. Swinging it around his head, he flings it hard against the concrete wall ten feet away.

It strikes with a crash and crumples into splinters.

The heads come up, the heads immediately go down. A door slams and a voice calls:

"Three minutes!"

He turns back. "You played like you were glued to the floor. Joe, you didn't make six passes all evening. Tom, ain't a mite o' use chuckin' from way out there, you know that. *Move that ball!"* His voice rises to a shriek as he glares at them. "Basketball is a game of movement; move to the strong side. Swing-it-wide-and-swing-it-true. You had things sewed up, then what happened? The roof fell in. So you lost your heads, you saw you might be beaten, and you quit. Bunch of quitters. You quit cold. You got scared, you didn't pass, you acted like you had boxcars in your shoes. . . ."

Back and forth, back and forth he stalks, suffering as they suffer, sharing their agony, yet pleading, abusing, entreating. "Watch that ball. Alla time, watch . . . that . . . ball. At no time . . . take . . . yer eyes . . . offa that ball. An' get those bricks outa your britches. This isn't kindergarten, it's basketball. How you gonna go back home and face those folks if you lose? Get out there and fight."

He turned, saw the table, kicked savagely, taking out some of his rage and disappointment upon it. The table overturned, fell, clattered to the floor with a bang, and a roll of Doc Showalter's adhesive tape jangled and bounced along the concrete.

Then he was back at them again.

"This is your last chance. The bread-and-butter quarter. Every shot counts. Have you got guts? Are you a bunch of quitters, that's what I wanna know? Have . . . you . . . got the . . . guts?"

They rose together. Benches scrape on the floor. Their voices, hoarse and husky from shouting, conquer the room.

"Les' go, big team . . . les' get those guys. Les' win this one. . . ."

Together they pour out the door onto the arena floor. You can hear the sudden cheers from the Springfield side as they appear.

This seldom-seen, little-mentioned part of basketball is merely a small slice of the American way in sport. For our sport is sentimental, true, sport is crazy, sport is lots of fun. But sport in the United States is also cruel, hard, ruthless, like so much in American life. Most Americans are half idealists and half realists; sometimes the one and then the other emerges dominant in our national character. A French girl exchange student, recently returning home after a year in this country, remarked that it was difficult for Europeans to understand how we could be so idealistic and so materialistic at the same time. All the idealism of the good American is in basketball. All his materialism, too.

Nobody in Indiana tolerates willingly a defeated team or a losing coach for long. It is obvious that only one team out of some eight hundred can win the State each year, yet every school, even the smallest, starts the season with hopes and dreams. We expect to win. America has no time for losers.

If this is so, why do coaches stay in basketball, why undergo this terrible punishment which soon makes a young man old? For the money? There isn't any. Most of them are underpaid for the hours they put in, the work they do with the youngsters aside from their actual coaching, the energy and effort they expend eighteen hours a day. Kids call a basketball coach by his first name in the middle land. But never a principal or a teacher.

What, then, is the reason coaches remain coaches? They stay in the sport for the adventure, partly, for the goal, the chance of becoming celebrated, a little. But mainly because they can do no other. They started basketball as little shavers in the Y, they played in grade school, they made the team in junior high, they played through high school and college. It's in their blood and cannot easily be put aside.

The pioneering spirit which we have seen is an important factor in American sport, that feel for competition deep within us; this keeps them coaching basketball. Even after defeats, disappointments, ulcers, nervous breakdowns, they stay with it. Since business has become a huge, impersonal thing, with men employed by bosses in New York or Chicago they never see, life can be a dullish thing. Sport is the great national adventure of the twentieth century. In his heart, the coach knows his life will inevitably be a short one. He does it because he prefers it to anything else.

How about the adults? What is their chief interest as parents? Are they interested in the schools? That their children should become educated citizens? Perhaps; but first of all their interest is in basketball and having the boy make the team. In fact, at times this furnishing amuse-ment to the town is their sole interest in the schools and education. As Russell Kirk remarked ironically, "What's a school for if not to give the community a good time?" The thing he terms "this expensive and purposeless athleticism" is actually the paramount issue in most schools. We never ask how successful a teacher is the girl presiding over the third grade, or the young man who teaches history. We ask what kind of a won-and-lost record Art Benson made over at Springfield. Jim Tatum, successful football coach at the University of North Carolina, made this point cogently. "I don't think winning is the most important thing. I think it's the only thing."

Americans believe in the happy ending. It is hard to make them accept the fact that if two football teams meet, one of them is pretty sure to lose. The American goes into sport as he goes into war, expecting, of course, to win. The only uncertainty in war is the actual time when we can get the hell out of this lousy country and get back to the Davis Drugstore at the corner of Market and Union, in Lima, Ohio.

Kids are imitative, and if everyone in Springfield thinks victory important, they concentrate on winning. What does the average boy in an Indiana school want to be when he grows up? A basketball coach, naturally, and of course a winning one, because he has been told that a loser is a poor thing indeed. This is the dream of most Americans today; in every sport the field is open. Here money, pull, family, or position don't count. May the best man win. It's the pioneer wagon again, the prairie and the plains, the unconquerable frontier, the urge and surge and the innate restlessness deep in the heart of every American boy.

Once upon a time, throughout this vast region which Sinclair Lewis liked to call The Valley of Democracy, there was growth in the arts and letters, there were statesmen of note and scholars turning out important work. The Hoosier poets such as James Whitcomb Riley, novelists such as Meredith Nicholson and Booth Tarkington and Theodore Dreiser, satirists such as George Ade, newspaper reporters including Elmer Davis and Roy Howard, historians such as William J. Beveridge came from this middle land. One of the finest publishing houses in the United States was and still is located there. Where are the successors to these creative talents? They don't exist since basketball has become the folk art of the region. Attention, creativeness, energy, talent, all are centered around basketball.

The game fills a place in this society that is unbelievable unless you have lived in it. Basketball is a rallying point for everyone of both sexes and all ages. The miner in the South, the farmer in the rich central plains, the steelworker along Lake Michigan, and the little old lady in the faded gray dress all respond to the quick break and a zone defense. Basketball unites the community, occasionally at two or three in the morning when thousands turn out to welcome home a winning—or even a losing—team from the State. It gives everyone in Springfield that sense of belonging so necessary to modern man.

Very seldom, and obviously very, very timidly, the growth, spread, and importance of basketball are questioned. The fact is that the majority of high school principals realize the drawbacks and defects of basketball better than anyone else. Most of them would leap with joy if the State Tournament with its obvious excesses were abolished. Someone occasionally does suggest curtailing it. As well ask an American to give up his Chevy!

But what about the ones who make the game possible: the boys? and also the girls? Save for a handful of cheerleaders, basketball gives nothing to the girls who become sport watchers like the adults, not participants, although in some states, as Iowa, girls also compete. (Observe that painfully few boys in high school participate in varsity basketball either, probably a fraction of one per cent in most places.)

Does basketball help these boys who play? Most emphatically, yes. The old phrase about the "muddied oafs at the wicket, the flanneled fools at the goal" may have been true in Kipling's time; not today. Basketball matures the boys, that is, those who compete. It teaches them quick thinking, resourcefulness, coordination, courage, and the values of the competitive spirit. No basketball player will ever end as a fatalist. And no youngster of fifteen or sixteen who has stood there before those shrieking thousands, with the fate of his team and his town depending on tossing that ball through a hoop on the wall, is ever quite the same afterward.

Granted. Yet does basketball induce those qualities we like to consider important for good citizens in a democracy, to name only a few, such as tolerance, compassion, generosity, kindness, respect for the rights of others? Does it? Not as a rule, if one wants to win.

And who in the United States doesn't? I do.

Further, in that field house, there are 16,000 watching while ten to fifteen boys compete. In every field house and gymnasium the country over, on every college and high school gridiron, we exploit the youngsters. Call this sport if you wish. The fact is they are there to furnish entertainment for the town.

They like it? Often, no doubt . . . The fact is that the professional approach to sport, which did not exist in 1900, has seeped down from the colleges to the schools. Intercollegiate sport has gradually developed into a first-class training ground for a jungle society. Now interscholastic sport is following the same road.

Understanding What You Read

1. Describe what basketball in Indiana means, as conveyed by John R. Tunis, to
   a. average residents
   b. high school principals
   c. high school girls
   d. basketball coaches

2. What specific criticisms does Tunis make of the way interscholastic basketball is regarded in Indiana?

3. How, according to Tunis, are American values reflected in the way Hoosiers care about their high school basketball teams? Be specific.

Writer's Workshop

An argumentative or persuasive essay tries to convince the reader of the correctness of the author's position. Write an argumentative essay convincing people of one of the following positions:
a. Tunis's essay is ultimately more positive than negative about interscholastic basketball in Indiana.
b. Tunis's essay has more negative than positive things to say about interscholastic basketball in Indiana.
To make your case, be as exact as possible in referring to specific points made by John Tunis in "Ain't God Good to Indiana!"

Attitude

Winning isn't everything. No, it's how you look that matters. Here's a handy lesson on how to comport yourself on the playing field.

Long ago I passed the point in life when major-league ball-players begin to be younger than yourself. Now all of them are, except for a few aging trigenarians and a couple of quadros who don't get around on the fastball as well as they used to and who sit out the second games of doubleheaders. However, despite my age (thirty-nine), I am still active and have a lot of interests. One of them is slow-pitch softball, a game that lets me go through the motions of baseball without getting beaned or having to run too hard. I play on a pretty casual team, one that drinks beer on the bench and substitutes freely. If a player's wife or girlfriend wants to play, we give her a glove and send her out to right field, no questions asked, and if she lets a pop fly drop six feet in front of her, nobody agonizes over it.

Except me. This year. For the first time in my life, just as I am entering the dark twilight of my slow-pitch career, I find myself taking the game seriously. It isn't the bonehead play that bothers me

especially—the pop fly that drops untouched, the slow roller juggled and the ball then heaved ten feet over the first baseman's head and into the next diamond, the routine singles that go through outfielders' legs for doubles and triples with gloves flung after them. No, it isn't our stone-glove fielding or pussy-foot base-running or limp-wristed hitting that gives me fits, though these have put us on the short end of some mighty ridiculous scores this summer. It's our attitude.

Bottom of the ninth, down 18–3, two outs, a man on first and a woman on third, and our third baseman strikes out. *Strikes out!* In slow-pitch, not even your grandmother strikes out, but this guy does, and after his third strike—a wild swing at a ball that bounces on the plate—he topples over in the dirt and lies flat on his back, laughing. *Laughing!*

Same game, earlier. They have the bases loaded. A weak grounder is hit toward our second baseperson. The runners are running. She picks up the ball, and she looks at them. She looks at first, at second, at home. We yell, "Throw it! Throw it!" and she throws it, underhand, at the pitcher, who has turned and run to back up the catcher. The ball rolls across the third-base line and under the bench. Three runs score. The batter, a fatso, chugs into second. The other team hoots and hollers, and what does she do? She shrugs and smiles ("Oh, silly me"); after all, it's only a game. Like the aforementioned strikeout artist, she treats her error as a joke. They have forgiven themselves instantly, which is unforgivable. It is *we* who should forgive them, who can say, "It's all right, it's only a game." They are supposed to throw up their hands and kick the dirt and hang their heads, as if this boner, even if it is their sixteenth of the afternoon—*this* is the one that really and truly breaks their hearts.

That attitude sweetens the game for everyone. The sinner feels sweet remorse. The fatso feels some sense of accomplishment; this is no bunch of rumdums he forced into an error but a team with some class. We, the sinner's teammates, feel momentary anger at her—dumb! dumb play!—but then, seeing her grief, we sympathize with her in our hearts (any one of us might have made that mistake or one worse), and we yell encouragement, including the

shortstop, who, moments before, dropped an easy throw for a force at second. "That's all right! Come on! We got 'em!" we yell. "Shake it off! These turkeys can't hit!" That makes us feel good, even though the turkeys now lead us by ten runs. We're getting clobbered, but we have a winning attitude.

Let me say this about attitude: Each player is responsible for his or her own attitude, and to a considerable degree you can *create* a good attitude by doing certain little things on the field. These are certain little things that ballplayers do in the Bigs, and we ought to be doing them in the Slows.

1. When going up to bat, don't step right into the batter's box as if it were an elevator. The box is your turf, your stage. Take possession of it slowly and deliberately, starting with a lot of back-bending, knee-stretching, and torso-revolving in the on-deck circle. Then, approaching the box, stop outside it and tap the dirt off your spikes with your bat. You don't have spikes, you have sneakers, of course, but the significance of the tapping is the same. Then, upon entering the box, spit on the ground. It's a way of saying, "This here is mine. This is where I get my hits."

2. Spit frequently. Spit at all crucial moments. Spit correctly. Spit should be *blown,* not ptuied weak-

ly with the lips, which often results in dribble. Spitting should convey forcefulness of purpose, concentration, pride. Spit down, not in the direction of others. Spit in the glove and on the fingers, especially after making a real knucklehead play; it's a way of saying, "I dropped the ball because my glove was dry."

3. At bat and in the field, pick up dirt. Rub dirt in the fingers (especially after spitting on them). Toss dirt, as if testing the wind for velocity and direction. Smooth the dirt. Be involved with dirt. If no dirt is available (e.g., in the outfield), pluck tufts of grass. Fielders should be grooming their areas constantly between plays, flicking away tiny sticks and bits of gravel.

4. Take your time. Tie your laces. Confer with your teammates about possible situations that may arise and conceivable options in dealing with them. Extend the game. Three errors on three consecutive plays can be humiliating if the plays occur within the space of a couple of minutes, but if each error is separated from the next by extensive conferences on the mound, lace-tying, glove adjustments, and arguing close calls (if any), the effect on morale is minimized.

5. Talk. Not just an occasional "Let's get a hit now" but continuous rhythmic chatter, a flow of sylla-bles: "Hey babe hey babe c'mon babe good stick now hey babe long tater take him downtown babe . . . hey good eye good eye."

Infield chatter is harder to maintain. Since the slow-pitch pitch is required to be a soft underhand lob, infielders hesitate to say, "Smoke him babe hey low heat hey throw it on the black babe chuck it in there back him up babe no hit no hit." Say it anyway.

6. One final rule, perhaps the most important of all: When your team is up and has made the third out, the batter and the players who were left on base do not come back to the bench for their gloves. *They remain on the field, and their teammates bring their gloves out to them.* This requires some organization and discipline, but it pays off big in morale. It says, "Although we're getting our pants knocked off, still we must conserve our energy."

Imagine that you have bobbled two fly balls in this rout[1] and now you have just tried to stretch a single into a double and have been easily thrown out sliding into second base, where the base runner ahead of you had stopped. It was the third out and a dumb play, and your opponents smirk at you as they run off the field. You are the

---

1 *rout:* a state of wild confusion and defeat.

goat, a lonely and tragic figure sitting in the dirt. You curse yourself, jerking your head sharply forward. You stand up and kick the base. How miserable! How degrading! Your utter shame, though brief, bears silent testimony to the worthiness of your teammates, whom you have let down, and they appreciate it. They call out to you now as they take the field, and as the second baseman runs to his position he says, "Let's get 'em now," and tosses you your glove. Lowering your head, you trot slowly out to right. There you do some deep knee bends. You pick grass. You find a pebble and fling it into foul territory. As the first batter comes to the plate, you check the sun. You get set in your stance, poised to fly. Feet spread, hands on hips, you bend slightly at the waist and spit the expert spit of a veteran ballplayer—a player who has known the agony of defeat but who always bounces back, a player who has lost a stride on the base paths but can still make the big play.

This is *ball*, ladies and gentleman. This is what it's all about.

Understanding What You Read

1. What is the author's age as he writes this piece? How does his age affect how he looks at
   a. baseball
   b. slow-pitch softball
2. Garrison Keillor is having some fun with baseball traditions in this short piece of prose. Name three conventions that baseball players observe that Keillor cites as being crucial to demonstrate if a player has the correct "attitude."

Writer's Workshop

Pick a sport other than baseball and write a few paragraphs about how to display the correct "attitude" in that sport. Try to come up with five or six essential things to do for players of your sport, as Garrison Keillor did in "Attitude." Remember, you are writing gentle satire about a sport whose mannerisms you know well.

. . . .

400-meter Freestyle

Experience the last 50 meters of a water race—note how this poet puts you right in the swim.

THE GUN full swing the swimmer catapults and cracks

s

i

x

feet away onto that perfect glass he catches at
a
n
d
throws behind him scoop after scoop cunningly moving

t

h

e

water back to move him forward. Thrift is his wonderful
s
e
c
ret; he has schooled out all extravagance. No muscle

r

i

p

ples without compensation wrist cock to heel snap to
h
i
s
mobile mouth that siphons in the air that nurtures

h

i

m

at half an inch above sea level so to speak.
T
h
e

400-meter Freestyle

astonishing whites of the soles of his feet rise
                              a
                              n
                              d
salute us on the turns. He flips, converts, and is gone
a
l
l
in one. We watch him for signs. His arms are steady at
                                   t
                                     h
                                     e
catch, his cadent feet tick in the stretch, they know
t
h
e
lesson well. Lungs know, too; he does not list for
                                a
                                  i
                                  r
he drives along on little sips carefully expended
b
u
t
that plum red heart pumps hard cries hurt how soon
                                   i
                                     t
                                     s
near one more and makes its final surge   TIME: 4:25:9

. . . .

Understanding What You Read

1. How does the shape of this poem—how the poem looks on the page—reflect its subject matter?

2. What does the writer mean by "Thrift is his wonderful secret; he has schooled out all extravagance"?

3. Why does the writer omit punctuation in the last several lines of the poem?

Writer's Workshop

This poem could be considered a concrete poem, one in which the arrangement of the words on the page reflects the subject matter of the piece. (e. e. cummings has a famous poem about autumn, and the poem is so arranged that the words look like leaves falling down the page.)

Now it's your turn. Take any moment in sports and write a poem about it, capturing it vividly, with specific details, the way Maxine W. Kumin captures a swim race. Be sure the look of the poem somehow captures the subject; for example, a poem about tennis might show the words "bouncing" back and forth across an imaginary net down the center of the page. Let your imagination go but be sure the reader will be able to make sense of the picture you create.

The Passer

*A pass thrown perfectly in a football game is like many other lines in
life.*

Dropping back with the ball ripe in my palm,
grained and firm as the flesh of a living charm,
I taper and coil myself down, raise arm to fake,
running a little, seeing my targets emerge
like quail above a wheat field's golden lake.   5

In boyhood I saw my mother knit my warmth
with needles that were straight. I learned to feel
the passage of the bullet through the bore,
its vein of flight between my heart and deer
whose terror took the pulse of my hot will.   10

I learned how wild geese slice arcs from hanging pear
of autumn noon; how the thought of love cleaves home,
and fists, with fury's ray, can lay a weakness bare,
and instinct's eye can mine fish under foam.

So as I run and weigh, measure and test,   15
the light kindles on helmets, the angry leap;
but secretly, cooly, as though stretching a hand to his chest,
I lay the ball in the arms of my planing end,
as true as metal, as deftly as surgeon's wrist.

---

8. *bore:* the inside diameter of a gun barrel.

Understanding What You Read

1. Poets are usually content to use a single figure of speech in a line, either a simile or a metaphor. In this poem George Abbe piles figures on figures. For instance, in line 11, a football pass is like a flight of geese seen against a setting sun that, in turn, is like a pear hanging from a tree. To understand this poem, you'll have to read it slowly and carefully.

   Name at least three comparisons that George Abbe uses to describe what happens to a football pass. For each of these, explain how the thing compared is like a football pass.

2. In what way is the passer performing "as deftly as surgeon's wrist"?

Writer's Workshop

Pick a moment in sports and describe it in terms of something else. This really is the essence of poetry: being nonliteral about the familiar. If you like, you may describe the moment in prose. The important thing is to compare the moment in sports to something outside of sports.

In the Pocket

Surrounded by his blockers, with the enemy approaching, a quarter-back looks out and tells us what it's like.

Going backward
All of me and some
Of my friends are forming a shell   my arm is looking
Everywhere and some are breaking
In   breaking down   5
And out   breaking
Across, and one is going deep   deeper
Than my arm.   Where is Number One hooking
Into the violent green alive
With linebackers?   I cannot find him he cannot beat   10
His man   I fall back more
Into the pocket   it is raging and breaking
Number Two has disappeared into the chalk
Of the sideline   Number Three is cutting with half
A step of grace   my friends are crumbling   15
Around me the wrong color
Is looming   hands are coming
Up and over between
My arm and Number Three: throw it hit him in
the middle   20
Of his enemies   hit move scramble
Before death and the ground
Come up LEAP STAND KILL DIE STRIKE
Now.

Understanding What You Read

1. What is the situation being described in this poem?

2. Remember that tone is the author's attitude toward his or her subject. How would you describe the tone of this poem?

3. Explain how the diction—the words used— and the arrangement of words on the page contribute to the tone and to the meaning of this poem.

Writer's Workshop

Pick a moment in sports that has a definite mood or emotional feeling associated with it, as does the moment described in "In the Pocket." In poetry or prose, describe the moment, letting the diction and the arrangement of words, with or without punctuation, set the tone you wish to convey. For example, if you want to convey something peaceful and graceful, would you be more likely to use short, choppy phrases or longer, flowing ones?

Lou Gehrig—
An American Hero

*"Yet today I consider myself the luckiest man on the face of the earth."
These words came from a baseball legend dying at the age of 38.*

O ut by the flagpole in center field of the Yankee Stadium, the ball park which during the glittering Golden Decade was the home of the greatest slugging team baseball has ever known, there stands a newly erected bronze plaque.

On it in relief is the bust of a man wearing a baseball cap and uniform. And the inscription reads:

HENRY LOUIS GEHRIG. JUNE 19, 1903–JUNE 2, 1941. A MAN, A GENTLEMAN, AND A GREAT BALL PLAYER, WHOSE AMAZING RECORD OF 2,130 CONSECUTIVE GAMES SHOULD STAND FOR ALL TIME. THIS MEMORIAL IS A TRIBUTE FROM THE YANKEE PLAYERS TO THEIR BELOVED CAPTAIN AND TEAMMATE, JULY 4, 1941.

Henry Louis Gehrig was born at 179th Street and Amsterdam Avenue, Manhattan, on June 19, 1903. His father, Henry Gehrig, was an artisan, an ironworker; that is,

he made ornamental grilles for doors and railings and balustrades—when he could get work at his trade. When he couldn't, he did odd jobs, until he landed a steady job as a janitor. Christina Gehrig, the mother, was a solid German hausfrau who knew her place in life was the kitchen, and her duty to feed and look after her family.

His early home life was European in the sense that less affection was shown Lou than is usual in, let us say, a typical American home. In the German home, the father is king, and among the poorer people who are engaged in a constant struggle for existence there is little time for a sentimental relationship between parents and children. Henry Louis was no stranger to corporal punishment at the hands of his father.

Early in life he became imbued with a sense of his own worthlessness which he never overcame to the end of his days. He just never understood how he could possibly be any good, or how anybody could really love him. When he married, he used to break his wife's heart with the constant reproaches he cast at himself. Her most difficult task was to build in him some slight sense of his true worth.

As a man, his greatest handicap was that he was supersensitive, shy, self-accusing, quick to take hurt and slow to recover therefrom.

His boyhood was responsible for this. He was a big boy for his age, and slow-witted. Smaller kids would gang up and chase him. They called him "chicken heart," threw stones at him, chased him away from their games, hooted his ineptness at things that came naturally to them.

Eventually, he won some measure of tolerance. He swam with the other boys off the old coal barge in the Harlem River near the High Bridge, got chased by cops and once was even arrested for swimming without trunks. There was a fine scandal in the Gehrig household when Pop had to come down to the police station and bring him home. Their boy in jail already! A bummer he was becoming with them good-for-nothing loafers. Louie got a good smacking.

But when he was fourteen, America entered the First World War and the inevitable witch hunts spread even to his neighborhood. His old folks were Germans, and Germans were enemies. That terrible time, too, had its effect on the character of the boy. Added to his poverty and awkwardness, it drove him still farther away from his own kind, pitched him still lower in his own estimation.

There was nothing at which he was very good: neither studies nor baseball. He was an undistinguished fifth wheel on the P. S. 132 ball team, a left-handed catcher who couldn't hit the length of his cap, a chicken heart who was so ball-shy at the plate that even when he reached college he had to be cured of batting with one foot practically in the dugout.

But no matter what the atmosphere of the Gehrig home or the handicaps of poverty, one thing must not be forgotten. Mama Gehrig was insistent that her Louie avail himself of the great opportunity provided by this new land—education. Poor they might be, and insignificant in the social scale, but he had the same opportunity to become educated as the richest boy in the land.

And so when Gehrig was graduated from P. S. 132, instead of being sent out to find work to augment the meager family budget, he entered New York's famous High School of Commerce at 65th Street near Amsterdam Avenue.

Commerce was a long distance from upper Amsterdam Avenue, but his parents provided him with carfare, or he walked or hitched on delivery wagons. He had his lunch box and a nickel for a bottle of milk in the General Organization lunchroom.

The rebuffs he suffered as a boy when he tried to play with the kids on the block had already had their effect upon him. Oliver Gintel, now a prosperous furrier in New York, writes:

"In my first year at Commerce, I was trying to get a berth on the soccer team. In practice one day, I kicked the ball accidentally towards a huskily built boy who booted the thing nonchalantly almost the length of the practice field.

"I approached him to try out for the team. He refused, stating that he wasn't good at athletics, and besides, his mother wouldn't give him permission. Later I went to work on him in earnest and eventually Lou did make the team, playing for three seasons as halfback. We won the winter championship for three successive years while he was a member of the team."

Apparently, Lou managed to convert his parents to the impor-

tance of sport in the life of an American boy, for he also played on the football team and returned to his first love, baseball. But the curious thing was that, whereas he was a brilliant soccer player and a capable prospect on the football field, he was a poor performer on the diamond. He was made a first baseman, and in his first year batted only .150.

But here entered two factors that were to follow him through life. The first was his own dogged persistence and his desire to learn and improve himself, and the second was the faith in him that somehow, in spite of his clumsiness and awkwardness, he inspired in the men who taught the game.

Harry Kane, coach of the Commerce baseball team, was the first of these, and Gehrig always gave him full credit for correcting his early faults as a hitter. Day after day, Kane would take the boy and pitch to him for fifteen-minute stretches. The next year he was already hitting .300.

Then, a crisis overtook the family, one that threatened to bring his education to an end. His father was stricken with some temporary form of paralysis and was no longer able to work.

But brave and determined, Mama Gehrig went to work as a cook and housekeeper for a fraternity house at Columbia University and took in washing on the side.

Young Lou went to work too, after school hours. He got jobs—in butcher shops and grocery stores, running errands, minding kids, delivering papers. And somehow he managed to attend baseball practice as well.

In his final year at Commerce, Gehrig caught his first real glimpses of the world into which he was soon to move. For one thing, he took a part-time job as a waiter in the fraternity house at Columbia where his mother was cooking and housekeeping. And for another he took his first trip away from home, when the then recently born *Daily News* sent the championship Commerce baseball team out to Chicago to play an inter-city game with Lane Tech High.

The New York boys beat the Chicago boys by the score of 12 to 6. Lou Gehrig, the first baseman, didn't get a hit in three times at bat, but the fourth time he appeared at the platter the bases were full and Gehrig poled one over the right field wall and out of the park.

It was a robust clout, and as a result for the first time the shadow of a Great Personage fell athwart the kid player. A reformed pitcher who had come to the New York Yankees from the Boston Red Sox had been hitting a prodigious number of home runs for them. His name, of course, was Babe Ruth. And the newspapers called Lou Gehrig the "Babe Ruth of the High Schools."

Babe Ruth! Lou Gehrig! Two names that were to be coupled for so long. And always Babe Ruth first and Lou Gehrig after. Strange that even on his first day of glory he should fall under the great shadow of the Babe. Strange, that is, now that we can see his career as a whole and realize how long Lou Gehrig played in the shadow of Ruth; how long it was before he came into his own, and how tragically short his glory was then.

Lou Gehrig was graduated from Commerce and in 1922 matriculated at Columbia University, aided by a scholarship awarded him, perhaps not for what lay between his ears so much as for his 210 pounds of bone and muscle and the fact that he was willing to give on the field of sport.

Lou Gehrig went out for baseball in the spring and brought the love-light to the eyes of Andy Coakley, Columbia coach and former pitcher for the Philadelphia Athletics. Andy made a pitcher out of him, took up the batting lessons where Kane had left off, and pretty soon Lou Gehrig was poling them high, wide and handsome over the college fences. He hit seven home runs in one season, one of them the longest ever seen at South Field, and batted over .540.

And he won a new name. They called him the "Babe Ruth of Columbia."

A collegian who could sock a baseball as far as Gehrig was hitting them would naturally attract the attention of the major-league scouts, and Paul Kritchell, famous Yankee scout, had seen enough of Gehrig to convince the management that he was worth signing.

Kritchell approached Andy Coakley and Gehrig, but at first all offers were turned down, because to Mama Gehrig a man who did nothing but play games, even if it was for money, was nothing but a loafer and a no-good.

Then for the second time disaster in the form of illness struck at Lou's home and his career, and Gehrig was called upon to make a stern and important choice. Mom Gehrig contracted double pneumonia, Pop Gehrig was still sickly and unable to work, and life closed in on the Gehrigs. Bills and more bills. Not a cent in the house, and nothing coming in.

There has been considerable discussion as to how much, in cold cash, Lou Gehrig actually cost the New York Yankees. According to Gehrig, he received $500 for making the momentous decision to sign a contract with organized baseball.

That $500 was the biggest sum of money that any of the Gehrigs had ever seen. It came at a time when it was desperately needed. It paid rent and doctors and hospital bills and nurses.

Education or no, Mom was ill and needed attention. That's all there was to it. Kritchell was there at the right time with the contract and the money, and Gehrig signed.

But there were to be many discouraging moments and frustrations before Gehrig heard Miller Huggins, the Yankee manager, say one spring, "All right, Gehrig. Get in there in place of Pipp."

Because for all his big frame, loud voice and quick smile, Lou Gehrig was one of those strange souls who seem born to be frustrated, to have glory and happiness always within their reach, even in their grasp, only to have them snatched away.

Although Gehrig did not realize it, when he was farmed out to Hartford in the Eastern League and then, in 1925, spent a lot of time on the Yankee bench, he was a carefully planned spark plug in the new baseball machine Miller Huggins was building to replace the worn-out one that had won three pennants in 1921–23. Ruth was still the big siege gun, but the rest of the team was getting old.

Teams fall apart that way, because most major-league teams are part seasoned veterans and part peppery youngsters. When the veterans go, replacements must be found, and it is in those periods that the big teams will be found out of the money.

But when he chafed on the Yankee bench in 1925, Lou Gehrig, young and ambitious, had no picture of the patient plans of such a master builder of championship ball teams as Miller Huggins. Once, when Huggins was shipping some ivory[1] off to St. Paul, Gehrig begged Hug to send him too. He was asking to be sent from a great major league club back to the minors, so that he might be able to play ball. He was tired of sitting on the bench.

From Huggins he got a lecture he never forgot. "Lou," Hug said, "I'm not going to send you off to St. Paul. You're going to stay right on that bench and learn baseball. You may think you know as much as those fellows out on the field, but you don't. You got a lot to learn, and there's no way to learn it right now except on the bench. Those fellers out there had to do the same thing when they were young. Your turn will come. I want you to sit next to me for a while on the bench. I'll help you."

It put an entirely new light on

things for Lou. The bench no longer was a penance and a trial; it became a school. Sitting next to Huggins, Lou learned to appraise every batter who came to the plate: he memorized the placement of the batter's hits, noted how the infield lined up to handle him. He learned to watch the pitchers: how they pitched, what they pitched, what their strategy was in a tight spot; their mannerisms, little telltale motions toward first—in short, he absorbed anything and everything that would help him to play the game when his time came. Baseball, he discovered, was a painstaking profession, an exhaustive and never-ending study.

Then in May, first baseman Wallie Pipp was beaned in batting practice and became subject to violent headaches. On June first, Gehrig replaced him. Thereafter, for fourteen years and 2,130 consecutive games, he was never off first base, except for one game which he started at shortstop merely to be in the line-up and preserve his great consecutive-games record at a time when he was bent double with lumbago.[2]

From now on the tale of Lou Gehrig is a continuous upward climb to fame and success beyond his dreams. In 1927 he was already

---

1 *ivory:* baseball slang: players.

2 *lumbago:* a rheumatic pain around the hips.

daring to challenge Babe Ruth for the home-run championship.

In 1926, the American League pitchers were unconvinced about Gehrig's hitting ability and still kept pitching those four wide ones to the Babe in times of crisis. Then Lou would come up and bust the lemon out of the county and there would go your old ball game.

By 1927 word went around the league: "Don't pass the Babe to get at Gehrig. Bad medicine!" So they had to pitch to Babe. And the Babe got sixty home runs. But Lou got the valuable-player award.

Success in full measure now came to Henry Louis Gehrig, the American-born son of immigrant German parents. He had fame, money, popularity, love and companionship, and thanks to his wife Eleanor, even a little self-assurance.

The awkward boy who could neither bat nor field as a youngster had, by his unswerving persistence, his gnawing ambition, his tenacity and iron will power, made himself into the greatest first baseman in the history of organized baseball.

In 1934 Lou won the triple batting championship of the American League and gave it to his league in hitting that year, batting .363, hitting 49 home runs, and driving in 165 runs.

In 1936, Lou was again named the most valuable player in the American League, exactly nine years after he had first achieved this honor. His salary had been mounting steadily, and in 1938 he signed for the largest sum he ever received for playing ball, $39,000.

Toward the end of the last decade, the name, the figure, and above all, the simple engaging personality of Lou Gehrig became welded into the national scene. Came the baseball season, came Gehrig. Came Gehrig, came home runs, triples, doubles, excitement and faultless play around first base. And his consecutive-games record went on and on. Sick or well, he never missed a game.

Lou played with colds. He played with fevers. He played so doubled over with lumbago that it was impossible for him to straighten up, and bent over at the plate, he still got himself a single.

In 1934, the year he won the triple crown, he fractured a toe. He played on. He was knocked unconscious by a wild pitch, suffered a concussion that would hospitalize the average man for two weeks. He was at his position the next day and collected four hits. When, late in his career, his hands were X-rayed, they found seventeen assorted fractures that had healed by themselves. He had broken every finger on both hands and some twice, and *hadn't even mentioned it* to anyone.

The fantastic thing about all this is not that he was able to endure the pain of breaks, strains, sprains, pulled and torn tendons, muscles and ligaments, but that it failed to impair his efficiency. On the contrary, if he had something the matter with him it was the signal for him to try all the harder, so that no one, least of all his own severe conscience, could accuse him of being a handicap to his team while playing in a crippled condition.

When, in 1939, Lou Gehrig found himself slow in spring training, he began to punish his body for failure that was unaccountable and drive it harder than ever before.

It had begun before that, the slow tragedy of disintegration. Signs and symptoms had been mistaken. During most of 1938, Gehrig had been on a strict diet. That year had not been a good one for him. In the early winter of 1939 he had taken a $5,000 salary slash. Baseball players are paid by the records they compile. That winter, as usual, Lou and Eleanor went ice skating together. Lou was a fine skater. But, strangely, he kept falling all the time.

The teams went South for the 1939 training season and the sports writers went along with them. And the boys with one accord began sending back stories that must have saddened them to write.

What they saw was not unfamiliar to them. The useful playing lifetime of a top-flight professional athlete is on the average shockingly short. A sports writer is quick to notice the first symptoms of slowing up. They were obvious with Gehrig at St. Petersburg. He was slow afoot, afield and at bat. And while he fought like a rookie to hold his position, no improvement was evident. Sadly the sports writers wrote that the old Iron Horse was running down.

But the players on the Yankee ball club were saying something else. They were close to Gehrig. They noticed things that worried and depressed them. And they had knowledge of their craft and of themselves. One of the things they knew was that a ballplayer slows up gradually. His legs go, imperceptibly at first, then noticeably as he no longer covers the ground in the field that he used to cover. But he doesn't come apart all at one time, and in chunks.

There are grim tales of things that happened in the locker room, and one is macabre with overtones of manly nobility. It tells of Gehrig dressing, leaning over to lace his spikes and falling forward to the floor, to lie momentarily helpless. And it tells further of tough men with the fine instincts to look away and not to hurt his already tortured soul the more by offering to help. Quickly they left the locker room, leaving him to struggle to his feet alone with no eyes to see his weakness.

Few men can have gone through the hell that Gehrig did during those days.

Picture the fear, the worry, the helpless bewilderment that must have filled Lou's soul as he found that he could not bat, could not run, could not field. The strain and terror of it lined his face in a few short months and brought gray to his hair. But it could not force a complaint from his lips.

His performance during the early part of 1939 was pitiful. And yet, so great was the spell cast by his integrity, his honest attempts to please and his service over the long years, that the worst-mannered, worst-tempered and most boorish individual in the world, the baseball fan, forebore to heckle him.

On Sunday, April 30, 1939, the Yankees played the Senators in Washington. Lou Gehrig came to bat four times with runners on base. He failed even to meet the ball, and the Yankees lost.

Monday was an off day. Lou went home. He did a lot of thinking, but he did it to himself. He had the toughest decision of his life to make. But he had to make it alone.

Tuesday, May second, the team met in Detroit to open a series against the Tigers. Joe McCarthy flew in from Buffalo. Lou met him in the dugout and said the fateful words:

"Joe, I always said that when I felt I couldn't help the team any more I would take myself out of the line-up. I guess that time has come."

"When do you want to quit, Lou?" asked McCarthy.

Gehrig looked at him steadily and said, "Now. Put Babe Dahlgren in."

Later, alone in the dugout, he wept.

The record ended at 2,130 games.

The newspapers and the sports world buzzed with the sensation of Lou Gehrig's departure from the Yankee line-up.

At the urging of Eleanor, Lou went to the Mayo Clinic at Rochester, Minnesota, for a check-up.

There was a lull in the news. Then out of a clear sky the storm burst again. Black headlines tore across the page tops like clouds and lightninged their messages: "GEHRIG HAS INFANTILE PARALYSIS." "GEHRIG FIGHTS PARALYZING ILLNESS."

The New York Yankees released the report of the doctors at the clinic. It was a disease diagnosed as amyotrophic lateral sclerosis, interpreted for the layman as a form of infantile paralysis, and the mystery of the too-sudden decline and passing of Henry Louis Gehrig, perennial Yankee first baseman, was solved.

Before Gehrig came home from the Mayo Clinic, Eleanor went to their family physician, gave him the name of the disease and asked to be told the truth. The doctor knew her well. He said quietly, "I think you can take it. And I think you should know."

Then he told her that her husband could not live more than two years.

Before she could give in to grief and shock for the first and last time, Eleanor phoned to the Mayo Clinic. She had but one question to ask of the doctors there. "Have you told my husband?"

Gehrig had so captivated the staff that they had not yet had the heart to tell him the truth, and they so advised Eleanor.

She begged, "Please promise me that you never will. Don't ever let him know. I don't want him to find out."

They promised. Only then did Eleanor permit herself to weep.

The time of weeping was short. Lou came home. He came home full of smiles and jokes, and the girl who met him was smiling and laughing too, though neither noticed that in the laughter of the other there was something feverish.

Lou's cheer was based outwardly on the fact that he hadn't been just an aging ballplayer; that his sudden disintegration had been caused by disease—a disease of which he promised Eleanor he would be cured before he learned to pronounce its name.

Eleanor fought a constant fight to keep the truth from Lou. She had to be on the spot always to answer the telephone; to watch over him so that people did not get to him; to look after the mail before he saw it. Ever present was the menace of the one crackpot who might slip through the shields of love she placed about her husband and tell him that his case was hopeless.

As to what Lou knew, he never told.

On July 4, 1939, there took place the most tragic and touching scene ever enacted on a baseball diamond—the funeral services for Henry Louis Gehrig.

Lou Gehrig attended them in person.

Lou Gehrig Appreciation Day, as it was called, was a gesture of love and appreciation on the part of everyone concerned, a spontaneous reaching out to a man who had been good and kind and decent, to thank him for having been so.

Everyone waited for what he would say. With a curled finger he dashed away the tears that would not stay back, lifted his head and brought his obsequies[3] to their heartbreaking, never-to-be-forgotten finish when he spoke his epitaph:

"For the past two weeks you have been reading about a bad break I got. Yet today I consider myself the luckiest man on the face of the earth . . ."

EPILOGUE

There is an epilogue, because although the tale of Lou Gehrig—An American Hero—really ends above, he lived for quite a while longer, and perhaps in the simple story of how he lived what time was left to him is to be found his greatest gallantry.

Almost two more years had to pass before the end came to Henry Louis Gehrig, and Eleanor says that during that time he was always laughing, cheerful, interested in everything, impatient only of unasked-for sympathy. In short, he lived his daily life.

But he did more. And here we come to the final bit of heroism. With his doom sealed and his parting inevitable from the woman who had given him the only real happiness he had ever known, he chose to spend his last days in work and service.

Mayor LaGuardia appointed him a city parole commissioner. And so for the next months, as long as he was able to walk even with the assistance of others, Gehrig went daily to his office and did his work. He listened to cases, studied them; he brought to the job his thoroughness and his innate kindness and understanding.

On June 2, 1941, Lou Gehrig died in the arms of his wife in their home in Riverdale, New York.

It is not so much the man whom our weary souls have canonized as the things by which he lived and died. And for the seeing of those we must all of us be very grateful.

---

3 *obsequies:* funeral or burial rites.

Understanding What You Read

1. One distinctive characteristic of Lou Gehrig's childhood was
   a. his unusual athletic ability
   b. his feelings of inferiority
   c. his popularity at school

2. How did Lou Gehrig's role on the Yankees complement Babe Ruth's role?

3. What changed for Lou Gehrig at the start of the 1939 season?

4. What record is Lou Gehrig most known for?
   a. 60 homeruns in a season
   b. 2,130 consecutive games played
   c. winning the Most Valuable Player trophy two years in a row

5. Why do you think, even in the face of a terrible disease, Lou Gehrig said, "Yet today I consider myself the luckiest man on the face of the earth"?

Writer's Workshop

1. Paul Gallico calls Lou Gehrig "an American hero." In a brief essay, explain why you think Gallico chose this phrase for Gehrig, then tell whether you think the label is accurate. Be specific in your support or refutation of Gallico's phrase.

2. Paul Gallico obviously admired Lou Gehrig greatly; it shows in the writing. Gehrig's life—and death—are made vital through all the specific and vivid details that Gallico uses in this biographical essay.

   Write an essay in which you bring to life someone you admire—in or out of sports. Relate at least two anecdotes that capture the essence of the person you are highlighting. Use details to make that person real. If you do research—and probably you will have to unless you interview someone you know—be sure to give credit to the sources of your information.

Princeton's Bill Bradley

Two highpoints in the career of a famous basketball player are recreated in this account of a memorable tournament. Princeton—Michigan, December 30, 1964; Princeton—Wichita, March 20, 1965

This season (1964–65), in the course of a tournament held during the week after Christmas, Bradley took part in a game that followed extraordinarily the pattern of his game against St. Joseph's. Because the stakes were higher, it was a sort of St. Joseph's game to the third power. Whereas St. Joseph's had been the best team in the East, Princeton's opponent this time was Michigan, the team that the Associated Press and the United Press International had rated as the best college team of all.

The chance to face Michigan represented to Bradley the supreme test of his capability as a basketball player. As he saw it, any outstanding player naturally hopes to be a member of the country's No. 1 team, but if that never happens, the next best thing is to be tested against the No. 1 team. And the Michigan situation seemed even more important to him because, tending as he sometimes does to question his own worth, he was uncomfortably conscious that a committee had picked him for the Olympic team, various committees had awarded him his status as an All-American, and, for that matter, committees had elected him a Rhodes Scholar. Michigan, he felt, would provide an exact measurement of him as an athlete.

The height of the Michigan players averages six feet five, and nearly every one of them weighs over two hundred pounds. Smoothly experienced, both as individuals and as a coordinated group, they have the appearance, the manner, and the assurance of a professional team. One of them, moreover, is Cazzie Russell, who like Bradley, was a consensus All-American last year. For a couple of days before the game, the sports pages of the New York newspapers were crammed with headlines, articles, and even cartoons comparing Bradley and Russell, asking which was the better player, and looking toward what one paper called the most momentous individual confrontation in ten years of basketball.

One additional factor—something that meant relatively little to Bradley—was that the game was to be played in Madison Square Garden. Bradley had never played in the Garden, but, because he mistrusts metropolitan standards, he refused to concede that the mere location of the coming test meant anything at all. When a reporter asked him how he felt about appearing there, he replied, "It's just like any other place. The baskets are ten feet high."

Bradley now says that he prepared for the Michigan game as he had prepared for no other. He slept for twelve hours, getting up at noon. Then, deliberately, he read the New York newspapers and absorbed the excited prose which might have been announcing a prizefight: FESTIVAL DUEL: BILL BRADLEY VS. CAZZIE RUSSELL . . . CAZZIE—BRADLEY: KEY TEST . . . BRADLEY OR CAZZIE? SHOWDOWN AT HAND . . . BILL BRADLEY OF PRINCETON MEETS CAZZIE RUSSELL OF MICHIGAN TONIGHT AT THE GARDEN!! This exposure to the newspapers had the effect he wanted; he developed chills, signifying a growing stimulation within him. During most of the afternoon, when any other player in his situation would probably have been watching television, shooting pool, or playing ping-pong or poker—anything to divert the mind—Bradley sat alone and concentrated on the coming game, on the components of his own play, and on the importance to him and his team of what would occur. As much as anything, he wanted to prove that an Ivy League team could be as good as any other team. Although no newspaper gave Princeton even the slightest chance of winning, Bradley did not just hope to do well himself—he intended that Princeton should win.

Just before he went onto the court, Bradley scrubbed his hands with soap and water, as he always does before a game, to remove any accumulated skin oil and thus increase the friction between his fingers and the ball. When the game was forty-two seconds old, he hit a jump shot and instantly decided, with a rush of complete assurance of a kind that sometimes comes over an athlete in action, that a victory was not only possible but probable.

Michigan played him straight, and he played Michigan into the floor. The performance he delivered had all the depth and variation of theoretical basketball, each move being perfectly executed against able opposition. He stole the ball, he went back door, he threw unbelievable passes. He reversed away from the best defenders in the Big Ten. He held his own man to one point. He played in the backcourt, in the post, and in the corners. He made long set shots, and hit jump shots from points so far behind the basket that he had to start them from arm's length in order to clear the backboard. He tried a hook shot on the dead run and hit that, too. Once, he found himself in a corner of the court with two Michigan players, both taller than he, pressing in on him shoulder to shoulder. He parted them with two rapid fakes—a move of the ball and a move of his head—and leaped up between them to sink a twenty-two-foot jumper. The same two players soon cornered him again. The fakes were different the second time, but the result was the same. He took a long stride between them and went up into the air, drifting forward, as they collided behind him, and he hit a clean shot despite the drift.

Bradley, playing at the top of his game, drew his teammates up to the best performances they could give, too, and the Princeton team as a whole outplayed Michigan. The game, as it had developed, wasn't going to be just a close and miraculous Princeton victory, it was going to be a rout. But, with Princeton twelve points ahead, Bradley, in the exuberance of sensing victory, made the mistake of playing close defense when he did not need to, and when he was too tired to do it well. He committed his fifth personal foul with four minutes and thirty-seven seconds to go, and had to watch the end of the game from the bench. As he sat down, the twenty thousand spectators stood up and applauded him for some three minutes. It was, as the sportswriters and the Garden management subsequently agreed, the most clamorous ovation ever given a basketball player, amateur or professional, in Madison Square Garden. Bradley's duel with Russell had long since become incidental. Russell scored twenty-seven points and showed his All-American caliber, but during the long applause the announcer on the Garden loudspeakers impulsively turned up the volume and said, "Bill Bradley, one of the greatest players ever to play in Madison Square Garden, scored forty-one points."

Bradley had ratified[1] his reputation—not through his point total

---

1 *ratified:* validated, confirmed.

nearly so much as through his total play. After he left the court—joining two of his teammates who had also fouled out—Michigan overran Princeton, and won the game by one basket. Bradley ultimately was given the trophy awarded to the most valuable player in the tournament, but his individual recognition meant next to nothing to him at the time, because of Princeton's defeat.

It had become fully apparent, however, that Bradley would be remembered as one of basketball's preeminent stars. And like Hank Luisetti, of Stanford, who never played professional basketball, he will have the almost unique distinction of taking only the name of his college with him into the chronicles of the sport.

Having won a great victory over Providence and having lost to Michigan, there was nothing that Princeton could do in its final game that would either supersede the one or salvage anything from the other. Hence van Breda Kolff—who had been voted Coach of the Year only hours before the Michigan game—seemed to have a sizable problem in preparing his team for their playoff with Wichita, the Midwestern regional champion. Princeton had a kind of responsibility in its final game not to move mechanically and dispirit-

edly around the court but to play as well as it could, to finish its season strongly, to prove to the remaining skeptic fringe that an Ivy League team was not out of place in a national final, and, in doing so, to make itself the third-ranking team in the United States. All of that was true enough, but the Princeton players knew who belonged there and the effect of such exhortations was only enough to get them about halfway up for the game. In the end, the remark that set the fire came when van Breda Kolff said that no team, after three years, should let a player like Bill Bradley play his last game in anything but a win that would not be forgotten.

The Princeton-Wichita game ended, as a contest, when it had only been underway for about five minutes and the score was Princeton 16, Wichita 4. Princeton's team, as a unit, was shooting, dribbling, passing, and rebounding at the top of its form. Wichita tried to confuse Princeton and break its momentum by shifting rapidly back and forth from one kind of defense to another, but Princeton, hitting sixty-two per cent from the floor, unconcernedly altered its attack to fit the requirements of each defense. The score at half time was Princeton 53, Wichita 39, and later, with nine minutes and some seconds to go, it was 84 to 58.

Princeton seemed to have proved what it needed to prove, and Bradley, who by then had scored thirty-two points, had been given the victory which van Breda Kolff had said he deserved. The thirteen thousand people in the coliseum, who had reacted to the previous games with a low hum and occasional polite clapping, had been more typical of a basketball crowd, apparently stirred by Princeton's ricochet passing and marvelously accurate shooting. Van Breda Kolff's team wasn't merely winning, it was winning with style.

But the game was over, and, one by one, van Breda Kolff began to take out his first team players, leaving Bradley in the game. Bradley hit a short one after taking the tap from a jump ball. He made two foul shots and a jumper from the top of the key. He put in two more foul shots, committed his own fourth personal foul, and looked toward van Breda Kolff in expectation of leaving the game; but van Breda Kolff ignored him. Getting the ball moments later, Bradley passed off to Don Roth. Smiling and shaking his head slightly, Roth returned the ball to Bradley.

There was a time-out and Bradley could hear people in the grandstands shouting at him that he ought to shoot when he got the ball. All of his teammates crowded around him and urged him to let it fly and not worry about anyone else on the floor. Van Breda Kolff, calmly enough, pointed out to him that his career was going to end in less than five minutes and this was his last chance just to have a gunner's go at the basket for the sheer fun of it. "So," remembers Bradley, "I figured that I might as well shoot."

In the next four minutes and forty-six seconds, Bradley changed almost all of the important records of national championship basketball. The most intense concentration of basketball people to collect anywhere in any given year is of course at the national championships, and as a group they stood not quite believing, and smiling with pleasure at what they were seeing. Bradley, having decided to do as everyone was urging him to do, went into the left-hand corner and set up a long, high, hook shot. "I'm out of my mind," he said to himself, but the shot dropped through the net. "O.K.," he thought, moving back up the court, "I'm going to shoot until I miss."

A moment later, sprinting up the floor through the Wichita defense, he took a perfect pass, turned slightly in the air and tossed the ball over his shoulder and into the basket, with his left hand. The thirteen thousand people in the crowd, Wichita's huge mission of fans included, reacted with an almost unbelievable roar to each shot as it went into the basket. It was an individual performer's last and in some ways greatest moment. Everyone in the coliseum knew it, and, to Bradley, the atmosphere was tangible. "There would be a loud roar," he remembered. "Then it was as if everyone were gathering their breath." Taking a pass at the base line, he jumped above a defender, extended his arm so that the shot would clear the backboard, and sent a sixteen-foot jumper into the basket. Someone in the crowd started to chant, "I believe! I believe!" and others took it up, until, after each shot, within the overall clamor, the amusing chant could be heard.

From the left side, Bradley went up for a jump shot. A Wichita player was directly in front of him, in the air, too, ready to block it. Bradley had to change the position of the ball, and, all in a second, let it go. He was sure that it was not going to go in, but it did. Coming up the floor again, he stopped behind the key and hit another long jumper from there. Within the minute, he had the ball again and was driving upcourt with it, but a Wichita player stayed with him and forced him into the deep right-hand corner. Suddenly, he saw that

he was about to go out of bounds, so he jumped in the air and—now really convinced that he was out of his mind—released a twenty-two-foot hook shot, which seemed to him to be longer and more haphazard than any hook shot he had ever taken and certain to miss. It dropped through the net. Thirty seconds later, he drove into the middle, stopped, faked, and hit a short, clean jumper. Twenty seconds after that, he had the ball again and went high into the air on the right side of the court to execute, perfectly, the last shot of his career. With thirty-three seconds left in the game, van Breda Kolff took him out.

Princeton had beaten Wichita 118 to 82 and had scored more points than any other team in any other game in the history of the national championships, a record which had previously been set and re-set in opening rounds of play. Bradley had scored fifty-eight points, breaking Oscar Robertson's individual scoring record, which had been set in a regional consolation game. Hitting twenty-two shots from the floor, he had also broken Robertson's field goal record. His one hundred and seventy-seven points made against Penn State, North Carolina State, Providence, Michigan, and Wichita were the most ever made by any player in the course of the national championships, breaking by seventeen points the record held by Jerry West, of West Virginia, and Hal Lear, of Temple. His sixty-five field goals in five games set a record, too. His team had also scored more points across the tournament than any other team ever had, breaking a record set six years earlier by West Virginia. It had made forty-eight field goals against Wichita, breaking a record set by U.C.L.A.; and it had made one hundred and seventy-three field goals in the tournament, twenty-one more than Loyola of Illinois made in 1963 while setting the previous record and winning the national championship. Where the names of three individuals and four universities once appeared in the records of the championships, only the names of Bradley and Princeton now appear, repeated and repeated again.

The team record for most field goals in five games was so overwhelming that it had already been set—at a lower level—before Bradley began his final sequence of scoring. But the other seven records had all been set during his remarkable display, and to establish them he had scored twenty-six points in nine minutes, missing once. After van Breda Kolff and the others had persuaded him to forget his usual standards and to shoot every time he got the ball, he had

scored—in less than five minutes—sixteen points without missing a shot.

When Bradley returned to Princeton, he stood on top of the bus which had brought the team from the airport and began to apologize to a crowd of undergraduates for letting them down. "We didn't produce," he said. "I don't know whether to say I'm sorry . . ."

"Say it fifty-eight times," someone shouted, and Bradley's apologies were destroyed by applause.

He had been voted the most valuable player in the national championships. His fifty-eight points, made in his last game, had been his career high—and, through the whole game, he had made three of every four shots he had taken. His .886 final free-throw average for the season was the highest in the United States. His season scoring average was over thirty points a game, and he had finished his career with 2,503 points, becoming, after Oscar Robertson, of Cincinnati, and Frank Selvy, of Furman, the third highest scorer in the history of college basketball.

Conquerors of this sort usually follow up their homecomings with a lingering parade through the streets of Rome, but Bradley disappeared less than twenty-four hours after his return, having arranged to live alone in a house whose owners were away. Far enough from the campus to be cut off from it almost completely, he stayed there for a month—while a couple of hundred reporters, photographers, ministers, missionaries, Elks, Lions, Rotarians, TV producers, mayors, ad men, and fashion editors tried unsuccessfully to find him. His roommates, who fought off the locusts that actually came to the campus, began to feel a little jaundiced about the invasions of society. Bradley, meanwhile, had gone into seclusion in order to write his senior thesis, and, working about fifteen hours a day for thirty days, he completed it. The thesis was thirty-three thousand words long, and he finished it one month to the day after the game with Wichita. It received a straight 1—grades at Princeton begin with 1 and end with 7—and Bradley was graduated with honors.

Meanwhile, a group of people in Princeton started the procedures necessary to change the name of their street to Bradley Court. The New York Knickerbockers, in order to protect themselves against any possibility that Bradley might change his mind about professional basketball and eventually play for another N.B.A. team, made him their first choice selection in the annual player draft. According to the guesses of newspapers, they offered him over fifty thousand dollars to sign. He heard from Oxford that, after his arrival there, he would be *in statu pupillari*[2] at Worcester College.

And finally, his classmates at Princeton, not long before their graduation, summed him up in their "1965 Senior Class Poll," a rambling, partly serious and partly comical list of superlatives, ranging through eighty-one categories including "Biggest Socialite," "Biggest Swindler," "Most Brilliant," "Most Impeccably Dressed," "Most Ambitious," "Roughest," "Smoothest," "Laziest," "Hairiest," and "Most Likely to Retire at Thirty." Bradley was elected to none of these distinctions. He was named as "Most Popular," and "Most Likely to Succeed." As "Princeton's Greatest Asset," the Class of 1965 selected Bradley and a deceased woman who had just left the university twenty-seven million dollars. One category read: "Biggest Grind: Niemann, Lampkin; Thinks He Is: Bradley." His classmates also designated Bradley as the person they most respected. And, as a kind of afterthought, they named him best athlete.

---

2 *in statu pupillari: Lat.,* granted a scholarship.

Understanding What You Read

1. Describe how Bill Bradley prepared for the Madison Square Garden game against Michigan and its All-American, Cazzie Russell.

2. The game against Michigan ended

   a. with a Princeton victory
   b. with a Michigan victory, Cazzie Russell having outplayed Bill Bradley
   c. with a Michigan victory but with Bradley having played exceptionally well

3. Why does the account of Bradley's performance in the last four minutes and forty-six seconds of the Wichita game read like a work of fiction?

4. Why did Bradley "disappear" after the Wichita triumph and stay hidden for a month?

Writer's Workshop

Since John McPhee first wrote about Bill Bradley, Bradley has gone on to be a Rhodes Scholar, an outstanding professional basketball player, and a United States Senator. Research any aspect of Bradley's life since 1964 and narrate one part of it in the kind of detail that McPhee uses to describe the moments in basketball. An encyclopedia will not give you enough detail to do this. You may have to go to newspaper accounts of Bradley's playing days or to newspaper or magazine accounts of his senatorial career. You might want to read Bradley's own book, **Life on the Run**, his account of playing professional basketball.

Whatever source material you use, your goal is to write a vivid, detailed narration of some aspect of Bradley's life, as John McPhee did. Aim for 1,000 to 2,000 words.

The Crucible of White Hot Competition

America had just fought and won a war against powers that stood for bigotry and racism; now, it was time for the country to practice the ideals thousands had died for.

Opening Day of the baseball season was always a festive occasion in Jersey City on the banks of the Passaic River. Each year Mayor Frank Hague closed the schools and required all city employees to purchase tickets, guaranteeing a sellout for the hometown Giants of the International League. The Giants sold 52,000 tickets to Roosevelt Stadium, double the ball park capacity. For those who could not be squeezed into the arena, Mayor Hague staged an annual pre-game jamboree. Jersey City students regaled the crowd outside the stadium with exhibitions of running, jumping, and acrobatics, while two bands provided musical entertainment.

On April 18, 1946, the air crackled with a special electricity. Hague's extravaganza marked the start of the first minor league baseball season since the end of the war. But this did not fully account for the added tension and excitement. Nor could it explain why people from nearby New York City had burrowed through the Hudson Tubes[1] for the event. Others had arrived from Philadelphia, Baltimore, and even greater distances to witness this contest. Most striking was the large number of blacks in the crowd, many undoubtedly attending a minor league baseball game for the first time. In the small area reserved for reporters chaotic conditions prevailed. "The press box was as crowded as the subway during rush hours," wrote one of its denizens[2] in the Montreal *Gazette*. On the field photographers "seemed to be under everybody's feet." The focus of their attention was a handsome, broad-shouldered athlete in the uniform of the visiting Montreal Royals. When he batted in the first inning, he would be the first black man in the twentieth century to play in organized baseball. Jackie Robinson was about to shatter the color barrier.

---

1 *Hudson Tubes:* subway tunnels under the Hudson River.

2 *denizens:* inhabitants.

"This in a way is another Emancipation Day for the Negro race," wrote sportswriter Baz O'Meara of Montreal's *Daily Star,* "a day that Abraham Lincoln would like." Wendell Smith, the black sportswriter of the Pittsburgh *Courier* who had recommended Robinson to Brooklyn Dodger President Branch Rickey, reported, "Everyone sensed the significance of the occasion as Robinson . . . marched with the Montreal team to deep centerfield for the raising of the Stars and Stripes and the 'Star-Spangled Banner.' We sang lustily and freely for this was a great day." And in the playing area, the black ballplayer partook in the ceremonies "with a lump in my throat and my heart beating rapidly, my stomach feeling as if it were full of feverish fireflies with claws on their feet."

Six months had passed since Rickey had surprised the nation by signing Robinson to play for the Dodgers' top farm club. It had been a period of intense speculation about the wisdom of Rickey's action. Many predicted that the effort to integrate baseball would prove abortive,[3] undermined by opposition from players and fans, or by Robinson's own inadequacies as a ballplayer. Renowned as a collegiate football and track star, Robinson had played only one season in professional baseball with the Kansas City Monarchs of the Negro National League. Upon Robinson's husky, inexperienced shoulders rested the fate of desegregation in baseball.

Robinson's experiences in spring training had dampened optimism. Compelled to endure the indignities of the Jim Crow[4] South, barred by racism from many ball parks, and plagued by a sore arm, Robinson had performed poorly in exhibition games. One reporter suggested that had he been white, the Royals would have dropped him immediately. Other experts also expressed grave doubts. Jim Semler, owner of the New York Black Yankees, commented before the opener, "The pace in the IL is very fast. . . . I doubt that Robinson will hit the kind of pitching they'll be dishing up to him." And Negro League veteran Willie Wells predicted, "It's going to take him a couple of months to get used to International League pitching."

Robinson, the second Montreal batter, waited anxiously as "Boss" Hague threw out the first ball and lead-off hitter Marvin Rackley advanced to the plate. Rackley, a speedy center fielder from South

---

3 *abortive:* unsuccessful.

---

4 *Jim Crow:* (from the name of a stereotype black in a musical act) discrimination against blacks by legal enforcement or traditional approval.

Carolina, grounded out to the shortstop. Robinson then strode to the batter's box, his pigeon-toed gait enhancing the image of nervousness. His thick neck and tightly muscled frame seemed more appropriate to his earlier gridiron exploits than to the baseball diamond.

Many had speculated about the crowd reaction. Smith watched anxiously from the press box to see "whether the fears which had been so often expressed were real or imagined." In the stands Jackie's wife, Rachel, wandered through the aisles, too nervous to remain in her seat. "You worry more when you are not participating than when you are participating," she later explained, "so I carried the anxiety for Jack." Standing at home plate, Jackie Robinson avoided looking at the spectators, "for fear I would see only Negroes applauding—that the white fans would be sitting stony-faced or yelling epithets."[5] The capacity crowd responded with a polite, if unenthusiastic welcome.

Robinson's knees felt rubbery; his palms, he recalled, seemed "too moist to grip the bat." Warren Sandell, a promising young lefthander, opposed him on the mound. For five pitches Robinson did not swing and the count ran to three and two. On the next pitch,

Robinson hit a bouncing ball to the shortstop who easily retired him at first base. Robinson returned to the dugout accompanied by another round of applause. He had broken the ice.

Neither side scored in the first inning. In the second the Royals tallied twice on a prodigious home run by right fielder Red Durrett. Robinson returned to the plate in the third inning. Sandell had walked the first batter and surrendered a single to the second. With two men on base and nobody out, the Giants expected Robinson, already acknowledged as a master bunter, to sacrifice. Sandell threw a letter-high fastball, a difficult pitch to lay down. But Robinson did not bunt. The crowd heard "an explosive crack as bat and ball met and the ball glistened brilliantly in the afternoon sun as it went hurtling high and far over the left field fence," 330 feet away. In his second at-bat in the International League, Robinson had hit a three-run home run.

Robinson trotted around the bases with a broad smile on his face. As he rounded third, Manager Clay Hopper, the Mississippian who reportedly had begged Rickey not to put Robinson on his team, gave him a pat on the back. "That's the way to hit 'em, Jackie," exclaimed Rackley in his southern drawl. All of the play-

---

5 *epithets:* abuse and insults.

ers in the dugout rose to greet him, and John Wright, a black pitcher recruited to room with Robinson, laughed in delight. In the crowded press box Wendell Smith turned to Joe Bostic of the *Amsterdam News* and the two black reporters "laughed and smiled. . . . Our hearts beat just a little faster and the thrill ran through us like champagne bubbles." Most of their white colleagues seemed equally pleased, though one swore softly, according to one account, and "there were some very long faces in the gathering" as well.

The black second baseman's day had just begun. In the fifth inning, with the score 6–0, Robinson faced Giant relief pitcher Phil Oates. The "dark dasher," as Canadian sportswriters came to call Robinson, bunted expertly and outraced the throw "with something to spare." During spring training Rickey had urged the fleet-footed Robinson "to run those bases like lightning. . . . Worry the daylights out of the pitchers." Robinson faked a start for second base on the first pitch. On the next he took off, easily stealing the base. Robinson danced off second in the unnerving style that would become his trademark. Tom Tatum, the Montreal batter, hit a ground ball to third. Robinson stepped backwards, but as the Jer-

sey City fielder released the ball, he broke for third, narrowly beating the return throw.

Robinson had stolen second base and bluffed his way to third. He now determined to steal home to complete the cycle. He took a long lead, prompting Oates to throw to third to hold him on base. On the pitch he started toward home plate, only to stop halfway and dash back. The crowd, viewing the Robinson magic for the first time, roared. On the second pitch, Robinson accelerated again, causing Oates to halt his pitching motion in mid-delivery. Oates had balked and the umpire waved Robinson in to score. Earlier Robinson had struck with power; now he had engineered a run with speed. The spectators, delighted with the daring display of baserunning, went wild, screaming, laughing, and stamping their feet. Blacks and whites, Royal fans and Giant fans, baseball buffs and those there to witness history, all joined in the ensuing pandemonium.[6]

One flaw marred Robinson's performance. "By manner of proving that he was only human after all," according to one reporter, Robinson scarred his debut with a fielding error in the bottom of the inning. Acting as middleman in a

---

6 *pandemonium:* confusion, wild uproar.

double play, he unleashed an errant throw that allowed the Giants to score their only run. Otherwise, Robinson affirmed his reputation as an exceptional fielder.

In the seventh inning Robinson triggered yet another Royal rally. He singled sharply to right field, promptly stole another base, and scored on a triple by Johnny Jorgenson. Before the inning had ended two more runs crossed the plate to increase the Royal lead to 10–1. In the eighth frame Robinson again bunted safely, his fourth hit in the contest. Although he did not steal any bases, he scrambled from first to third on an infield hit. Once again he unveiled his act, dashing back and forth along the baseline as the pitcher wound up. Hub Andrews, the third Jersey City pitcher, coped with this tactic no better than his predecessor. Andrews balked and for the second time in the game umpires awarded Robinson home plate. According to a true baseball aficionado,[7] this established "some kind of a record for an opening day game."

The Royals won the game 14–1. Montreal pitcher Barney DeForge threw an effortless eight-hitter and Durrett clubbed two home runs. But, as the Pittsburgh *Courier's* front page headline gleefully

announced, JACKIE "STOLE THE SHOW." "He did everything but help the ushers seat the crowd," crowed Bostic. In five trips to the plate Robinson made four hits, including a three-run home run, scored four times, and drove in three runs. He also stole two bases and scored twice by provoking the pitcher to balk. "Eloquent as they were, the cold figures of the box score do not tell the whole story," indicated the New York *Times* reporter in an assessment that proved prophetic of Robinson's baseball career. "He looked as well as acted the part of a real baseball player."

"This would have been a big day for any man," reported the *Times*, "but under the special circumstances, it was a tremendous feat." Joe Bostic, who accompanied his story in the *Amsterdam News* with a minute-by-minute account of Robinson's feats in the game, waxed lyrical. "Baseball took up the cudgel[8] for Democracy," wrote Bostic, "and an unassuming, but superlative Negro boy ascended the heights of excellence to prove the rightness of the experiment. And prove it in the only correct crucible[9] for such an experiment—the crucible of white hot competition."

---

8 *cudgel:* a short, heavy club.

9 *crucible:* a place where forces interact to produce change; a vessel used for melting substances that require great heat.

---

7 *aficionado:* fan.

Understanding What You Read

1. Why was there such a crowd on opening day at Roosevelt Stadium?

2. Why was Jackie Robinson's first hit in the International League so startling?

3. Suppose that Jackie Robinson had struck out each time he came to bat. What effect do you think this would have had on his career? On the careers of other African Americans in professional sports?

Writer's Workshop

It may be difficult today to realize that there was a time when African-Americans were not allowed to play professional sports with white players. But there was such a time. Use your imagination and try to picture yourself as a spectator in Roosevelt Stadium on April 18, 1946. Describe your feelings before and after the game. If you are white, imagine that you are black. If you are black, imagine that you are white. Again, use your imagination and avoid stereotypes.

• CHAPTER THREE •

Moments of Glory Past

Nearly everyone, at least once in life, experiences a moment of glory, feels the exultation of achievement, of praise, of joy, of triumph, of splendor. But that moment passes—very quickly. For a select few, the moment may recur. But for no one can the moment be sustained, fixed in a freeze-frame forever. For everyone there is a return to the ordinary jolts and jars of day-to-day living. How, then, do people deal with the memory of these moments? In this chapter, you'll see how several people managed when the moment of glory passed.

Notes and Comment

The evil that men do lives after them;
The good is oft interred with their bones.
— *Shakespeare*

It often happens with the *Times* that when a man dies certain unpleasant aspects of his life are given charitably short shrift in his obituary.[1] For example, if a once-honored member of Congress has been convicted of a crime and put in prison, the *Times* obituary writer nearly always makes as little as possible of this ugly, necessary fact; in the writing up of his life the dead man receives a sort of posthumous[2] pardon by ellipses[3] and abbreviation. There is an exception to this rule. When it comes to sports, and especially to baseball, the *Times* rarely follows the principle of *de mortuis nil nisi bonum;*[4] it would seem that our so-called national pastime is too important a subject to be tampered with in the name of kindness. A characteristically frank obituary

1 *obituary:* a brief biography, usually written after a person's death.

2 *posthumous:* occurring after death.

3 *ellipses:* omission.

4 *de mortuis . . . :Lat.,* of the dead, say nothing but good.

appeared in the *Times* just the other day. It was headed FRED SNODGRASS, 86, DEAD: BALLPLAYER MUFFED 1912 FLY. With a brisk matter-of-factness that the *Times* might have hesitated to employ in the obituary of an unregenerate mass murderer, the account began, "Fred Carlisle Snodgrass, who muffed an easy fly that helped to cost the New York Giants the 1912 World Series, died Friday at the age of eighty-six." Note that the deed took place *sixty-two years ago*. The passage of six long and presumably penitent decades has done nothing to soften the heart of the implacable obituary writer. Mr Snodgrass isn't to be let off with a simple, unmodified "fly." Oh, no—it was an "easy" fly that Mr. Snodgrass had the misfortune to muff.

Mr. Snodgrass gave up big-league baseball after nine more years, moved to California, became mayor of Oxnard, and was a successful banker and rancher. Surely he could be thought to have discharged his debt to society by now? Not at all. The *Times* is relentless. It spells out his offense with what amounts to relish: "Mr. Snodgrass made a two-base muff of pinch-hitter Clyde Engle's easy pop fly to set up the tying run. One man walked and another singled, driving in Mr. Engle to tie the game and put the winning run on third. A long outfield fly scored the winning run. He is survived by his widow, Josephine; two daughters, Mrs. Eleanor Lefever and Mrs. Elizabeth Garrett; and five grandchildren."

How lucky we are, those of us who go to the grave without having played a professional sport! Our errors, whatever they may be, are not in the record books; the *Times* will be gentle with us, and a miscalculation that occupied less than a second on a sunny fall day when we were twenty-four will not be made the means by which we win a place in history.

Understanding What You Read

1. What did the **New York Times** highlight in the obituary of Fred Snodgrass?
   a. Snodgrass's political career in California
   b. Snodgrass's career as a banker and a rancher
   c. Snodgrass's error in the 1912 World Series

2. In two or three sentences, explain why the writer for the **New Yorker** magazine says, "How lucky we are, those of us who go to the grave without having played a professional sport!"

3. How would you describe the tone of the **New Yorker** piece? Is it angry? Amused? Ironic? Cite evidence from the piece to support your opinion.

Writer's Workshop

The writer for the **New Yorker** takes the **New York Times** to task for emphasizing a single incident in the long career of Frank Snodgrass. But isn't the **New Yorker** writer guilty of the same thing? In a few paragraphs explain whether you feel that the **New Yorker** writer is genuinely protesting a lack of fairness or simply taking a cheap shot at the **New York Times**.

. . . .

The Day I Quit Playing Baseball for Good

When is it time to quit? Some athletes hang on too long, desperate for one more triumph. This amateur knew when his playing days were over.

Baseball was never my best game. But I played it: softball in summer camp, hardball in the Army until, as a catcher, I reached a gloveless right hand for a riser and it knocked a bone clear through the knuckle of one finger. I still have the scar. And that finger, the one next to my pinkie, often locks when I put my hand into my pocket for change. It helps me remember.

I mostly played basketball then: half court in Brooklyn, off the bench with a ranked college team in Army leagues in France, where I had moments of great unobserved glory.

At 55 years old, I'd be a lunatic to return to the cement courts at the playground, though that's where my heart leans, even now. In fact, I played on and off, even with my weight soaring, until it became a clown's act. And then a guy my age died out there, just like that, taking a layup. I didn't play any more after that.

So when my old friend Sandy Bing called last year and asked if I'd like to play "a little precision baseball," I thought perhaps I'd found myself a middle-age diversion.

He played with a guy named Lou Osterwell and they'd been playing their game of precision baseball for more than 10 years, until two years ago, with Lou's twin brother Julius as their third man. Then Julius died and the weekly Sunday game almost collapsed until Sandy brilliantly thought of me; we'd played baseball and basketball together in the Army. Sandy was my age and Lou was 76. That, I thought, is my kind of game.

It wasn't.

The game was for two guys to field, about 120 feet out on one of the dirt lots in Central Park, and one guy to bat; even with fairly precise batting, without me, one fielder would be one too few for the job. Since there was no back-up, the fielder's pitch, from that distance, had to be quite accurate, and if the batter had a bad eye, the ball would roll a couple of hundred yards behind him.

I discovered quickly that Lou played like a 25-year-old and Sandy like someone half his age. At bat, they missed no more than one out of a dozen pitches, except when I threw wildly. They went into the dirt for grounders and came up with the ball. Lou regularly caught pop-ups in a glove held behind his back.

Lou and Julius had once gotten letters from Leo Durocher, asking them to try out for the Dodgers; they'd played for the Merchant Marines, then for a brewery, then in Panama, the West Indies, Jamaica; they might have been the only twins in the majors. Then someone said it was probably a joke, which Lou later doubted and they didn't even answer Durocher. Still, Lou hadn't stopped. He even had a theory about stopping: "You never get it back. First your legs go, and then your eye. DiMaggio never got it back."

I missed a couple of easy grounders and Lou said, "He can't see the ball, Sandy. He can't see below his stomach. That's why he misses it, Sandy."

I tried harder and what happened when I bent over was that lunch rushed to my head, my pants ripped in the crotch; I felt a tiny tear, as of hernia muscles. Once the ball took a bad bounce and caught me high on the cheekbone; once I came out of the dirt with a handful of pebbles. "Pick it up," growled Lou. "That ball ain't horse dung." I threw wildly to the batter, tripped on my laces and my pride, tried to hide, or slow down, or stop panting, but couldn't.

Standing there on the sidelines, my pants torn, the buttons on my shirt ripped off, breathing in gasps, my palm and cheekbone throbbing, I let Sandy and Lou take the last 10 minutes by themselves. They were a joy to watch. They picked up the pace, threw harder, fungoed the ball with more authority, and then came over toward me, Lou talking loudly. I heard him say that if "he" was going to fit into the little precision baseball game, he'd have to start by losing 50 pounds of blubber, putting on a sweat shirt instead of something from Brooks Brothers, wearing a cap, *looking* like a ballplayer.

"This joker looks like he walked out of some office downtown, Sandy," Lou said. "And I never saw someone who could play while *carrying* a base under his belt."

When they got close enough, I said, "I used to play basketball . . . Sandy will. . . . "

But Lou interrupted, "Out here,

what you used to do, don't count."

I remembered those words the following spring when Sandy called to say the new season was starting and Lou had agreed to let me try once more. I wanted another chance and I wanted to come back; I wanted someday to see my toes again. But to Sandy's words of encouragement, his knowledge of a fearless kid who caught hardballs gloveless, I could only mumble, "DiMaggio never got it back, either."

Understanding What You Read

An important skill is the ability to read a text, however long or short, and then summarize briefly its essence. This skill demonstrates not only your reading ability but also your ability to think clearly and precisely.

In no more than two sentences, explain why Nick Lyons "quit playing baseball for good."

Writer's Workshop

Think of a time when you made a decision that had a sense of finality about it, as Nick Lyons's decision had for him. Your situation doesn't have to involve sports. Narrate what led up to that decision and how you actually made your choice.

If possible, use one of Lyons's writing techniques in your essay: the use of a quotation (in Lyons's case about Joe DiMaggio) midway through the narrative and again at the end to pull your writing together.

A Snapshot for Miss Bricka Who Lost in the Semi-Final Round of the Pennsylvania Lawn Tennis Tournament at Haverford, July, 1960

In sports everyone focuses on the winner. But here's a portrait of someone who lost a tennis match one hot July day.

Applause flutters onto the open air
like starlings bursting from a frightened elm,
and swings away across the lawns
in the sun's green continuous calm

of far July. Coming off the court,   5
you drop your racket by the judge's tower
and towel your face, alone, looking off,
while someone whispers to the giggling winner,

and the crowd rustles, awning'd in tiers
or under umbrellas at court-end tables,   10
glittering like a carnival
against the mute distance of maples

along their strumming street beyond
the walls of afternoon. Bluely, loss
hurts in your eyes—not loss merely,   15
but seeing how everything is less

that seemed so much, how life moves on
past either defeat or victory,
how, too old to cry, you shall find steps
to turn away. Now others volley   20

behind you in the steady glare;
the crowd waits in its lazy revel,
holding whiskey sours, talking, pointing,
whose lives (like yours) will not unravel

to a backhand, a poem, or a sunrise,   25
though they may wish for it. The sun
brandishes softly his swords of light
on faces, grass, and sky. You'll win

hereafter, other days, when time
is kinder that this worn July   30
that keeps you like a snapshot: losing,
your eyes, once, made you beautiful.

---

22. *revel:* celebration.

Understanding What You Read

1. Identify two similes that Robert Wallace creates in this poem. What two things are compared in each simile? Do you feel each simile is apt? Why or why not?

2. How is the crowd portrayed in this "snapshot"? Refer to specific lines in the poem.

3. In what way do Miss Bricka's eyes make this snapshot memorable for Robert Wallace?

Writer's Workshop

1. In a poem, preferably without rhyme, capture a moment in sports. Take your "snapshot" as vividly as Robert Wallace takes his in this poem. Show the main actor but also the scenes around that central focus.

2. Watch a sports event. Pay careful attention to a person on the losing side. Try to capture in words the essence of that scene and that person's demeanor. You may write in either prose or poetry.

Outdoors: Fishing with Hemingway as a Guide

This man tried to relive an Ernest Hemingway short story; can truth be as good as fiction?

Anyone who spends much time outdoors in Michigan is likely to find himself crossing the trails of legends. Many of the most impressive trails tend to follow trout streams, and to have been made by one legend in particular: a young fellow from Oak Park, Ill., named Ernest Hemingway. Young Hemingway surveyed much of the best fishing in northern Michigan, and documented it so thoroughly and memorably that on certain waters it is difficult to find a stretch free of literary associations. Consequently, some of us, instead of ignoring legends altogether and just going fishing, end up turning our fishing trips into pilgrimages.

Like many people, I first read Hemingway's short story, "Big Two-Hearted River," in a high-school English class. Although bothered that the author did not specify the size and species of the trout Nick Adams caught, I became determined to fish the Two-Hearted with live grasshoppers on a fly rod, eat peaches from a can, and snuff mosquitos on the side of my tent with a flaring match. It would be years before I learned how difficult (and dangerous) that could be, and before I learned that Hemingway had duped us with his Two-Hearted River title. The story was about the Fox, not the Two-Hearted. Hemingway was a liar.

By now the great Fox/Two-Hearted question creates little debate, but in those days it was a matter of some controversy. Literary sleuths retraced Nick Adams's route over the rolling country north of the town of Seney. Others sifted for evidence through Hemingway's still-unpublished letters. Upper Peninsula trout laureate[1] John Voelker theorized that Hemingway simply disguised the name of a favorite trout stream. In the

---

1 *laureate*: an honored expert in a certain field; most often used in the honorary title *poet laureate*.

end, it was agreed that the Two-Hearted River was the Fox, and that Hemingway, as he said himself to a friend, had chosen the more colorful name because it "is poetry."

During my sophomore year in college, I finally made my pilgrimage to the Fox. I lived in Marquette—a city of 25,000, the largest metropolis in the Upper Peninsula—passing my weekdays in college classrooms and my weekends and holidays fishing nearby creeks and rivers. In the library I learned of Hemingway's trip to the Fox in 1919, the year he returned home wounded from Italy. He and two friends camped for a week along the Fox, near Seney, catching nearly 200 brook trout, some up to 15 inches long. Hemingway, describing the trip in a letter, wrote that one fish broke his line and was the "biggest trout I've ever seen . . . and fell like a ton of the Bricks."

Early on a humid Saturday in June, I set out to hitch-hike the 150 miles to Seney. I wore a backpack with my sleeping bag, tent, food, and chest waders in it, and carried my fly rod and a paperback.

It took most of the morning to reach Seney, in three rides, including an unforgettable 40-mile hitch from Munising to Seney through the infamous Seney Stretch—23

miles of straight-as-an-arrow highway through marshes and swamps—in a pickup truck driven by a skinny, wild-eyed old man who was coming off a three-day drinking binge. He had once walked the 23 miles of the Seney Stretch, at night, after missing his ride back to lumber camp at the end of a weekend in Seney. He tried to hitch-hike, he recalled, but in those days traffic was rare as pocket-money (his words) and he was forced to walk the entire distance, arriving in camp barely in time to eat breakfast and follow the crew to the woods.

Seney, once a rough and tumble lumber town famed for its brothels and bars, had been destroyed by forest fires in 1891 and 1895 and was a virtual ghost town when Hemingway saw it in 1919. Now it is complete again, or as complete as it may ever be, with a service station, restaurant, motel and tavern strung out along M-28. The bridge over the Fox River is a quarter-mile west of all that industry, as if the town, when it was rebuilt, was shifted slightly askew by a surveyor's miscalculation.

I grew up in northern Michigan. I know biting insects intimately, but I have never seen mosquitos like those that rose from the weeds and grasses along the Fox River that day. Larger and more aggressive than the bugs of ordinary experience, they surrounded me in a whining, frenzied, desperate search for blood. Repellent was useless. Any insects that might have been repelled were forced against me by those behind. Even when I sprayed the aerosol directly at them they scarcely altered their flight. They absorbed the poison and developed genetic immunity instantly.

Panicked, I ran north, upstream, in the direction Nick Adams hiked. But every mosquito in the area was alerted to my presence and there was no outrunning them. I met a man wearing netting over his head and carrying an impressively stout bait-casting rod. I asked in passing how the fishing was. Terrible, he said.

That decided it. I turned around, ran back to the highway, and caught a ride west with a young family in a Toyota. They were from Wisconsin and had been camping near Tahquamenon Falls. I squeezed into the back seat with the two sons, whose faces were swollen with insect bites. The parents wanted local color. I told them the old man's tale about the Seney Stretch, and explained that the river they had just crossed was the model for the famous Hemingway story, "Big Two-Hearted River." The information seemed to disappoint them.

They let me out along the Lake Superior shoreline near Munising. I set my tent on the beach, in the perpetual bug-free wind, and passed the remainder of the weekend reading my book and considering the folly of angling/literary pilgrimages. I never uncased my fly rod.

Understanding What You Read

1. What did literary "sleuths" discover about Hemingway's story, "Big Two-Hearted River"?
    a. Hemingway was writing about the Two-Hearted River and called it that in his fiction.
    b. Hemingway had never, in fact, been fishing anywhere in that area.
    c. Hemingway was describing another river but called it the Two-Hearted in his story because of literary considerations.
2. What did Dennis find when he went fishing in Hemingway land?
3. What does the writer of this essay conclude about "literary pilgrimages"?

Writer's Workshop

A comparison and contrast essay (as noted earlier in the text) looks for similarities (comparisons) and differences (contrasts) in two works. Read "Big Two-Hearted River" and then write an essay in which you compare and contrast Ernest Hemingway's fictionalized river with what Jerry Dennis found when he went fishing on the Fox River, presumably the model for Hemingway's fiction.

My Fights with Jack Dempsey

Here's a boxer who's as good with a pen as he is with his fists. He recounts moments from a glorious past, when planning and cleverness were as important as a solid right.

The laugh of the twenties was my confident insistence that I would defeat Jack Dempsey for the heavyweight championship of the world. To the boxing public, this optimistic belief was the funniest of jokes. To me, it was a reasonable statement of calculated probability, an opinion based on prize-ring logic.

The logic went back to a day in 1919, to a boat trip down the Rhine River. The first World War having ended in victory, the Army was sending a group of A.E.F.[1] athletes to give exhibitions for doughboys in the occupation of the German Rhineland. I was light heavyweight champion of the A.E.F. Sailing past castles on the Rhine, I was talking with the Corporal in charge of the party. Corporal McReynolds was a peacetime sportswriter at Joplin, Missouri, one of those Midwestern

newspapermen who combined talent with a copious assortment of knowledge. He had a consummate[2] understanding of boxing, and I was asking him a question of wide interest in the A.E.F. of those days.

We had been hearing about a new prizefight phenomenon in the United States, a battler burning up the ring back home. He was to meet Jess Willard for the heavyweight championship. His name was Jack Dempsey. None of us knew anything about him, his rise to the challenging position for the title had been so swift. What about him? What was he like? American soldiers were interested in prizefighting. I was more than most—an A.E.F. boxer with some idea of continuing with a ring career in civilian life.

The Corporal said yes, he knew Jack Dempsey. He had seen Dempsey box a number of times,

---

1 *A.E.F.:* American Expeditionary Force—troops sent to aid the Allies during World War I.

2 *consummate:* extremely skilled.

and covered the bouts for his Midwestern newspaper. Dempsey's career had been largely in the West.

"Is he good?" I inquired.

"He's tops," responded Corporal McReynolds. "He'll murder Willard."

"What's he like?" I asked.

The Corporal's reply was vividly descriptive. It won't mean anything to most people nowadays, but at that time it was completely revealing to anyone who read the sports pages. McReynolds said: "He's a big Jack Dillon."

I knew about Jack Dillon, as who didn't thirty years ago? He was a middleweight whose tactics in the ring were destructive assault—fast, shifty, hard-hitting, weaving in with short, savage punches, a knocker-out, a killer. Dillon even looked like Dempsey, swarthy, beetle-browed, and grim—a formidable pair of Jacks.

I thought the revelation over for a moment, and recalled: "Jack Dillon was beaten by Mike Gibbons, wasn't he?"

"Yes," replied the Corporal. "I saw that bout. Gibbons was too good a boxer. He was too fast. His defense was too good. Dillon couldn't lay a glove on him."

Mike Gibbons was the master boxer of his time, the height of defensive skill, a perfectionist in the art of sparring.

I said to the Corporal: "Well, maybe Jack Dempsey can be beaten by clever boxing."

His reply was reflective, thought out. "Yes," he said, "when Dempsey is beaten, a fast boxer with a good defense will do it."

This, coming from a brainy sports writer, who knew so much about the technique of the ring and who had studied the style of the new champion, aroused a breathless idea in me. My own ambition in the ring had always been skillful boxing, speed and defense—on the order of Mike Gibbons.

As a West Side kid fooling around with boxing gloves, I had been, for some reason of temperament, more interested in dodging a blow than in striking one. Fighting in preliminary bouts around New York, I had learned the value of skill in sparring. In A.E.F. boxing I had emphasized skill and defense—the more so as during this time I had hurt my hands. Previously I had been a hard hitter. Now, with damaged fists, I had more reason than ever to cultivate defensive sparring.

Sailing down the Rhine, I thought maybe I might be a big Mike Gibbons for the big Jack Dillon. It was my first inkling that someday I might defeat Jack Dempsey for the Heavyweight Championship of the World, which all assumed Jack was about to acquire.

This stuck in mind, and presently the time came when I was able to make some observation firsthand. I was one of the boxers on the card of that first Battle of the Century, the Dempsey-Carpentier fight. I was in the semifinal bout. This place of honor and profit was given to me strictly because of my service title. The ex-doughboys were the heroes of that postwar period, and the light heavyweight championship of the A.E.F. was great for publicity. I was ballyhooed as the "Fighting Marine."

Actually, I had no business in the bout of second importance on that occasion of the first Million Dollar Gate. I was an A.E.F. champ, but we service boxers knew well enough that our style of pugilism was a feeble amateur thing, compared with professional prizefighting in the United States. The best of us were mere former prelim fighters, as I was. There were mighty few prominent boxers in Pershing's A.E.F. In World War II you saw champs and near-champs in uniform, but the draft was not so stern in such matters during the war against the Kaiser's Germany.

In the semifinal bout of the Dempsey-Carpentier extravaganza, I, with my bad hands, fought poorly. Nobody there could have dreamed of me as a possible future conqueror of the devastating champ—least of all Jack himself, if he had taken any notice of the semifinal battlers. I won on a technical K.O. from my opponent, but that was only because he was so bad—Soldier Jones of Canada, who, like myself, was in the big show only because he too had an army title—the war covering a multitude of sins.

After the bout, clad in a bathrobe, I crouched at one corner of the ring, and watched the Manassa Mauler exchange blows with the Orchid Man of France. As prize-ring history records, the bout was utterly one-sided; the frail Carpentier was hopelessly overmatched. But it afforded a good look at the Dempsey style.

The Corporal on the boat sailing down the Rhine had been exact in his description of Dempsey. The Champ was, in every respect, a big Jack Dillon—with all the fury and destruction implied by that. No wonder they called him the Man Killer. But, studying intently, I saw enough to confirm the Corporal's estimate that when Dempsey was defeated it would be by a skillful defensive boxer, a big Mike Gibbons. Correct defense would foil the shattering Dempsey attack.

This estimate was confirmed again and again during subsequent opportunities. I attended Dempsey fights, and studied motion pictures of them. More and more I saw how accurate defense could baffle the Man Killer's assault. The culmination was the Shelby, Montana, meeting of Dempsey and Tom Gibbons, the heavyweight younger brother of Mike. Tom, like Mike, was a consummate boxer, and Dempsey couldn't knock him out. For the first time in his championship and near-championship career, the Man Killer failed to flatten an opponent. The public, which had considered Tom Gibbons an easy mark, was incredulous and thought there must have been something peculiar about it. For me there was nothing peculiar, just final proof that good boxing could thwart the murder in the Dempsey fists. There was a dramatic twist in the fact that the final proof was given by a brother of Mike Gibbons.

At the Dempsey-Carpentier fight, I had seen one other thing. Another angle flashed, as at a corner of the ring I watched and studied. Famous in those days was the single dramatic moment, the only moment when the Orchid Man seemed to have a chance. That was when, in the second round, Carpentier lashed out with a right-hand punch. He was renowned for his right, had knocked out English champions with it. He hit Dempsey high on the jaw with all his power.

I was in a position to see the punch clearly and note how Carpentier threw it. He drew back his right like a pitcher with a baseball. The punch was telegraphed all over the place. Yet it landed on a vulnerable spot. How anybody could be hit with a right launched like that was mystifying to one who understood boxing. Dempsey went back on his heels, jarred. Carpentier couldn't follow up, and in a moment Jack was again on the relentless job of wrecking the Orchid Man with body blows. But it was a vivid demonstration that the champion could be hit with a right.

Dempsey was no protective boxer. He couldn't do defensive sparring. He relied on a shifty style, his own kind of defense, and couldn't be hit just any way. His weakness was that he could be nailed with a straight right. Later on, I saw this confirmed in other Dempsey battles. It was dramatized sensationally at the Polo Grounds when the powerful but clumsy Firpo smashed him with a right at the very beginning of the first round, and later blasted Dempsey out of the ring with right-hand punches—the Wild Bull of the Pampas almost winning the championship.

To me it signified that the strategy of defensive boxing might be supplemented by a right-hand punch—everything thrown into a right. It would never do for me to start mixing with the Champ in any knock-down, drag-out exchange of haymakers. He'd knock me out. It would have to be a surprise blow, and it could easily be that. Both Carpentier and Firpo, who had nailed the Champ, were noted for their right—all they had. But Jack would never suspect a Sunday punch from me, stepping in and trying to knock him out with a right.

I was catalogued not only as a defensive boxer but also as a light hitter, no punch. I might wear an opponent down and cut him to pieces, but I couldn't put him to sleep with a knockout slam. That had been true—previously. I had been going along with the handicap of bad hands. I could hit hard enough, but didn't dare for fear of breaking my hands. So I was a comparatively light hitter—and typed as one.

Finally, in desperation, I had to do something about my fragile hands. I went to a lumber camp in Canada for one winter and worked as a woodsman, chopping down trees. The grip of the ax was exercise for my damaged mitts. Months of lumber camp wood chopping and other hand exercises worked a cure. My hands grew strong and hard, my fists rugged enough to take the impact of as powerful a blow as I could land. In subsequent bouts I had little trouble with my hands. This I knew, and others might have been aware of the change, but I was tagged as a feather duster puncher—and that was that. The old philosophy of giving a dog a bad name.

Prizefight publicity often resorts to the ballyhoo of a secret punch, a surprise blow, nearly always a fraud—but I really had the chance. At the beginning of the first round I would step in and put everything I had in a right-hand punch, every ounce of strength. I might score a knockout, or the blow would daze the champion sufficiently to make it easier to outbox him the rest of the way.

I was, meanwhile, fighting my way to the position of challenger. I won the light heavyweight championship from Battling Levinsky and subsequently fought Carpentier, the Orchid Man, and went through a series of savage bouts with Harry Greb, one of the greatest of pugilists. In our first bout, Greb gave me a murderous mauling. In our last, I beat him almost as badly. After a long series of matches with sundry light heavies and heavies I went on to establish myself as heavyweight contender by defeating Tom Gibbons.

It was dramatic irony that I earned my shot at the title at the expense of Tom, brother of my model, Mike.

Public opinion of my prospects with Dempsey was loud and summary. The champion is always the favorite, and Dempsey was one of the greatest champions, as destructive a hitter as the prize ring has ever known. He was considered unbeatable, and I was rated as a victim peculiarly doomed to obliteration, pathetic, absurd.

It was argued that I was a synthetic fighter. That was true. As a kid prelim battler, my interest had been in romantic competition and love of boxing, while holding a job as a shipping clerk with a steamship company. As a marine in France, my love of boxing and a distaste for irksome military duties after the armistice brought me back as a competitor in A.E.F. boxing tournaments. We gave our best to entertain our buddies and, incidentally, to avoid guard duty. After the war, when I had grown up, my purpose simply was to develop the sparring ability I had as a means of making money—seeing in the heavyweight championship a proud and profitable eminence.

They said I lacked the killer instinct—which was also true. I found no joy in knocking people unconscious or battering their faces. The lust for battle and massacre was missing. I had a notion that the killer instinct was really founded in fear, that the killer of the ring raged with ruthless brutality because deep down he was afraid.

Synthetic fighter, not a killer! There was a kind of angry resentment in the accusation. People might have reasoned that, to have arrived at the position of challenger, I must have won some fights. They might have noted that, while the champion had failed to flatten Tom Gibbons, I had knocked him out. But then the Dempsey-Gibbons bout was ignored as rather mystifying, one of "those things."

The prizefight "experts" were almost unanimous in not giving me a chance. The sports writers ground out endless descriptions of the doleful things that would happen to me in the ring with Dempsey. There were, so far as I know, only a few persons prominent in sports who thought I might win, and said so. One was Bernard Gimbel, of the famous mercantile family, a formidable amateur boxer and a student of ring strategy. The others included that prince of sportswriters, the late W. O. McGeehan, and a few lesser lights in the sports-writing profession. They picked me to win, and were ridiculed. The consensus of the experts was echoed by the public, though with genuine sadness on the part of some.

Suspicion of a hoax started following a visit by a newspaperman to my training camp at Speculator, New York. Associated Press reporter Brian Bell came for an interview. He noticed a book lying on the table next to my bed. Books were unexpected equipment in a prizefight training camp. He was curious and took a look at the volume—*The Way of All Flesh*. That surprised him. The Samuel Butler opus[3] was, at that time, new in its belated fame, having been hugely praised by George Bernard Shaw as a neglected masterpiece. It was hardly the thing you'd expect a prizefighter to be reading, especially while training for a bout with Jack Dempsey.

Brian Bell knew a story when he saw one. He later became one of the chief editors of the Associated Press. Instead of talking fight, he queried me about books. I told him I like to read Shakespeare. That was the gag. That was the payoff. The A.P. flashed the story far and wide—the challenger, training for Jack Dempsey, read books, literature—Shakespeare. It was a sensation. The Shakespeare-Tunney legend was born.

The story behind it all went back to a day in 1917 when a young marine named Gene Tunney was getting ready to embark with his company bound for the war in France. We were stowing things in our kits, when I happened to glance at the fellow next to me. I noticed that among the belongings he was packing were two books. That surprised me.

In the marines you kept the stuff you took to the minimum. You carried your possessions on your back in the long marches favored by the Marine Corps. Every ounce would feel like a ton. Yet here was a leatherneck[4] stowing away two books to add to his burden. I was so curious that I sneaked a look at the two books and saw—Shakespeare. One was *Julius Caesar,* the other, *A Winter's Tale*. He must be a real professor, I thought.

The leatherneck in question was the company clerk. I had known him when in recruit camp—a young lawyer in civilian life, quiet and intelligent. Now, my respect for him went up many notches. He must be educated indeed to be taking two volumes of Shakespeare to carry on his back on the long marches we would have in France.

We sailed in the usual transport style, piled in bunks in a stuffy hold. The weather was rough, and

---

3 *opus:* a work or composition.

4 *leatherneck:* a member of the U.S. Marine Corps.

virtually the whole division of marines became seasick. The few good sailors poked unmerciful fun at their seasick comrades. I happened to be one of the fortunate, and joined in the ridicule of the miserable sufferers.

Sickest of all was the company clerk. He writhed in misery. He would lie on deck all day, an object of groaning filth. At night he was equally disgusting in his bunk. This was the tier next to mine, and I saw more of him than most. The high respect I had formed for him went down those many notches. He might be educated, he might take Shakespeare to war with him, but he was a mess at sea.

We put in at Brest, and promptly the order came—prepare to march. We were to put on a show at the dock for inspection by the brass hats. I started to get ready, and then came the appalling discovery. I couldn't find the tunic of my uniform. I knew I had stowed it in my kit, but it was gone. I hunted everywhere. In the Marine Corps it was practically a capital offense for a leatherneck to be without an article of issue, and here I was without my tunic for the long march upon arrival in France.

I heard a marine asking: "Whose is this?" He was on a cleaning job, and was holding up a disreputable object that he had fished from under the bunks. "Somebody's blouse," he announced with a tone of disgust, "and look at it."

I did—it was my blouse, a mess of seasick filth.

The explanation was easy to guess. The company clerk in the tier of bunks next to mine had done it. Having befouled all his clothes, he had, in his dumb misery, reached into my bunk and taken my blouse. He had worn it until it was too filthy to wear—after which he had chucked it under the bunks.

There was nothing I could do. There was no time to get the blouse cleaned, and there was no use blaming it on the company clerk. It was strictly up to me to have possession of every article of issue in good shape. I could only inform our company commander that I didn't have my tunic—and take the penalty, extra guard duty and kitchen police.

When, ashore, the company clerk came out of his seasickness and realized what had happened, he was duly remorseful. He was a decent fellow, his only real offense having been seasickness. He told me how sorry he was, and asked what he could do to make up for the trouble he had got me into. What could he give me? That was the way things were requited[5] among the marines—handing something over to make up for something. What did he have that I might want? He hadn't anything I could take, except those two books. I told him, "Give me one of them and call things square." He did. He retained *Julius Caesar* and gave me *A Winter's Tale.* He knew what he was about, as anyone who knows Shakespeare will attest.

Having the book, I tried to read it but couldn't make any sense of it. I kept on trying. I always had a stubborn streak, and figured the book must mean something. But it didn't so far as I could make out. I went to the company clerk. He had given me the book, and it might mean something to him. It did, and he proceeded to explain.

He coached me, led me through *A Winter's Tale,* which turned out to be interesting. That was practically my introduction to Shakespeare—the hard way. After training on *A Winter's Tale,* I read such works as *Hamlet, Macbeth, Othello,* with ease.

I had always liked reading—and this had a practical side. I found that books helped in training for boxing bouts. One of the difficulties of the prizefight game is that of relieving tension in training camp, getting one's mind

off the fight. The usual training camp devices were jazz phonograph records and the game of pinochle. I didn't like jazz, and the mysteries of pinochle were too deep for me. So I resorted to reading as a way to ease the dangerous mental strain during training. I found that books were something in which I could lose myself and get my mind off the future—like *The Way of All Flesh,* which Brian Bell of the Associated Press found me reading while training for Dempsey.

Hitherto, as just another prizefighter, my personal and training camp habits had been of little news interest, and nobody had bothered to find out whether I read books or not. Now, as the challenger for the heavyweight title, I was in a glare of publicity, and the disclosure that I read books, literature, Shakespeare, was a headline. The exquisite twist was when one of Dempsey's principal camp followers saw the newspaper story. He hurried to Jack with a roar of mirth. "It's in the bag, Champ. The so-and-so is up there reading a book!"

The yarn grew with the telling—training for Dempsey on Shakespeare. It simplified itself down to the standing joke— Tunney, the great Shakespearean. This put the finishing touch to the laugh over my prospects in the

---

5 *requited:* repaid.

ring with Dempsey.

It made me angry and resentful. I was an earnest young man with a proper amount of professional pride. The ridicule hurt. It might have injured my chances. To be consigned so unanimously to certain and abject defeat might have been intimidating, might have impaired confidence. What saved me from that was my stubborn belief in the correctness of my logic. The laugh, in fact, helped to defeat itself and bring about the very thing that it ridiculed. It could only tend to make the champion overconfident.

For a boxer there's nothing more dangerous than to underestimate an opponent. Jack Dempsey was not one to underestimate. It was not his habit of mind to belittle an antagonist. He was far too intelligent for that. In fact, Jack rather tended to underestimate himself. With all his superb abilities in the ring, he was never arrogant or cocky, never too sure of himself. But not even Jack Dempsey could escape the influence of opinion so overwhelming, such mockery as "It's in the bag, Champ. The so-and-so is up there reading a book." That could help my strategy of a surprise blow to knock him out or daze him for the rest of the fight.

•   •   •

When we finally got into the ring at Philadelphia things went so much according to plan that they were almost unexciting to me. During the first minute of sparring, I feinted Dempsey a couple of times, and then lashed out with the right-hand punch, the hardest blow I ever deliberately struck. It failed to knock him out. Jack was tough, a hard man to flatten. His fighting style was such that it was difficult to tag him on the jaw. He fought in a crouch, with his chin tucked down behind his left shoulder. I hit him high, on the cheek. He was shaken, dazed. His strength, speed, and accuracy were reduced. Thereafter it was a methodical matter of outboxing him, foiling his rushes, piling up points, clipping him with repeated, damaging blows, correct sparring.

There was an element of the unexpected—rain. It drizzled and showered intermittently throughout the fight. The ring was wet and slippery, the footing insecure. That was bad for a boxer like me, who depended on speed and sureness of foot for maneuvering. One false step with Jack Dempsey might bring oblivion. On the other hand, the slippery ring also worked to the disadvantage of the champion. A hitter needs secure footing from which to drive his punches, and any small uncertainty underfoot may rob him of his power. So the rain was an even thing except that it might have the therapeutic value of a shower for a dazed man, and Dempsey was somewhat dazed during the ten rounds. Jack was battered and worn out at the end, and I might have knocked him out if the bout had gone a few rounds more. The decision was automatic, and I was heavyweight champion of the world.

The real argument of the decade grew out of my second bout with Dempsey, at Chicago, the following year—the "long count" controversy. It produced endless talk, sense and nonsense, logic and illogic. To this day in any barroom you can work up a wrangle on the subject of the long count. How long was Tunney on the floor after Dempsey knocked him down? Could he have got up if the count had been normal?

To me the mystery has always been how Dempsey contrived to hit me as he did. In a swirl of action, a wild mix-up with things happening fast, Jack might have nailed the most perfect boxer that ever blocked or side-stepped a punch, he was that swift and accurate a hitter. But what happened to me did not occur in any dizzy confusion of flying fists. In an ordinary exchange Dempsey simply stepped in and hit me with a left hook.

It was in the seventh round. I had been outboxing Jack all the way. He hadn't hurt me, hadn't hit me with any effect. I wasn't dazed or tired. I was sparring in my best form, when he lashed out.

For a boxer of any skill to be hit with a left swing in a commonplace maneuver of sparring is sheer disgrace. It was Dempsey's most effective blow, the one thing you'd watch for—you'd better, for the Dempsey left, as prize-ring history relates, was murder. I knew how to evade it, side-step or jab him with a left and beat him to the punch. I had been doing that all along.

I didn't see the left coming. So far as I was concerned, it came out of nowhere. That embarrassed me more than anything else—not to mention the damage done. It was a blow to pride as well as to the jaw. I was vain of my eyesight. My vision in the ring was always excellent. I used to think I could see a punch coming almost before it started. If there was anything I could rely on, it was my sharpness of eye—and I utterly failed to see that left swing.

The only explanation I have ever been able to think of is that in a training bout I had sustained an injury to my right eye. A sparring partner had poked me in the eye with thumb extended. I was rendered completely blind for an instant, and after some medical treatment was left with astigmatism which could easily have caused a blind spot, creating an area in which there was no vision. Our relative position, when Dempsey hit me, must have been such that the left swing came up into the blind spot, and I never saw it.

With all his accuracy and power Dempsey hit me flush on the jaw, the button. I was knocked dizzy. Whereupon he closed for the kill, and that meant fighting fury at its most destructive. When Dempsey came in for a knockout he came with all his speed and power. I didn't know then how many times he slugged me. I had to look at the motion pictures the next day to find out. There were seven crashing blows, Dempsey battering me with left and right as I fell against the ropes, collapsing to a sitting position on the canvas.

Of what ensued during the next few seconds, I knew nothing. I was oblivious of the most debated incident of the long count and had to be told later on what happened.

The story went back to the Dempsey-Firpo fight, to that wild first round during which Firpo hit the floor in one knockdown after another. This was in New York, where the rule was that a boxer scoring a knock-down must go to a neutral corner and remain there until the referee had completed the count. In the ring with the Wild

Bull of the Pampas, Dempsey undoubtedly through excitement of battle violated that rule, as the motion pictures showed clearly afterward.

Jack confesses he remembers nothing that took place during that entire fight. Firpo landed a terrific first blow. Dempsey, after suffering a first-blow knock-down, apparently jumped up to the fray by sheer professional instinct—the fighting heart of a true champion. Instead of going to a corner, Jack would stand over Firpo and slug him as he got up. After one knock-down, Jack stepped over his prostrate opponent to the other side, to get a better shot at him—the referee was in the way. After another knock-down, Dempsey slugged Firpo before the South American had got his hands off the floor, when he was still technically down. The Champ might well have been disqualified after that—not to mention the fact that he was pushed back into the ring when Firpo battered him out. The referee, however, in his confusion permitted all the violations.

The Dempsey-Firpo brawl aroused a storm of protest and brought about a determination that in the future Dempsey should be kept strictly to the rules. In our Chicago bout the regulation applied—go to a neutral corner upon scoring a knock-down. The referee had been especially instructed to enforce this. He was told that, in case of a knock-down, he was not to begin a count until the boxer who had scored the knockdown had gone to a neutral corner.

This was the reason for the long count. Dempsey, having battered me to the canvas, stood over me to hit me the moment I got up—if I did get up. The referee ordered him to a neutral corner. He didn't go. The referee, in accordance with instructions, refrained from giving count until he did go. That imposed on Jack a penalty of four seconds. It was that long before he went to the corner and the referee began the count.

When I regained full consciousness, the count was at two. I knew nothing of what had gone on, was only aware that the referee was counting two over me. What a surprise! I had eight seconds in which to get up. My head was clear. I had trained hard and well, as I always did, and had that invaluable asset—condition. In the proverbial pink, I recovered quickly from the shock of the battering I had taken. I thought—what now? I'd take the full count, of course. Nobody but a fool fails to do that. I felt all right, and had no doubt about being able to get up. The question was what to do when I was back on my feet.

I never had been knocked down before. In all the ring battles and training bouts I had engaged in, I had never previously been on the canvas. But I had always thought about the possibility, and had always planned before each bout what to do if I were knocked down, what strategy to use upon getting up. That depended on the kind of opponent.

I had thought the question out carefully in the case of Jack Dempsey. If he were to knock me down, he would, when I got up, rush me to apply the finisher. He would be swift and headlong about it. Should I try to clinch and thus gain some seconds of breathing space? That's familiar strategy for a boxer after a knock-down. Often it's the correct strategy—but not against Dempsey, I figured. He hit too hard and fast with short punches for it to be at all safe to close for a clinch. He might knock me out.

Another possibility was to get set and hit him as he rushed. That can be effective against a fighter who, having scored a knockdown, comes tearing in wide open, a mark for a heavy blow. If you are strong upon getting to your feet, you can sometimes turn the tables by throwing everything into a punch. Bob Fitzsimmons often did it. But that wouldn't do against Dempsey, I reckoned. He was too tough and hit too hard. He would welcome a slugging match. After having been knocked down, I might not be in any shape to take the risk of stepping in and hitting him.

For my second bout with Dempsey the plan that I decided upon, in case I was knocked down, was based on the thing I had learned about Jack. Word from his training camp had indicated that his legs were none too good. I had learned that his trainers had been giving him special exercises for footwork, because he had slowed down in the legs. That was the cue—match my legs against his, keep away from him, depend on speed of foot, let him chase me until I was sure I had recovered completely from the knock-down.

The plan would work if my own legs were in good shape, after the battering I had taken. That was what I had to think about on the floor in Chicago. My legs felt all right. At the count of nine I got up. My legs felt strong and springy.

Jack came tearing in for the kill. I stepped away from him, moving to my left—circling away from his left hook. As I side-stepped swiftly, my legs had never been better. What I had heard about Dempsey's legs was true. As I circled away from him, he tried doggedly, desperately, to keep up with me—but

he was slow. The strategy was okay—keep away from him until I was certain that all the effects of the knock-down had worn off. Once, in sheer desperation, Jack stopped in his tracks and growled at me to stand and fight.

I did—but later, when I knew that my strength, speed, and reflexes were completely normal. I started to close with him and hit him with the encyclopedia of boxing. Presently Dempsey's legs were so heavy that he couldn't move with any agility at all, and I was able to hit him virtually at will. He was almost helpless when the final bell rang—sticking it out with stubborn courage.

I have often been asked—could I have got up and carried on as I did without those extra four seconds of the long count? I don't know. I can only say that at the count of two I came to, and felt in good shape. I had eight seconds to go. Without the long count, I would have had four seconds to go. Could I, in that space of time, have got up? I'm quite sure that I could have. When I regained consciousness after the brief period of black-out, I felt that I could have jumped up immediately and matched my legs against Jack's, just as I did.

The long count controversy, with all the heated debate, produced a huge public demand for another Dempsey-Tunney fight, number three. Tex Rickard was eager to stage it. He knew, as everybody else did, that it would draw the biggest gate ever. The first Dempsey-Tunney fight grossed over a million seven hundred thousand; the second, over two million and a half. Rickard was sure a third would draw three million. I was willing, eager. I planned to retire after another championship bout, wanted to get all that I could out of it.

But Jack refused. He was afraid of going blind. The battering he had taken around the eyes in his two fights with me alarmed him. The very thing that kept him from being hit on the jaw, his style of holding his chin down behind his shoulder, caused punches to land high. He dreaded the horror that has befallen so many ring fighters and is the terror of them all—the damage that comes from too many punches around the eyes, blindness.

Jack Dempsey was a great fighter—possibly the greatest that ever entered a ring. Looking back objectively, one has to conclude that he was more valuable to the sport or "The Game" than any prizefighter of his time. Whether you consider it from his worth as a gladiator or from the point of view of the box office, he was tops. His name in his most glorious days was magic among his people, and today, twenty years after, the name Jack Dempsey is still magic. This tells a volume in itself. As one who has always had pride in his profession as well as his professional theories, and possessing a fair share of Celtic romanticism, I wish that we could have met when we were both at our unquestionable best. We could have decided many questions, to me the most important of which is whether "a good boxer can always lick a good fighter."

I still say yes.

Understanding What You Read

1. Before Gene Tunney had even seen Jack Dempsey fight, why did he take heart from Mike Gibbons?

2. What did Tunney conclude was the best way to defeat Dempsey?
    a. By overpowering the Manassa Mauler
    b. By a clever, quick defensive style combined with a right-hand punch
    c. By a series of left-handed punches

3. How did Tunney's interest in reading work for him before the first fight with Jack Dempsey?

4. Gene Tunney writes of his marine friend, "He retained **Julius Caesar** and gave me **A Winter's Tale**. He knew what he was about, as anyone who knows Shakespeare will attest." What did Tunney mean by, "He knew what he was about"?

5. Why might you say that "Moments of Glory Past" is an accurate description of Jack Dempsey after Tunney got up from the "long count"?

Writer's Workshop

Write a compare-and-contrast essay about Gene Tunney and Jack Dempsey. Remember that in this type of essay you compare similarities and contrast differences. Make the first half of your essay deal with comparisons and the second half with contrasts between the two noted fighters.

The Loser

Floyd Patterson couldn't get over losing the championship. He retreated from his family and from the world. This essay takes you there.

At the foot of a mountain in upstate New York, about sixty miles from Manhattan, there is an abandoned country clubhouse with a dusty dance floor, upturned barstools, and an untuned piano; and the only sounds heard around the place at night come from the big white house behind it—the clanging sounds of garbage cans being toppled by raccoons, skunks, and stray cats making their nocturnal raids down from the mountain.

The white house seems deserted, too; but occasionally, when the animals become too clamorous, a light will flash on, a window will open, and a Coke bottle will come flying through the darkness and smash against the cans. But mostly the animals are undisturbed until daybreak, when the rear door of the white house swings open and a broad-shouldered Negro appears in gray sweat clothes with a white towel around his neck.

He runs down the steps, quickly passes the garbage cans and proceeds at a trot down the dirt road beyond the country club toward the highway. Sometimes he stops along the road and throws a flurry of punches at imaginary foes, each jab punctuated by hard gasps of his breathing— *"hegh-hegh-hegh"*—and then reaching the highway, he turns and soon disappears up the mountain.

At this time of morning farm trucks are on the road, and the other drivers wave at the runner. And later in the morning other motorists see him, and a few stop suddenly at the curb and ask:

"Say, aren't *you* Floyd Patterson?"

"No," says Floyd Patterson. "I'm his brother, Raymond."

The motorists move on, but recently a man on foot, a disheveled man who seemed to have spent the night outdoors, staggered behind the runner along the road and yelled, "Hey, Floyd Patterson!"

"No, I'm his brother, Raymond."

"Don't tell *me* you're not Floyd Patterson. I know what Floyd

Patterson looks like."

"Okay," Patterson said, shrugging, "if you want me to be Floyd Patterson, I'll be Floyd Patterson."

"So let me have your autograph," said the man, handing him a rumpled piece of paper and a pencil.

He signed it—"Raymond Patterson."

One hour later Floyd Patterson was jogging his way back down the dirt path toward the white house, the towel over his head absorbing the sweat from his brow. He lives alone in a two-room apartment in the rear of the house, and has remained there in almost complete seclusion since getting knocked out a second time by Sonny Liston.

In the smaller room is a large bed he makes up himself, several record albums he rarely plays, a telephone that seldom rings. The larger room has a kitchen on one side and, on the other, adjacent to a sofa, is a fireplace from which are hung boxing trunks and T-shirts to dry, and a photograph of him when he was the champion, and also a television set. The set is usually on except when Patterson is sleeping, or when he is sparring across the road inside the clubhouse (the ring is rigged over what was once the dance floor), or when, in a rare moment of painful

honesty, he reveals to a visitor what it is like to be the loser.

"Oh, I would give up anything to just be able to work with Liston, to box with him somewhere where nobody would see us, and to see if I could get past three minutes with him," Patterson was saying, wiping his face with the towel, pacing slowly around the room near the sofa. "I *know* I can do better. . . . Oh, I'm not talking about a rematch. Who would pay a nickel for another Patterson-Liston fight? I know *I* wouldn't. . . . But all I want to do is get past the first round."

Then he said, "You have no idea how it is in the first round. You're out there with all those people around you, and those cameras, and the whole world looking in, and all that movement, that excitement, and 'The Star Spangled Banner,' and the whole nation hoping you'll win, including the president. And do you know what all this does? It blinds you, just blinds you. And then the bell rings, and you go at Liston and he's coming at you, and you're not even aware that there's a referee in the ring with you.

". . . Then you can't remember much of the rest, because you don't want to. . . . All you recall is, all of a sudden you're getting up, and the referee is saying, 'You all right?' and you say, 'Of *course* I'm all right,' and he says, 'What's your name?' and you say, 'Patterson.'

"And then, suddenly, with all this screaming around you, you're down again, and you know you have to get up, but you're extremely groggy, and the referee is pushing you back, and your trainer is in there with a towel, and the people are all standing up, and your eyes focus directly at no one person—you're sort of floating.

"It is not a *bad* feeling when you're knocked out," he said. "It's a *good* feeling, actually. It's not painful, just a sharp grogginess. You don't see angels or stars; you're on a pleasant cloud. After Liston hit me in Nevada, I felt, for about four or five seconds, that everybody in the arena was actually in the ring with me, circled around me like a family, and you feel warmth toward all the people in the arena after you're knocked out. You feel lovable to all the people. And you want to reach out and kiss everybody—men and women— and after the Liston fight somebody told me I actually blew a kiss to the crowd from the ring. I don't remember that. But I guess it's true because that's the way you feel during the four or five seconds after a knockout. . . .

"But then," Patterson went on, still pacing, "this good feeling leaves you. You realize where you are, and what you're doing there, and what has just happened to you. And what follows is a hurt, a confused hurt—not a physical hurt—it's a hurt combined with anger; it's a what-will-people-think hurt; it's an ashamed-of-my-own-ability hurt . . . and all you want then is a hatch door in the middle of the ring—a hatch door that will open and let you fall through and land in your dressing room instead of having to get out of the ring and face those people. The worst thing about losing is having to walk out of the ring and face those people . . . ."

Then Patterson walked over to the stove and put on the kettle for tea. He remained silent for a few moments. Through the walls could be heard the footsteps and voices of the sparring partners and the trainer who live in the front of the house. Soon they would be in the clubhouse getting things ready should Patterson wish to spar. In two days he was scheduled to fly to Stockholm and fight an Italian named Amonti, Patterson's first appearance in the ring since the last Liston fight.

Next he hoped to get a fight in London against Henry Cooper. Then, if his confidence was restored, his reflexes reacting, Patterson hoped to start back up the ladder in this country, fighting all the leading contenders, fighting often, and not waiting so long between each fight as he had done when he was a champion in the 90 percent tax bracket.

His wife, whom he finds little time to see, and most of his friends think he should quit. They point out that he does not need the money. Even he admits that, from investments alone on his $8 million gross earnings, he should have an annual income of about thirty-five thousand dollars for the next twenty-five years. But Patterson, who is only twenty-nine years old and barely scratched, cannot believe that he is finished. He cannot help but think that it was something more than Liston that destroyed him—a strange, psychological force was also involved, and unless he can fully understand what it was, and learn to deal with it in the boxing ring, he may never be able to live peacefully anywhere but under this mountain. Nor will he ever be able to discard the false whiskers and mustache that, ever since Johansson beat him in 1959, he has carried with him in a small attaché case into each fight so he can slip out of the stadium unrecognized should he lose.

"I often wonder what other fighters feel, and what goes through their minds when they lose," Patterson said, placing the cups of tea on the table. "I've wanted so much to talk to another fighter about all this, to compare thoughts, to see if he feels some of the same things I've felt. But who can you talk to? Most fighters don't talk much anyway. And I can't even look another fighter in the eye at a weigh-in, for some reason.

"At the Liston weigh-in, the sportswriters noticed this, and said it showed I was afraid. But that's not it. I can never look *any* fighter in the eye because . . . well, because we're going to fight, which isn't a nice thing, and because . . . well, once I actually did look a fighter in the eye. It was a long, long time ago. I must have been in the amateurs then. And when I looked at this fighter, I saw he had such a nice face . . . and then he looked at *me* . . . and *smiled* at me . . . and *I* smiled back! It was strange, very strange. When a guy can look at another guy and smile like that, I don't think they have any business fighting.

"I don't remember what happened in that fight, and I don't remember what the guy's name was. I only remember that, ever since, I have never looked another fighter in the eye."

The telephone rang in the bedroom. Patterson got up to answer it. It was his wife, Sandra. So he excused himself, shutting the bedroom door behind him.

Sandra Patterson and their four children live in a $100,000 home in an upper-middle-class white neighborhood in Scarsdale, New York. Floyd Patterson feels uncomfortable in this home surrounded by a manicured lawn and stuffed with furniture, and since losing his title to Liston, he has preferred living full time at his camp, which his children have come to know as "daddy's house." The children, the eldest of whom is a daughter named Jeannie now seven years old, do not know exactly what their father does for a living. But Jeannie, who watched the last Liston-Patterson fight on closed-circuit television, accepted the explanation that her father performs in a kind of game where the men take turns pushing one another down; he had his turn pushing them down, and now it is their turn.

The bedroom door opened again, and Floyd Patterson, shaking his head, was very angry and nervous.

"I'm not going to work out today," he said. "I'm going to fly down to Scarsdale. Those boys are picking on Jeannie again. She's the only Negro in this school, and the older kids give her a rough time, and some of the older boys tease her and lift up her dress all the time. Yesterday she went home crying, and so today I'm going down there and plan to wait outside the school for those boys to come out, and . . . "

"How old are they?" he was asked.

"Teenagers," he said. "Old enough for a left hook."

Patterson telephoned his pilot friend, Ted Hanson, who stays at the camp and does public-relations work for him, and has helped teach Patterson to fly. Five minutes later Hanson, a lean white man with a crew cut and glasses, was knocking on the door; and ten minutes later both were in the car that Patterson was driving almost recklessly over the narrow, winding country roads toward the airport, about six miles from the camp.

"Sandra is afraid I'll cause trouble; she's worried about what I'll do to those boys; she doesn't want trouble!" Patterson snapped, swerving around a hill and giving his car more gas. "She's just not firm enough! She's afraid . . . she was afraid to tell me about that groceryman who's been making passes at her. It took her a long time before she told me about that dishwasher repairman who comes over and calls her 'baby.' They all know I'm away so much. And that dishwasher repairman's been to my home about four, five times this month already. That machine breaks down every week. I guess he fixes it so it breaks down every week. Last time, I laid a trap. I waited forty-five minutes for him to come, but then he didn't show up. I was going to grab him and say, 'How would you like it if I called *your* wife *baby?* You'd feel like punching me in the nose, wouldn't you? Well, that's what I'm going to do—if you ever call her *baby* again. You call her Mrs. Patterson; or Sandra, if you know her. But you don't know her, so call her Mrs. Patterson.' And then I told Sandra that these men, this type of white man, he just wants to have some fun with colored women. He'll never marry a colored woman, just wants to have some fun. . . ."

Now he was driving into the airport's parking lot. Directly ahead, roped to the grass airstrip, was the single-engine green Cessna that Patterson bought and learned to fly before the second Liston fight. Flying was a thing Patterson had always feared—a fear shared by, maybe inherited from, his manager, Cus D'Amato, who still will not fly.

D'Amato, who took over training Patterson when the fighter was seventeen or eighteen years old and exerted a tremendous influence over his psyche, is a strange but fascinating man of fifty-six who is addicted to Spartanism and self-denial and is possessed by suspicion and fear: He avoids subways because he fears someone might push him onto the tracks; never has married, never reveals his home address.

"I must keep my enemies confused," D'Amato once explained. "When they are confused, then I can do a job for my fighters. What I do not want in life, however, is a sense of security; the moment a person knows security, his senses are dulled—and he begins to die. I also do not want many pleasures in life; I believe the more pleasures you get out of living, the more fear you have of dying."

Until a few years ago, D'Amato did most of Patterson's talking, and ran things like an Italian *padrone*. But later Patterson, the maturing son, rebelled against the Father Image. After losing to Sonny Liston the first time—a fight D'Amato had urged Patterson to resist—Patterson took flying lessons. And before the second Liston fight, Patterson had conquered his fear of height, was master at the controls, was filled with renewed confidence—and knew, too, that even if he lost, he at least possessed a vehicle that could get him out of town, fast.

But it didn't. After the fight, the little Cessna, weighed down by too much luggage, became overheated ninety miles outside of Las Vegas. Patterson and his pilot companion, having no choice but to turn back, radioed the airfield and arranged for the rental of a larger plane. When they landed, the Vegas air terminal was filled with people leaving town after the fight. Patterson hid in the shadows behind a hangar. His beard was packed in the trunk. But nobody saw him.

Later the pilot flew Patterson's Cessna back to New York alone. And Patterson flew in the larger, rented plane. He was accompanied on his flight by Hanson, a friendly, forty-two-year-old, thrice-divorced Nevadan who once was a crop duster, a bartender, and a cabaret hoofer; later he became a pilot instructor in Las Vegas, and it was there that he met Patterson. The two became good friends. And when Patterson asked Hanson to help fly the rented plane back to New York, Hanson did not hesitate, even though he had a slight hangover that night—partly due to being depressed by Liston's victory, partly due to being slugged in a bar by a drunk after objecting to some unflattering things the drunk had said about the fight.

Once in the airplane, however, Ted Hanson became very alert. He had to, because after the plane had cruised a while at ten thousand feet, Floyd Patterson's mind seemed to wander back to the ring, and the plane would drift off course, and Hanson would say, "Floyd, Floyd, how's about getting back on course?", and then Patterson's head would snap up and his eyes would flash toward the dials.

And everything would be all right for a while. But then he was back in the arena, reliving the fight, hardly believing that it had really happened. . . .

". . . And I kept thinking, as I flew out of Vegas that night, of all those months of training before the fight, all the roadwork, all the sparring, all the months away from Sandra . . . thinking of the time in camp when I wanted to stay up until eleven-fifteen P.M. to watch a certain movie on The Late Show. But I didn't because I had roadwork the next morning. . . .

". . . And I was thinking about how good I'd felt before the fight, as I lay on the table in the dressing room. I remember thinking, 'You're in excellent physical condition, you're in good mental condition—but are you vicious?' But you tell yourself, 'Viciousness is not important now, don't think about it now; a championship fight's at stake, and that's important enough and, who knows? maybe you'll get vicious once the bell rings.'

". . . And so you lay there trying to get a little sleep . . . but you're only in a twilight zone, half asleep, and you're interrupted every once in a while by voices out in the hall, some guy's yelling 'Hey, Jack,' or 'Hey, Al,' or 'Hey, get those four-rounders into the ring.' And when you hear that, you think, 'They're not ready for you yet.' So you lay *there . . . and wonder, 'Where will I be tomorrow? Where will I be three hours from now?' Oh, you think all kinds of thoughts, some thoughts completely unrelated to the fight . . . you wonder whether you ever paid your mother-in-law back for all those stamps she bought a year ago . . . and you remember that time at two A.M. when Sandra tripped on the steps while bringing a bottle up to the baby . . . and then you get mad and ask: 'What am I thinking about these things for?' . . . and you try to sleep . . . but then the door opens and somebody says to somebody else, 'Hey, is somebody gonna go to Liston's dressing room and watch 'em bandage up?'*

"*. . . And so then you know it's about time to get ready. . . . You open your eyes. You get off the table. You glove up, you loosen up. Then Liston's trainer walks in. He looks at you, he smiles. He feels the bandages and later he says, 'Good luck, Floyd,' and you think, 'He didn't have to say that; he must be a nice guy.'*

"*. . . And then you go out, and it's the long walk, always a long walk, and you think, 'What am I gonna be when I come back this way?' Then you climb into the ring. You notice Billy Eckstine at ringside leaning over to talk to somebody, and you see the reporters—some you like, some*

you don't like—and then it's 'The Star-Spangled Banner,' and the cameras are rolling, and the bell rings. . . .

"*. . . How could the same thing happen twice? How? That's all I kept thinking after the knockout . . . . Was I fooling these people all these years? . . . Was I ever the champion? . . . And then they lead you out of the ring . . . and up the aisle you go, past those people, and all you want is to get to your dressing room, fast . . . but the trouble was in Las Vegas they made a wrong turn along the aisle, and when we got to the end there was no dressing room there . . . and we had to walk all the way back down the aisle, past the same people, and they must have been thinking, 'Patterson's not only knocked out, but he can't even find his dressing room. . . .'*

"*. . . In the dressing room I had a headache. Liston didn't hurt me physically—a few days later I only felt a twitching nerve in my teeth—it was nothing like some fights I've had: like that Dick Wagner fight in fifty-three when he beat my body so bad I was urinating blood for days. After the Liston fight, I just went into the bathroom, shut the door behind me, and looked at myself in the mirror. I just looked at myself, and asked, 'What happened?' and then they started pounding on the door, and saying,*

'Com' on out, Floyd, com' on out; the press is here, Cus is here, com' on out, Floyd. . . .'

". . . And so I went out, and they asked questions, but what can you say? What you're thinking about is all those months of training, all the conditioning, all the depriving; and you think, 'I didn't have to run that extra mile, didn't have to spar that day, I could have stayed up that night in camp and watched The Late Show. *. . . . I could have fought this fight tonight in no condition. . . .'"*

"Floyd, Floyd," Hanson had said, "let's get back on course. . . ."

Again Patterson would snap out of his reverie, and refocus on the omniscope,[1] and get his flying under control. After landing in New Mexico, and then in Ohio, Floyd Patterson and Ted Hanson brought the little plane into the New York airstrip near the fight camp. The green Cessna that had been flown back by the other pilot was already there, roped to the grass at precisely the same spot it was on this day five months later when Floyd Paterson was planning to fly it toward perhaps another fight—this time a fight with some schoolboys in Scarsdale who had been lifting up his little daughter's dress.

Patterson and Ted Hanson untied the plane, and Patterson got

a rag and wiped from the windshield the splotches of insects. Then he walked around behind the plane, inspected the tail, checked under the fuselage, then peered down between the wing and the flaps to make sure all the screws were tight. He seemed suspicious of something. D'Amato would have been pleased.

"If a guy wants to get rid of you," Patterson explained, "all he has to do is remove these little screws here. Then when you try to come in for a landing, the flaps fall off, and you crash."

Then Patterson got into the cockpit and started the engine. A few moments later, with Hanson beside him, Patterson was racing the little plane over the grassy field, then soaring over the weeds, then flying high above the gentle hills and trees. It was a nice takeoff.

Since it was only a forty-minute flight to the Westchester airport, where Sandra Patterson would be waiting with a car, Floyd Patterson did all the flying. The trip was uneventful until, suddenly behind a cloud, he flew into heavy smoke that hovered above a forest fire. His visibility gone, he was forced to the instruments. And at this precise moment, a fly that had been buzzing in the back of the cockpit flew up front and landed on the instrument panel in front of Patterson. He glared at

---

1 *omniscope:* an optical instrument.

the fly, watched it crawl slowly up the windshield, then shot a quick smash with his palm against the glass. He missed. The fly buzzed safely past Patterson's ear, bounced off the back of the cockpit, circled around.

"This smoke won't keep up," Hanson assured. "You can level off."

Patterson leveled off.

He flew easily for a few moments. Then the fly buzzed to the front again, zigzagging before Patterson's face, landed on the panel and proceeded to crawl across it. Patterson watched it, squinted. Then he slammed down at it with a quick right hand. Missed.

Ten minutes later, his nerves still on edge, Patterson began the descent. He picked up the radio microphone—"Westchester tower . . . Cessna 2729 uniform . . . three miles northwest . . . land in one-six on final . . . "—and then, after an easy landing, he climbed quickly out of the cockpit and strode to his wife's station wagon outside the terminal.

But along the way a small man smoking a cigar turned toward Patterson, waved at him, and said, "Say, excuse me, but aren't you . . . aren't you . . . Sonny Liston?"

Patterson stopped. He glared at the man, bewildered. He wasn't sure whether it was a joke or an insult, and he really did not know what to do.

"Aren't you Sonny Liston?" the man repeated, quite serious.

"No," Patterson said, quickly passing by the man, "I'm his brother."

When he reached Mrs. Patterson's car, he asked, "How much time till school lets out?"

"About fifteen minutes," she said, starting up the engine. Then she said, "Oh, Floyd, I just should have told Sister, I shouldn't have . . . "

"*You* tell Sister; *I'll* tell the boys . . . ."

Mrs. Patterson drove as quickly as she could into Scarsdale, with Patterson shaking his head and telling Ted Hanson in the back, "Really can't understand these school kids. This is a religious school, and they want twenty thousand dollars for a glass window—and yet, some of them carry these racial prejudices, and it's mostly the Jews who are shoulder to shoulder with us, and. . . . "

"Oh, Floyd," cried his wife, "Floyd, I have to get along here . . . you're not here, you don't live here, I . . . ."

She arrived at the school just as the bell began to ring. It was a modern building at the top of a hill, and on the lawn was the statue of a saint, and behind it a large white cross. "There's Jeannie," said Mrs. Patterson.

"Hurry, call her over here," Patterson said.

"Jeannie! Come over here, honey."

The little girl, wearing a blue school uniform and cap, and clasping books in front of her, came running down the path toward the station wagon.

"Jeannie," Floyd Patterson said, rolling down his window, "point out the boys who lifted your dress."

Jeannie turned and watched as several students came down the path; then she pointed to a tall, thin curly-haired boy walking with four other boys, all about twelve to fourteen years of age.

"Hey," Patterson called to him. "can I see you for a minute?"

All five boys came to the side of the car. They looked Patterson directly in the eye. They seemed not at all intimidated by him.

"You the one that's been lifting up my daughter's dress?" Patterson asked the boy who had been singled out.

"Nope," the boy said casually.

"Nope?" Patterson said, caught off guard by the reply.

"Wasn't him, mister," said another boy. "Probably was his little brother."

Patterson looked at Jeannie. But she was speechless, uncertain. The five boys remained there, waiting for Patterson to do something.

"Well, er, where's your little brother?" Patterson asked.

"Hey, kid!" one of the boys yelled. "Come over here."

A boy walked toward them. He resembled his older brother; he had freckles on his small, upturned nose, had blue eyes, dark curly hair and, as he approached the station wagon, he seemed equally unintimidated by Patterson.

"You been lifting up my daughter's dress?":

"Nope," the boy said.

"Nope!" Patterson repeated, frustrated.

"Nope, I wasn't lifting it. I was just touching it a little. . . ."

The other boys stood around the car looking down at Patterson, and other students crowded behind them, and nearby Patterson saw several white parents standing next to their parked cars; he became self-conscious, began to tap nervously with his fingers against the dashboard. He could not raise his voice without creating an unpleasant scene, yet could not retreat gracefully; so his voice went soft, and he said, finally:

"Look, boy, I want you to stop it. I won't tell your mother—that might get you in trouble—but don't do it again, okay?"

"Okay."

The boys calmly turned and walked, in a group, up the street.

Sandra Patterson said nothing.

Jeannie opened the door, sat in the front seat next to her father, and took out a small blue piece of paper that a nun had given her and handed it across to Mrs. Patterson. But Floyd Patterson snatched it. He read it. Then he paused, put the paper down, and quietly announced, dragging out the words, *"She didn't do her religion. . . ."*

Patterson now wanted to get out of Scarsdale. He wanted to return to camp. After stopping at the Patterson home in Scarsdale and picking up Floyd Patterson, Jr., who is three, Mrs. Patterson drove them all back to the airport. Jeannie and Floyd, Jr., were seated in the back of the plane and then Mrs. Patterson drove the station wagon alone up to camp, planning to return to Scarsdale that evening with the children.

It was four P.M. when Floyd Patterson got back to the camp, and the shadows were falling on the clubhouse, and on the tennis court routed by weeds, and on the big white house in front of which not a single automobile was parked. All was deserted and quiet; it was a loser's camp.

The children ran to play inside the clubhouse; Patterson walked slowly toward his apartment to dress for the workout.

"What could I do with those schoolboys?" he asked. "What can you do to kids of that age?"

It still seemed to bother him—the effrontery[2] of the boys, the realization that he had somehow failed, the probability that, had those same boys heckled someone in Liston's family the school yard would have been littered with limbs.

While Patterson and Liston both are products of the slum, and while both began as thieves, Patterson had been tamed in a special school with help from a gentle Negro spinster; later he became a Catholic convert, and learned not to hate. Still later he bought a dictionary, adding to his vocabulary such words as "vicissitude" and "enigma." And when he regained his championship from Johansson, he became the Great Black Hope of the Urban League.

He proved that it is not only possible to rise out of a Negro slum and succeed as a sportsman, but also to develop into an intelligent, sensitive, law-abiding citizen. In proving this, however, and in taking pride in it, Patterson seemed to lose part of himself. He lost part of his hunger, his anger—and as he walked up the steps into his apartment, he was saying, "I became the good guy . . . . After Liston won the title, I kept hoping that he would change

---

2 *effrontery:* shameless boldness; insolence.

. . . .

into a good guy, too. That would have relieved me of the responsibility, and maybe I could have been more of the bad guy. But he didn't. . . . It's okay to be the good guy when you're winning. But when you're losing, it is no good being the good guy."

Patterson took off his shirt and trousers and, moving some books on the bureau to one side, put down his watch, his cuff links and a clip of bills.

"Do you do much reading?" he was asked.

"No," he said. "In fact, you know I've never finished reading a book in my whole life? I don't know why. I just feel that no writer today has anything for me; I mean, none of them has felt any more deeply than I have, and I have nothing to learn from them. Although Baldwin to me seems different from the rest. What's Baldwin doing these days?"

"He's writing a play. Anthony Quinn is supposed to have a part in it."

"Quinn doesn't like me."

"Why?"

"I read or heard it somewhere; Quinn had been quoted as saying that my fight was disgraceful against Liston, and Quinn said something to the effect that he could have done better. People often say that—*they* could have done better! Well, I think that if *they* had to fight, *they* couldn't even go through the experience of waiting for the fight to begin. They'd be up the whole night before, and would be drinking, or taking drugs. They'd probably get a heart attack. I'm sure that, if I was in the ring with Anthony Quinn, I could wear him out without even touching him. I would do nothing but pressure him, I'd stalk him, I'd stand close to him. I wouldn't touch him, but I'd wear him out and he'd collapse. But Anthony Quinn's an old man, isn't he?"

"In his forties."

"Well, anyway," Patterson said, "getting back to Baldwin, he seems like a wonderful guy. I've seen him on television and, before the Liston fight in Chicago, he came by my camp. You meet Baldwin on the street and you say, 'Who's this poor slob?—he seems just like another guy; and this is the same impression *I* give people when they don't know me. But I think Baldwin and me, we have much in common, and someday I'd just like to sit somewhere for a long time and talk to him. . . .'"

Patterson, his trunks and sweat pants on, bent over to tie his shoelaces, and then, from a bureau drawer, took out a T-shirt across which was printed *Deauville*. He has several T-shirts bearing the same name. He takes good care of them. They are souvenirs from the high point of his life. They are from the Deauville Hotel in Miami Beach, which is where he trained for the third Ingemar Johansson match in March of 1961.

Never was Floyd Patterson more popular, more admired than during that winter. He had visited President Kennedy; he had been given a thirty-five-thousand-dollar jeweled crown by his manager; his greatness was conceded by sportswriters—and nobody had any idea that Patterson, secretly, was in possession of a false mustache and dark glasses that he intended to wear out of Miami Beach should he lose the third fight to Johansson.

It was after being knocked out by Johansson in their first fight that Patterson, deep in depression, hiding in humiliation for months in a remote Connecticut lodge, decided he could not face the public again if he lost. So he bought false whiskers and a mustache, and planned to wear them out of his dressing room after a defeat. He had also planned, in leaving his dressing room, to linger momentarily within the crowd and perhaps complain out loud about the fight. Then he would slip undiscovered through the night and into a waiting automobile.

Although there proved to be no need for bringing disguise into the second or third Johansson fights, or into a subsequent bout in Toronto against an obscure heavyweight named Tom McNeeley, Patterson brought it anyway; and, after the first Liston fight, he not only wore it during his thirty-hour automobile ride from Chicago to New York, but he also wore it while in an airliner bound for Spain.

"As I got onto this plane, you'd never have recognized me," he said. "I had on this beard, mustache, glasses and hat—and I also limped, to make myself look older. I was alone. I didn't care what plane I boarded; I just looked up and saw this sign at the terminal reading 'Madrid,' and so I got on that flight after buying a ticket.

"When I got to Madrid I registered at a hotel under the name Aaron Watson. I stayed in Madrid about four or five days. In the daytime I wandered around to the poorer sections of the city, limping, looking at the people, and the people stared back at me and must have thought I was crazy because I was moving so slow and looked the way I did. I ate food in my hotel room. Although once I went to a restaurant and ordered soup. I hate soup. But I thought it was what old people would order. So I ate it. And after a week of this, I began to actually think I was somebody else. I began to believe it.

And it is nice, every once in a while, being somebody else."

Patterson would not elaborate on how he managed to register under a name that did not correspond to his passport; he merely explained, "With money, you can do anything."

Now, walking slowly around the room, his black silk robe over his sweat clothes, Patterson said, "You must wonder what makes a man do things like this. Well, I wonder too. And the answer is, I don't know . . . but I think that within me, within every human being, there is a certain weakness. It is a weakness that exposes itself more when you're alone. And I have figured out that part of the reason I do the things I do, and cannot seem to conquer that one word—*myself*—is because . . . is because . . . I am a coward. . . ."

He stopped. He stood very still in the middle of the room, thinking about what he had just said, probably wondering whether he should have said it.

"I am a coward," he then repeated softly. "My fighting has little to do with that fact, though. I mean you can be a fighter—and a *winning* fighter—and still be a coward. I was probably a coward on the night I won the championship back from Ingemar. And I remember another night, long ago, back when I was in the amateurs, fighting this big tremendous man named Julius Griffin. I was only a hundred fifty-three pounds. I was petrified. It was all I could do to cross the ring. And then he came at me, and moved close to me . . . and from then on I don't know anything. I have no idea what happened. Only thing I know is, I saw him on the floor. And later somebody said, 'Man, I never saw anything like it. You just jumped up in the air, and threw thirty different punches. . . .'"

"When did you first think you were a coward?" he was asked.

"It was after the first Ingemar fight."

"How does one see this cowardice you speak of?"

"You see it when a fighter loses. Ingemar, for instance, is not a coward. When he lost the third fight in Miami, he was at a party later in the Fountainebleu. Had I lost, I couldn't have gone to that party. And I don't see how he did. . . ."

"Could Liston be a coward?"

"That remains to be seen," Patterson said. "We'll find out what he's like after somebody beats him, how he takes it. It's easy to do anything in victory. It's in defeat that a man reveals himself. In defeat I can't face people. I haven't the strength to say to people, 'I did my best, I'm sorry, and whatnot.'"

"Have you no hate left?"

"I have hated only one fighter," Patterson said. "And that was Ingemar in the second fight. I had been hating him for a whole year before that—not because he beat me in the first fight, but because of what he did after. It was all that boasting in public, and his showing off his right-hand punch on television, his thundering right, his 'toonder and lightning.' And I'd be home watching him on television, and *hating* him. It is a miserable feeling, hate. When a man hates, he can't have any peace of mind. And for one solid year I hated him because, after he took everything away from me, deprived me of everything I was, he *rubbed it in.* On the night of the second fight, in the dressing room, I couldn't wait until I got into the ring. When he was a little late getting into the ring, I thought, 'He's holding me up; he's trying to unsettle me—well, I'll get him!'"

"Why couldn't you hate Liston in the second match?"

Patterson thought for a moment, then said, "Look, if Sonny Liston walked into this room now and slapped me in the face, then you'd see a fight. You'd see the fight of your life because, then, a principle would be involved. I'd forget he was a human being. I'd forget I was a human being. And I'd fight accordingly."

"Could it be, Floyd, that you made a mistake in becoming a prizefighter?"

"What do you mean?"

"Well, you say you're a coward; you say you have little capacity for hate; and you seemed to lose your nerve against those schoolboys in Scarsdale this afternoon. Don't you think you might have been better suited for some other kind of work? Perhaps a social worker, or. . . . "

"Are you asking why I continue to fight?"

"Yes."

"Well," he said, not irritated by the question, "first of all, I love boxing. Boxing has been good to me. And I might just as well ask you the question 'Why do you write?' Or, 'Do you retire from writing everytime you write a bad story?' And as to whether I should have become a fighter in the first place, well, let's see how I can explain it. . . . Look, let's say you're a man who has been in an empty room for days and days without food . . . and then they take you out of that room and put you into another room where there's food hanging all over the place . . . and the first thing you reach for, you eat. When you're hungry, you're not choosy, and so I chose the thing that was closest to me. That was boxing. One day I just wandered into a gymnasium and boxed a boy. And I beat him. Then I boxed another boy. I beat him, too. Then I kept boxing. And winning. And I said, 'Here, finally, is something I can do!'

"Now I wasn't a sadist," he quickly added. "But I liked beating people because it was the only thing I could do. And whether boxing was a sport or not, I wanted to make it a sport because it was a thing I could succeed at. And what were the requirements? Sacrifice. That's all. To anybody who comes from the Bedford-Stuyvesant section of Brooklyn, sacrifice comes easy. And so I kept fighting, and one day I became heavyweight champion, and I got to know people like you. And you wonder how I can sacrifice, how I can deprive myself so much. You just don't realize where I've come from. You don't understand where I was when it began for me.

"In those days, when I was about eight years old, everything I got—I stole. I stole to survive, and I did survive, but I seemed to hate myself. My mother told me I used to point to a photograph of myself hanging in the bedroom and say, 'I don't like that boy!' One day my mother found three large X's scratched with a nail or something over that photograph of me. I don't remember doing it. But I do remember feeling like a parasite at home. I remember how awful I used to feel at night when my father, a longshoreman, would come home so tired that, as my mother fixed food before him, he would fall asleep at the table because he was that tired. I would always take his shoes off and clean his feet. That was my job. And I felt so bad because here I was, not going to school, doing nothing, just watching my father come home; and on Friday nights it was even worse. He would come home with his pay, and he'd put every nickel of it on the table so my mother could buy food for all the children. I never wanted to be around to see that. I'd run and hide. And then I decided to leave home and start stealing—and I did. And I would never come home unless I brought something that I had stolen. Once I remember I broke into a dress store and stole a whole mound of dresses, at two A.M. and there I was, this little kid, carrying all those dresses over the wall, thinking they were all the same size, my mother's size, and thinking the cops would never notice me walking down the street with all those dresses piled over my head. They did, of course . . . . I went to the Youth House . . . ."

Floyd Patterson's children, who had been playing outside all this time around the country club, now became restless and began to call him, and Jeannie started to pound on his door. So Patterson picked up his leather bag, which contained his gloves, his mouthpiece and adhesive tape, and walked with the children across the path toward the clubhouse.

He flicked on the light switches behind the stage near the piano. Beams of amber streaked through the dimly lit room and flashed onto the ring. Then he walked to one side of the room, outside the ring. He took off his robe, shuffled his feet in the rosin, skipped rope, and then began to shadowbox in front of the spit-stained mirror, throwing out quick combinations of lefts, rights, lefts, rights, each jab followed by a *"hegh-hegh-hegh-hegh."* Then, his gloves on, he moved to the punching bag in the far corner, and soon the room reverberated to his rhythmic beat against the bobbing bag—rat-tat-tat-*tetteta*, rat-tat-tat-*tetteta*, rat-tat-tat-*tetteta*, rat-tat-tat-*tetteta!*

The children, sitting on pink leather chairs, moved from the bar to the fringe of the ring, watched him in awe, sometimes flinching at the force of his pounding against the leather bag.

And this is how they would probably remember him years from now; a dark, solitary, glistening figure punching in the corner of a forlorn spot at the bottom of a mountain where people once came to have fun—until the clubhouse became unfashionable, the paint began to peel, and Negroes were allowed in.

As Floyd Patterson continued to bang away with lefts and rights, his gloves a brown blur against the bag, his daughter slipped quietly off her chair and wandered past the ring into the other room. There, on the other side of the bar and beyond a dozen round tables, was the stage. She climbed onto the stage and stood behind a microphone, long dead, and cried out imitating a ring announcer, "Ladieeees and gentlemen . . . tonight we present. . . ."

She looked around, puzzled. Then seeing that her little brother had followed her, she waved him up to the stage and began again: "Ladiees and gentlemen . . . tonight we present . . . *Floydie Patterson.* . . ."

Suddenly, the pounding against the bag in the other room stopped. There was silence for a moment. Then Jeannie, still behind the microphone and looking down at her brother, said, "Floydie, come up here!"

"No," he said.

"Oh, come up here!"

"No," he cried.

Then Floyd Patterson's voice from the other room, called: "Cut it out. . . . I'll take you both for a walk in a minute."

He resumed punching—rat-tat-tat-*tetteta*—and they returned to his side. But Jeannie interrupted, asking, "Daddy, how come you sweating?"

"Water fell on me," he said, still

pounding.

"Daddy," asked Floyd, Jr., "how come you spit water on the floor before?"

"To get it out of my mouth."

He was about to move over to the heavier punching bag when the sound of Mrs. Patterson's station wagon could be heard moving up the road.

Soon she was in Patterson's apartment cleaning up a bit, patting the pillows, washing the teacups that had been left in the sink. One hour later the family was having dinner together. They were togeth-er for two more hours; then, at ten P.M., Mrs. Patterson washed and dried all of the dishes, and put the garbage out in the can—where it would remain until the raccoons and skunks got to it.

And then, after helping the children with their coats and walking out to the station wagon and kissing her husband good-bye, Mrs. Patterson began the drive down the dirt road toward the highway. Patterson waved once, and stood for a moment watching the taillights go, and then he turned and walked slowly back toward the house.

Understanding What You Read

1. Does the first paragraph of this essay set the atmosphere for what is to follow? Explain.

2. Make a list of five major personality characteristics of Floyd Patterson that you feel are revealed in this essay. For each one, list the incident or words that led you to conclude this was a major personality characteristic.

3. "All was deserted and quiet; it was a loser's camp." What does Gay Talese mean by this?

4. Look up the words **vicissitude** and **enigma.** Why do both words, symbolic of Patterson's educating himself, also represent his life?

Writer's Workshop

1. Every year the Achievement Test in English Composition produced by the Educational Testing Service includes a 20-minute essay as part of its one-hour test in December. The 20-minute essay begins with a quotation and each student is asked to either agree or disagree with the quotation and then to support his or her answer with examples from history or current affairs, literature, or personal experience.

   In "The Loser" Floyd Patterson says, "It's easy to do anything in victory. It is in defeat that a man reveals himself."

   Do you agree or disagree with these words? Take about five minutes to plan an essay, then fifteen minutes to write it. Support your answer with examples from history or current affairs, literature, or personal experience.

2. Every writer carefully chooses material and then arranges it to create an effect. Write an essay in which you analyze the details Gay Talese has included in the last fifteen paragraphs of "The Loser." In your thinking, consider why Talese chose to end his essay this way. Why did he include the details he did? What effect do they have on the reader?

Who Killed Benny Paret?

Norman Cousins asks a question about boxing. He supplies his own angry answer.

Sometime about 1935 or 1936 I had an interview with Mike Jacobs, the prizefight promoter. I was a fledgling[1] reporter at that time; my beat was education but during the vacation season I found myself on varied assignments, all the way from ship news to sports reporting. In this way I found myself sitting opposite the most powerful figure in the boxing world.

There was nothing spectacular in Mr. Jacobs' manner or appearance; but when he spoke about prizefights, he was no longer a bland little man but a colossus who sounded the way Napoleon must have sounded when he reviewed a battle. You knew you were listening to Number One. His saying something made it true.

We discussed what to him was the only important element in successful promoting—how to please the crowd. So far as he was concerned, there was no mystery to it. You put killers in the ring and the people filled your arena. You hire boxing artists—men who are adroit at feinting, parrying, weaving, jabbing, and dancing, but

who don't pack dynamite in their fists—and you wind up counting your empty seats. So you searched for the killers and sluggers and maulers—fellows who could hit with the force of a baseball bat.

I asked Mr. Jacobs if he was speaking literally when he said people came out to see the killer.

"They don't come out to see a tea party," he said evenly. "They come out to see the knockout. They come out to see a man hurt. If they think anything else, they're kidding themselves."

Recently, a young man by the name of Benny Paret was killed in the ring. The killing was seen by millions; it was on television. In the twelfth round, he was hit hard in the head several times, went down, was counted out, and never came out of the coma.

The Paret fight produced a flurry of investigations. Governor Rockefeller was shocked by what happened and appointed a committee to assess the responsibility. The New York State Boxing Commission decided to find out what was wrong. The District Attorney's office expressed its concern. One

---

1 *fledgling:* beginner.

question that was solemnly studied in all three probes concerned the action of the referee. Did he act in time to stop the fight? Another question had to do with the role of the examining doctors who certified the physical fitness of the fighters before the bout. Still another question involved Mr. Paret's manager; did he rush his boy into the fight without adequate time to recuperate from the previous one?

In short, the investigators looked into every possible cause except the real one. Benny Paret was killed because the human fist delivers enough impact, when directed against the head, to produce a massive hemorrhage in the brain. The human brain is the most delicate and complex mechanism in all creation. It has a lacework of millions of highly fragile nerve connections. Nature attempts to protect this exquisitely intricate machinery by encasing it in a hard shell. Fortunately, the shell is thick enough to withstand a great deal of pounding. Nature, however, can protect man against everything except man himself. Not every blow to the head will kill a man—but there is always the risk of concussion and damage to the brain. A prizefighter may be able to survive even repeated brain concussions and go on fighting, but the damage to his brain

may be permanent.

In any event, it is futile to investigate the referee's role and seek to determine whether he should have intervened to stop the fight earlier. That is not where the primary responsibility lies. The primary responsibility lies with the people who pay to see a man hurt. The referee who stops a fight too soon from the crowd's viewpoint can expect to be booed. The crowd wants the knockout; it wants to see a man stretched out on the canvas. This is the supreme moment in boxing. It is nonsense to talk about prizefighting as a test of boxing skills. No crowd was ever brought to its feet screaming and cheering at the sight of two men beautifully dodging and weaving out of each other's jabs. The time the crowd comes alive is when a man is hit hard over the heart or the head, when his mouthpiece flies out, when the blood squirts out of his nose or eyes, when he wobbles under the attack and his pursuer continues to smash at him with poleax[2] impact.

Don't blame it on the referee. Don't even blame it on the fight managers. Put the blame where it belongs—on the prevailing mores[3] that regard prizefighting as a per-

---

2 *poleax:* medieval weapon combining blade, ax, hammer, and spike.

3 *mores:* customs or moral attitudes.

fectly proper enterprise and vehicle of entertainment. No one doubts that many people enjoy prizefighting and will miss it if it should be thrown out. And that is precisely the point.

Understanding What You Read

1. According to promoter Mike Jacobs, people come to see prize fights to
   a. Witness the artistry of fine athletes at work
   b. Cheer for a favorite boxer
   c. See violence and brutality

2. What were the official responses to Paret's death?

3. Why do you think that Cousins does not reveal what the investigations concluded?

4. According to Norman Cousins, the ultimate responsibility for Benny Paret's death lies with
   a. The fans who pay the money to see and support boxing
   b. The boxing commission that certified Paret's good health
   c. The referee who might have stopped the fight too late

Writer's Workshop

Norman Cousins is trying to sway your opinion on an issue he feels strongly about. But he doesn't begin his persuasive essay by announcing his stand. Instead, he starts with an anecdote (a little story) about his interview with Mike Jacobs. Then he offers an example—the death of Benny Paret. Next, Cousins considers who is responsible for Paret's death, rejects several alternatives, and states his own opinion.

Use the structure of Cousins's essay to write a persuasive essay about the effect of sports on society. You might even argue against Cousins's stand; in your persuasive essay you might argue that the aggressive nature of a sport helps release tension among those who watch it. Take any position you wish about the broad effect of sports on society, but be sure to have examples in your essay that support your argument—or use one effective extended example as Norman Cousins did.

Pancho Gonzales, the Lone Wolf of Tennis

A very private person, he had his own lifestyle. Writer Dick Schaap tries to figure out the legend of Pancho Gonzales.

R ichard Gonzales is the greatest tennis player in the world today. He has considerable wealth and prestige, plus an incredible amount of ability—almost everything a man could want. But on his strong right shoulder sits the same chip that marks so many men who have overcome odds not of their own making. It is the chip that has made him the fiercest competitor in tennis, a relentless champion who must prove again and again that in all the world there is no one else so skillful. But it also has had a deeper, more significant effect. It has shaped Gonzales into the lone wolf of tennis, a dark, brooding figure silhouetted against a rococo backdrop of fame, fortune, and talent.

Gonzales is a loner in the strictest sense of the word. While he was winning the pro tennis tour four years ago, he did not travel with Lew Hoad, Tony Trabert, and Pancho Segura in the spacious station wagons provided by promoter Jack Kramer. He drove alone in his own car, a souped-up Ford Thunderbird, picking his own routes and his own way stations. When the rest of the troupe checked in at one hotel he generally stayed at another. Usually he ate by himself, away from the bright lights and the noise. He rarely attended social functions, and when he did, he seemed to generate electric tension.

Once, the night before the tour made its annual stop in Madison Square Garden, Gonzales went to a party on New York City's swank East End Avenue. Among the other guests was Gina Lollobrigida, the Italian movie actress who has been described as the most tempting seven syllables since "Come up and see me sometime." At the party, a press photographer suggested, quite logically, that Gina and Pancho pose for a picture together. Gina warmly agreed. Gonzales seemed somewhat cooler. While the subjects waited, the photographer carefully adjusted his camera.

"Come on," Gonzales snapped. "Let's get this over with."

Gina took a deep breath—and smiled.

The photographer checked his flash attachment.

"What are you waiting for?" Gonzales demanded.

Gina smoothed her dress, wet her lips and laughed lightly.

"Stand a little closer together," the cameraman said. "Would you please smile, Pancho?"

Gonzales scowled. "Take the damn picture," he said, and then delivered a brief lecture on the social and technological failings of press photographers. A short while later, Gina was still smiling and Gonzales was still fuming. He left the party.

Yet the same man who verbally dissected the photographer can be genuinely pleasant and cooperative. It is one of the paradoxes[1] of Gonzales that he deeply wants to be friendly, but he instinctively fears anyone who might hurt or misuse him. On his most recent tour, he seems to have relaxed a little bit, but not much.

The genial, relaxed Gonzales appears at strange times. Late one evening in 1958, he stopped in a restaurant for a light snack. It was after midnight and the match with Hoad, which had ended only thirty minutes earlier, had lasted more than two hours. He was thoroughly exhausted. Blisters seared his feet.

He could easily have been curt and irascible.[2]

As he entered the restaurant, Gonzales spotted men seated around a table in a corner, all sipping tall glasses of white milk. "What's this," he asked, "the local milk club?" One of the men grinned. "No," he said. "We saw you play tonight and decided it was about time we got in shape."

For the first time all night, Gonzales cracked a broad smile. He walked over to the milk table, postponing his own meal, and chatted for several minutes about tennis, conditioning, and sports in general. When he was finished, he had won five lifelong fans.

His fellow professionals recognize Gonzales' aloofness and changeability, but for the most part, they can neither predict nor explain his moods. Even Segura, the little Ecuadorian who is closer to Gonzales than any other tennis player admits that he is often puzzled by the champion. "Gorg's a funny guy," Segura says. "He's independent. He likes to be alone. I don't know why."

(The nickname of Gorg, or Gorgo, has stuck with Gonzales since he won the 1948 U. S. Singles championship and promptly lost half a dozen matches in a row to Ted Schroeder. Tennis writer Jim

---

1 *paradox:* seeming contradictory qualities.

---

2 *irascible:* irritable.

Burchard called Pancho "The Cheese Champ" which inevitably became Gorgonzales—from Gorgonzola, an Italian cheese— and eventually Gorgo.)

Lew Hoad found Pancho's outward coolness no easier to handle than his service. "I guess," Hoad says, "that Gorg feels he can't be friendly with a fellow he has to try to beat every night. Maybe he's right. He does rather well, you know."

The only pro who advances a definite theory about Gonzales is Tony Trabert. "He's got a persecution complex," Trabert insists. "I don't blame him for having had it originally. He was persecuted. Even his nickname was a form of persecution. In California, many prejudiced people call all persons of Mexican descent 'Pancho.' But things have changed since he was a kid. When people call him 'Pancho' now, they say it admiringly. It's time he got over his complex."

But as any psychiatrist will confirm, it is not easy to erase a feeling that has deep roots in childhood and adolescence. The first of Carmen and Manuel Gonzales' seven children, Richard was born in Los Angeles on May 9, 1928. His father was a house painter and, although the family was never destitute, there was no extra money for luxuries. The Gonzaleses lived in a section of the south side of Los Angeles where a boy was considered an unqualified success if he grew up to become an auto mechanic.

One day, when Richard was seven years old, his father reluctantly gave him permission to cross the street alone and visit South Park, a local playground. The youngster set out on a scooter he had built from two-by-fours and roller skate wheels. When he reached the intersection, he did not stop or look or listen. He barreled into the street just as an automobile was approaching. The driver braked hard, but before the car could stop, its door handle hooked Richard's cheek. The accident left a scar several inches long. Today Pancho scarcely notices it. "Sometimes I forget which side it's on," he says.

But later there were less violent incidents that left more serious scars. Gonzales suffered one particularly depressing setback when he was fifteen. By then he was the best tennis player his age in Southern California. An above-average student, he decided his future was not in the classroom. He quit high school to spend all his spare time on the tennis court. As soon as Perry Jones, the czar of Southern California tennis, learned that Gonzales had left school, he called the boy into his office.

"Richard," Jones began, evenly,

"it isn't fair for you to play anybody who goes to school all day while you practice tennis."

"But Mr. Jones," Gonzales said, "I don't want to go to school any more. I want to play tennis."

Jones paused and leaned forward. "Until you return to school," he said, "I must bar you from all tournaments."

Gonzales was crushed. He had embraced tennis, and tennis, in turn, had spurned him. Rumors spread that Jones barred Gonzales because he was of Mexican descent. This was not true, but by repetition, it became a popular theory. Even now, although Pancho concedes that the ban was justified, he still seems to think that somehow he should have been eligible for the junior tournaments.

Not until after four years had elapsed, including fifteen months spent swabbing decks in the Navy, was Gonzales reinstated. Then, suddenly, he received another emotional slap in the face. He had been dating an attractive blond tennis player from the Los Angeles area. Everyone who saw them agreed that the dark, handsome Gonzales and the pale, beautiful girl made a stunning couple. Everyone, that is, except her father. He told her to stop seeing Pancho. For a while, the girl tried deception. She took her school books, said she was going to the

library and, instead, met Pancho. But, finally, the subterfuge[3] proved too burdensome. They stopped dating.

No sensitive adolescent could experience such difficulties without absorbing considerable pain, and Richard Gonzales was a sensitive boy. His hands were sensitive to the feel of a tennis racquet and his mind was sensitive to the string of an antagonistic society. He reacted naturally; he withdrew into himself.

"I remember Pancho at the first tournament he ever played away from home," says Gussie Moran, the former Wimbledon sensation who is now an entertaining sportscaster. "He was a quiet, shy boy who sat alone in the clubhouse. He had a forlorn look on his face and a chip on his shoulder. But when he stepped onto the tennis court, he was someone else. He was a god, patrolling his personal heaven."

Gonzales, basically, is not much different today. He is a far better tennis player. He has sharpened his strokes to the point of perfection. Yet he still sits by himself in the locker room, his head sunk in his hands, the sweat dripping from his brow.

Until one night a couple of years ago, we had seen Gonzales play as a pro only in big cities

---

3 *subterfuge:* deception.

where a sizable press corps, an army of tennis stars and the attendant fanfare always acted as a buffer against reality. The best way to understand and appreciate Richard Alonzo Gonzales, we decided, was to see him on tour in small towns, winning most matches, living alone, traveling alone, eating alone. Late one rainy and foggy afternoon, after a quick stop at the insurance vending machine, we boarded a DC-3 and flew from Newark to join the pro tour in Corning, New York.

Corning is an industrial town on the southern tier of upstate New York, nestled near the Finger Lakes. It is known for producing Steuben crystal, the finest glass in the country, and Ted Atkinson, one of the finest jockeys. In Corning everything revolves around the glassworks, and there, in a modern gymnasium, Pancho Gonzales and Lew Hoad played the sixty-seventh match of their current series.

The picture of Gonzales in action is unforgettable. For pure artistry, it rates with Musial, coiled and ready to strike; Cousy, flipping a backhanded pass; Snead, at the top of his backswing; and Arcaro, whipping a horse down the stretch. When he serves Gonzales strains, rears back and fires. Despite his size, he rushes catlike to the net, defying an opponent to

pass him. His long, light strides carry him to shots that lesser men never reach. On an overhead slam, he kicks up and follows through with frightening force. His nervous energy is never wasted. It is stacked up into a huge pile until the sheer weight of Pancho's ability falls upon an opponent, startling him at first, then bewildering him and, finally, crushing him.

For thirty-two games in the first set at Corning, Hoad refused to crack. Then Gonzales broke service, held his own and won the set, 18–16. He took the second set, 7–5, and stretched his series lead to five matches, 36–31. After the final point, champion and challenger shook hands perfunctorily, posed for several photographs, and retired to the dressing room.

Hoad entered first, shuffled to his locker in the far corner and sat down. Gonzales slumped onto a bench five feet away. For fully three minutes, neither said a word. The tension slowly ebbed from their faces. Then Gonzales spoke. "Give me a towel, will you," he said to Hoad. The taut, hard lines that striped both men's brows began to disappear. Gonzales drained half a Coke with one swallow. "I was lucky," he said. "I hit two shots I never saw."

They changed their shirts and socks and walked back to the court for a doubles match. Just as Hoad's right arm swept up for the first serve, Gonzales dropped his racquet loudly to the floor. "Excuse me, Lew," he said. "Did I disturb you?" The doubles served as an escape valve and, throughout the match, Gonzales clowned openly, hitting balls behind his back and swinging vainly at shots ten feet beyond his reach. On one serve he tossed up three balls and smacked two of them. As the crowd laughed, Pancho relaxed.

Afterward, in the locker room, he stripped off his shoes and socks and poked at huge callouses beneath the large toe of each foot. "Look at this one," he said. "Full of fluid." A trace of fatigue darkened his face. "This is the toughest sport of all," he said. "Even in pro basketball, they don't play every night. Besides, when they're tired, they get a substitute. We don't. We play even when we're hurt. I've played with a sprained ankle. Lew finished a match one night after colliding with a wall and being knocked unconscious."

Gonzales showered and put on a pair of slacks and a red polo shirt. Then he turned to me. "I'm going to get something to eat," he said. "Want to come along?" It was a stunning reversal in mood. Only six hours earlier, I had asked Gonzales if I might ride with him. His answer had been pointed. "No," he had said. "I don't have

any room."

As we walked from the locker room, a spectator shouted, "Good exhibition, Pancho." Gonzales frowned. "It was not an exhibition," he said. "If it had been, it would not have gone on so long."

Outside, in a parking lot behind the glassworks, Gonzales unlocked his Thunderbird. Even in the dark, its yellow body and white top shimmered brightly. He switched on the electric ignition and a modified Cadillac engine roared mightily.

For Gonzales, there is only one object more fascinating and more challenging than a tennis racket. It is a hot rod. The tennis champion of the world owns four automobiles that are constantly being tuned for drag-strip racing in California. Usually Pancho works as a mechanic, adjusting the steering, changing the gear ratio, pampering the engine. But sometimes he puts on crash helmet and goggles, settles into the driver's seat and hurtles down an old, abandoned air strip at speeds of more than 150 miles an hour.

Gonzales let the motor idle for several minutes before he slipped into gear. Then he pulled out of the parking lot, turned right, crossed a bridge over the Chemung River, and turned right again on Market Street. A few blocks down, he parked at the Athens

Restaurant. He walked in and sat down on a stool by the counter. "Give me a rare hamburger steak," he told the waitress, "and a cup of coffee."

Gonzales leaned forward, resting his elbows on the counter. "When I gain extra weight," he said, "I eat nothing but meat and liquids for a week to ten days. Then I get an awful hunger. It is something you cannot imagine. I see a piece of pie and I want it terribly."

While he ate, Gonzales said nothing. After a second cup of coffee and a glass of milk, he smoked a cigarette and went out to the Thunderbird. By 1 A.M. he was back in his single room at the Centerway Motel. At five, he fell asleep. "I replayed the match in my mind," he explained the next day. "I tried to figure out what I did right, why I won. Then I tried to decide how I would play the next match."

The next morning, while Hoad, Trabert and Segura toured the museum at the Corning Glass Works, Gonzales tried to sleep. At eleven-thirty, a steady, driving rain fell as I walked to the motel to meet Pancho. He was standing outside, conspicuous in his red polo shirt and a yellow sleeveless sweater, bent over the motor of his car. While the rain drenched him, he changed spark plugs. "You have to have two sets of spark plugs,"

he said, "one for the city and one for the open road."

For fifteen minutes he fastened, checked and adjusted. Then he went into the motel's restaurant and ordered a bowl of Wheaties, two $3\frac{1}{2}$ minute soft-boiled eggs, two cups of coffee and a glass of milk. After breakfast he returned to the car, checked it once more and packed his clothes and equipment. At twelve-fifteen, he climbed into the driver's seat and I got in beside him. We pulled away from the motel on Route 414 and started toward the next town on the tour—Clinton, New York, some 160 miles from Corning. Gonzales began to relax. His hands slipped easily into the ten o'clock and four o'clock positions favored by race drivers. Two miles outside Corning the motor suddenly sputtered, coughed and died. Despite Pancho's checks and double checks, we were out of gas.

The road from Corning to Watkins Glen, roughly 30 miles away, is a bumpy one, but after we refueled, Gonzales cruised along at 60 to 70 miles an hour. It was fast, but not dangerous driving. "I don't open it up," he said. "The T-Bird can do 145 miles an hour if I let it out. It'll go from zero to 115 in fifteen seconds."

Then, abruptly, we headed into a sharp curve. I braked, involuntarily, where there was no brake.

Gonzales did not even take his foot off the accelerator. We whipped around the bend into a straightaway. "That's how I make up time," he said. "I don't slow down on the curves."

After we passed Watkins Glen, bounced through a long stretch of highway under construction and picked up Route 414, Lake Seneca glimmered in the rain on our right. Gonzales ignored the scenery and concentrated on the road. "I like to travel alone," he said. "I can leave when I want. I don't have to wait for the others and they don't have to wait for me. When I want to stop and rest, I can."

Water leaked slowly through the windshield on the driver's side. "Is the feud between you and Kramer really bitter?" I asked.

"You're damn right it is," Gonzales said. "The main reason I don't like Kramer is simple. Money."

He lit a cigarette and continued. "I'm the best player and I deserve the most money. Kramer has me over a barrel now. He's got me under contract and I can't do a thing about it. After it runs out, we'll see. Some people have suggested that I start my own tour, but that's not my idea. I'll probably stick with this. I want a better deal, though. Somebody's going to get hurt and it's not going to be me."

Under his contract, Gonzales earns twenty percent of the gross receipts, an income of close to $75,000 a year.

Gonzales once dragged Kramer into court, seeking to have the contract changed. The judge threw out the case. Pancho had no legal complaint, he ruled; the contract was binding. Since then, even when they played gin rummy together at a nickel a point, Gonzales and Kramer have not spoken. "Pancho never says a social word to me," Kramer says.

Gonzales passed three cars easily, pulled into the right lane and began to talk about his family. "I've got three boys," he said, "Richard, Michael, and Danny. Richard, the oldest, is ten and looks like he's going to be a good tennis player."

He leaned back and rubbed the scar on his left cheek. He might have been thinking about his personal troubles. He is divorced from his wife, Henrietta, and was planning to marry Madelyn Darrow, a former Miss Rheingold.

We passed Syracuse and the sun threatened to break through the heavy rain clouds. "Pro tennis is a funny game," Gonzales said. "It's hard not to relax when you get far ahead. That's what Hoad did when he had me 18–9 in matches. That's what I did when I had him 32–23. He almost caught up and I had to bear down. I had to diet, practice, sleep, train. I'm training harder this year than I ever did before. I'm in the best shape of my life."

A few miles before Utica, we turned onto a side road that led into Clinton. On the outskirts of Clinton, we stopped at a service station. "Change the oil and fill it up," Gonzales told the attendant. We ran down the road, dodging puddles, to a small restaurant. It was almost three-thirty and Pancho wanted a large meal before the night's matches. He finished off a bowl of soup, a sirloin steak, a lettuce and tomato salad, and a bottle of 7-Up. Then he hesitated. "I'll have a piece of apple pie," he said.

While he ate, Gonzales read the Utica newspaper. Next to a story announcing the arrival of the tour, there was an AP dispatch praising Jack Kramer for his work in training young Barry MacKay for the Davis Cup matches with Australia.

"Kramer's always taking the credit," Gonzales grumbled. "I don't think he played once with the kid. We did all the work."

We hurried back to the service station and, after Pancho supervised the changing of his oil filter and bought a new set of spark plugs, we drove to the Clinton Arena, a barnlike construction that serves as home for the Clinton Comets in the Eastern Hockey League. We got out of the car,

walked inside and shivered. It felt cold enough for a hockey game.

Jerry Dashe and Don Westergard, the tour's equipment managers, were installing the tour's portable canvas tennis court. "When's it going to be ready?" Gonzales asked. "I want to get some practice."

"Not before five," Westergard called back. "You might as well go out until then."

We went back to the car and drove to a nearby hardware store. Gonzales bought a set of wrenches, then visited the local Mercury agency. "I want some floor mats for a T-Bird," he said. "Have any?"

The owner picked out two black mats and handed them to Gonzales. He started to fill out a sales slip. "Could you give me your name sir?" he said.

"Sure," Pancho answered "Gonzales."

"How do you spell that?"

"G-O-N-Z-A-L-E-S."

"Oh," said the proprietor, "like the tennis player."

"Same guy," said Gonzales.

"You're Pancho Gonzales," the owner said, with considerable awe. "I've read about you."

Gonzales turned his head away, slightly embarrassed. He didn't say a word, took his change and brought the mats out to the car. We returned to the arena, but the court still was not ready. Gonzales stepped outside and, with his new wrenches, began working on the car. Shortly after five, he went inside, dressed and went on the court for a practice session with Segura. For half an hour, Big Pancho and Little Pancho volleyed back and forth, concentrating on lobs and backhands. Then they went into the locker room. Trabert and Hoad had just arrived. "Hey, Gorg," Trabert said, "what's that big bubble sticking out of the hood on your car?"

"That's an air filter," Gonzales said, seriously. "I found that particles of dirt were getting into the motor and causing . . ."

"Okay, okay," said Trabert. "That's enough. You start to lose me when you get technical."

Before the preliminary match between Segura and Trabert began, Gonzales walked outside and climbed into one of the Kramer station wagons. He tried to sleep, but had no success. Spectators, waiting in line for tickets, approached the station wagon and stared at Pancho as though he were the firing unit in a NIKE display. Children banged on the windows and asked for autographs.

Gonzales gave up and went back into the locker room. In a few minutes, Trabert and Segura came through the door. "How'd it go, Segoo?" Gonzales asked.

"No good, Gorg," Segura said.

"He beat me again. He was really serving the ball tonight."

"How bad are the lights?"

"Not bad," Segura said. "Sometimes you lose the ball in them."

About fifteen minutes before match time, the lines in Gonzales' face started to harden again. By the time he ran onto the court, he was wearing his mean face, the one that he reserves for frightening opponents and reporters. But in the first set, Hoad refused to be frightened. His serve boomed across the net and skidded past Gonzales. His passing shots and net game were superb. He polished off the champion 6–2.

Then Pancho loosened up and, in forty minutes, swept two sets, 6–3, 6–1, extending his tour lead to six matches.

When the match was finished, Pancho dressed quickly. The next day's match was scheduled in New Castle, Pennsylvania, almost 400 miles away. There was a good deal of driving to be done and not much time for pleasantries. "I'll try to reach at least Buffalo tonight," he said. "Maybe I'll drive all the way." Then he climbed into the Thunderbird, switched on the ignition and, delicately, patiently, let the motor warm up. Alone in the small car, away from the crowds, the dark night enveloping him, Richard Gonzales looked like a traveling salesman, a Willie Loman[4] without samples. He shifted into reverse, backed out of his parking spot and started off, alone, on a 400-mile trip to a tennis match. He intended to win it.

---

4 *Willie Loman:* the aging salesman in Arthur Miller's play *Death of a Salesman.*

Understanding What You Read

1. What personality characteristic made Pancho Gonzales a distinctive athlete?
   a. his sense of humor
   b. his openness to all people including strangers
   c. his moody behavior
2. What explanation does author Dick Schaap put forth for Gonzales's manner?
3. What connection does Dick Schaap make between Pancho Gonzales's personality and his success at tennis?

Writer's Workshop

Dick Schaap creates a marvelous character portrait of Pancho Gonzales. Schaap succeeds because he watched Gonzales closely and recorded telling events that capture and reveal Gonzales's character.

Observe closely someone you know. Then write a sketch of 750 to 1,000 words in which you show the person speaking and acting in ways that reveal his or her personality.

. . . .

Arthur Ashe Looks Back at a Year of Troubles and Triumph

It was the best of times and the worst of times, both for America and for tennis-great Arthur Ashe.

Arthur Ashe really did not have much of a choice in the matter. Quiet, unassuming, almost bookish-looking in the hornrimmed glasses he wore then, he was nonetheless cast as a symbol in the late 1960s, that often turbulent period of political and social change in this country. Ashe was black and he was a tennis player, a combination that made many people uneasy in a sport in which everyone wore white. And because he was a celebrity, he had a forum for his views.

In 1968, Ashe was 25 years old and a lieutenant in the United States Army. He was an amateur in the first year of open tennis, when those who presided over the game finally lifted the barriers to professionals.

But it was Ashe and not one of the professionals who won the first United States Open, played on the grass courts of Forest Hills that year. He defeated Tom Okker of the Netherlands, 14–12, 5–7, 6–3, 3–6, 6–3, also becoming the first black man to win a Grand Slam event. Althea Gibson had won the United States Nationals at Forest Hills in 1957, and Wimbledon in 1958.

Because amateurs were entitled to only $28 a day in expenses, Okker was awarded the first-place prize of $14,000. This year, the twentieth anniversary of the first Open, the men's and women's singles winner will each take home $275,000 when the last ball is hit at the National Tennis Center in Flushing Meadows Park.

"I'm thrilled to see the game generating so much money," Ashe said, "because that was what we were fighting for. But I'm also actually appalled. I'm not trying to be holier than thou, but when our association said, 'Jump,' in 1968, we said, 'How high?'

"Now, everyone is a law unto themselves and there is a total lack of cooperation from the top players. They don't care what happened 20 years ago."

The United States Open was memorable for Ashe, but only one in a series of events that made 1968 what he calls a tumultuous year. As a soldier assigned to the United States Military Academy at West Point, Ashe had to maintain a delicate balance between his responsibilities as a young spokesman for blacks and his commitment to his country. That was not easy to do during the Vietnam War.

He attended meetings with prominent black athletes who were planning a protest for the Olympic Games that summer in Mexico City. In March 1968, Ashe made a speech to a church group in Washington and was criticized by the superintendent at West Point, who said the speech was too political.

There was sadness and anger when Dr. Martin Luther King, Jr., and then Robert F. Kennedy were assassinated. It was a time when rebellious young whites and disenfranchised blacks took to the streets in sometimes violent protests.

Playing tennis, even for the Davis Cup team, must have seemed frivolous at times. At West Point, where Ashe was a data-processing instructor, the Vietnam War was an ominous dark cloud over the scenic campus on the Hudson River. There were funeral processions almost daily, he said.

And Ashe remembered visiting hospitals in South Vietnam with his Davis Cup teammates Clark Graebner, Bob Lutz, and Stan Smith after they won the Cup in Australia. They found it difficult to celebrate. "Bob Lutz had a guy die right in front of him," Ashe said. "It was a very sobering experience."

It has helped him keep his perspective. Ashe had many joyful moments in 1968, too. In addition to his Davis Cup success, he strung together a two-month winning streak, which included four tournament victories, among them the United States Open triumph. He was on the cover of *Life* magazine.

When he returned to West Point—the conquering hero—after the Open, the entire Corps of Cadets gave him a standing cheer in the mess hall during dinner.

"It makes your heart leap," Ashe said. "It was one of the nicest ovations I ever got. It was a heckuva year. I was big news in 1968."

Ashe is 45 now, a husband and father, living in Mount Kisco, N.Y. A heart attack and subsequent bypass surgery ended his playing career in 1979, but he remains a presence in tennis, doing television commentary, writing for magazines and newspapers, serving in various capacities for the United States Tennis Association, but still an activist in promoting tennis for blacks. Ashe heads the Black Tennis and Sports Foundation.

His three-volume work, *A Hard Road to Glory,* will be published this fall. It is a history of the black athlete in the United States.

Twenty years seem like a long time ago to Ashe, but it frustrates him that blacks have progressed slowly in tennis. His success did not open the door to eager young protégés. Instead, he is an aberration.

"The biggest problem still is money," Ashe said. With lessons, it will cost a family $50,000 to pay for a developing tennis player.

A pair of sneakers and a playground can launch a basketball career. A sandlot and a broom handle can do the same for an aspiring young baseball player. But the parents of disadvantaged youths cannot begin to afford the price of a tennis career. Even middle-class parents must often borrow to pay the costs.

And Ashe points out the psychological problems that members of minorities from the inner city encounter when they play at private clubs, where their counterparts are better dressed and carry several racquets. He said they often suffer from a lack of confidence, feeling they do not belong. An all-black tennis club in Boston, he said, enlisted the aid of a psychologist to prepare the young players for matches at clubs in more affluent neighborhoods.

There are widespread incidents of discrimination, too, he added. But there is also hope. Four blacks are among the top-ranked collegiate players in the country. And several big cities, Detroit, Atlanta, Indianapolis, Kansas City, Mo., and Newark among them, have initiated ambitious public-parks programs to help popularize tennis among blacks.

Ashe said that Mayor Sharpe James of Newark—a tennis nut, Ashe said—had allocated funds for the construction of a new tennis facility with indoor and outdoor courts. "Prince is giving us a bunch of racquets, we're getting eight gross of balls, we're going to touch 52,000 kids at 62 schools," Ashe said.

"The growth of tennis has been spotty in the open era," he said. "The problem is how to raise money on a local level. We have tons of catching up to do."

Understanding What You Read

1. List and explain three reasons why Arthur Ashe found both "troubles and triumph" in 1968.
2. How has professional tennis changed from the way it was in 1968?
   a. There are significantly higher financial rewards.
   b. There are more blacks playing the game.
   c. Some key rules of play have been changed.
3. Why do some members of minorities have psychological problems playing tennis at private clubs?

Writer's Workshop

In this article Peter Alfano skillfully leads Arthur Ashe through a discussion of his past and at the same time contrasts it with the present. Some things may seem the same today for Arthur Ashe as they did in 1968 and some—or many—things may be different.

Do a compare-and-contrast essay about yourself. Pick a time—say two or three years ago—and find things that are similar in your life now (your personality, your basic direction in life) and things that are significantly different (a specific interest, a career goal). You might want to write your essay using quotations as Peter Alfano did. In other words, write an essay based on an interview with yourself.

Mark Fidrych

Fans filled stadiums to watch him play. And before each pitch, he talked to the ball. Then, a sore arm cut short his career in the major leagues.

Nobody ever rode a higher wave or gave us more
       back of what it taught
Or thought less of it,
Shrugging off the fame it
      brought, calling it "no big deal"   5
And, once it was taken
     away, refusing bitterness with such
Amazing grace.
Absence of damage limits one's perception
       of existence.   10
Suffering, while not to be pursued,
Yields at least what Mark
      termed "trains of thoughts,"
Those late, sad milk runs to Evansville
       and Pawtucket   15
Which he viewed
     not simply as pilgrimages
Of loss, but as interesting trips
In themselves—tickets to ride
     that long dark tunnel through   20
Which everybody—even those less gifted—must sooner
Or later pass
Because, "hey, that's what you call life."

Understanding What You Read

1. What characteristic of Mark Fidrych does poet Tom Clark celebrate in this poem?

2. Fidrych is a rare professional athlete. He started an All-Star game as a rookie—and then never made it through his second season. According to Tom Clark, Mark Fidrych was rare as an ex-athlete, too. Do you agree? Explain your view.

Writer's Workshop

You have twenty-three lines of poetry—or fewer, if you wish. Celebrate an athlete whom you admire. It may be someone you read about once or someone you watch and cheer for today or someone in your own school. In your poem, let your readers know exactly what it is that makes that athlete admirable. See if you can touch on more than the athlete's performance on the field. Avoid writing rhymes because the quest for rhymes may restrict your communicating your meaning.

Ex-Basketball Player

Is there a Flick Webb starring at your school this year?

Pearl Avenue runs past the high-school lot,
Bends with the trolley tracks, and stops, cut off
Before it has a chance to go two blocks,
At Colonel McComsky Plaza. Berth's Garage
Is on the corner facing west, and there,   5
Most days, you'll find Flick Webb, who helps Berth out.

Flick stands tall among the idiot pumps—
Five on a side, the old bubble-head style,
Their rubber elbows hanging loose and low.
One's nostrils are two S's, and his eyes   10
An E and O. And one is squat, without
A head at all—more of a football type.

Once Flick played for the high-school team, the Wizards.
He was good: in fact, the best. In '46
He bucketed three hundred ninety points,   15
A county record still. The ball loved Flick.
I saw him rack up thirty-eight or forty
In one home game. His hands were like wild birds.

He never learned a trade, he just sells gas,
Checks oil, and changes flats. Once in a while,   20
As a gag, he dribbles an inner tube,
But most of us remember anyway.
His hands are fine and nervous on the lug wrench.
It makes no difference to the lug wrench, though.

Off work, he hangs around Mae's Luncheonette.   25
Grease-grey and kind of coiled, he plays pinball,
Sips lemon cokes, and smokes those thin cigars;
Flick seldom speaks to Mae, just sits and nods
Beyond her face towards bright applauding tiers
Of Necco Wafers, Nibs, and Juju Beads.   30

Understanding What You Read

1. Which of the following statements, do you feel, best sums up the theme of this poem?
   a. Great performance in sports comes from hard work.
   b. Some people reach their life's high point while in high school.
   c. The past is always better than the present.

2. What does the poet mean by "The ball loved Flick"?

3. How can the poem's first four lines ("Pearl Avenue . . . Plaza") be seen as a metaphor for Flick Webb's life?

4. What is the point of the last two lines of the fourth stanza ("His hands . . . lug wrench, though")?

5. Which of the following best characterizes the poet's tone in the poem?
   a. Heartily expressed admiration of Flick Webb's basketball ability.
   b. Bitter sarcasm and mockery of Flick Webb.
   c. Sympathy and perhaps some regret at the lack of fulfillment in Flick Webb's adult life.

Writer's Workshop

This poem is set in the late 1940s, after Flick Webb finished high school and began work at Berth's Garage. A lot of things have changed since then, but people like Flick Webb are still around. Would a present-day version of Flick be at work today in a gas station? What do you think he would be doing, maybe bagging groceries in a supermarket?

Try to imagine a present-day Flick Webb and write about him either in a short prose sketch or in a poem. Notice that the poet, John Updike, uses many proper nouns—Pearl Avenue, Berth's Garage, Necco Wafers, Juju Beads—to create for the reader the world Flick lives in. Do the same for the character in your poem or sketch.

Hub Fans Bid Kid Adieu

"The Hub" is Boston. "The Kid" is baseball-great Ted Williams. The occasion is Williams's last at bat in Fenway Park.

F enway Park, in Boston, is a lyric little bandbox of a ball park. Everything is painted green and seems in curiously sharp focus, like the inside of an old-fashioned peeping-type Easter egg. It was built in 1912 and rebuilt in 1934, and offers, as do most Boston artifacts, a compromise between Man's Euclidean determinations and Nature's beguiling irregularities. Its right field is one of the deepest in the American League, while its left field is the shortest; the high left-field wall, three hundred and fifteen feet from home plate along the foul line, virtually thrusts its surface at right-handed hitters. On the afternoon of Wednesday, September 28, as I took a seat behind third base, a uniformed groundkeeper was treading the top of this wall, picking batting-practice home runs out of the screen, like a mushroom gatherer seen in Wordsworthian perspective on the verge of a cliff. The day was overcast, chill, and unin-spirational. The Boston team was the worst in twenty-seven seasons. A jangling medley of incompetent youth and aging competence, the Red Sox were finishing in seventh place only because the Kansas City Athletics had locked them out of the cellar. They were scheduled to play the Baltimore Orioles, a much nimbler blend of May and December, who had been dumped from pennant contention a week before by the insatiable Yankees. I, and 10,453 others, had shown up primarily because this was the Red Sox's last home game of the season, and therefore the last time in all eternity that their regular left fielder, known to the headlines as TED, KID, SPLINTER, THUMPER, TW and, most cloyingly, MISTER WONDERFUL, would play in Boston. "WHAT WILL WE DO WITHOUT TED? HUB FANS ASK" ran the headline on a newspaper being read by a bulb-nosed cigar smoker a few rows away. Williams's retirement had been announced, doubted (he had been threatening retirement for years), confirmed by Tom Yawkey, the Red Sox owner, and at last widely accepted as the sad but probable truth. He was forty-two and had redeemed his abysmal season of 1959 with a—considering his advanced age—fine one. He had been giving away his gloves and bats and had grudgingly consented to a sentimental ceremony today. This was not necessarily his last game; the Red Sox were scheduled to travel to New York and wind up the season with three games there.

I arrived early. The Orioles were hitting fungos on the field. The day before, they had spitefully smothered the Red Sox 17–4, and neither their faces nor their drab gray visiting-team uniforms seemed very gracious. I wondered who had invited them to the party. Between our heads and the lowering clouds a frenzied organ was thundering through, with an appositeness[1] perhaps accidental, "You *maaaade* me love you, I didn't wanna do it, I didn't wanna do it . . ."

The affair between Boston and Ted Williams has been no mere summer romance; it has been a marriage, composed of spats, mutual disappointments, and toward the end, a mellowing hoard of shared memories. It falls into three stages, which may be termed Youth, Maturity, and Age; or Thesis, Antithesis, and Synthesis; or Jason, Achilles, and Nestor.

First, there was the by now legendary epoch when the young bridegroom came out of the West, and announced "All I want out of life is that when I walk down the street folks will say 'There goes the greatest hitter who ever lived.'" The dowagers of local journalism attempted to give elementary deportment lessons to this child who spake as a god, and to their horror were themselves rebuked. Thus began the long exchange of backbiting, hat-flipping, booing, and spitting that has distinguished Williams's public relations. The spitting incidents of 1957 and 1958 and the similar dockside courtesies that Williams has now and then extended to the grandstand should be judged against this background: The left-field stands at Fenway for twenty years have held a large number of customers who have bought their way in primarily for the privilege of showering abuse on Williams. Greatness necessarily attracts debunkers, but in Williams's case the hostility has been systematic and unappeasable. His basic offense against the fans has been to wish that they weren't there. Seeking a perfectionist's vacuum, he has quixotically[2] desired to

---

1 *appositeness:* appropriateness; relevance.

2 *quixotically:* [from *Don Quixote*] foolishly; impractically.

sever the game from the ground of paid spectatorship and publicity that supports it. Hence his refusal to tip his cap to the crowd or turn the other cheek to newsmen. It has been a costly theory—it has probably cost him among other evidences of goodwill, two Most Valuable Player awards, which are voted by reporters—but he has held to it from his rookie year on. While his critics, oral and literary, remained beyond the reach of his discipline, the opposing pitchers were accessible, and he spanked them to the tune of .406 in 1941. He slumped to .356 in 1942 and went off to war.

In 1946, Williams returned from three years as a marine pilot to the second of his baseball avatars,[3] that of Achilles, the hero of incomparable prowess and beauty who nevertheless was to be found sulking in his tent while the Trojans (mostly Yankees) fought through to the ships. Yawkey, a timber and mining maharajah, had surrounded his central jewel with many gems of slightly lesser water, such as Bobby Doerr, Dom DiMaggio, Rudy York, Birdie Tebbetts, and Johnny Pesky. Throughout the late forties, the Red Sox were the best paper team in baseball, yet they had little three-dimensional to show for it, and if this was a tragedy, Williams was Hamlet. A succinct review of the

3 *avatars:* gods come down to earth.

indictment—and a fair sample of appreciative sports-page prose—appeared the very day of Williams's valedictory, in a column by Huck Finnegan in the *Boston American* (no sentimentalist, Huck):

Williams's career, in contrast [to Babe Ruth's], has been a series of failures except for his averages. He flopped in the only World Series he ever played in (1946) when he batted only .200. He flopped in the playoff game with Cleveland in 1948. He flopped in the final game of the 1949 season with the pennant hinging on the outcome (Yanks 5, Sox 3). He flopped in 1950 when he returned to the lineup after a two-month absence and ruined the morale of a club that seemed pennant-bound under Steve O'Neill. It has always been Williams's records first, the team second, and the Sox non-winning record is proof enough of that.

There are answers to all this, of course. The fatal weakness of the great Sox slugging teams was not-quite-good-enough pitching rather than Williams's failure to hit a home run every time he came to bat. Again Williams's depressing effect on his teammates has never been proved. Despite ample coaching to the contrary, most insisted that they *liked* him. He has been generous with advice to any player who asked for it. In an increasingly combative baseball atmosphere, he continued to duck beanballs docilely. With umpires he was gracious to a fault. This courtesy itself annoyed his critics, whom there was no pleasing. And against the ten crucial games (the seven World Series games with the St. Louis Cardinals, the 1948 playoff with the Cleveland Indians, and the two-game series with the Yankees at the end of the 1949 season, winning either one of which would have given the Red Sox the pennant) that make up the Achilles' heel of Williams's record, a mass of statistics can be set showing that day in and day out he was no slouch in the clutch. The correspondence columns of the Boston papers now and then suffer a sharp flurry of arithmetic on this score; indeed, for Williams to have distributed all his hits so they did nobody else any good would constitute a feat of placement unparalleled in the annals of selfishness.

Whatever residue of truth remains of the Finnegan charge, those of us who love Williams must transmute as best we can, in our own personal crucibles. My personal memories of Williams begin when I was a boy in Pennsylvania, with two last-place teams in Philadelphia to keep me company. For me, "W'ms, if" was a figment of the box scores who always seemed to be going 3-for-5. He radiated, from afar, the hard blue glow of high purpose. I remember listening over the radio to the All-Star Game of 1946, in which Williams hit two singles and two home runs, the second one off a Rip Sewell "blooper" pitch; it was like hitting a balloon out of the park. I remember watching one of his home runs from the bleachers of Shibe Park; it went over the first baseman's head and rose meticulously along a straight line and was still rising when it cleared the fence. The trajectory seemed qualitatively different from anything anyone else might hit. For me, Williams is the classic ballplayer of the game on a hot August weekday, before a small crowd, when the only thing at stake is the tissue-thin difference between a thing done well and a thing done ill. Baseball is a game of the long season, of relentless and gradual averaging-out. Irrelevance—since the reference point of most individual games is remote and statistical—always threatens its interest, which can be maintained not by the occasional heroics that sportswriters feed upon but by players who always *care*; who care, that is to say, about themselves and their art. Insofar as the clutch hitter is not a sportswriter's myth, he is a vulgarity, like a writer who writes only for money. It may be that, compared to managers' dreams such as Joe DiMaggio and the always helpful Stan Musial, Williams is an icy star. But of all team sports, baseball, with its graceful intermittences of action, its immense and tranquil field sparsely settled with poised men in white, its dispassionate mathematics, seems to me best suited to accommodate, and be ornamented by, a loner. It is an essentially lonely game. No other player visible to my generation has concentrated within himself so much of the sport's poignance, has so assiduously[4] refined his natural skills, has so constantly brought to the plate that intensity of competence that crowds the throat with joy.

By the time I went to college, near Boston, the lesser stars Yawkey had assembled around Williams had faded, and his craftsmanship, his rigorous pride, had become itself a kind of heroism. This brittle and temperamental player developed an unexpected quality of persistence. He was always coming back—back from Korea, back from a broken collarbone, a shattered elbow, a bruised heel, back from drastic bouts of flu and ptomaine poisoning. Hardly a season went by without some enfeebling mishap, yet he always came back, and always looked like himself. The delicate mechanism of timing and power seemed locked, shockproof, in some case outside his body. In addition to injuries, there were a heavily publicized divorce, and the usual storms with the press, and the Williams Shift—the maneuver, custom-built by Lou Boudreau, of the Cleveland Indians, whereby three infielders were concentrated on the right side of the infield, where a left-handed pull hitter like Williams generally hits the ball. Williams could easily have learned to punch singles through the vacancy on his left and fattened his average hugely. This was what Ty Cobb, the Einstein of average, told him to do. But the game had changed since Cobb; Williams believed that his value to the club and to the game was as a slugger, so he went on pulling the ball, trying to blast it through three men, and paid the price of perhaps fifteen points of lifetime average. Like Ruth before him, he bought the occasional home run at the cost of many directed singles—a calculated sacrifice certainly not, in the case of a hitter as average-minded as Williams, entirely selfish.

---

4 *assiduously:* persistently applied.

. . . .

After a prime so harassed and hobbled, Williams was granted by the relenting fates a golden twilight. He became at the end of his career perhaps the best *old* hitter of the century. The dividing line came between the 1956 and the 1957 seasons. In September of the first year, he and Mickey Mantle were contending for the batting championship. Both were hitting around .350, and there was no one else near them. The season ended with a three-game series between the Yankees and the Sox, and living in New York then, I went up to the Stadium. Williams was slightly shy of the four hundred at-bats needed to qualify; the fear was expressed that the Yankee pitchers would walk him to protect Mantle. Instead, they pitched to him—a wise decision. He looked terrible at the plate, tired and discouraged and unconvincing. He never looked very good to me in the Stadium. (Last week, in *Life,* Williams, a sportswriter himself now, wrote gloomily of the Stadium, "There's the bigness of it. There are those high stands and all those people smoking—and, of course, the shadows. . . . It takes at least one series to get accustomed to the Stadium and even then you're not sure.") The final outcome in 1956 was Mantle .353, Williams .345.

The next year, I moved from New York to New England, and it made all the difference. For in September of 1957, in the same situation, the story was reversed. Mantle finally hit .365; it was the best season of his career. But Williams, though sick and old, had run away from him. A bout of flu had laid him low in September. He emerged from his cave in the Hotel Somerset haggard but irresistible; he hit four successive pinch-hit home runs. "I feel terrible," he confessed, "but every time I take a swing at the ball it goes out of the park." He ended the season with thirty-eight home runs and an average of .388, the highest in either league since his own .406, and, coming from a decrepit man of thirty-nine, an even more supernal[5] figure. With eight or so of the 'leg hits' that a younger man would have beaten out, it would have been .400. And the next year, Williams, who in 1949 and 1953 had lost batting championships by decimal whiskers to George Kell and Mickey Vernon, sneaked in behind his teammate Pete Runnels and filched his sixth title, a bargain at .328.

In 1959, it seemed all over. The dinosaur thrashed around in the .200 swamp for the first half of the

---

5 *supernal:* heavenly.

season, and was even benched ("rested," Manager Mike Higgins tactfully said). Old foes like the late Bill Cunningham began to offer batting tips. Cunningham thought Williams was jiggling his elbows; in truth, Williams's neck was so stiff he could hardly turn his head to look at the pitcher. When he swung, it looked like a Calder mobile with one thread cut; it reminded you that since 1953 Williams's shoulders had been wired together. A solicitous pall settled over the sports pages. In the two decades since Williams had come to Boston, his status had imperceptibly shifted from that of a naughty prodigy to that of a municipal monument. As his shadow in the record books lengthened, the Red Sox teams around him declined, and the entire American League seemed to be losing life and color to the National. The inconsistency of the new superstars—Mantle, Colavito, and Kaline—served to make Williams appear all the more singular. And off the field, his private philanthropy—in particular, his zealous chairmanship of the Jimmy Fund, a charity for children with cancer—gave him a civic presence somewhat like that of Richard Cardinal Cushing. In religion, Williams appears to be a humanist, and a selective one at that, but he and the cardinal, when their good works intersect and they appear in the public eye together, make a handsome and heartening pair.

Humiliated by this 1959 season, Williams determined, once more, to come back. I, as a specimen Williams partisan, was both glad and fearful. All baseball fans believe in miracles; the question is, how *many* do you believe in? He looked like a ghost in spring training. Manager Jurges warned us ahead of time that if Williams didn't come through he would be benched, just like anybody else. As it turned out, it was Jurges who was benched. Williams entered the 1960 season needing eight home runs to have a lifetime total of 500; after one time at bat in Washington, he needed seven. For a stretch, he was hitting a home run every second game that he played. He passed Lou Gehrig's lifetime total, then the number 500, then Mel Ott's total, and finished with 521, thirteen behind Jimmy Foxx, who alone stands between Williams and Babe Ruth's unapproachable, 714. The summer was a statistician's picnic. His two-thousandth walk came and went, his eighteen-hundredth run batted in, his sixteenth All-Star game. At one point, he hit a home run off a pitcher, Don Lee, off whose father, Thornton Lee, he had hit a home run a generation before. The only comparable season for a forty-two-year-old man was Ty Cobb's in 1928. Cobb batted .323 and hit one homer. Williams batted .316 but hit twenty-nine homers.

In sum, though generally conceded to be the greatest hitter of his era, he did not establish himself as "the greatest hitter who ever lived." Cobb, for average, and Ruth, for power, remain supreme. Cobb, Rogers Hornsby, Joe Jackson, and Lefty O'Doul, among players since 1900, have higher lifetime averages than Williams's .344. Unlike Foxx, Gehrig, Hack Wilson, Hank Greenberg, and Ralph Kiner, Williams never came close to matching Babe Ruth's season home-run total of sixty. In the list of major league batting records, not one is held by Williams. He is second in walks drawn, third in home runs, fifth in lifetime averages, sixth in runs batted in, eighth in runs scored and in total bases, fourteenth in doubles, and thirtieth in hits. But if we allow him merely average seasons for the four-plus seasons he lost to two wars, and add another season for the months he lost to injuries, we get a man who in all the power totals would be second, and not a very distant second, to Ruth. And if we further allow that these years would have been not merely average but prime years, if we allow for all the months when Williams was playing in sub-par condition, if we permit his early and later years in baseball to be some sort of index of what the middle years could have been, if we give him a right-field fence that is not, like Fenway's, one of the most distant in the league, and if—the least excusable "if"—we imagine him condescending to outsmart the Williams Shift, we can defensibly assemble, like a colossus induced from the sizable fragments that do remain, a statistical figure not incommensurate with his grandiose ambition. From the statistics that are on the books, a good case can be made that in the *combination* of power and average Williams is first; nobody else ranks so high in both categories. Finally, there is the witness of the eyes; men whose memories go back to Shoeless Joe Jackson—another unlucky natural—rank him and Williams together as the best-looking hitters they have seen. It was for our last look that ten thousand of us had come.

Two girls, one of them with pert buckteeth and eyes as black as vest buttons, the other with white skin and flesh-colored hair, like an underdeveloped photograph of a redhead, came and sat on my right. On my other side was one of those frowning, chestless young-old men who can frequently be seen, often wearing sailor hats, attending ball games alone. He did not once open his program but instead tapped it, rolled up, on his knee as he gave the game his disconsolate attention. A young lady, with freckles and a depressed, dainty nose that by an optical illusion seemed to thrust her lips forward for a kiss, sauntered down into the box seats and with striking aplomb took a seat right behind the roof of the Oriole dugout. She wore a blue coat with a Northeastern University emblem sewed to it. The girls beside me took it into their heads that this was Williams's daughter. She looked too old to me, and why would she be sitting behind the visitors' dugout? On the other hand, from the way she sat there, staring at the sky and French-inhaling, she clearly was *some-body*. Other fans came and eclipsed her from view. The crowd looked less like a weekday ball park crowd than like the folks you might find in Yellowstone National Park, or emerging from automobiles at the top of scenic Mount Mansfield. There were a lot of competitively well-dressed couples of tourist age, and not a few babes in arms. A row of five seats in front of me was abruptly filled with a woman and four children, the youngest of them two years old, if that. Someday, presumably, he could tell his grandchildren that

he saw Williams play. Along with these tots and second-honey-mooners, there were Harvard freshmen, giving off that peculiar nervous glow created when a quantity of insouciance[6] is saturated with insecurity; thick-necked army officers with brass on their shoulders and lead in their voices; pepperings of priests; perfumed bouquets of Roxbury Fabian fans; shiny salesmen from Albany and Fall River; and those gray, hoarse men— taxidrivers, slaughterers, and bartenders—who will continue to click through the turnstiles long after everyone else has deserted to television and trampo-ramas. Behind me, two young male voices blossomed, cracking a joke about God's five proofs that Thomas Aquinas exists—typical Boston College levity.

The batting cage was trundled away. The Orioles fluttered to the sidelines. Diagonally across the field, by the Red Sox dugout, a cluster of men in overcoats were festering like maggots. I could see a splinter of white uniform, and Williams's head, held at a self-dep-recating and evasive tilt. Williams's conversational stance is that of a six-foot-three-inch man under a six-foot ceiling. He moved away to the patter of flash bulbs, and

---

6 *insouciance:* unconcern.

began playing catch with a young Negro outfielder named Willie Tasby. His arm, never very powerful, had grown lax with the years, and his throwing motion was a kind of muscular drawl. To catch the ball, he flicked his glove hand onto his left shoulder (he batted left but threw right, as every schoolboy ought to know) and let the ball plop into it comically. This catch session with Tasby was the only time all afternoon I saw him grin.

A tight little flock of human sparrows who, from the lambent[7] and pampered pink of their faces, could only have been Boston politicians moved toward the plate. The loudspeakers mammothly coughed as someone huffed on the microphone. The ceremonies began. Curt Gowdy, the Red Sox radio and television announcer, who sounds like everybody's brother-in-law, delivered a brief sermon, taking the two words "pride" and "champion" as his text. It began, "Twenty-one years ago, a skinny kid from San Diego, California . . ." and ended, "I don't think we'll ever see another like him." Robert Tibolt, chairman of the board of the Greater Boston Chamber of Commerce, presented Williams with a big Paul Revere silver bowl. Harry Carlson, a member

of the sports committee of the Boston Chamber, gave him a plaque, whose inscription he did not read in its entirety, out of deference to Williams's distaste for this sort of fuss. Mayor Collins presented the Jimmy Fund with a thousand-dollar check.

Then the occasion himself stooped to the microphone, and his voice sounded, after the others, very Californian; it seemed to be coming, excellently amplified, from a great distance, adolescently young and as smooth as a butternut. His thanks for the gifts had not died from our ears before he glided, as if helplessly, into "In spite of all the terrible things that have been said about me by the maestros of the keyboard up there . . ." He glanced up at the press rows suspended above home plate. (All the Boston reporters, incidentally, reported the phrase as "knights of the keyboard," but I heard it as "maestros" and prefer it that way.) The crowd tittered, appalled. A frightful vision flashed upon me, of the press gallery pelting Williams with erasers, of Williams clambering up the foul screen to slug journalists, of a riot, of Mayor Collins being crushed." . . . And they *were* terrible things," Williams insisted, with level melancholy, into the mike. "I'd like to forget them, but I can't." He paused, swallowing his memories,

---

7 *lambent:* bright, radiant.

. . . .

and went on. "I want to say that my years in Boston have been the greatest thing in my life." The crowd, like an immense sail going limp in a change of wind, sighed with relief. Taking all the parts himself, Williams then acted out a vivacious little morality drama in which an imaginary tempter came to him at the beginning of his career and said, "Ted, you can play anywhere you like." Leaping nimbly into the role of his younger self (who in biographical actuality had yearned to be a Yankee), Williams gallantly chose Boston over all the other cities, and told us that Tom Yawkey was the greatest owner in baseball and we were the greatest fans. We applauded ourselves heartily. The umpire came out and dusted the plate. The voice of doom announced over the loudspeakers that after Williams's retirement his uniform number, 9, would be permanently retired—the first time the Red Sox had so honored a player. We cheered. The national anthem was played. We cheered. The game began.

Williams was third in the batting order, so he came up in the bottom of the first inning, and Steve Barber, a young pitcher who was not yet born when Williams began playing for the Red Sox, offered him four pitches, at all of which he disdained to swing, since none of

them were within the strike zone. This demonstrated simultaneously that Williams's eyes were razor-sharp and that Barber's control wasn't. Shortly, the bases were full, with Williams on second. "Oh, I hope he gets held up at third! That would be wonderful," the girl beside me moaned, and, sure enough, the man at bat walked and Williams was delivered into our foreground. He struck the pose of Donatello's David, the third-base bag being Goliath's head. Fiddling with his cap, swapping small talk with the Oriole third baseman (who seemed delighted to have him drop in), swinging his arms with a sort of prancing nervousness, he looked fine—flexible, hard, and not unbecomingly substantial through the middle. The long neck, the small head, the knickers whose cuffs were worn down near his ankles—all these points, often observed by caricaturists, were visible in the flesh.

One of the collegiate voices behind me said, "He looks old, doesn't he, old; big deep wrinkles in his face . . ."

"Yeah," the other voice said, "but he looks like an old hawk, doesn't he?"

With each pitch, Williams danced down the baseline, waving his arms and stirring dust, ponderous but menacing, like an attacking goose. It occurred to about a dozen humorists at once to shout "Steal home! Go, go!" Williams's speed afoot was never legendary. Lou Clinton, a young Sox outfielder, hit a fairly deep fly to center field. Williams tagged up and ran home. As he slid across the plate, the ball, thrown with unusual heft by Jackie Brandt, the Oriole center fielder, hit him on the back.

"Boy, he was really loafing, wasn't he?" one of the boys behind me said.

"It's cold," the other explained. "He doesn't play well when it's cold. He likes heat. He's a hedonist."[8]

The run that Williams scored was the second and last of the inning. Gus Triandos, of the Orioles, quickly evened the score by plunking a home run over the handy left-field wall. Williams, who had had this wall at his back for twenty years, played the ball flawlessly. He didn't budge. He just stood there, in the center of the little patch of grass that his patient footsteps had worn brown, and, limp with lack of interest, watched the ball pass overhead. It was not a very interesting game. Mike Higgins, the Red Sox manager, with nothing to lose, had restricted his major league players to the left-field line—along with

Williams, Frank Malzone, a first-rate third baseman, played the game—and had peopled the rest of the terrain with unpredictable youngsters fresh, or not so fresh, off the farms. Other than Williams's recurrent appearances at the plate, the *maladresse*[9] of the Sox infield was the sole focus of suspense; the second baseman turned every grounder into a juggling act, while the shortstop did a breathtaking impersonation of an open window. With this sort of assistance, the Orioles wheedled their way into a 4–2 lead. They had early replaced Barber with another young pitcher, Jack Fisher. Fortunately (as it turned out), Fisher is no cutie; he is willing to burn the ball through the strike zone, and inning after inning this tactic punctured Higgins's string of test balloons.

Whenever Williams appeared at the plate—pounding the dirt from his cleats, gouging a pit in the batter's box with his left foot, wringing resin out of the bat handle with his vehement grip, switching the stick at the pitcher with an electric ferocity—it was like having a familiar Leonardo appear in a shuffle of *Saturday Evening Post* covers. This man, you realized— and here, perhaps, was the difference, greater than the difference in gifts—really

---

8 *hedonist:* pleasure-lover.

9 *maladresse:* clumsiness.

intended to hit the ball. In the third inning, he hoisted a high fly to deep center. In the fifth, we thought he had it; he smacked the ball hard and high into the heart of his power zone, but the deep right field in Fenway and the heavy air and a casual east wind defeated him. The ball died. Al Pilarcik leaned his back against the big "380" painted on the right-field wall and caught it. On another day, in another park, it would have been gone. (After the game, Williams said, "I didn't think I could hit one any harder than that. The conditions weren't good.")

The afternoon grew so glowering that in the sixth inning the arc lights were turned on—always a wan sight in the daytime, like the burning headlights of a funeral procession. Aided by the gloom, Fisher was slicing through the Sox rookies, and Williams did not come to bat in the seventh. He was second up in the eighth. This was almost certainly his last time to come to the plate in Fenway Park, and instead of merely cheering, as we had at his three previous appearances, we stood, all of us—stood and applauded. Have you ever heard applause in a ball park? Just applause—no calling, no whistling, just an ocean of hand-claps, minute after minute, burst after burst, crowding and running together in continuous succession like the pushes of surf at the edge of the sand. It was a somber and considered tumult. There was not a boo in it. It seemed to renew itself out of a shifting set of memories as the kid, the marine, the veteran of feuds and failures and injuries, the friend of children and the enduring old pro evolved down the bright tunnel of twenty-one summers toward this moment. At last, the umpire signaled for Fisher to pitch; with the other players, he had been frozen in position. Only Williams had moved during the ovation, switching his bat impatiently, ignoring everything except his cherished task. Fisher wound up, and the applause sank into a hush.

Understand that we were a crowd of rational people. We knew that a home run cannot be produced at will; the right pitch must be perfectly met and luck must ride the ball. Three innings before, we had seen a brave effort fail. The air was soggy; the season was exhausted. Nevertheless, there will always lurk, around a corner in a pocket of our knowledge of the odds, an indefensible hope, and this was one of the times, which you now and then find in sports, when a density of expectation hangs in the air and plucks an event out of the future.

Fisher, after his unsettling wait, was wide with the first pitch. He put the second one over, and Williams swung mightily and missed. The crowd grunted, seeing that classic swing, so long and smooth and quick, exposed, naked in its failure. Fisher threw the third time, Williams swung again and there it was. The ball climbed on a diagonal line into the vast volume of air over center field. From my angle, behind third base, the ball seemed less an object in flight than the tip of a towering, motionless construct, like the Eiffel Tower or the Tappan Zee Bridge. It was in the books while it was still in the sky. Brandt ran back to the deepest corner of the outfield grass; the ball descended beyond his reach and struck in the crotch where the bullpen met the wall, bounced chunkily, and, as far as I could see, vanished.

Like a feather caught in a vortex, Williams ran around the square of bases at the center of our beseeching screaming. He ran as he always ran out home runs—hurriedly, unsmiling, head down, as if our praise were a storm of rain to get out of. He didn't tip his cap. Though we thumped, wept, and chanted "We want Ted" for minutes after he hid in the dugout, he did not come back. Our noise for some seconds passed beyond excitement into a kind of immense open anguish, a wailing, a cry to be saved. But

immortality is nontransferable. The papers said that the other players, and even the umpires on the field, begged him to come out and acknowledge us in some way, but he never had and did not now. Gods do not answer letters.

Every true story has an anticlimax. The men on the field refused to disappear, as would have seemed decent, in the smoke of Williams's miracle. Fisher continued to pitch, and escaped further harm. At the end of the inning, Higgins sent Williams out to his left-field position, then instantly replaced him with Carrol Hardy, so we had a long last look at Williams as he ran out there and then back, his uniform jogging, his eyes steadfast on the ground. It was nice, and we were grateful, but it left a funny taste.

One of the scholasticists behind me said, "Let's go. We've seen everything. I don't want to spoil it." This seemed a sound aesthetic decision. Williams's last word had been so exquisitely chosen, such a perfect fusion of expectation, intention, and execution, that already it felt a little unreal in my head, and I wanted to get out before the castle collapsed. But the game, though played by clumsy midgets under the feeble glow of the arc lights, began to tug at my attention, and I loitered in the runway until it was over. Williams's homer had, quite incidentally, made the score 4–3. In the bottom of the ninth inning, with one out, Marlin Coughtry, the second-base juggler, singled. Vic Wertz, pinch-hitting, doubled off the left field wall, Coughtry advancing to third. Pumpsie Green walked, to load the bases. Willie Tasby hit a double-play ball to the third baseman, but in making the pivot throw Billy Klaus, an ex-Red Sox infielder, reverted to form and threw the ball past the first baseman and into the Red Sox dugout. The Sox won, 5–4. On the car radio as I drove home I heard that Williams had decided not to accompany the team to New York. So he knew how to do even that, the hardest thing. Quit.

Understanding What You Read

1. What does John Updike mean when he calls the Baltimore Orioles a "much nimbler blend of May and December" than the Red Sox?

2. Updike writes, "But of all team sports, baseball, with its graceful intermittences of action, its immense and tranquil field sparsely settled with poised men in white, its dispassionate mathematics, seems to me best suited to accommodate, and be ornamented by, a loner. It is an essentially lonely game." Why does Updike say this? Do you agree or disagree? Support your answer.

3. John Updike, a poet, short-story writer, novelist, and literary critic, is a master of using figurative language to bring alive his writing. What does he mean when he says the Red Sox's "second baseman turned every grounder into a juggling act, while the shortstop did a breathtaking impersonation of an open window"?

4. What does Updike mean when he says of Ted Williams's refusal to take a final bow after his homerun, "Gods do not answer letters"?

Writer's Workshop

In this essay John Updike used a dozen similes and metaphors; he pitches them at us, to use a simile, like so many unexpected curve balls over the plate. Describing fans seated near him at the game, Updike says, "Two girls, one of them with pert buckteeth and eyes as black as vest buttons, the other with white skin and flesh-colored hair, like an underdeveloped photograph of a red-head, came and sat on my right."

Describe two people or two objects in terms of something else—in other words, use similes or metaphors the way Updike used similes to describe the two girls.

To an Athlete Dying Young

Can an early death be looked on favorably? A poet ponders the question.

The time you won your town the race
We chaired you through the market place;
Man and boy stood cheering by,
And home we brought you shoulder-high.

Today, the road all runners come,   5
Shoulder-high we bring you home,
And set you at your threshold down,
Townsman of a stiller town.

Smart lad, to slip betimes away
From fields where glory does not stay   10
And early though the laurel grows
It withers quicker than the rose.

Eyes the shady night has shut
Cannot see the record cut,
And silence sounds no worse than cheers   15
After earth has stopped the ears:

Now you will not swell the rout
Of lads that wore their honors out,
Runners whom renown outran
And the name died before the man.   20

---

11. *laurel:* a flower symbolizing victory.
17. *rout:* a disorderly retreat.

So set, before its echoes fade,
The fleet foot on the sill of shade,
And hold to the low lintel up
The still-defended challenge-cup.

And round that early-laureled head   25
Will flock to gaze the strengthless dead,
And find unwithered on its curls
The garland briefer than a girl's.

---

23. *lintel:* the crossbar above a door.
28. *garland:* a wreath of flowers.

Understanding What You Read

1. What caused the celebration narrated in stanza 1?
2. What is being referred to in stanza 2? Remember figurative, or nonliteral, language. What might "the road all runners come" be? Why is the person being talked of now a "Townsman of a stiller town"?
3. Why does A. E. Housman call the lad (stanza 3) "smart"? Why was it "smart" to be an "athlete dying young"? Support your answer with references to the poem.

Writer's Workshop

In this poem the author takes a point of view about athletes who die young. In a short essay or poem, take your own point of view on some aspect of life—it doesn't have to be sports—and argue it well. Stay on only one side of the issue as Housman takes only one point of view here, lamenting "Runners whom reknown outran/ And the name died before the man."

Clemente!

*A believer—but, more important—someone who acted on his beliefs,
Roberto Clemente died at the age of 38 trying to help the victims of an
earthquake in Nicaragua.*

In a treatise about his own breed, Paul Gallico once said that sports writers are often cynics[1] because they "learn eventually that, while there are no villains, there are no heroes either." But, he warned, "until you make the final discovery that there are only human beings, who are therefore all the more fascinating, you are liable to miss something."

Roberto Clemente Walker[2] of Puerto Rico—the first Latin American to enter baseball's Hall of Fame—was a fascinating human being. And if, as Gallico observes, there are no heroes, there are men who achieve deeds of heroic dimension. Roberto Clemente was one of these gifted few.

---

1 *cynics:* fault-finders; those with a low opinion of human nature.

2 *Walker:* In the United States *Walker* was incorrectly used as Roberto's middle name. It was actually his second surname. Hispanic people use the surnames of both parents, with *Clemente*, the father's first, followed by *Walker*, his mother's maiden name.

"Without question the hardest single thing to do in sport is to hit a baseball," says the great Boston slugger Ted Williams. "A .300 hitter, that rarest of breeds, goes through life with the certainty that he will fail at his job seven out of ten times." A baseball is a sphere with a diameter of $2^7/_8$ inches. The batter stands at home plate and grips a tapering wood cylinder that has a maximum diameter of $2^3/_4$ inches; he tries to defend a strike zone that is approximately seven baseballs wide and eleven high. The pitcher, from $60^1/_2$ feet away, throws the ball at a speed of about 90 miles per hour. As it spins toward the plate—hopping, sinking, or curving—the hitter has four-tenths of one second to decide whether he should let it pass by, jump away to avoid being maimed, or swing. To get "good wood" on it, he must connect squarely with a $3/_4$-inch portion of the ball's round surface—and then hope that none of the nine defensive players catches it. Roberto

Clemente had enormous success in this complex, difficult task. In September, 1972, when he smashed his 3,000th hit, he scaled a peak where only ten other men in the hundred-year history of baseball ever set foot. In his eighteen years as a major league player, he made a memorable impact upon a great sport. A lifetime average of .317, four league batting championships, a Most Valuable Player award, and twelve Golden Gloves for superior defensive play are just a few souvenirs that attest to his marvelous talent. During the 1971 World Series, his devastating *tour de force,*[3] witnessed by millions on television, at last evoked the national recognition that he felt was long overdue. Roger Angell, in his superb book *The Summer Game,* says, "Now and again— very rarely—we see a man who seems to have met all the demands, challenged all the implacable averages, spurned the mere luck. He has defied baseball, even altered it, and for a time at least the game is truly his." During the 1971 World Series, and on many other occasions, the game was Roberto Clemente's.

But these great moments cost him dearly. Another famous Latin, Enrico Caruso, once said, "To be great, it is necessary to suffer."

Roberto Clemente endured severe physical pain and sacrificed a good portion of his life to perfect his skills.

There is much more to a great athlete than the one-dimensional view of his performance on the playing field. Roberto Clemente was a human being like all the rest of us, but when you peel away from each man the frailties that we share, there is a residue[4] that defines each man's uniqueness.

The classical poets of ancient Greece would have rejoiced over Roberto Clemente. Unlike the Goliath-sized supermen of basketball and football, his physique was a nearly perfect match for the "normal" ideal that one sees in time-weathered marble friezes and statues. He was strikingly handsome, with a superbly sculpted body: five feet, eleven inches tall, one hundred and eighty pounds, broad-shouldered with powerful arms and hands, slender of waist, fleet of foot. His simple, traditional values might seem hopelessly naïve to the cynic, but they would have inspired the ancient lyricists. He saw himself as a fine craftsman and viewed his craft, baseball, as deserving of painstaking labor. He believed passionately in the virtue and dignity of hard work. He believed, with equal fervor, that a

---

3 *tour de force:* feat of strength or skill.

4 *residue:* the remainder; what is left.

. . . .

man should revere his parents, his wife and children, his country, and God. But he was not a docile man. He believed just as fiercely in his personal worth and integrity. "From head to toes, Roberto Clemente is as good as the President of the United States," he proclaimed. "I believe that, and I think every man should believe that about himself."

It was this belief that caused Roberto Clemente to become deeply involved during a period of major social change, the 1950s and 1960s, when black and Spanish-speaking people quickened their pace in the struggle for equality. That long march is far from over, but Clemente's brilliance in his craft and his unyielding demands for respect off the field advanced the cause by great distances. His immense pride in his Puerto Rican heritage and in his blackness inspired many others to hold their own heads high.

Those who knew Roberto Clemente offer an appealing portrait of a remarkable man: a serious artist who wrote his own style of poetry in the air, with powerful strokes of a bat, leaping catches, and breathtaking throws; a man with an enormous well of sentiment, who could inspire tears and could himself be driven to tears by symbolic gestures of kindness and nobility; a man whose temper was quick and terrible like a tropical storm, but who bore no grudge; a man with an almost childlike zest for life, who spoke from the heart and damn the consequences; a man with a very special sense of humor that he shared with only a few friends. But above all, in talking with the people whose lives were touched by Roberto Clemente—in Puerto Rico, in the spring training camp at Bradenton, Florida, in Pittsburgh—one hears of the empathy, the deep concern for others, the concern that moved him one rainy New Year's Eve to fly off on a mission to help others, and to perish in the effort. In her book *Nobody Ever Died of Old Age,* Sharon R. Curtin tells of an elderly woman who "was near the end of her life and had never experienced magic, never challenged the smell of brimstone, never clawed at the limit of human capability." In his all-too-brief life—in those rich, eventful thirty-eight years—Roberto Clemente experienced magic often, and others felt his magic. He knew many people, some for only a brief time, whom he touched very deeply. Through them, he touched me, too.

Understanding What You Read

1. Kal Wagenheim quotes Paul Gallico in the first paragraph. What is Gallico's point? Put the quotation in your own words.

2. What is the effect of Wagenheim's description of the measurements of a baseball? Why did Wagenheim include them?

3. Roberto Clemente is quoted as saying, "From head to toes, Roberto Clemente is as good as the President of the United States. I believe that, and I think every man should believe that about himself." In your opinion, was Clemente being arrogant or simply proud? Explain.

4. In addition to Clemente's athletic skills, what characteristics of the man does Wagenheim admire?

Writer's Workshop

Choose a person whom you admire, either in or out of sports, and write a character sketch of that person. Include at lease two anecdotes that reveal your subject's personality. Use these to support any general statements. If your subject is someone you don't know personally, you may have to do some research to find the anecdotes.

• CHAPTER FOUR •

Parents and Children

Parents pass along not only height and eye color to their children but values and principles, too. In this chapter you'll read about parents and children engaged in sports and interacting, sometimes even competing.

Donald Hall believes that "fathers playing catch with sons" is a kind of metaphor for an ideal relationship. Robert D. Behn, on the other hand, sees this treasured connection broken by distorted values. Tracee Talavera is eager to make the sacrifices necessary to become a topflight gymnast, but her parents are not. Tom Wicker discovers in his son a previously unrevealed competence and a sense of command.

As in the other chapters of this book, you'll find something of yourself in these pages, something that may transcend sports.

Fathers Playing Catch with Sons

"Baseball is fathers and sons," says poet and essayist Donald Hall, who finds meaning in one generation tossing a ball to another.

My father and I played catch as I grew up. Like so much else between fathers and sons, playing catch was tender and tense at the same time. He wanted to play with me. He wanted me to be good. He seemed to *demand* that I be good. I threw the ball into his catcher's mitt. Attaboy. Put her right there. I threw straight. Then I tried to put something on it; it flew twenty feet over his head. Or it banged into the sidewalk in front of him breaking stitches and ricocheting off a pebble into the gutter of Greenway Street. Or it went wide to his right and lost itself in Mrs. Davis's bushes. Or it went wide to his left and rolled across the street while drivers swerved their cars.

I was wild, I was *wild.* I had to be wild for my father. What else could I be? Would you have wanted me to have *control?*

But I was, myself, the control on him. He had wanted to teach school, to coach and teach history at Cushing Academy in Ashburnham, Massachusetts, and he had done it for two years before he was married. The salary was minuscule and in the twenties people didn't get married until they had the money to live on. Since he wanted to marry my mother, he made the only decision he could make: he quit Cushing and went into the family business, and he hated business, and he wept when he fired people, and he wept when he was criticized, and his head shook at night, and he coughed from all the cigarettes, and he couldn't sleep, and he almost died when an ulcer hemorrhaged when he was forty-two, and ten years later, at fifty-two, he died of lung cancer.

But the scene I remember—at night in the restaurant, after a happy, foolish day in the uniform of a Pittsburgh Pirate—happened when he was twenty-five and I was almost one year old. So I do not "remember" it at all. It simply rolls itself before my eyes with the intensity of a lost memory suddenly found again, more intense than the moment itself ever is.

It is 1929, July, a hot Saturday afternoon. At the ballpark near East Rock, in New Haven Connecticut, just over the Hamden line, my father is playing semipro baseball. I don't know the names of the teams. My mother has brought me in a basket, and she sits under a tree, in the shade, and lets me crawl when I wake up.

My father is very young, very skinny. When he takes off his cap—the uniform is gray, the bill of the cap blue—his fine hair is parted in the middle. His face is very smooth. Though he is twenty-five, he could pass for twenty. He plays shortstop, and he is paid twenty-five dollars a game. I don't know where the money comes from. Do they pass the hat? They would never raise so much money. Do they charge admission? They must charge admission, or I am wrong that it was a semipro and that he was paid. Or the whole thing is wrong, a memory I concocted. But of course the reality of 1929—and my mother and the basket and the shade and the heat—does not matter, not to the memory of the living nor to the bones of the dead nor

even to the fragmentary images of broken light from that day which wander light-years away in unrecoverable space. What matters is the clear and fine knowledge of this day as it happens now, permanently and repeatedly, on a deep layer of the personal Troy.[1]

There, where this Saturday afternoon of July in 1929 rehearses itself, my slim father performs brilliantly at shortstop. He dives for a low line drive and catches it backhand, somersaults, and stands up holding the ball. Sprinting into left field with his back to the plate, he catches a fly ball that almost drops for a Texas leaguer. He knocks down a ground ball, deep in the hole and nearly to third base, picks it up, and throws the man out at first with a peg as flat as the tape a runner breaks. When he comes up to bat, he feels lucky. The opposing pitcher is a side-armer. He always hits side-armers. So he hits two doubles and a triple, drives in two runs and scores two runs, and his team wins 4 to 3. After the game a man approaches him, while he stands, sweating and tired, with my mother and me in the shade of the elm tree at the rising side of the field. The man is a baseball scout. He offers my father

---

1 *Troy:* ancient city of Homeric epic, discovered in 1873 by Heinrich Schliemann under the layers of later cities.

a contract to play baseball with the Baltimore Orioles, at that time a double-A minor league team. My father is grateful and gratified; he is proud to be offered the job, but he must refuse. After all, he has just started working at the dairy for his father. It wouldn't be possible to leave the job that had been such a decision to take. And besides, he adds, there is the baby.

My father didn't tell me he turned it down because of me. All he told me, or that I think he told me: he was playing semipro at twenty-five dollars a game; he had a good day in the field, catching a ball over his shoulder running away from the plate; had a good day hitting, too, because he could always hit a side-armer. But he turned down the Baltimore Oriole offer. He couldn't leave the dairy then, and besides, he knew that he had just been lucky that day. He wasn't really that good.

But maybe he didn't even tell me that. My mother remembers nothing of this. Or rather she remembers that he played on the team for the dairy, against other businesses, and that she took me to the games when I was a baby. But she remembers nothing of semipro, of the afternoon with the side-armer, of the offered contract. Did I make it up? Did my father exaggerate? Men tell stories to their sons, loving and being loved.

I don't care.

Baseball is fathers and sons. Football is brothers beating each other up in the backyard, violent and superficial. Baseball is the generations, looping backward forever with a million apparitions of sticks and balls, cricket and rounders, and the games the Iroquois played in Connecticut before the English came. Baseball is fathers and sons playing catch, lazy and murderous, wild and controlled, the profound archaic song of birth, growth, age, and death. This diamond encloses what we are.

This afternoon—March 4, 1973—when I played ball and was not frightened, I walked with the ghost of my father, dead seventeen years. The ballplayers would not kill me, nor I them. This is the motion, and the line that connects me now to the rest of the world, the motion past fear and separation.

Understanding What You Read

1. Why do you think Donald Hall felt that "like so much else between fathers and sons, playing catch was tender and tense at the same time"?

2. Do you agree with Hall's appraisal of father-and-son relationships? Why or why not?

3. Why did Donald Hall's father quit teaching?

4. Why did Donald Hall's father not accept a contract to go into professional baseball?

Writer's Workshop

In 500 to 750 words of prose, capture a scene between parent and child (it doesn't have to involve sports) that reflects what you think of as a universal moment. You're writing about the kind of experience that Donald Hall says reflects "The profound archaic song of birth, growth, age, and death," an experience that connects the child "to the rest of the world, the motion past fear and separation."

So that the task doesn't seem too overwhelming, think of it this way: If you write about something that meant a great deal to you, you can probably be assured that you weren't the first person to experience such a moment. Your story, then, should have the kind of universality Hall writes of.

Tracee

There are no days off on the road to the Olympics, and that's the way Tracee wanted it.

Dawn breaks chilly and damp, and Tracee Talavera feels crummy. Her muscles ache, her throat is sore, she has a slight headache. She would like to stay burrowed in this warm bed in this cozy room crowded with five other girls and dozens of cuddly stuffed animals. From the muffled groans around her, she can tell that the others feel the same way.

She sits up. There are no days off on the road to the Olympics. Besides, she thinks, a crummy day may be just what she needs. She's been feeling too good lately. Maybe she needs the experience of working out while she feels bad.

That way, if she goes to a championship meet with a sore throat and a headache she'll be prepared. The difference between winning and losing in gymnastics is sometimes just a sneeze, a twitch, a frown. Maybe this lousy day will pay off.

The difference between Tracee Talavera and the millions of other teenaged girls who do gymnastics is more than muscle strength and balance and coordination. It is the willingness to get up at 4:45 A.M. no matter how she feels, and, perhaps even more important, the motivation to find a golden glimmer in a gray funk.

By 6 A.M. Tracee and the other young Elite (top competitive level) gymnasts who live together are limbering up for their daily workout in a chilly, chalk-dusty gym in Eugene, Oregon. If Tracee is still feeling crummy, she isn't showing it. Once warmed up, she races across the gym, somersaults over a leather vaulting horse, and plunges into a pond of foam rubber.

She bounds to her feet and glances at coach Dick Mulvihill for approval. He turns away from Tracee to watch another girl.

Tracee's expression hardens, her eyes narrow. She jogs back to her starting position, waits until Mulvihill is looking at her, then starts again, charging down the narrow runway, leaping into the air, flipping over the horse. This time, as she rises from the foam,

Mulvihill is nodding at her. Tracee smiles. She hurries away to try it again.

"She's hungry," says Mulvihill, a few minutes later. We are standing together in the gym as the camera crew shoots Tracee making an entry in the precise workout journal that every serious gymnast keeps. "She's the first one on the apparatus and just about the last to leave. She sets the pace for all the kids and she hustles all the time."

"Hunger, is that what you look for in a beginning gymnast?" I ask Mulvihill.

"I like to look at their eyes," he says. "If they're looking around and they sort of have a hungry, steely, squinty look, like they're sizing up the other girls."

"You sound like a prizefight manager," I say.

"I used to box myself," he says.

Six hundred miles away, Tracee's parents, Nancy and Rip Talavera, are just getting up. They think about Tracee every day, and their thoughts are mixed with pride and sorrow.

"Tracee went up to Eugene when she was eleven," says Nancy. "She's now sixteen. We've lost five years of her youth that we can never regain. It's a situation where you've given your child to someone else to raise and it's a loss."

Tracee calls home once a week from Eugene, and chitchats with her mother about grandma, the pets, neighbors. Nancy always felt it was important to keep Tracee up to date on family trivia so she wouldn't feel like a stranger when she came home. But Rip rarely talks to Tracee when she calls. He says it's too painful, he misses her so much. And Rip seems to be protecting himself from further hurt when he says, "In fact, when she does come back, it really is disappointing, because she's not the kid who left here." When I ask him about the eleven-year-old Tracee who left, his voice cracks. "That's like a dream."

Allowing Tracee to leave home was an emotionally painful decision, and an expensive one. It cost almost $10,000 a year in tuition and living expenses for Tracee to attend Mulvihill's National Academy of Artistic Gymnastics. And the decision was a gamble—balanced against the hope that Tracee would become a champion was the fear that she could be physically hurt or become psychologically stunted, a gym rat instead of a well-rounded person.

But the Talaveras had been heading toward that decision ever since Tracee was an infant, a nonstop crib bouncer, living-room rug flipper, a trampoline tumbler. She was pure energy looking for an outlet.

She found that outlet when she was five. Like millions of others around the world, she was captivated by Olga Korbut, the tiny gymnast from the Soviet Union who won a gold medal in the 1972 Olympics. Watching the Games on television, Tracee, and her sister, Coral, who was eight, determined to become gymnasts, too.

This wasn't as easy in 1972 as it would become a few years later when children's gymnastics classes sprang up like fast-food franchises. The Talaveras found no lessons available in San Francisco. They enrolled their daughters in acrobatics classes (after a year, the girls complained that the classes weren't "hard enough"), in ballet ("too slow"), and trampoline, before they eventually found a gymnastics club south of the city.

In the next few years, gymnastics came to dominate the Talaveras' family life. The girls moved up the levels of competition and their parents became their cheerleaders, chauffeurs, trainers. They searched for better coaching. They found a good coach in Walnut Creek, a suburb within driving distance of their San Francisco home. After a while, they moved to Walnut Creek.

During summer vacations, they traveled to Eugene so the girls could work out with Mulvihill and his wife, Linda Metheny, a gymnast in three Olympics.

Both sisters were strong and light for their body size, graceful, energetic, and talented. But Tracee had the kid sister advantage of growing up with an older, more advanced gymnast; whatever Coral learned, Tracee learned, too. She also had what one Japanese coach called "konjo," an inner drive, a fighter's fire to keep going, to never quit.

In 1976, Nadia Comaneci of Rumania replaced Olga Korbut as the Olympic gymnastic darling and all over the world strong little girls fantasized about replacing Nadia. Tracee's potential was recognized. She was a California champion at nine, she was on track to the Olympic trials. Excitement grew in the Talavera household. If Tracee continued to develop, she might be the darling of the 1980 Olympics in Moscow. When the girls' Walnut Creek coach left California for a better job, Tracee and Coral went to live at the Academy in Eugene, to train full time with Mulvihill.

"She was the imp," remembers Mulvihill. "The vivacious little teeny-bopper that darted around and really didn't know what was going on but was having a good time."

Coral was injured and became discouraged. She left after a year. The Talaveras thought that Tracee would come home, too, but she stayed. She began winning local, state, and regional titles. She won two United States championships and a bronze medal at the World Games in Moscow. She won a place on the 1980 Olympic team.

She also seemed to flourish in the cloistered life at the Academy, a carefully regulated existence that allows no dating and hardly any activities beyond gymnastics and regular public school. Even school was bent around gymnastics. Tracee attended only three or four classes a day, mostly math, English, and foreign languages. She got credit for gym, music, art, and social studies because of gymnastics and the international travel—she got to China, Japan, and Europe even if she never got to the school cafeteria.

"Sometimes you wish you could go to dances and football games and people's parties and stuff," says Tracee, "but then you sort of think, well, I'm getting more out of life right now than they are and I can always go to parties later. So it's sort of . . . it's worth it, I think."

The girls of the Academy work out six days a week, three on the compulsory exercises that every gymnast must perform in competition, three days for the optional exercises that each performs to show off her own particular strength. Six hours a day of the

vaulting horse and the tumbling mat and the uneven parallel bars and the balance beams, the endless floor routines practiced until each muscle has a memory of its own, pushing through pain and boredom and the low days when the coach scowls or, worse, ignores her, coming back after sprained ankles and pulled muscles and torn tendons and broken toes, ignoring the clouds of chalk dust and the chilly dawns and the constant "rips," the little skin tears in the palm that plague most gymnasts.

Many girls drop out of high-level competitive gymnastics, particularly those who have been pushed by their parents after their own interest waned. Some of those girls, afraid to confront their parents, will "eat their way out" of competition, or purposely get hurt.

Tracee's conflict was different. Her passion for gymnastics was growing, even as her parents began to doubt that her life was taking the right course.

In the summer of 1980, Tracee's world came apart. First, President Carter canceled United States participation in the Olympics; there would be no trip to Moscow, no chance to become the first American female gymnast to ever win an Olympic medal, no shot at becoming the imp of the world.

Then, her father demanded that

she leave the Academy and come home to stay.

"She was hooked on gymnastics, she wanted to do gymnastics at all costs," explains Rip now. He wanted her to concentrate on her studies so she could attend a good college. "Tracee has to be prepared for life, and gymnastics isn't going to prepare her for life. It's a good experience in life, but it's not what's essential. Nobody is going to ask her how her double back was when she's looking for a job."

Tracee came home to Walnut Creek in the fall of 1980. She was fourteen. She never stopped nagging her mother and father to send her back to Eugene.

"She made it sufficiently tough," says Nancy, "that my husband and I let her go back. We wanted it to work so bad, but she didn't want it to work. She'd go to a local gym and she'd complain about everything."

Nancy's eyes fill with tears when she remembers the four months that Tracee was home. "She made us feel guilty that she wasn't doing her gymnastics in what she felt was the best place. Anytime there was a little problem, she'd say, 'Well, in Eugene we did it like this.'"

Nancy and Rip wanted Tracee to lead a "normal" life. But Walnut Creek wasn't "normal" for Tracee anymore.

"My gymnastics wasn't going anywhere," remembers Tracee. "I wanted to come back the whole time."

"She made it real impossible," says Rip. The final incident was a meet in Oakland, California. Coach Mulvihill was there, and Rip couldn't help noticing their easy rapport, how Tracee brightened up. After four months, Rip gave up and let Tracee return to Eugene.

"My dad just got sick of my nagging," says Tracee.

When she said that, she gave a little laugh. It sounded cold. I wondered how much guilt might be behind that little laugh. Tracee wanted to become the best that she could be, she obviously burned to be great. Her parents were ambitious for her, too. And yet, the pride they all felt was mixed with so much pain. They had all made sacrifices so Tracee could go for the gold.

When I interviewed Rip in the fall of 1982, he said that he no longer pays any money to the Academy. Coach Mulvihill would not discuss his financial arrangements. But there was no doubt that Tracee was a prime attraction at the Academy. Her picture was on the cover of Academy publications, her poster was on sale in the office. The Academy has a local booster club of people who donate money.

I wondered how many Eugene girls attended classes at the Academy because Tracee was there. How many girls from other cities came to live at the Academy because they dreamed of becoming Olympians, too.

But staying there may be harder than getting there.

"It's not for everyone," says Tracee. We're sitting in the upstairs living room of the Mulvihill house rather than the downstairs lounge area of the dormitory, because one of the girls is sick and we don't want to disturb her. The interview, one of an increasing number that Tracee undergoes, is just an interruption in this day that broke chill and damp and crummy. After her workout, she lifted weights, jogged, and went to school.

Meanwhile, six hundred miles to the south, Rip and Nancy are thinking about her, wishing they were there to monitor her studies, wondering if the Mulvihills care as much about her life outside gymnastics as they do.

Rip thinks about the addiction to glory, and what will happen to her psyche and her body as she pounds away toward the next Olympics. Nancy thinks about what will happen to her when her gymnastics career is over.

"I've seen a lot of kids who haven't had the same success they had as a gymnast feel they're a fail-ure," she says. "A couple of kids have gone anorexic[1] because they're still striving to be that cute little gymnast that they were at eleven and twelve and thirteen and now they're seventeen and they're not getting that attention."

The family is still deeply involved in gymnastics. Coral coaches at her college, Nancy judges meets, and Rip teaches at a small local club. He says he is more relaxed with other people's daughters than he ever was with his own.

"So I lose Tracee," he says, glancing around the gym, "but I got about thirty other kids here that I work with. So these are like my, you know, almost like my family."

Nancy nods when I ask her if she ever thinks about that decision they made years ago to let their daughters become gymnasts, and the decisions that followed to let Tracee devote her life to it. "She had a talent and we were lucky enough to be able to let her pursue it. I don't think what we've done would be much different than what most parents would do. Most parents want to do what's best for

---

1 *anorexic:* affected with anorexia nervosa, a psychological disorder, primarily among young women, characterized by fear of gaining weight, and often leading to malnutrition and excessive weight loss.

their kids. And I feel that's what we've done."

Back in Eugene, Tracee does her homework, has supper with the other girls, then watches some television, "General Hospital" or another soap taped earlier in the day. She will go to sleep early. She has to get up tomorrow morning at 4:45.

"Some girls just can't take it," said Tracee when I saw her. "First of all, they're used to their own rooms. They're used to, like, having the whole room, everything of theirs and they get this little space."

She talked about the trouble she has readjusting to her parents' house when she returns a few times a year on brief vacations.

"It's really weird going back home," she says. "You know, here, all fourteen of us go here, then all fourteen go there. It's done in such large groups and like at home I'm sort of by myself a lot. And you know, there's only four people in my family so it's just like, gosh it's so empty you know, there's no one there."

But in June of 1983, Tracee responded to her parents' wishes and came home again. Her grandmother was dying and her father, Rip, was more upset than ever by Tracee's absence.

Tracee settled into the life of the family. She spent the summer working out in the gym where Rip volunteered. She still planned to try out for the Olympic team.

Was Tracee going to stay home this time? The last time I called, her mother's voice sounded uncertain as she said, "I'm keeping my fingers crossed."

Understanding What You Read

1. What is the main reason Tracee Talavera has to awaken every morning at 4:45?
   a. To get her schoolwork done before practice
   b. To get to practice, because at her level of skill every practice session counts
   c. She has practice at 5 A.M.

2. What is **konjo**? Did Tracee have this characteristic? Explain.

3. Why was 1980 a particularly bad year for Tracee Talavera? Give two reasons.

Writer's Workshop

1. Where do your emotions go in this piece of writing? Do you think Tracee's father is right in wanting her to come home and live a more well-rounded life, or do you think Tracee is right in her determination to be the best she can be in gymnastics? Support your point of view as strongly and effectively as you can in an essay of about 500 to 750 words.

2. Do you think Tracee Talavera is a spoiled brat with an obsession? Or is she a hard-driving dedicated person? Convince your reader in an essay of 500 to 750 words. In your essay consider the following question: What responsibility does a person have to develop his or her abilities?

That Dark Other Mountain

A father and his son go mountain climbing.

My father could go down a mountain faster than I
Though I was first one up.
Legs braced or with quick steps he slid the gravel slopes
Where I picked cautious footholds.

Black, Iron, Eagle, Doublehead, Chocorua   5
Wildcat and Carter Dome—
He beat me down them all. And that last other mountain
And that dark other mountain.

Understanding What You Read

1. In what way does the poet use mountain climbing to capture both a young person's and an older person's characteristics?

2. What is "that dark other mountain"? What words in the poem helped you to determine this?

Writer's Workshop

The mountain in this poem represents more than a heap of rock, dirt, and ice. It has a larger meaning. It is a symbol for life. But notice that the mountain does not lose its actuality for the poet; it is still a mountain. Choose some other object—a tree, an automobile, a clock—or some other action—laughing, washing your hands, throwing a Frisbee—and try to suggest a larger meaning from it in a brief poem.

Playing to Win

A mother sees the intensity in her athlete daughter, an intensity that affects the entire family.

My daughter is an athlete. Nowadays, this statement won't strike many parents as unusual, but it does me. Until her freshman year in high school, Ann was only marginally interested in sport of any kind. When she played, she didn't swing hard, often dropped the ball, and had an annoying habit of tittering on field or court.

Indifference combined with another factor that did not bode well for a sports career. Ann was growing up to be beautiful. By the eighth grade, nature and orthodontics had produced a 5-foot 8-inch, 125-pound, brown-eyed beauty with a wonderful smile. People told her, too. And, as many young women know, it is considered a satisfactory accomplishment to be pretty and stay pretty. Then you can simply sit still and enjoy the unconditional positive regard. Ann loved the attention too, and didn't consider it demeaning when she was awarded "Best Hair," female category, in the eighth-grade yearbook.

So it came as a surprise when she became a jock. The first indication that athletic indifference had ended came when she joined the high school cross-country team. She signed up in early September and ran third for the team within three days. Not only that. After one of those 3.1-mile races up hill and down dale on a rainy November afternoon, Ann came home muddy and bedraggled. Her hair was plastered to her head, and the mascara she had applied so carefully that morning ran in dark circles under her eyes. This is it, I thought. Wait until Lady Astor sees herself. But the kid with the best eighth grade hair went on to finish the season and subsequently letter in cross-country, soccer, basketball, and softball.

I love sports, she tells anyone who will listen. So do I, though my midlife quest for a doctorate leaves me little time for either playing or watching. My love of sports is bound up with the goals in my life and my hopes for my three daughters. I have begun to hear the message of sports. It is very different from many messages that women receive about living, and I think it is good.

My husband, for example, talked to Ann differently when he realized that she was a serious competitor and not just someone who wanted to get in shape so she'd look good in a prom dress. Be aggressive, he'd advise. Go for the ball. Be intense.

Be intense. She came in for some of the most scathing criticism from her dad, when, during basketball season, her intensity waned. You're pretending to play hard, he said. You like it on the bench? Do you like to watch while your teammates play?

I would think, how is this kid reacting to such advice? For years, she'd been told at home, at school, by countless advertisements, "Be quiet, Be good, Be still." When teachers reported that Ann was too talkative, not obedient enough, too flighty. When I dressed her up in frilly dresses and admonished her not to get dirty. When ideals of femininity are still, quiet, cool females in ads whose vacantness passes for sophistication. How can any adolescent girl know what she's up against? Have you ever really noticed intensity? It is neither quiet nor good. And it's definitely not pretty.

In the end, her intensity revived. At half time, she'd look for her father, and he would come out of the bleachers to discuss tough defense, finding the open player, squaring up on her jump shot. I'd watch them at the edge of the court, a tall man and a tall girl, talking about how to play.

Of course, I'm particularly sensitive at this point in my life to messages about trying hard, being active, getting better through individual and team effort. Ann, you could barely handle a basketball two years ago. Now you're bringing the ball up against the press. Two defenders are after you. You must dribble, stop, pass. We're depending on you. We need you to help us. I wonder if my own paroxysms[1] of uncertainty would be eased had more people urged me—be active, go for it!

Not that dangers don't lurk for the females of her generation. I occasionally run this horror show in my own mental movie theater: an unctuous[2] but handsome lawyerlike drone of a young man spies my Ann. Hmmm, he says, unconsciously to himself, good gene pool, and wouldn't she go well with my BMW and the condo? Then I see Ann with a great new

---

1 *paroxysms:* sudden or violent emotions.

2 *unctuous:* smug and falsely earnest.

hairdo kissing the drone goodby-honey and setting off to the nearest mall with splendid-looking children to spend money.

But the other night she came home from softball tryouts at 6 in the evening. The dark circles under her eyes were from exhaustion, not makeup. I tried too hard today, she says. I feel like I'm going to puke.

After she has revived, she explains. She wants to play a particular position. There is competition for it. I can't let anybody else get my spot, she says, I've got to prove that I can do it. Later we find out that she has not gotten the much-wanted third-base position, but she will start with the varsity team. My husband talks about the machinations[3] of coaches and tells her to keep trying. You're doing fine, he says. She gets that I-am-going-to-keep-trying look on her face. The horror-show vision of Ann-as-Stepford-Wife fades.

Of course, Ann doesn't realize the changes she has wrought, the power of her self-definition. I'm an athlete, Ma, she tells me when I suggest participation in the school play or the yearbook. But she has really caused us all to rethink our views of existence: her younger sisters who consider sports a natural activity for females, her father whose advocacy of women has

3 *machinations:* crafty actions and schemes.

increased, and me. Because when I doubt my own abilities, I say to myself, Get intense, Margaret. Do you like to sit on the bench?

And my intensity revives.

I am not suggesting that participation in sports is the answer for all young women. It is not easy—the losing, jealousy, raw competition and intense personal criticism of performance.

And I don't wish to imply that the sports scene is a morality play either. Girls' sports can be funny. You can't forget that out on that field are a bunch of people who know the meaning of the word cute. During one game, I noticed that Ann had a blue ribbon tied on her ponytail, and it dawned on me that every girl on the team had an identical bow. Somehow I can't picture the Celtics gathered in the locker room of the Boston Garden agreeing to wear the same color sweatbands.

No, what has struck me, amazed me and made me hold my breath in wonder and in hope is both the ideal of sport and the reality of a young girl not afraid to do her best.

I watch her bringing the ball up the court. We yell encouragement from the stands, though I know she doesn't hear us. Her face is red with exertion, and her body is concentrated on the task. She dribbles, draws the defense to her, passes, runs. A teammate passes the ball back to her. They've beaten the press. She heads toward the hoop.

Her father watches her, her sisters watch her, I watch her. And I think, drive, Ann, drive.

Understanding What You Read

1. How did the way Ann grew up conflict with her need to be "intense" on the athletic field in order to succeed there?

2. In the "horror show in my own mental movie theater" that the narrator describes, what is it that she fears for her daughter's future? Be specific.

3. How did Ann's becoming an athlete affect the attitudes of the following:
     a. her younger sisters
     b. her father
     c. her mother

4. After this essay was published in a magazine, this letter-to-the-editor from Malvine Cole of Jamaica, Vermont, was printed:

As a competitive swimmer when I was a girl, I lived for those moments when, body poised, toes tingling, I would hear the official intone: "Judges and timers ready? On your mark, get set . . ." I would crack-splash into the pool and go for it, to the piercing cries of my mother, at the pool's edge: "C'mon Mal!" Between events, my father would boast, in my presence, "You should see that kid swim!"

I had to swim, I had to win because I was loved for doing—for winning—and not for being who I was otherwise. This feeling has shadowed me since.

So I must caution Mrs. Whitney to relax about her daughter the athlete, and make it clear that she loves her on the court and off, when she wins or loses.

What is the letter-writer's point? Do you think it is something Mrs. Whitney should be concerned about? Why or why not?

Writer's Workshop

1. Capture in words an intense moment you have had in sports—a moment where you were giving your all, totally caught up in the action and needs of that moment, the way Ann was portrayed in the last paragraph of this piece .

2. If you are a girl and you can relate to Ann and "the ideal of sport and the reality of a young girl not afraid to do her best," explain how you came to know that feeling. Describe at least two incidents that capture the experience you have had.

"Can't Anybody Here Play This Game?"

One of the joys of growing older is being able to wag your finger at the younger generation.

It used to be that on the Fourth of July you'd see doubleheaders in the major league ballparks—and, in the parks and backyards all over the country, fathers and sons throwing the ball back and forth. But while some fathers will be traipsing off to the ballparks with their sons to watch single games, you won't see much of that other tradition vital to this country's heritage.

Yuppie[1] fathers and modern kids—well, they just hardly know how to throw and play catch anymore. As Casey Stengel said of the once inept Amazin' Mets, "Can't anybody here play this game?"

Some see this neglect of catch as part of the widespread view that America's youth is in ruins. Young people cannot add three-digit numbers without a pocket calculator. They use drugs. They think Japan is located between Britain and Egypt—you know, just south of Mexico City.

It's true that many teenage boys know as much about baseball as they know about cricket.

Still, watch many a male adolescent try to throw a baseball. Some throw off the wrong foot. Some fail to follow through. Many are off balance. Few can throw a ball with a smooth, fluid motion. And when they try to catch the ball, they stab at it.

The reason for these shortcomings is simple: They have not done it enough to become proficient.

When we (the model generation for America) grew up, we all knew about baseball. We learned about the game on the radio—from such announcers as Red Barber, Russ Hodges, Mel Allen, or Curt Gowdy.

And we learned to throw and catch by, well, throwing and catching. Even those of us who could never make the team knew how to perform these vital functions.

---

1 *yuppie:* a *y*oung *u*rban *p*rofessional; term is usually used negatively.

That was really the American pastime—playing catch. It is simple to do. You do not need much space. All you really need is two people, two gloves and one ball. You can do it for a few minutes or for hours.

But it is only through days, weeks, and months of playing catch that you feel the rhythm, the union of the two players, the sense of surmounting klutziness.

Today, however, America's youth plays video games. They ride skateboards. They may kick a soccer ball a little or practice their slam dunk. But when was the last time you saw some kids in your neighborhood playing catch?

"Baseball is fathers and sons," wrote the poet Donald Hall. "Baseball is fathers and sons playing catch, the long arc of the years between."

But the arc has been broken. Fathers, it seems, no longer play catch with their sons. One reason for this is obvious: There are simply fewer fathers around. Playing catch is not likely to be a central activity in a one-parent family.

Yet, even when father and son live under the same roof, there may not be two baseball gloves in the basement. There may be a videocassette recorder, running shoes, 10-speed bikes, and squash rackets.

But when was the last time you saw a mail-order catalogue that offered a baseball glove? Yuppies are not into baseball gloves.

(Last summer, for my wife's birthday, my son and I gave her a new baseball glove. But then, she can throw a baseball better than most teenage boys.)

On this day, we celebrate baseball: the Giants play the Cubs in San Francisco, the Mets host the Cincinnati Reds, the Yankees play the Rangers in Texas, the Boston Red Sox take on the Royals in Kansas City, and the sons of the Boys of Summer, the Los Angeles Dodgers, play the Cardinals in Los Angeles.

And yet, to boys nowadays, summer is not only synonymous with baseball. Not only is the significance of July being lost—so too is the how and the why of that essential pregame warm-up: playing catch.

It's a connection between kids, between fathers and sons, with forgotten moments of coordination, with hot dogs and beer, with the Fourth of July, with America.

Understanding What You Read

1. Which of the following statements best describes the tone of Robert D. Behn's essay?
    a. He is sympathetic to the problems faced by modern youth.
    b. He teases the present generation about losing touch with the past.
    c. He applauds youth for the progress they have made in sports.
    d. He views playing catch as a boring pastime.

2. What reasons does Behn give for the decline of "fathers and sons playing catch"?

3. This essay was published on the Fourth of July. Why is that an appropriate day for this kind of writing?

Writer's Workshop

1. Write an essay of your own in reply to Robert D. Behn's essay. If you disagree with him, offer reasons to back up your opinions. If you agree, add some examples of your own to his.

2. Although you lack the perspective of age, you have probably noticed changes that have occurred in the relationships of parents and their offspring since you were a child. Some of these changes you may regret. Others, you may applaud. Write an essay in which you describe the more significant changes and explain how you feel about them.

See How They Run

The Boston Marathon sees Johnny Burke running in place of his father.

T he bus stopped at the side of the road opposite the country lane, and as he waited for the door to open, Johnny Burke could see the farmhouse and the sea of parked cars in the yard beyond.

"It's going to be hot out there today," the driver said. "And, brother, I sure don't envy you any. When I go twenty-six miles I want to do it sitting down."

Johnny swung to the ground, leather carryall in hand. The smell of the countryside was fresh and fragrant in his nostrils, but he knew the driver was right. It would be hot. In the seventies now by the feel of it. He was right about the twenty-six miles too. Why anyone should want to run that distance had always been a mystery that not even his father could satisfactorily explain.

Going up the lane he remembered the farmhouse from that other trip, years ago, but he did not remember the yard. Like a picnic ground or Gypsy carnival, with the relatives of the contestants milling around and laughing and eating basket lunches. Already there were some who stood about in track suits and sweaters, and Johnny Burke smiled a little scornfully. Coming here that other time with his father he had been thrilled and excited, but that, he realized now, was because he had been so young.

On the porch of the rambling farmhouse which had for this one day been turned into the marathon headquarters of the world, the hubbub of voices lay thick about him. Inside there would be places to change, for his father had told him how the furniture would be carted to the barn beforehand. Somehow this seemed as fantastic as the crowd outside or the race itself. Why should the owner turn her house inside out for a couple hundred maniacs? A Mrs. Tebeau, the papers had said. And although she was seventy-three years old she had, with the help of her daughter, served as hostess to the marathoners for sixteen years, furnishing sandwiches and milk for all who wanted them.

He noticed the girl as he climbed the steps. She was standing a few feet away, talking to some man; a slim, straight, pleasant-faced girl, looking strangely out of place here with her trim, heather-colored suit. She glanced toward him as he stopped, and smiled, and it was such a friendly smile that he smiled back and felt a sudden tingling ripple through him.

"Aren't you Johnny Burke?" The man, moving forward now, was a lank, lazy-looking individual, all but his eyes, which were blue and quizzical[1] and direct. "I thought so," he said when Johnny nodded. "I saw you at the Intercollegiates last year. That was a nice mile you ran. I'm Dave Shedden, of the *Standard*."

Johnny shook hands and thanked him. Shedden glanced at a list in his hand.

"So you're the John Burke that entered this year? We thought it was your dad. This would have been his twentieth."

"He couldn't make it," Johnny said, and then, because he could not explain: "So I thought I'd come up and take his place."

"It'll take some running to do that."

"So I understand."

"And what about the invitation mile in New York tomorrow?"

"I'm passing it up."

"Oh? I thought that was sup-

posed to be your dish."

Johnny began to dislike Shedden. There was an undertone of sarcasm in his words, a skepticism that Johnny found annoying.

"I'd rather win this," he said.

"Just like that?"

"Don't you think I can?"

"Could be." Shedden shrugged. "Only you're stepping out of your class, aren't you? You won't be running against a select little group of college boys today."

Johnny gave him back his sardonic[2] grin. "Select, maybe; but they all know how to run or they couldn't get entered."

"They've got reputations, you mean," Shedden said. "Well, out here a guy needs more than that. It's pretty tough on prima donnas."

Johnny let it go and would have moved on had it not been for a sturdy, bronzed man of forty-five or so who bustled up to take the reporter's arm.

"Hey, Dave, where's Burke? You seen Burke anywhere?"

"This is Burke," said Shedden, and Johnny saw the man's wide-eyed glance and then his grin.

"Johnny Burke!" he was pumping Johnny's hand now and slapping his shoulder. "Young Johnny, huh? I'm Tom Reynolds. I've run with your old man for nineteen years. Did he ever tell you? Where is he? Is he quittin'? Old age getting

---

1 *quizzical:* inquisitive, questioning.

2 *sardonic:* mocking, sarcastic.

. . . .

him? . . . Oh, Kay."

And then, miraculously, the girl Johnny had been watching was standing in front of him. Her hand was firm and warm in his and he saw that there were auburn lights in her dark hair, that her nose was cute and lightly freckled.

"I saw you in the meet at the Garden two years ago," she said. "And I think it's grand, your running in place of your father today. He wanted to make it twenty races in a row, didn't he? And I heard what you said to Mr. Shedden about the race in New York. Will you mind so awfully?"

Johnny Burke said he wouldn't. He was used to the idea now, but two weeks ago it had been different. He had not known until then that his father would never run again, and he remembered too vividly coming down the stairs with the doctor that evening and going out on the porch where, with the darkness masking their faces, they had talked of Johnny, senior, and the verdict had been given. No more than six months, the doctor said. Probably not that.

It had been a bad night for Johnny, and before he fell asleep at dawn he knew what he wanted to do. His father, not yet aware how sick he was, had entered the marathon months before, and so, the next afternoon, Johnny told him he was going to use that entry

and run this year's race by proxy and make the record an even twenty.

Even now he could see the thin wan face brighten as his father lay there in bed with the pillows propping him up.

"You will? You'll take my place?" he'd said. "Honest, Johnny?" And then, thinking, the doubt had come. "But the race in New York you've been talking about? That's the next day."

"The invitation mile?" Johnny had said. "What's that? I've beaten all those guys before, one time or another."

"You could win that race, though."

"I'll win the marathon too."

His father had laughed at that. "You're crazy! I only won twice in nineteen years and I was better than most."

"Ah, you were never anything but a fair country runner."

"I could outrun you the best day you ever saw," his father had cracked, and Johnny had jeered at him past the hardness in his throat because he saw how good it made his father feel.

There had been but two weeks in which to train, and he had worked diligently, following the schedule his father mapped out, wanting to cry sometimes when he saw how thrilled and proud his father seemed when he listened to the nightly reports. Johnny had worked up to twenty miles the day before yesterday, and when his father heard the time he admitted that Johnny might have a chance.

"Only don't try to win it, Johnny," he said. "This is no mile. You've been running races where only the first three places count. In this one the first thirty-five get listed in the papers."

Johnny hadn't argued then, nor had he told anyone the truth.

He knew how the newspapers would pounce on the sentimental elements of the story if they knew his father had run his last race. Not even his father must know that. And there was no sacrifice involved anyway. He had looked forward to that New York race, but he was glad to run this race instead, for he loved his father and knew how much this day meant to him each year.

He saw that Shedden and Tom Reynolds had moved on and realized the girl was waiting for him to speak. "No, I don't mind," he said again. "I've been arguing with Dad for years about this race and now I want to find out for myself."

"Arguing?"

"I can't figure it out. Dad has won twice, but in the past ten years he hasn't even been in the first five."

"My father hasn't been in the first five lately either."

"That's what I mean. Twenty-six miles, three hundred and eighty-five yards is an awful grind. If a guy feels he can't win–"

"You think no one should enter unless he feels he can win?"

"Not unless he's young and on the way up. There's maybe a dozen runners in the bunch. The rest of it's a farce." She looked at him strangely, but he did not notice and waved his hand to include the yard and farmhouse. "Look at them," he said, and in his laugh there was something superior, unconscious perhaps, but noticeable, for his was the viewpoint of one who has been at the top. "Anybody can get in that mails in an entry. Anybody."

"Yes," Kay Reynolds said. "It's a poor man's race. You don't have to go to college or belong to any club, and there's nothing in it but a medal and a cup if you win. And yet they've been running this race for over forty years. There have been marathons ever since the Greeks defeated the Persians."

"Sure," Johnny said. "But why do they let all the clowns in? I read in the paper about some of them that even smoke–"

"Benny 'Cigars' Kelly and Jim 'Tobacco' Lane."

"Yes," Johnny said. "And the papers say they flatfoot the whole distance, puffing cigars and making faces at the crowd."

"Yes," Kay Reynolds said, "there are clowns. There always are in any event that's truly open. And there is Clarence De Mar, who is fifty-two and has won seven times. And Kennedy. He's fifty-seven. He's run twenty-eight times and finished twenty-seven races. And Semple, who's been running for twenty-four years. And your father and mine. That's why the papers call this race the biggest and freest sport spectacle on earth. Did you ever run before a half-million people?"

Johnny looked at her then. Her eyes were steady now and she wasn't smiling. "That's a lot of people," he said, and grinned. "Let's settle for a spectacle."

"But still a little beneath you."

Johnny's grin went away and his cheeks got hot. Who did she think she was, bawling him out? "What difference does it make? If a couple hundred fellows want to come out and run twenty-six miles, that's their business. I didn't come up here to make a spectacle; I came to win a race."

"Yes," the girl said, not looking at him now, and distance in her voice. "And I can see why you think you will. You've had every advantage, haven't you? The best coaches, and trainers and special food and privileges and expense money. These others have nothing but enthusiasm and determination.

They are self-taught and trained and what food they get they work for six days a week."

"Okay," said Johnny, "I'm a snob. I came up to run this race, but I don't have to like it." He turned away, stopped to say stiffly: "It's nice to know you'll be rooting for me."

"I will," Kay Reynolds said, "because I'll be remembering your father, like thousands of others. I only hope you can do as well today as he would if he were here."

Johnny went inside, red-faced and angry, and the sight that met his eyes served only to heighten the irritation and bear out his argument. Like a side show at a circus. Skins of every shade from skim milk to chocolate. Fuzzy-chinned kids, gray-thatched and bald-topped oldsters; fat boys with pillow stomachs and skinny ones with pipestem legs.

He made his way into a side room that smelled of wintergreen oil and stale perspiration and old shoes. He found a place to sit down and began to change, not listening to the babble about him until someone addressed him.

"Your first race?" The thin Yankee drawl came from a blond, shaggy-haired fellow beside him. "It's my fifth. My name's Bronson."

Johnny had to take the outthrust hand. "Burke," he said.

"Not Johnny Burke's boy?" Bronson's face lit up. "Hey, fellows! What do you think? This is Johnny Burke's boy."

They flocked about him then, fifteen or twenty of them, shaking hands and asking questions and wanting to know about his father and wishing him luck. And though he was proud of his father when he heard their tributes, he was scornful, too, because, of the group, only a few made mention of his own achievements; even then the others did not seem impressed, cataloguing him not as Johnny Burke who'd done a 4:10 mile but only as Johnny Burke's boy.

"I'll never forget him," Bronson said as they went out on the porch. "Hadn't been for your dad I'd never finished my first race. I was down around Lake Street, running about twentieth when your dad came up. You know they got official cars that have paper cups of water and lemon halves and things like that to hand out when you need 'em, but they're catering to the leaders mostly. And I think I'm about done when a car comes past and your dad hollers and they pull alongside to give him a cup of water and he douses it on my head." Bronson grinned. "I finished. Twenty-third."

Johnny looked at him. "Did you ever win?"

"Oh, no. Finished ninth once, though. Got me a medal for it. I figure to be in the first ten this year too. Look, I'd like you to meet my wife. She's heard me talk about your dad–" He turned and was waving to someone, and Johnny Burke saw the sturdy apple-cheeked girl on the running board of a five-year-old sedan. She had a child on her knee and waved back. Johnny drew away, confused and a little embarrassed.

"Thanks," he said, "but hadn't we better get along to the starting line? Where you from?" he asked, to change the subject.

"Over Pittsfield way. Got a farm there."

"That's quite a jaunt, isn't it?"

"Oh, no. Lots come from Canada, even. We make a day of it. Start early, you know, and stop for a bite somewhere."

"And drive back afterwards?"

"You bet. Alice now, that's my wife, will ride along after we start and find some spot down around Brookline to watch the fellows go by; then she'll pick me up at Exeter Street after I finish. The official car'll have our bags all there waiting for us; and say–" He smiled with some embarrassment. "I guess you know a lot more about running than I do, but if this is your first marathon–well, I don't want to try and tell you, but don't let these front runners bother you. It's an awful long haul and –"

Johnny signed. "I guess I can make out," he said, and then Tom Reynolds was there, looking bronzed and sturdy and fit, Johnny thought, like his father before that illness came.

"Been looking for you." He took Johnny's arm and drew him aside. "Don't let any of those fancy Dans fool you after we start. They'll dance away from the rest of us for three or four miles and then they'll get a stitch and get picked up by the Red Cross car and watch the rest of the race over a tailboard. They're like some of the other phonies."

"I'll remember," Johnny said, but Reynolds wasn't through.

"Your old man and I've been doing this for nineteen years. This was to be our last—we're no Clarence De Mars or Bill Kennedys—and we're old enough to quit. But now you've got to take old Johnny's place. Stick with me. I know the pace."

Johnny nodded his thanks. "We'll see," he said. "I never ran the course, but I think I can go the distance all right." Funny. To hear them talk you'd think he wasn't even going to finish without everybody helping him. "I'll make out."

"Sure you will. And say, Coolidge Corner in Brookline was always a bad spot for Johnny and me. That's gettin' near the end, you know, with lots of autos around, and not bein' front runners we couldn't always count on an official car bein' near. So Kay's always been there since she was a little girl, with lemon halves in case we needed 'em. She'll have one for you today." He paused and Johnny's glance faltered before the steady eyes because it seemed as though Reynolds had read his thoughts. "But maybe you won't need anything," he said abruptly. "Anyway, good luck."

The starter got them away promptly at the stroke of twelve and down the lane they went, stretched clear across its width and fifteen or twenty deep. To Johnny, it was nothing but a mob and he moved out briskly to get away from the dust and jostling.

By the time he reached the main highway he was running fifth and satisfied with his position, and for a while then he did not think about the race, but only how he felt. He felt good. Loose, with lots of juice in his flat-muscled body and an easy animal grace that brought the road back under him in long effortless strides. He didn't think about his pace until he heard someone pounding up beside him and then a voice in his ear.

"Easy, son." It was Tom Reynolds and he looked worried.

"This is no mile."

Johnny nodded, a little irritated that this man should tell him how to run. He shortened his stride slightly and fell off the pace. Two chunky individuals went by him, one young and one old, flat-footed runners, making it tough for themselves already. Another came alongside, a string bean with pasty skin and a handkerchief, knotted at the corners, on his head, to keep the sun off.

He saw that Tom Reynolds was at his shoulder and thought about his advice. He thought of other things Tom Reynolds did not know about. He'd grown up knowing of this hobby of his father's, and how he trained, and hearing over and over the details of all the B.A.A.[3] marathons. As a boy the race had seemed a colorful and exciting climax that he might sometime reach himself, but later, as he grew older and there were no more victories for his father, the idea of this annual contest had become an object of secret ridicule. Even his mother had sometimes acted ashamed in those last few years before her death. It wasn't dignified for a man of his age, she said. And what did he get out of it? It was probably the other women in her bridge club, Johnny thought, who asked her

questions that she could not answer because she herself did not know why her husband ran on, year after year.

His own training had started while he was a junior in high school, and he could remember his father making him jog along with him sometimes, short distances at first, and working up in easy stages until he could do three or four loping miles without too much uneasiness. He had never lost a race in high school, and in college, though he was the son of a machinist and had to earn part of his expenses, he had become a figure of some importance on the campus solely because of the training his father had given him. That's why he was running today: to pay back a little of what he owed while it would do some good.

He saw now that they were running through a town and knew it must be Framingham. About five miles, he guessed, and he still felt good and there was no tightness in his lungs. There were crowds along the curbing now and he could hear them yelling encouragement up ahead of him. Then he was going by the checking station and from somewhere at the side he heard a roar that made him smile.

"Yeah, Burke," they said, and he waved back, thinking of the times he'd heard that same cry in the Sta-

---

3 *B.A.A.:* Boston Athletic Association.

dium and Franklin Field and in the Garden.[4]

He thought then of Tom Reynolds and glanced over his shoulder. Runners were strung out behind him as far as he could see, but Reynolds was not among them and he knew he must have stepped up his pace while he had been thinking.

Well, that was all right. There were other things Reynolds did not know. He and Bronson and those runners who had shaken hands. Some had probably never heard of him because they had no racing interest but the marathon distance; the others who knew of his reputation—Shedden, the reporter, and Kay Reynolds included—did not give him a chance. To them he was just another miler, and a cocky one at that.

Perhaps he was. And this race was as he'd always maintained in good-natured arguments with his father: a bunch of screwballs out to make an exhibition of themselves for the most part, with a dozen or so real runners in the pack. Well, he was running this one race and he was going to win it and that would be that. What the others did not know was that even while he was in college he had often trained with his father during vacations,

_____

4 *Stadium and Franklin Field and in the Garden:* sites of athletic contests.

sometimes driving the car slowly behind him to protect him from the other cars along the road, and sometimes jogging alongside him, mile after mile. He knew what it was to go twenty miles—he'd once gone twenty-five. Today he was going to do twenty-six miles and three hundred and eighty-five yards.

He brought the race back into the focus of his thoughts and found himself approaching the center of Natick with perhaps ten miles behind him. Across the square some enthusiasts had stretched a banner as a token of encouragement for a local contestant and as Johnny drew near he heard his name called from the edges of the road and found the tribute a cheerful sound, warmly stimulating. But the race was already taking its toll of impudent front runners. Of the dozen or more who had been in front of him, seven had dropped out. Approaching Wellesley he saw the pasty fellow with the handkerchief on his head sitting at the roadside waiting for a lift.

"Blisters," he said as Johnny went by. "Terrible blisters," he said, and waved cheerfully.

Along by the college the girls were out in force. Bright-faced, smiling girls in sweaters and gay skirts and saddle-strapped shoes. There would be girls like that in New York tomorrow night, and though he would not run he would be there for the meet and the parties and dancing afterward. He'd get the four o'clock down this afternoon, and Stan Tarleton would meet him, and with no racing tomorrow he could step out.

"Halfway," he said as he passed the checking station and took stock of himself and the race.

He was breathing pretty well, but he could feel his legs and the pounding of the pavement now, realizing that the roadbed was a lot harder on his feet than a cinder track. He lengthened his stride for a hundred yards to get a kink out of his right thigh and it went away all right and he dropped back to his former pace.

Between Wellesley and Auburndale two runners passed him and he let them go. Like the third quarter in a mile run, he thought, when it's still a long way to the end, but you have to keep the pace up. He was conscious of the heat now and it was harder to breathe. The pain was coming slowly, not real bad yet, but frightening when he counted the miles. Eighteen behind him. The hills of Newton and eight more to go.

The first hill seemed endless, slowing him down until he was practically walking at the top. Then, not sure how much longer he could go, he gained the downslope and his strength came back

and he was struggling upward again. Gradually, as he fought that rise, a curious giddiness he had never experienced before came upon him and he did not know he was walking until he heard someone speak his name.

"Come on, young Johnny," the voice said. "Only a couple more hills to go."

It was an effort for Johnny to put the voice and the tanned blond face together and then, through the curtain of his giddiness, he knew it was Bronson, and picked up his stride again to match the other. The car, coming up from behind, meant nothing to him until there came a sudden icy shock upon his head and the feel of water trickling through his hair and down his neck. Then, abruptly, his giddiness had gone and he saw Bronson grinning at him, an empty paper cup in his hand as the official car moved on ahead.

"Thanks," Johnny Burke said. "I guess it was the heat." And he was both grateful and angry with himself for not remembering that in this race there were accompanying cars and refreshments for those lucky enough to get them.

"Sure," Bronson said. "Let's go now."

He started out in front, grinning over his shoulder, and Johnny went after him, seeing the other draw ahead until he realized that a country boy from Pittsfield was showing him his heels; then he pulled his shoulders back a little and sardonic resentment at his near collapse kept him dogging Bronson's footsteps all the way up the College hill and down the long slope to Cleveland Circle.

Here it was flat and he knew there were only five miles to go. The pain was coming again and a numbness crept along his legs and he thought, *It's like the last lap*, and then a new and horrible awareness came to him and he forgot the man up ahead. This last-lap pain for him had never lasted longer than a minute or so; now it must go on for five more miles.

"You went out a little fast, boy. You got anything left?"

Tom Reynolds was at his shoulder, though he seemed a block away. His face was twisted and set, too, but he was breathing all right and his stride was firm and solid.

"Sure I've got something left." Johnny got the words out one at a time, laboriously, angrily.

"Show me. Come on. Match me for a hundred strides. Your old man could do it if he was here."

Anger drove Johnny Burke along for quite a while. He matched Tom Reynolds' pace, forgetting the torture in his lungs and the aching numbness in his legs. He wanted to talk back to this man who drove him on, but he knew he could not speak, and kept pounding on, not counting the strides any longer but always matching them until, somewhere down along the misty row of faces on the curbstone, Reynolds spoke again.

"This is the place," he said heavily. "This is where your dad and I always find out who's the better man each year. You're on your own now, Johnny Burke."

He moved out in front then, Reynolds did, an inch at a time, and Johnny saw the number on his back pull away and dissolve into soft focus. Somewhere, dim and thin and faraway, he could hear the voice of the crowd. "Come on, Burke," it said.

And he kept on, holding his own as a new nausea began to fasten about his stomach. Not cramps, but a simple sickness he could not understand until he realized that over the past few miles the poisonous smell of automobile exhausts had become much stronger as traffic increased. The thought that a contest must be run under such conditions infuriated him, and yet, even as he raged, he knew that this was but another hazard in the race to be shared by all who dared to try it.

For a step or two he ran bent over to see if this would help. There were more people here, he knew, and he could see some kind of square with shops and store fronts and streetcar tracks down the middle of the street. He staggered finally, fighting the nausea rather than his weariness. He looked about for an official car and found none near him. Then, his stride breaking now, he saw something loom out from the edge of the crowd. A hand found his and a girl's voice was in his ear.

"Suck on this," it said. "It's not far now. You can do it."

There was something in his hand and he put it to his lips and there was a tart strong taste of lemon in his mouth, laving his throat and starting the saliva again. He felt it going down his throat, the quick contraction of his stomach. He sucked greedily, breathing around the lemon, and gradually his head cleared and the nausea fled and there was nothing left but the pain and torment that come near the end for every runner who goes all out.

Someone drew alongside him. He could hear the slap of shoes against the asphalt pavement. The sound angered him and he pulled away, finding the strength somehow and knowing then that he was running better.

Up ahead he saw a bobbing figure and focused on it, watching it come nearer, drawing even and then hearing Bronson's voice as he went past: "Give it to 'em, Burke! Give 'em hell for me!"

Vaguely he remembered passing someone else, for the sound of labored breathing was not his own, and as he came into the approach of Kenmore Square he saw a familiar number just ahead and then he was matching strides with Tom Reynolds.

"Go on," the older man called, though it must have been an effort now. "What're you waitin' for? It's only a mile and you've got two ahead of you."

He saw them out in front as he pulled away from Reynolds. They were running shoulder to shoulder, raggedly, and he set out after them, blindly in his exhaustion, yet no longer worried or afraid. His running was detached, all but the torment of pain in his chest, and though below his waist there was nothing but fringe, he somehow found himself thinking with a curious clarity that explained many things in that last mile.

It was the cheering that started those thoughts. The sound of his name, like the pounding of rain, refreshing him, beating out a monotone of encouragement. "Burke . . . Burke . . . Burke!"

He remembered the cheering back in Framingham, the vague sounds of applause and enthusiasm that had accompanied him mile after mile. Not a brief, concerted cheer for a stretch run and victory that he had so often heard, but something new and different that he had never before experienced. For more than two hours he had heard these sounds, and the thought of this helped carry him now, filling him with wonderment until, struggling closer to those twin bobbing figures up ahead, the question came to him—how did they know him, this crowd? They had never seen him before. His name was in the papers' starting lineup. Number 18. Johnny Burke. And then, all at once, he knew. Those half million along the course who cheered were cheering a name, the memory of a name, the memory of other races back through the years. Not him, but his father, whom they had known and loved as a great competitor who always gave his best.

There were twin shadows at his shoulder now and the blood was boiling into his eyes along with the tears, and under his heart were red-hot coals. Loose bird shot filled his throat and the faces of the crowd went swimming by like painted faces in a dream. He lifted his elbows a little higher to give his lungs more clearance. He made a staggering turn into Exeter Street for the last hundred yards, and the sound of his name beat against his eardrums and he knew, finally, why his father had come back to

run for nineteen years, why the others, not the clowns but the good competitors, came out on this day each year. Whether he finished first or fifty-first, each heard, for a little while, the sound of his name, a bit of acclaim to treasure secretly, to set him apart from his fellow man and make brighter an existence that otherwise was humdrum and monotonous; not an easy thing for any man to give up, for there is a need of such tribute in all men of heart and spirit, and each must find his little share in whatever way he can.

They said it was the closest finish in many years, but Johnny Burke did not know it. He did not feel the tape at his chest and would have run on had not strong hands grabbed him, supporting his arms so that he stood straddle-legged in the street with a sick stupor enveloping him until someone threw water in his face. Gradually then, the opaque[5] shutter of his vision lifted and he straightened, seeing other faces about him and the cameras of the press photographers. When he felt someone prying at his hand he opened it and looked down and found the lemon, now squeezed to yellow pulp.

The reporters were kind to him as he stretched out on the white-

5 *opaque:* blocking light.

sheeted cot in the basement of the old brick building. They stood about patiently until his heart had slowed and the strength began to flow again along his muscles. When he sat up someone put the laurel wreath upon his head. He had to keep it on while the flash-bulbs popped, and then he had to talk, though there was little he could say except that he was glad he'd won and knew his father would be pleased.

Later, under the shower, he thought of all the things he might have said, and of them all the thing he wanted most to say could be told to no one but his father. He knew how it would sound to those reporters—falsely modest, preten-tious; corny, they'd call it. How could he tell them that he had not won this race alone, could not have won but for his father? Oh, it was his legs and lungs that did the job, but, faltering back there in the hills of Newton, it was Bronson who had pulled him through. Bronson, talking to him, getting water from the official car and reviving him. Not because Bronson liked him or cared particularly whether he finished or not, but because in him he saw the other Johnny Burke. And Tom Reynolds, taunting him into matching strides when he started to lag again, reminding him always of his father so that he would not quit.

These two who had helped him had been thinking of his father, and yet, even with their help, he could not have won without the lemon that stilled his nausea and comforted him. Now, letting the cold water play along his spine, he had to know whether this, too, had been offered because of his father or whether that gesture Kay Reynolds had made was in some part for him alone.

Upstairs in the corridors of the old clubhouse the wives and moth-ers and families of those who had already finished clustered about their men; others, still waiting, gathered round to greet the front runners with the camaraderie born of good-natured competition. None seemed disgruntled, and when Johnny Burke appeared they came to him with their congratulations as though he had long been one of them. He thanked them as best he could, the cords in his throat tight-ening as he spoke of his father and parried questions he could not answer.

How long he stood there he was never sure; he only knew that it was an anxious time because he was looking over heads and shoul-ders for a dark head and a heather-colored suit. Then, finally, he was by himself and an official had come up to ask him how the cup and medal were to be engraved.

"The way the entry read," Johnny Burke said, and the official, not understanding, smiled.

"But you're Johnny Burke, junior, aren't you?"

"Yes," Johnny said, and could neither explain nor say he wanted his father's record to read an even twenty races run. "Yes," he said again, "but I don't use the junior much. John Burke is the way I want it."

Then a soft voice was at his elbow, and his heart skipped and went racing on as he turned and saw Kay Reynolds' friendly smile. He had to clear his throat before he could reply to her congratulations, but there was a curious glow in his breast now; for as he took her offered hand in his he found something in her eyes that made him forget New York, something that told him from here on he was on his very own.

Understanding What You Read

1. What role does Johnny Burke's father play in the son's running of the marathon?

2. What is Johnny Burke's attitude as the race is about to start?
    a. Modesty and a lack of confidence in his ability to win
    b. A warm friendliness toward his father's old friends at the race
    c. An arrogant superiority toward most of the people around him

3. What function does the lemon serve Burke near the race's end?

4. Near the finish of the race, Burke sees his fellow runners in a new way. What is that new view and how does Burke come to it?

5. Who is Kay Reynolds and why is she an appropriate person to help young Burke?

Writer's Workshop

"See How They Run" takes the time to help the reader feel exactly what a marathon is like—almost mile by mile. A marathon couldn't be summarized in a few words, except, perhaps, by a skilled poet. Your job here is to capture with great detail all the physical aspects of some extended moment in sports, whether it is one game in tennis or an inning in baseball or one swimming race. The goal is to envelop the reader in the details that will bring alive the athletic experience. Try to make the reader feel as if he or she is living that moment, as George Harmon Coxe makes us almost double over right along with Johnny Burke in the home stretch of the grueling marathon. The way to accomplish this is by taking your time and being specific and detailed. Notice also that the writer does not provide you with a yard-by-yard description of the race. He mixes his description with the thoughts passing through Johnny's mind. In this way he avoids monotony and tedious repetition.

Tennis

Like father, like son.

The thing you ought to know about my father is that he plays a lovely game of tennis. Or rather, he used to, up to last year, when all of a sudden he had to give the game up for good. But even last summer, when he was fifty-five years of age, his game was something to see. He wasn't playing any of your middle-aged tennis, even then. None of that cute stuff, with lots of cuts and drop shots and getting everything back, that most older men play when they're beginning to carry a little fat and don't like to run so much. That wasn't for him. He still played all or nothing—the big game with a hard serve and coming right in behind it to the net. Lots of running in that kind of game, but he could still do it. Of course, he'd begun to make more errors in the last few years and that would annoy the hell out of him. But still he wouldn't change—not him. At that, his game was something to see when he was on. Everybody talked about it. There was always quite a little crowd around his court on the weekends, and when he and the other men would come off the court after a set of doubles, the wives would see their husbands all red and puffing. And then they'd look at my old man and see him grinning and not even breathing hard after *he'd* been doing all the running back after the lobs and putting away those overheads, and they'd say to him, "Honestly, Hugh, I just don't see how you do it, not at your age. It's *amazing*! I'm going to take my Steve [or Bill or Tom] off cigarettes and put him on a diet. He's ten years younger and just look at him." Then my old man would light up a cigarette and smile and shake his head and say, "Well, you know how it is. I just play a lot." And then a minute later he'd look around at everybody lying on the lawn there in the sun and pick out me or one of the other younger fellows and say, "Feel like a set of singles?"

If you know north Jersey at all, chances are you know my father. He's Hugh Minot—the Montclair one, not the fellow out in New Brunswick. Just about the biggest realty man in the whole section, I guess. He and my mother have this place in Montclair, thirty-five acres, with a swimming pool and a big vegetable garden and this En-Tout-Cas[1] court. A lovely home. My father got a little name for himself playing football at Rutgers, and that helped him when he went into business, I guess. He never played tennis in college, but after getting out he wanted something to sort of fill in for the football—something he could do well, or do better than the next man. You know how people are. So he took the game up. Of course, I was too little to remember his tennis game when he was still young, but friends of his have told me that it was really hot. He picked the game up like nothing at all, and a couple of pros told him if he'd only started earlier he might have gotten up there in the big time— maybe even with a national ranking, like No. 18 or so. Anyhow, he kept playing and I guess in the last twenty years there hasn't been a season where he missed more than a couple of weekends of tennis in the summertime. A few years back, he even joined one of these fancy clubs in New York with indoor courts, and he'd take a couple of days off from work and go in there just so he could play in the wintertime. Once,

I remember, he played doubles in there with Alice Marble and I think Sidney Wood.[2] He told my mother about that game lots of times, but it didn't mean much to her. She used to play tennis years ago, just for fun, but she wasn't too good and gave it up. Now the garden is the big thing with her, and she hardly ever comes out to their court, even to watch.

I play a game of tennis just like my father's. Oh, not as good. Not nearly as good, because I haven't had the experience. But it's the same game, really. I've had people tell me that when they saw us playing together—that we both made the same shot the same way. Maybe my backhand was a little better (when it was on), and I used to think that my old man didn't get down low enough on a soft return to his forehand. But mostly we played the same game. Which isn't surprising, seeing that he taught me the game. He started way back when I was about nine or ten. He used to spend whole mornings with me, teaching me a single shot. I guess it was good for me and he did teach me a good, all-round game, but even now I can remember that those morning lessons would somehow discour-

---

1 *En-Tout-Cas: Fr.,* in any event.

2 *Alice Marble . . . Sidney Wood:* two famous American tennis champions of the 1940s.

age both of us. I couldn't seem to learn fast enough to suit him, and he'd get upset and shout across at me, "Straight arm! Straight arm!" and then *I'd* get jumpy and do the shot even worse. We'd both be glad when the lesson ended.

I don't mean to say that he was so *much* better than I was. We got so we played pretty close a lot of the time. I can still remember the day I first beat him at singles. It was in June of 1937. I'd been playing quite a lot at school and this was my first weekend home after school ended. We went out in the morning, no one else there, and as usual, he walked right through me the first set—about 6–1 or so. I played much worse than my regular game then, just like I always did against him for some reason. But the next set I aced him in the second game and that set me up and I went on and took him, 7–5. It was a wonderful set of tennis and I was right on top of the world when it ended. I remember running all the way back to the house to tell Mother about it. The old man came in and sort of smiled at her and said something like, "Well, I guess I'm old now, Amy."

But don't get the idea I started beating him then. That was the whole trouble. There I was, fifteen, sixteen years old and getting my size, and I began to think, Well, it's

about time you took him. He wasn't a young man any more. But he went right on beating me. Somehow I never played well against him and I knew it, and I'd start pressing and getting sore and of course my game would go blooey.

I remember one weekend when I was in college, a whole bunch of us drove down to Montclair in May for a weekend—my two roommates and three girls we knew. It was going to be a lot of fun. But then we went out for some tennis and of course my father was there. We all played some mixed doubles, just fooling around, and then he asked me if I wanted some singles. In that casual way of his. And of course it was 6–2, 6–3, or some such thing. The second set we were really hitting out against each other and the kids watching got real quiet, just as if it was Forest Hills. And then when we came off, Alice, my date, said something to me. About him, I mean. "I think your father is a remarkable man," she said. "Simply remarkable. Don't you think so?" Maybe she wanted to make me feel better about losing, but it was a dumb question. What could I say except yes?

It was while I was in college that I began to play golf a little. I liked the game and I even bought clubs and took a couple of lessons. I broke ninety one day and wrote home to my father about it. He'd never played golf and he wrote back with some little gag about its being an old man's game. Just kidding, you know, and I guess I should have expected it, but I was embarrassed to talk about golf at home after that. I wasn't really very good at it, anyway.

I played some squash in college, too, and even made the B team, but I didn't try out for the tennis team. That disappointed my father, I think, because I wasn't any good at football, and I think he wanted to see me make some team. So he could come and see me play and tell his friends about it, I guess. Still, we did play squash a few times and I could beat him, though I saw that with time he probably would have caught up with me.

I don't want you to get the idea from this that I didn't have a good time playing tennis with him. I can remember the good days very well—lots of days where we'd played some doubles with friends or even a set of singles where my game was holding up or maybe even where I'd taken one set. Afterward we'd walk back together through the orchard, with my father knocking the green apples off the path with his racket the way he always did and the two of

us hot and sweaty while we smoked cigarettes and talked about lots of things. Then we'd sit on the veranda and drink a can of beer before taking a dip in the pool. We'd be very close then, I felt.

And I keep remembering a funny thing that happened years ago—oh, away back when I was thirteen or fourteen. We'd gone away, the three of us, for a month in New Hampshire in the summer. We played a lot of tennis that month and my game was coming along pretty fast, but of course my father would beat me every single time we played. Then he and I both entered the little town championship there the last week in August. Of course, I was put out in the first round (I was only a kid), but my old man went on into the finals. There was quite a big crowd that came to watch that day, and they had a referee and everything. My father was playing a young fellow—about twenty or twenty-one, I guess he was. I remember that I sat by myself, right down beside the court, to watch, and while they were warming up I looked at this man playing my father and whispered to myself, but almost out loud, "Take him! Take him!" I don't know why, but I just wanted him to beat my father in those finals, and it sort of scared me when I found that out. I wanted him to give him a real shellacking. Then they began to play and it was a very close match for a few games. But this young fellow was good, really good. He played a very controlled game, waiting for errors and only hitting out for winners when it was a sure thing. And he went on and won the first set, and in the next my father began to hit into the net and it was pretty plain that it wasn't even going to be close in the second set. I kept watching and pretty soon I felt very funny sitting there. Then the man won a love game off my father and I began to shake. I jumped up and ran all the way up the road to our cabin and into my room and lay down on my bed and cried hard. I kept thinking how I'd wanted to have the man win, and I knew it was about the first time I'd ever seen my father lose a love game. I never felt so ashamed. Of course, that was years and years ago.

I don't think any of this would have bothered me except for one thing—I've always *liked* my father. Except for this game, we've always gotten along fine. He's never wanted a junior-partner son, either in his office or at home. No Judge Hardy stuff or "Let me light your cigar, sir." And no backslapping, either. There have been times where I didn't see much of him for a year or so, but when we got together (at a ball game, say, or during a long trip in a car), we've always found we could talk and argue and have a lot of laughs, too. When I came back on my last furlough[3] before I went overseas during the war, I found that he'd chartered a sloop.[4] The two of us went off for a week's cruise along the Maine coast, and it was swell. Early-morning swims and trying to cook over charcoal and the wonderful quiet that comes over those little coves after you've anchored for the night and the wind has dropped and perhaps you're getting ready to shake up some cocktails. One night there, when we were sitting on deck and smoking cigarettes in the dark, he told me something that he never even told my mother—that he'd tried to get into the Army and had been turned down. He just said it and we let it drop, but I've always been glad he told me. Somehow it made me feel better about going overseas.

Naturally, during the war I didn't play any tennis at all. And when I came back I got married and all, and I was older, so of course the game didn't mean as much to me.

---

3 *furlough:* leave from duty given to a soldier.

4 *sloop:* a sailing ship with a single mast and a single jib sail.

But still, the first weekend we played at my father's—the very first time I'd played him in four years—it was the same as ever. And I'd have sworn I had outgrown the damn thing. But Janet, my wife, had never seen me play the old man before and *she* spotted something. She came up to our room when I was changing afterward. "What's the matter with you?" she asked me. "Why does it mean so much to you? It's just a game, isn't it? I can see that it's a big thing for your father. That's why he plays so much and that's why he's so good at it. But why you?" She was half kidding, but I could see that it upset her. "This isn't a contest," she said. "We're not voting for Best Athlete in the County, are we?" I took her up on that and tried to explain the thing a little, but she wouldn't try to understand. "I just don't like a sorehead," she told me as she went out of the room.

I guess that brings me down to last summer and what happened. It was late in September, one of those wonderful weekends where it begins to get a little cool and the air is so bright. Father had played maybe six or seven sets of doubles Saturday, and then Sunday I came out with Janet, and he had his regular tennis gang there—Eddie Earnshaw and Mark O'Connor and that Mr. Lacy. I guess we men had played three sets of doubles,

changing around, and we were sitting there catching our breath. I was waiting for Father to ask me for our singles. But he'd told me earlier that he hadn't been able to get much sleep the night before, so I'd decided that he was too tired for singles. Of course, I didn't even mention that out loud in front of the others—it would have embarrassed him. Then I looked around and noticed that my father was sitting in one of those canvas chairs instead of standing up, the way he usually did between sets. He looked awfully pale, even under his tan, and while I was looking at him he suddenly leaned over and grabbed his stomach and was sick on the grass. We all knew it was pretty bad, and we laid him down and put his cap over his eyes, and I ran back to the house to tell Mother and phone up the doctor. Father didn't say a word when we carried him into the house in the chair and then Dr. Stockton came and said it was a heart attack and that Father had played his last game of tennis.

You would have thought after that and after all those months in bed that my father would just give up his tennis court—have it plowed over or let it go to grass. But Janet and I went out there for the weekend just last month and I was surprised to find that the court was in good shape, and Father said he had asked the gang to come over, just so I could have some good men's doubles. He'd even had a chair set up in the orchard, halfway out to the court, so he could walk out there by himself. He walked out slow, the way he has to, and then sat down in the chair and rested for a couple of minutes, and then made it the rest of the way.

I haven't been playing much tennis this year, but I was really on my game there that day at my father's. I don't think I've ever played better on that court. I hardly made an error and I was relaxed and I felt good about my game. The others even spoke about how well I played.

But somehow it wasn't much fun. It just didn't seem like a real contest to me, and I didn't really care that I was holding my serve right along and winning my sets no matter who my partner was. Maybe for the first time in my life, I guess,

I found out that it was only a game we were playing— only that and no more. And I began to realize what my old man and I had done to that game. All that time, all those years, I had only been trying to grow up and he had been trying to keep young, and we'd both done it on the tennis court. And now our struggle was over. I found that out that day, and when I did I suddenly wanted to tell my father about it. But then I looked over at him, sitting in a chair with a straw hat on his head, and I decided not to. I noticed that he didn't seem to be watching us at all. I had the feeling, instead, that he was *listening* to us play tennis and perhaps imagining a game to himself or remembering how he would play the point—the big, high-bouncing serve and the rush to the net for the volley, and then going back for the lob and looking up at it and the wonderful feeling as you uncoil on the smash and put the ball away.

Understanding What You Read

1. How does the father in this story differ from other men his age?
    a. He is much happier.
    b. He plays tennis "all out," not just as a polite social game.
    c. He doesn't get along with his son.

2. This story is set in the 1930s and 1940s and contains numerous references to the characters' smoking and drinking. If the story had a contemporary setting, do you think these references would appear? Why or why not? How critical are they to the atmosphere of the story?

3. Considering the number of years covered in this story, you might have expected the narrator to furnish more details about his years in college, his time in the service, and his marriage. He doesn't. Why do you think he skips over these events?

Writer's Workshop

In a famous exchange between the writers F. Scott Fitzgerald and Ernest Hemingway, Fitzgerald said, "The very rich are different from you and me." Hemingway replied, "Yes, they have more money."

The family in this story is very well-off. The members live on a thirty-five acre estate, complete with a swimming pool, garden, and tennis court. But are they that different? Could a similar conflict between a father and a son develop in a family with less money? Does their money really isolate the Minots from all the problems that affect ordinary people?

On the basis of this story, which side do you take, Fitzgerald's or Hemingway's? Give reasons for your choice in a brief essay. You might title the essay "The very rich are different" or "The very rich aren't that different."

Rough Passage: A Family's Voyage of Discovery

It was supposed to be so peaceful, a three-week sail from Hawaii to Tahiti.

Any grandfather might be pleased to be invited to join his son's family on a sailing expedition. Any 62-year-old man contemplating mortality and Social Security might leap at the chance for a late-life adventure—three weeks on a 38-foot boat, crossing the Pacific Ocean from Hawaii to Tahiti.

But on May 20, seven days out of Honolulu, with nothing but ocean for hundreds of miles in any direction, I was no longer thinking of adventure or of grandfatherly acquaintance. After a hurried inspection below, my son Grey climbed into the cockpit of his sloop[1] *Vamonos* and gave us the bad news in a carefully restrained voice: "The sleeve's cracked and moving, and we're taking water below the waterline."

It was late afternoon, and the relentless Pacific sun was mercifully far down the western sky. My 3-year-old granddaughter, Stacey Kathleen, was playing quietly in her safety harness beside Sarah, her mother, who was at the wheel. I, more than half-seasick and a total newcomer to any but the most sedate forms of sailing, did not have to be told that a leak below the waterline was a serious matter, especially on a small boat alone in the middle of the ocean. I had no idea what "sleeve" Grey was talking about except that it had something to do with the steering gear and was causing the wheel on deck to feel "stiff."

Grey and Sarah stared at each other, and I looked at both of them in consternation.[2] Though my son had suffered nearly as much as I from seasickness—Sarah and Stacey seemed to have "iron stomachs"—Grey went immediately into action. First, by radio, he alert-

---

1 *sloop:* a sailing ship with a single mast and a single jib sail.

2 *consternation:* amazement and confusion.

ed a ham network[3] that keeps track of sailing traffic in that part of the Pacific, establishing our position, reporting our problem, seeking advice on emergency procedures, courses, and weather conditions.

Next, he and Sarah hauled into the cockpit the heavy bundle that, when opened and put overboard, would be our well-equipped life raft, together with a waterproof container of extra life-raft supplies. Then Grey took the wheel and sent Sarah below to tighten the cracked and leaking sleeve, through which, I later learned, ran the boat's vital steering post connecting the rudder to the wheel. (Grey is bulky; Sarah's small size made it easier for her to work below.)

Darkness came on and rain began to fall; *Vamonos* was tossing about in winds of more than 15 knots. There was nothing I could do but keep out of the way—not always easy on a small vessel—though I also tried, without much success, to ease things for little Stacey. Normally unintimidated[4] by life at sea, she had sensed the tension of the adults, as children will, and was upset and crying.

With more time to think than I wanted, and a crying child to goad me, I could not escape the incongruity of a sedentary grandfather and a frightened 3-year-old harnessed side-by-side to a tiny fiberglass platform at sea, a good bit closer to the Equator than to the assurances and comforts of everyday life. And as I watched my son moving about his boat, the darkening hours began to pose not only the seagoing emergency with which he was dealing, but a hard passage for me in my sense of myself as his father.

More than two years earlier, I had agreed to make the Hawaii-Tahiti trip with Grey and Sarah. After delaying it until 1988, while they built up their savings, we settled on May, the time of best sailing weather in that part of the Pacific. I scheduled a month's vacation, laid in outsize supplies of seasick medicine and suntan lotion, purchased a yachting cap, and arrived in Honolulu on April 30.

My son and his wife had been living in Hawaii for several years, after sailing on *Vamonos* from Catalina[5] in 1984. That year, Grey earned a history degree from the University of California at Berkeley

---

3 *ham network:* a group of amateur radio operators.

4 *unintimidated:* not frightened by.

---

5 *Catalina:* an island off the southwest coast of California.

and Sarah—a paleontology student to whom he had been married for a year—dropped out to be with him. Using funds from Grey's substantial earnings as electronics expert and soundman for the Lemmings, a Berkeley rock group, they had bought at a fire-sale price an old sailboat that was tied up and deteriorating in a local marina.

Sarah Austin is a West Coast fishing captain's daughter who grew up on and knows a lot about boats. Grey had had summer sailing experience and had attended an advanced and demanding French sailing school on the English Channel. Together, over many months and mostly by their own labor, he and Sarah had redeemed that first boat, then sold it for enough to make a substantial down payment on the craft they first named *Sarah*, later *Vamonos*—a sleek Canadian-built ocean racer, 38-feet long, sloop-rigged, and light in the water.

After they sailed to Hawaii, the Berkeley history graduate first worked as an assistant in a diving shop on Maui, becoming a licensed diving instructor; then, moving to Honolulu, he worked in the boatyard at the Keehi Marine Center. The erstwhile paleontology student, meanwhile, brought my first grandchild into the world in 1985, and still managed to work most nights in various island restaurants.

I was uneasy at these deviations from the usual career paths. So I asked Grey once if he wasn't afraid that at perhaps age 40 he might regret not having used his postcollege years to get started as a professional or in business.

"A lot of people my age," he replied, "at about 40, are going to look back and regret they didn't do in their younger years the kind of thing I'm doing in mine. And it'll be too late for most of them."

I found no way or wish to argue with that. I knew that by living on *Vamonos*, they could live on Sarah's earnings and bank most of Grey's for their "grand design"—a round-the-world, three-year sail through the South Pacific to Australia, then through the Indian Ocean, the Red Sea, the Mediterranean, and the Atlantic. If all went well—and they were young enough to be sure that it would—they would return to the United States in time to put Stacey in first grade, not too far behind schedule.

It was on the first leg of this extravagant voyage—Honolulu to Tahiti, a trip of some 2,382 miles—that a dubious but flattered grandfather was invited to sail. I welcomed the chance to be with Grey and Sarah and Stacey; and I looked forward a little tentatively to something that I feared a reasonably full life had not quite afforded me—an adventure, an experience beyond the ordinary.

My only venture into ocean sailing had come a year earlier, when I had visited Hawaii briefly and cruised in *Vamonos* with Grey and family from Oahu around Diamond Head to the Hawaiian island of Lanai. That rough, 16-hour passage deluded[6] me into thinking that I had an "iron stomach," and that an ocean crossing might have regular way stations and moments of rest.

After arriving for the Tahiti run, I learned quickly that there's always at least one more thing to be done before you cast off. In our case, Grey said, among lesser problems, that a brand-new and expensive part was faulty, so that the depth-finder on *Vamonos* wouldn't work.

I was expressing so much impatience to leave—my vacation period was finite[7]—that Grey decided to sail without a functional depth-finder. Only if we wanted to explore certain ill-charted harbors—and he didn't, he assured me—would it really matter. We set our sailing date for Sunday, May 8.

That hot and sunny day, the weather service reported no problems in any direction within 1,000 miles of Honolulu. There were a few on board, but nothing to delay us, so we loaded up with ice blocks, fresh water, and gasoline. We sailed at 3:40 P.M.—three or four days late by my expectations, amazingly near schedule in Grey's and Sarah's more sophisticated opinion. . . .

Seven days later, with Tahiti more than a thousand miles still ahead, as Grey dashed over me the small allotment of fresh water that was supposed to rinse off the salt from my first bath in a week, I wanted only two things: to feel well again, and to be back on terra firma.[8] Neither seemed likely.

I had lost any sense of proportion when I learned that the horizon was closer than the sea floor. We had been out of ice for several days—try surviving for long without that, middle-class America—and I had been mostly eating plain bread for about a week. Nausea had made me unable to read so much as a page of the books I had brought along to occupy the pleasant seagoing days.

All the way from Honolulu, we had been sailing southeast (mostly south), making six knots or more on constant trade winds—"smoking along," as Sarah put it. (A knot

---

6 *deluded:* fooled.

7 *finite:* limited.

8 *terra firma: Lat.,* solid ground.

is one nautical mile, or 2,000 yards, per hour.) But in her log for May 17, she had noted "monster seas," and the wind that night sometimes exceeded 30 knots; waves crashed over the open cockpit about every five minutes.

Monster seas, indeed; it does not encourage a seasick landsman, lashed into a constricted cockpit, to look up and see the ocean towering above him, or to feel the frail hull beneath him shooting up one side of a 12-to-15 foot wave and down the other like a roller coaster without a track; or, worse, to have one of those monster seas break like a tidal wave on top of the bisected eggshell to which he is clinging.

By that seventh day, May 20, wind and sea had moderated enough for us to venture baths on deck and I could conceive, at least, of smooth sailing and a settled stomach. Tumbling sleekly in the water alongside, schools of porpoises had been chasing about the boat like children in a backyard pool. Even so, after a week at sea, I had acquired two more hard-learned maritime axioms.

First, life aboard a 38-footer at sea is, at best, crowded, cramped, smelly, wet, and free of even elemental privacy, not to mention comfort. Second, contrary to my illusions from the preparatory cruise to Lanai in 1987, ocean sailing does not cease at sundown, or when a motel is reached, or when one is tired of it. It goes on and on, day and night, hour after hour, seasickness and discomfort notwithstanding, hammering seas be damned.

Grey and Sarah were standing four-hour watches apiece during the dangerous nighttime hours—a tanker coming over the horizon can bear down on a sailing yacht in a few minutes. Despite my nearly paralyzing state of greenish illness, I shakily took over the watch at 6 A.M.

So when, in the cooling dusk of May 20, Grey first sensed the "stiffness" in the steering that alerted him to danger, I was not jolted out of utter euphoria. As *Vamonos* was then located, Grey and the helpful ham-radio operators had concluded, we could sail on course mostly south and a little east about 10 more days to Papeete on Tahiti, where there would be haul-out facilities for the repair of *Vamonos's* steering gear, or perhaps a day or so less to one of the nearer French Polynesian islands. Alternatively, we could change course to westward and sail two or three days, about 350 miles—and downwind, which would make sailing more comfortable—to Christmas Island, a mere speck of land and lagoon 1,160 miles from Honolulu, and found just above the Equator on only the most detailed charts of the Pacific.

The second choice, drastically curtailing time at sea in a damaged boat, offered the best safeguard against further breakdown of the steering gear. But since on Christmas there were no haul-out facilities, and not much else, it might also mean the longest and most serious delay in the long-planned round-the-world cruise.

Grey and Sarah nevertheless altered course from 150 to about 240 degrees, and headed for Christmas Island. When informed of this decision, my first, ungenerous thought was not that the danger had been lessened, but that they had lopped seven or eight days off the hard time I was serving in *Vamonos.*

For unexplained reasons, following the change of course, the steering post slipped back into proper alignment and again turned easily within the cracked sleeve. This was a considerable relief—Grey let out a whoop when he felt the stiffness go out of the steering gear—but not a guarantee against new slippage, further damage to the sleeve or increasing leakage.

Grey and Sarah understood, as I did not at the time, that our relatively small leak threatened us only remotely with sinking; the more immediate and specific problem had been that we might lose the

ability to steer *Vamonos.*

Precisely what such a loss might have meant to our safety, I did not then know to ask, and they never told me; but in those seas and at our distance from land and help, the threat clearly was enough to cause a real night of anxiety for these reasonably experienced sailors. Nor was the horrendous possibility of sinking totally out of their minds.

"You always keep a life raft on board, but you never think you'll really have to use it," Grey told me later. "When I went down and shined a light on that water coming in below the waterline, I suddenly could see all of us actually sitting out there in a raft in the middle of the ocean. My blood literally turned cold."

For me, the sense of helplessness while in ill-understood but palpable danger was the worst problem; it brought me, moreover, into a strange new relationship with my son.

Grey was 29 years old. Though he was married, a father, and long absent from my house, I still thought of him in some ways as a dependent, certainly as a junior (he is, in fact, Thomas Grey Wicker, Jr.), subject to my advice and consent, if not control. I had changed his diapers, dried his tears, taught him to catch a baseball, seen him through school and the pitfalls of adolescence; he was, as I had always known him, my child, to whom I had read "Winnie the Pooh" and lectured learnedly on life.

That night, rocked by those gusty winds, strapped in, rain-soaked, uselessly huddled near my granddaughter on the downwind side of the cockpit—*Vamonos* was heeled sharply to starboard—that version of my son slipped forever behind me. I had no choice but to put my life in his hands—just as, it came to me, the child he had been had often, if unknowingly, put his in mine. I saw that the father involuntarily had become the child; struggling with wheel, halyards, sails, compass, the child necessarily had become the man.

Such a passage, I suppose, sooner or later comes to most fathers and sons. It can never be easy for either; it was not for me, accustomed as I was to being in charge, being heard, taking responsibility. Perhaps the change actually had happened a week earlier when, in brilliant sunshine and high spirits, with Diamond Head rising on the beam, Grey had steered *Vamonos* for the open ocean. I had been no more able then than I was a week later to take care of that boat, or myself, at sea. But even far from familiar shores, it had taken a leak below

the waterline to make me recognize that the time had come to give over.

Later that night, Grey told me to keep on my life jacket while I slept—much as I once had instructed a small boy at bedtime on a winter night to keep his blankets pulled up. I felt finally—even in the squally night and the unresolved emergency—a sense of relief, of real accomplishment. I had brought this man that far; I had done my part, after all, and it had not been a small one.

I knew a secret pride, because I had watched Grey handle his boat and our trouble, and seen that he knew what to do. Now that his time was here, the man my son had become would see us safely through. I slept soundly.

May 21 dawned gray, drizzly, and as chilly as the South Pacific gets. We were sailing easily before the wind, more comfortably than at anytime since leaving Honolulu. No further steering or leakage problems had developed overnight and by prearrangement the reassuring ham operators soon were on the air. They had comforting news: the United States Coast Guard in Hawaii had been alerted to our plight, with the result that what the hams described as a "commercial vessel"—otherwise unidentified and never seen—was standing by in our vicinity, ready to steam to the rescue if that became necessary.

In daylight and after reflection, however, Grey and Sarah took a more relaxed view of the steering problem; they decided, and convinced the ham network, that the help of the "commercial vessel" would not be needed. When its radio operator entered the far-flung conversation, they thanked him but urged his ship on its way. And *Vamonos*, in lighter but favorable winds, proceeded without further event, for nearly three days, toward landfall on Christmas Island shortly after noon May 23.

Christmas is some 30 miles long and surrounded by tricky waters, including something menacingly labeled on the charts the "Bay of Wrecks." Although we had approached the island's most favorable mooring area, we were still at sea long after dark and remained offshore all night. But shortly after dawn on Tuesday, May 24, with Sarah at the wheel—it had turned stiff again the day before—Grey dropped anchor just off the tiny village of London, near the unnavigably shallow entrance to the lagoon that occupies the center of the island (and offers, I later learned, some of the world's best bonefishing).

Christmas is so low-lying that it probably would be covered over by hurricane seas, if hurricanes struck so near the Equator. There's one telephone on the island, one airstrip, one flight in and one out every week, one hotel, and evidently no radiation left over from the atomic bomb tests the British conducted in the 1950s and the Americans in 1962.

Coconuts and fish are the main products, and about 2,000 native folk, unimpressed by visitors, live under the multi-island aegis[9] of the Kiribati Republic. Don't expect to find Sadie Thompson or Rita Hayworth[10] in the decidedly undecadent bar of the Captain Cook Hotel, where visiting fishermen can choose to pay 50 Australian dollars extra for an air-conditioned room.

But to me, the day we landed, the island looked as charming as the setting of an old Dorothy Lamour[11] movie. As we went ashore by dinghy[12]—a half-hour trip through choppy waters—that dauntless sailor, 3-year-old Stacey, fell sound asleep. I was not that

---

9 *aegis:* protection.

10 *Sadie Thompson and Rita Hayworth:* heroine of short story by Somerset Maugham; actress who played the role in movie version.

11 *Dorothy Lamour:* actress of the 1940s who starred in several movies set on tropical islands.

12 *dinghy:* a small rowboat.

worn out, but I had few regrets about leaving the canting[13] decks of *Vamonos*. Ocean sailing clearly was not my sport, although, in the last calm days and nights of cruising to Christmas, I finally had seen why going to sea held such attraction for Grey and Sarah and so many dedicated sailors.

Nothing matches sunrise or sunset over a vast and empty ocean. On a clear night, the display of stars in the vaulting heavens, moonlit paths across gently rolling waves, the occasional excitement of a shooting star or the literally unearthly passage of an orbiting satellite—such nights at sea can fill anyone with peaceful joy, and the humility of man returned to nature.

On our last easy day of sailing, as a strong current carried *Vamonos* in a light breeze, I lay on the foredeck in the shade of the mainsail, indolent and dozing, no longer sick, singularly free of care, with the water murmuring past the hull—the voice of the sea in a soothing mood. Across its limitless vista, as into a fire, I thought I could gaze forever; against its depths and power, the strains of life on shore seemed petty and false.

I had, besides, as I had wished, become better acquainted with Sarah and Stacey; in a 38-foot boat at sea, not much can be hidden. Whether I knew them better, or they me, is something else. I fear my granddaughter may remember mostly a queasy and querulous[14] old man with 10 days of grizzled beard. I will remember her not least for a certain acerbic[15] independence—a child, like her parents, not easily to be incorporated within the world's demanding routines.

Escape from those routines seems to me a prime reason why people are drawn to the sea. Not that ocean sailing doesn't make its demands and impose its rules, severe ones at that; but these are shaped from the fundamental need to survive in nature—a far different thing from the inculcated[16] desire to flourish in society. The sea's rules can be ignored only at real, physical peril, not at mere risk of social or financial penalty.

For those who can meet the demands of sea and weather—elemental challenges long lost to modern technological societies— the boatman's life can be unhurried, footloose, rewarding in itself rather than as a passage to something else, whether affluence or power or both. Such a life can be

---

13 *canting:* tilting; leaning.

14 *querulous:* complaining.

15 *acerbic:* sour or harsh.

16 *inculcated:* instilled or taught.

content—the opposite of the rat race.

Having accidentally arrived, for example, at Christmas Island, Grey and Sarah—taking things as they came—determined to stay awhile. They would fish, snorkel, dive, enjoy life in the sun with Stacey; and one day, someday, they would get around to the rudder repairs that would have to be made before they could sail on.

The next day, however, a shaven, chastened grandfather gratefully caught the weekly three-hour flight from Christmas to Hon-

olulu. I was eager to get back to my life, the kind of demands with which I had more or less learned to cope—back, as I had so often wished in the grimmest hours at sea, to terra firma.

But as I tried vainly, after take-off, to catch a last glimpse of *Vamonos* anchored offshore, I still could hear Grey's exultant voice, as we finally departed Honolulu and he explained himself and his life better than he ever had:

"Now all I have to do is what I've got to do to sail my boat!"

Understanding What You Read

1. "I was uneasy at these deviations from the usual career paths," writes Tom Wicker. What did he feel his son should be doing, and how did his son reply?

2. What two principles did Tom Wicker learn after a week at sea?

3. How did father and son exchange roles aboard the **Vamonos**?

4. What positive feelings about ocean sailing did Tom Wicker come to have despite "the rough passage"?

5. What do you think Grey Wicker meant when he said, "Now all I have to do is what I've got to do to sail my boat"?

Writer's Workshop

Another writer, Joseph Conrad, whose subject was often the sea, called that period in the life of Grey Wicker "the shadow line." It was a time, Conrad wrote, when one realized "that the region of early youth, too, must be left behind." It was a time of "rash moments. I mean moments when the young are inclined to commit rash actions, such as getting married suddenly or else throwing up a job for no reason."

Describe an event involving you or one of your parents in which the way you saw them or they saw you changed. Take your readers through the event and changed attitudes the way Tom Wicker did in his essay.

• CHAPTER FIVE •

The Fun
Side

*As games go, life is a pretty serious one. But even during its
worst moments, there is always a funny side.
Laughter is what keeps people sane.*

*In this chapter, ten writers who care deeply about sports
take a look at the fun side. They expose the silliness and
the exaggeration, the confused and confusing language,
the intensity and the daydreams in the world of sports.
And the hope is that you'll be in on the joke.*

Who's on First?

Here it is, the classic comedy routine about baseball. For best results, read it aloud.

Sebastian: Peanuts!

Dexter: Peanuts!

Sebastian: Popcorn!

Dexter: Popcorn!

Sebastian: Crackerjack!

Dexter: Crackerjack!

Sebastian: Get your packages of Crackerjack here!

Dexter:—Crackerjack—will you keep quiet? Sebastian! Sebastian, please! Don't interrupt my act!

Sebastian: Ladies and gentlemen and also the children—will you excuse me for a minute, please? Thank you.

Dexter: What do you want to do?

Sebastian: Look, Mr. Broadhurst—

Dexter: What are you doing?

Sebastian: I love baseball!

Dexter: Well, we all love baseball.

Sebastian: When we get to St. Louis, will you tell me the guys' names on the team so when I go to see them in that St. Louis ballpark I'll be able to know those fellows?

Dexter: Then you'll go and peddle your popcorn and don't interrupt the act anymore?

Sebastian: Yes, sir.

Dexter: All right. But you know, strange as it may seem, they give ballplayers nowadays very peculiar names.

Sebastian: Funny names?

Dexter: Nicknames. Nicknames.

Sebastian: Not—not as funny as my name—Sebastian Dinwiddie.

Dexter: Oh, yes, yes, yes!

Sebastian: Funnier than that?

Dexter: Oh, absolutely. Yes. Now on the St. Louis team we have Who's on first, What's on second, I Don't Know is on third—

Sebastian: That's what I want to find out. I want you to tell me the names of the fellows on the St. Louis team.

Dexter: I'm telling you. Who's on first, What's on second, I Don't Know is on third—

Sebastian: You know the fellows' names?

Dexter: Yes.

Sebastian: Well, then, who's playin' first?

Dexter: Yes!

Sebastian: I mean the fellow's name on first base.

Dexter: Who.

Sebastian: The fellow playin' first base for St. Louis.

Dexter: Who.

Sebastian: The guy on first base.

Dexter: Who is on first.

Sebastian: Well, what are you askin' me for?

Dexter: I'm not asking you—I'm telling you. *Who is on first.*

Sebastian: I'm asking you—who's on first?

Dexter: That's the man's name!

Sebastian: That's whose name?

Dexter: Yes.

Sebastian: Well, go ahead and tell me!

Dexter: Who.

Sebastian: The guy on first.

Dexter: Who.

Sebastian: The first baseman.

Dexter: Who is on first.

Sebastian: Have you got a first baseman on first?

Dexter: Certainly.

Sebastian: Then who's playing first?

Dexter: Absolutely.

Sebastian: When you pay off the first baseman every month, who gets the money?

Dexter: Every dollar of it. And why not, the man's entitled to it.

Sebastian: Who is?

Dexter: Yes.

Sebastian: So who gets it?

Dexter: Why shouldn't he? Sometimes his wife comes down and collects it.

Sebastian: Whose wife?

Dexter: Yes. After all, the man earns it.

Sebastian: Who does?

Dexter: Absolutely.

Sebastian: Well, all I'm trying to find out is what's the guy's name on first base.

Dexter: Oh, no, no. What is on second base.

Sebastian: I'm not asking you who's on second.

Dexter: Who's on first.

Sebastian: That's what I'm trying to find out.

Dexter: Well, don't change the players around.

Sebastian: I'm not changing nobody.

Dexter: Now, take it easy.

Sebastian: What's the guy's name on first base?

Dexter: What's the guy's name on second base.

Sebastian: I'm not askin' ya who is on second.

Dexter: Who's on first.

Sebastian: I don't know.

Dexter: He's on third. We're not talking about him.

Sebastian: How could I get on third base?

Dexter: You mentioned his name.

Sebastian: If I mentioned the third baseman's name, who did I say is playing third?

Dexter: No, Who's playing first.

Sebastian: Stay offa first, will ya?

Dexter: Well, what do you want me to do?

Sebastian: Now what's the guy's name on first base?

Dexter: What's on second.

Sebastian: I'm not asking ya who's on second.

Dexter: Who's on first.

Sebastian: I don't know.

Dexter: He's on third.

Sebastian: There I go back on third again.

Dexter: Well, I can't change their names.

Sebastian: Say, will you please stay on third base, Mr. Broadhurst.

Dexter: Please. Now, what is it you want to know?

Sebastian: What is the fellow's name on third base?

Dexter: What is the fellow's name on second base.

Sebastian: I'm not askin' ya who's on second.

Dexter: Who's on first.

Sebastian: I don't know.

Dexter and Sebastian: *Third base!*

Sebastian: You got a pitcher on the team?

Dexter: Wouldn't this be a fine team without a pitcher?

Sebastian: I don't know. Tell me the pitcher's name.

Dexter: Tomorrow.

Sebastian: You don't want to tell me today?

Dexter: I'm telling you, man.

Sebastian: Then go ahead.

Dexter: Tomorrow.

Sebastian: What time?

Dexter: What time what?

Sebastian: What time tomorrow are you gonna tell me who's pitching?

Dexter: Now listen, Who is not pitching. Who is on—

Sebastian: I'll break your arm if you say who's on first.

Dexter: Then why come up here and ask?

Sebastian: I want to know what's the pitcher's name.

Dexter: What's on second.

Sebastian: I don't know.

Sebastian and Dexter: *Third base!*

Sebastian: Gotta catcher?

Dexter: Yes.

Sebastian: I'm a good catcher, too, you know.

Dexter: I know that.

Sebastian: I would like to play for the St. Louis team.

Dexter: Well, I might arrange that.

Sebastian: I would like to catch. Now, I'm being a good catcher, Tomorrow's pitching on the team, and I'm catching.

Dexter: Yes.

Sebastian: Tomorrow throws the ball and the guy up bunts the ball.

Dexter: Yes.

Sebastian: Now, when he bunts

the ball—me being a good catcher— I want to throw the guy out at first base, so I pick up the ball and throw it to who?

Dexter: Now that's the first thing you've said right.

Sebastian: I DON'T EVEN KNOW WHAT I'M TALKING ABOUT.

Dexter: Well, that's all you have to do.

Sebastian: Is to throw it to first base.

Dexter: Yes.

Sebastian: Now who's got it?

Dexter: Naturally.

Sebastian: Who has it?

Dexter: Naturally.

Sebastian: Naturally.

Dexter: Naturally.

Sebastian: O. K.

Dexter: Now you've got it.

Sebastian: I pick up the ball and I throw it to Naturally.

Dexter: No you don't, you throw the ball to first base.

Sebastian: Then who gets it?

Dexter: Naturally.

Sebastian: O. K.

Dexter: All right.

Sebastian: I throw the ball to Naturally.

Dexter: You don't. You throw it to Who.

Sebastian: Naturally.

Dexter: Well, naturally. Say it that way.

Sebastian: That's what I said.

Dexter: You did not.

Sebastian: I said I'd throw the ball to Naturally.

Dexter: You don't. You throw it to Who.

Sebastian: Naturally.

Dexter: Yes.

Sebastian: So I throw the ball to first base and Naturally gets it.

Dexter: No. You throw the ball to first base—

Sebastian: Then who gets it?

Dexter: Naturally.

Sebastian: That's what I'm saying.

Dexter: You're not saying that.

Sebastian: Excuse me, folks.

Dexter: Now, don't get excited. Now, don't get excited.

Sebastian: I throw the ball to first base.

Dexter: Then Who gets it.

Sebastian: He better get it.

Dexter: That's it. All right now, don't get excited. Take it easy.

Sebastian: Now I throw the ball to first base, whoever it is grabs the ball, so the guy runs to second.

Dexter: Uh-huh.

Sebastian: Who picks up the ball and throws it to What. What throws it to I Don't Know. I Don't Know throws it back to Tomorrow—a triple play.

Dexter: Yeah. It could be.

Sebastian: And I don't care.

Dexter: What was that?

Sebastian: I said, *I don't care.*

Dexter: Oh, that's our shortstop!

Understanding What You Read

No one can **not** understand this hilarious and brilliant piece of writing. Of course, its humor is based on an almost total lack of communication between two people and the ensuing frustration. But the two characters communicate to their audience very well. The hilarity of this comic dialogue has lasted over forty years.

Would the dialogue work so well if it took place between the following?
a. two women
b. a man and a child
c. an American and a foreigner who speaks English

Explain your answers.

Writer's Workshop

The starting point of this routine is a little artificial—nicknames like "Who" and "What." But after that, notice how well Dexter and Sebastian stay in character in every change of dialogue. Each maintains his own point of view. This is a trait of all well-written dialogue. The writer restricts himself or herself completely to the mind of the character who is doing the talking.

Now, write your own comic dialogue about sports. You might, for example, try to explain baseball to a foreign student seeing the game for the first time.

> "Well, the object of this game is to score more runs than the other team."
> "What's a run?"
> "Every time you get around to home, it's a run."
> "What's 'home'? A house?"

Try it with any sport and see how much vernacular—language exclusive to a special activity—is built into all sports. If you try this suggestion—an American explaining a sport to a foreigner—your comic dialogue will be focused on misunderstanding just as Abbott and Costello's was. Let the person doing the explaining be the one getting frustrated in your scene; the foreigner in all innocence will be the foil, or straight man.

Who Flang That Ball?

English is consistent in its inconsistency.

My assignment was to interview Infield Ingersoll, one-time shortstop for the Wescosville Wombats and now a radio sports announcer. Dizzy Dean, Red Barber, and other sportscasters had taken back seats since the colorful Ingersoll had gone on the air. The man had practically invented a new language. "I know just what you're gonna ask," Infield began. "You wanna know how come I use all them ingrammatical expressions like 'He swang at a high one.' You think I'm illitrut."

"No, indeed," I said. Frankly, I *had* intended to ask him what effect he thought his extraordinary use of the King's English might have on future generations of radio listeners.

But a gleam in Infield's eyes when he said "illitrut" changed my mind. "What I'd really like to get," I said, "is the story of how you left baseball and became a sportscaster."

Infield looked pleased. "Well," he said, "it was the day us Wombats plew the Pink Sox. . ."

"Plew the Pink Sox?" I interrupted. "Don't you mean played?"

Infield's look changed to disappointment. "Slay, slew. Play, plew. What's the matter with that?"

"Slay is an irregular verb," I pointed out.

"So who's to say what's regular or irregular? English teachers! Can an English teacher bat three hundred?"

He paused belligerently, and then went on. "What I'm tryin' to do is easify the languish. I make all regular verbs irregular. Once they're all irregular, then it's just the same like they're all regular. That way I don't gotta stop and think."

He had something there. "Go on with your story," I said.

"Well, it was the top of the fifth, when this Sox batter wang out a high pop fly. I raught for it."

"Raught?"

"Past tense of verb to Reach. Teach, taught. Reach,—"

"Sorry," I said. "Go ahead."

"Anyhow I raught for it, only the sun blound me."

"You mean blinded?"

"Look," Infield said patiently, "you wouldn't say a pitcher winded up, would you? So there I was, blound by the sun, and the ball just nuck the tip of my glove—that's nick, nuck; same congregation as stick, stuck. But luckily I caught it just as it skam the top of my shoe."

"Skam? Could that be the past tense of to skim?"

"Yeah, yeah, same as swim, swam. You want this to be a English lesson or you wanna hear my story?"

"Your story, please, Mr. Ingersoll."

"Okay. Well, just then the umpire cell, 'Safe!' Naturally I was surprise. Because I caught that fly, only the ump cell the runner safe."

"Cell is to call as fell is to fall, I suppose?" I inquired.

"Right. Now you're beginning to catch on." Infield regarded me happily as if there was now some hope for me. "So I yold at him, 'Robber! That decision smold!'"

"Yell, yold. Smell, smold," I mumbled. "Same idea as tell, told."

Infield rumbled on, "I never luck that umpire anyway."

"Hold it!" I cried. I finally had tripped this backhand grammarian. "A moment ago, you used nuck as the past for nick, justifying it by the verb to stick. Now you use luck as a verb. Am I to assume by this that

luck is the past tense of lick?"

"Luck is past for like. To like is a regular irregular verb of which there are several such as strike, struck. Any farther questions or should I go on?"

"Excuse me," I said. "You were saying you never luck that umpire."

"And neither did the crowd. Everyone thrould at my courage. I guess I better explain thrould," Infield said thoughtfully. "Thrould comes from thrill just like would comes from will. Got that? Now to get back to my story: 'Get off the field, you bum, and no back talk!' the umpire whoze."

"Whoze?"

"He had asthma," Infield pointed out patiently.

I saw through it instantly. Wheeze, whoze. Freeze, froze.

"And with those words, that ump invote disaster. I swang at him and smeared him with a hard right that lood square on his jaw."

"Lood? Oh, I see—Stand, stood. Land, lood—it lood on his jaw."

"Sure. He just feld up and went down like a light. As he reclone on the field, he pept at me out of his good eye."

"Now wait. What's this pept?" I asked.

"After you sleep, you've did what?" Infield inquired.

"Why, slept—oh he peeped at you, did he?"

"You bet he pept at me. And in that peep I saw it was curtains for me in the league henceforward. So I beat him to it and just up and quat."

"Sit, sat. Quit—well, that gets you out of baseball," I said. "Only you still haven't told me how you got to be on radio and television."

"I guess that'll have to wait," Infield said, "on account I gotta hurry now to do a broadcast."

As he shade my hand good-by, Infield grun and wank at me.

Understanding What You Read

1. Which of the following statements do you feel best expresses W. F. Miksch's purpose in this essay? Be ready to give reasons for your choice.
   a. Miksch is making fun of the low educational level of professional athletes.
   b. Miksch is using Ingersoll to poke fun at the irregularities of the English language.
   c. Miksch doesn't want English teachers to determine what correct usage is.

2. Infield Ingersoll says, "I make all regular verbs irregular. Once they're all irregular, then it's just the same like they're all regular." Is this true? Are irregular verbs all irregular in the same way?

Writer's Workshop

W. F. Miksch uses the device of the naive, or innocent, character to point out some inconsistencies that most people are unaware of. Some writers will use a creature from outer space. Miksch and others are aware of the power of asking, "But why do you do it that way?"

Create your own naive character to ask pointed questions and poke fun at some practice, custom, or fad. The character you create does not have to be a professional athlete.

The Decline of Sport

The seasons are getting longer and the crowds bigger. Where will it all end? Here's one tongue-in-cheek answer to the sports craze.

In the third decade of the supersonic age, sport gripped the nation in an ever-tightening grip. The horse tracks, the ballparks, the fight rings, the gridirons, all drew crowds in steadily increasing numbers. Every time a game was played, an attendance record was broken. Usually some other sort of record was broken, too—such as the record for the number of consecutive doubles hit by left-handed batters in a Series game, or some such thing as that. Records fell like ripe apples on a windy day. Customs and manners changed, and the five-day business week was reduced to four days, then to three, to give everyone a better chance to memorize the scores.

Not only did sport proliferate but the demands it made on the spectator became greater. Nobody was content to take in one event at a time, and thanks to the magic of radio and television nobody had to. A Yale alumnus, class of 1962, returning to the Bowl with 197,000 others to see the Yale-Cornell football game would take along his pocket radio and pick up the Yankee Stadium, so that while his eye might be following a fumble on the Cornell twenty-two-yard line, his ear would be following a man going down to second in the top of the fifth, seventy miles away. High in the blue sky above the Bowl, skywriters would be at work writing the scores of other major and minor sporting contests, weaving an interminable record of victory and defeat, and using the new high-visibility pink news-smoke perfected by Pepsi-Cola engineers. And in the frames of the giant video sets, just behind the goal posts, this same alumnus could watch Dejected win the Futurity before a record-breaking crowd of 349,872 at Belmont, each of whom was tuned to the Yale Bowl and following the World Series game in the video and searching the sky for further news of events either under way or just completed. The effect of this vast cyclorama of sport was to divide the spectator's attention, over-subtilize his appreciation, and deaden his passion. As the fourth super-sonic decade was ushered in, the picture changed and sport began to wane.

A good many factors contributed to the decline of sport. Substitutions in football had increased to such an extent that there were very few fans in the United States capable of holding the players in mind during play. Each play that was called saw two entirely new elevens lined up, and the players whose names and faces you had familiarized yourself with in the first period were seldom seen or heard of again. The spectacle became as diffuse as the main concourse in Grand Central at the commuting hour.

Express motor highways leading to the parks and stadia had become so wide, so unobstructed, so devoid of all life except automobiles and trees that sport fans had got into the habit of traveling enormous distances to attend events. The normal driving speed had been stepped up to ninety-five miles an hour, and the distance between cars had been decreased to fifteen feet. This put an extraordinary strain on the sport lover's nervous system and he arrived home from a Saturday game, after a road trip of three hundred and fifty miles, glassy-eyed, dazed, and spent. He hadn't really had any relaxation and he had failed to see Czlika (who had gone in for Trusky) take the pass from Bkeeo (who had gone in for Bjallo) in the third period, because at that moment a youngster named Lavagetto had been put in to pinch-hit for Art Gurlack in the bottom of the the ninth with the tying run on second, and the skywriter who was attempting to write "Princeton 0—Lafayette 43" had banked the wrong way, muffed the "3," and distracted everyone's attention from the fact that Lavagetto had been whiffed.

Cheering, of course, lost its stimulating effect on players, because cheers were no longer associated necessarily with the immediate scene but might as easily apply to something that was happening somewhere else. This was enough to infuriate even the steadiest performer. A football star, hearing the stands break into a roar before the ball was snapped, would realize that their minds were not on him and would become dispirited and grumpy. Two or three of the big coaches worried so about this that they considered equipping all players with tiny ear sets, so that they, too, could keep abreast of other sporting events while playing, but the idea was abandoned as impractical, and the coaches put it aside in tickler files, to bring up again later.

I think the event that marked

the turning point in sport and started it downhill was the Midwest's classic Dust Bowl game of 1975, when Eastern Reserve's great right end, Ed Pistachio, was shot by a spectator. This man, the one who did the shooting, was seated well down in the stands near the forty-yard line on a bleak October afternoon and was so saturated with sport and with the disappointments of sport that he had clearly become deranged. With a minute and fifteen seconds to play and the score tied, the Eastern Reserve quarterback had whipped a long pass over Army's heads into Pistachio's waiting arms. There was no other player anywhere near him, and all Pistachio had to do was catch the ball and run it across the line. He dropped it. At exactly this moment, the spectator—a man named Homer T. Parkinson, of 35 Edgemere Drive, Toledo, O.—suffered at least three other major disappointments in the realm of sport. His horse, Hiccough, on which he had a five-hundred-dollar bet, fell while getting away from the starting gate at Pimlico and broke its leg (clearly visible in the video); his favorite shortstop, Lucky Frimstitch, struck out and let three men die on base in the final game of the Series (to which Parkinson was tuned); and the Governor Dummer soccer team, on which Parkinson's youngest son played goalie, lost to

Kent, 4–3, as recorded in the sky overhead. Before anyone could stop him, he drew a gun and drilled Pistachio, before 954,000 persons, the largest crowd that had ever attended a football game and the *second* largest crowd that had ever assembled for any sporting event in any month except July.

This tragedy, by itself, wouldn't have caused sport to decline, I suppose, but it set in motion a chain of other tragedies, the cumulative effect of which was terrific. Almost as soon as the shot was fired, the news flash was picked up by one of the skywriters directly above the field. He glanced down to see whether he could spot the trouble below, and in doing so failed to see another skywriter approaching. The two planes collided and fell, wings locked, leaving a confusing trail of smoke, which some observers tried to interpret as a late sports score. The planes struck in the middle of the nearby eastbound coast-to-coast Sunlight Parkway, and a motorist driving a convertible coupé stopped so short, to avoid hitting them, that he was bumped from behind. The pile-up of cars that ensued involved 1,482 vehicles, a record for eastbound parkways. A total of more than three thousand persons lost their lives in the highway accident, including the two pilots, and when panic broke out in the stadium, it cost another 872 in dead and injured. News of the disaster spread quickly to other sports arenas, and started other panics among the crowds trying to get to the exits, where they could buy a paper and study a list of the dead. All in all, the afternoon of sport cost 20,003 lives, a record. And nobody had much to show for it except one small Midwestern boy who hung around the smoking wrecks of the planes, captured some aero news-smoke in a milk bottle, and took it home as a souvenir.

From that day on, sport waned. Through long, noncompetitive Saturday afternoons, the stadia slumbered. Even the parkways fell into disuse as motorists rediscovered the charms of old, twisty roads that led through main streets and past barnyards, with their mild congestions and pleasant smells.

Understanding What You Read

1. What is E. B. White satirizing in these two sentences:

   . . . the record for the number of consecutive doubles hit by left-handed batters in a Series game. . . .

   . . . the **second** largest crowd that had ever assembled for any sporting event in any month except July.

   This piece of satire was written in 1947. Do the two quotations sound like exaggeration, as they did when they were written, or do they sound like actual broadcasts today? Explain.

2. What is the writer's point in the last paragraph? What do you think E. B. White thinks of "old, twisty roads that led through main streets and past barnyards, with their mild congestion and pleasant smells"? Does White like that world? How do you know?

3. On a sheet of paper create two columns. In the left-hand column, list aspects of "The Decline of Sport" that have come true since 1947, and in the right-hand column list aspects that today are still exaggeration. Which column is longer? How do you appraise White's insights of 1947?

Writer's Workshop

In creating satire a writer exaggerates to poke fun or to ridicule. In 1947 there was much exaggeration in "The Decline of Sport," though today much of White's story seems like prophesy.

Now it is your turn to create a satire about some aspect of sports that you think deserves teasing or outright criticism. But you are not writing an argumentative essay. A satire uses fictional techniques to make its points indirectly. Write a short story that exaggerates some aspect of sports that bothers you.

Death of Red Peril

Here's a tall tale about a racing caterpillar as told in the language of the folks who worked on the barges of the Erie Canal.

A horse race is a handsome thing to watch if a man has his money on a sure proposition. My pa was always a great hand at a horse race. But when he took to a boat and my mother he didn't have no more time for it. So he got interested in another sport.

Did you ever hear of racing caterpillars? No? Well, it used to be a great thing on the canawl. My pa used to have a lot of them insects on hand every fall, and the way he could get them to run would make a man have his eyes examined.

The way we raced caterpillars was to set them in a napkin ring on a table, one facing one way and one the other. Outside the napkin ring was drawed a circle in chalk three feet acrost. Then a man lifted the ring and the handlers was allowed one jab with a darning needle to get their caterpillars started. The one that got outside the chalk circle the first was the one that won the race.

I remember my pa tried out a lot of breeds, and he got hold of some pretty fast steppers. But there wasn't one of them could equal Red Peril. To see him you wouldn't believe he could run. He was all red and kind of stubby, and he had a sort of a wart behind that you'd think would get in his way. There wasn't anything fancy in his looks. He'd just set still studying the ground and make you think he was dreaming about last year's oats; but when you set him in the starting ring he'd hitch himself up behind like a man lifting on his galluses, and then he'd light out for glory.

Pa come acrost Red Peril down in Westernville. Ma's relatives resided there, and it being Sunday we'd all gone in to church. We was riding back in a hired rig with a dandy trotter, and Pa was pushing her right along and Ma was talking sermon and clothes, and me and my sister was setting on the back seat playing poke your nose, when all of a sudden Pa hollers, "Whoa!" and set the horse right down on the breeching. Ma let out a holler and come to rest on the dashboard with her head under the horse. "My gracious land!" she says. "What's happened?" Pa was out on the other side of the road right down in the mud in his Sunday pants, a-wropping up something in his yeller handkerchief. Ma begun to get riled. "What you doing, Pa?" she says. "What you got there?" Pa was putting his handkerchief back into his inside pocket. Then he come back over the wheel and got him a chew. "Leeza," he says, "I got the fastest caterpillar in seven counties. It's an act of Providence I seen him, the way he jumped the ruts." "It's an act of God I ain't laying dead under the back end of that horse," says Ma. "I've gone and spoilt my Sunday hat." "Never mind," says Pa; "Red Peril will earn you a new one." Just like that he named him. He was the fastest caterpillar in seven counties.

When we got back onto the boat, while Ma was turning up the supper, Pa set him down to the table under the lamp and pulled out the handkerchief. "You two devils stand there and there," he says to me and my sister, "and if you let him get by I'll leather the soap out of you."

So we stood there and he undid the handkerchief, and out walked one of them red, long-haired caterpillars. He walked right to the middle of the table, and then he took a short turn and put his nose in his tail and went to sleep.

"Who'd think that insect could make such a break for freedom as I seen him make?" says Pa, and he got out a empty Brandreth box and filled it up with some towel and put the caterpillar inside. "He needs a rest," says Pa. "He needs to get used to his stall. When he limbers up I'll commence training him. Now then," he says, putting the box on the shelf back of the stove, "don't none of you say a word about him."

He got out a pipe and set there smoking and figuring, and we could see he was studying out just how he'd make a world-beater out of that bug. "What you going to feed him?" asks Ma. "If I wasn't afraid of spoiling his stomach," Pa says, "I'd try him out with milkweed."

Next day we hauled up the Lansing Kill Gorge. Ned Kilbourne, Pa's driver, come aboard in the morning, and he took a look at that caterpillar. He took him out of the box and felt his legs and laid him down on the table and went clean over him. "Well," he says, "he don't look like a great lot, but I've knowed some of that red variety could chug along pretty smart." Then he touched him with a pin. It was a sudden sight.

It looked like the rear end of that caterpillar was racing the front end, but it couldn't never quite get by. Afore either Ned or Pa could get a move Red Peril had made a turn around the sugar bowl and run solid aground in the butter dish.

Pa let out a loud swear. "Look out he don't pull a tendon," he says. "Butter's a bad thing. A man has to be careful. Jeepers," he says, picking him up and taking him over to the stove to dry, "I'll handle him myself. I don't want no rum-soaked bezabors dishing my beans."

"I didn't mean harm, Will," says Ned. "I was just curious."

There was something extraordinary about that caterpillar. He was intelligent. It seemed he just couldn't abide the feel of sharp iron. It got so that if Pa reached for the lapel of his coat Red Peril would light out. It must have been he was tender. I said he had a sort of a wart behind, and I guess he liked to find it a place of safety.

We was all terrible proud of that bird. Pa took to timing him on the track. He beat all known time holler. He got to know that as soon as he crossed the chalk he would get back safe in his quarters. Only when we tried sprinting him across the supper table, if he saw a piece of butter he'd pull up short and bolt back where he came from. He had a mortal fear of butter.

Well, Pa trained him three

nights. It was a sight to see him there at the table, a big man with a needle in his hand, moving the lamp around and studying out the identical spot that caterpillar wanted most to get out of the needle's way. Pretty soon he found it, and then he says to Ned, "I'll race him agin all comers at all odds." "Well, Will," says Ned, "I guess it's a safe proposition."

We hauled up the feeder to Forestport and got us a load of potatoes. We raced him there against Charley Mack, the bank walker's, Leopard Pillar, one of them tufted breeds with a row of black buttons down the back. The Leopard was well liked and had won several races that season, and there was quite a few boaters around that fancied him. Pa argued for favorable odds, saying he was racing a maiden caterpillar; and there was a lot of money laid out, and Pa and Ned managed to cover the most of it. As for the race, there wasn't anything to it. While we was putting him in the ring—one of them birchbark and sweet-grass ones Indians make— Red Peril didn't act very good. I guess the smell and the crowd kind of upset him. He was nervous and kept fidgeting with his front feet; but they hadn't more'n lifted the ring than he lit out under the edge as tight as he could make it, and Pa touched him with the needle just as he lepped the line. Me and my sister was supposed to be in bed, but Ma had gone visiting in Forestport and we'd snuck in and was under the table, which had a red cloth onto it, and I can tell you there was some shouting. There was some couldn't believe that insect had been inside the ring at all; and there was some said he must be a cross with a dragon fly or a side-hill gouger; but old Charley Mack, that'd worked in the camps, said he guessed Red Peril must be descended from the caterpillars Paul Bunyan used to race. He said you could tell by the bump on his tail, which Paul used to put on all his caterpillars, seeing as how the smallest pointed object he could hold in his hand was a peavey.[1]

Well, Pa raced him a couple of more times and he won just as easy, and Pa cleared up close to a hundred dollars in three races. That caterpillar was a mammoth wonder, and word of him got going and people commenced talking him up everywhere, so it was hard to race him around these parts.

But about that time the lock keeper of Number One on the feeder come across a pretty swift

---

1 *peavey:* a lumberjack's tool having a hook and a metal spike at one end.

article that the people around Rome thought high of. And as our boat was headed down the gorge, word got ahead about Red Peril, and people began to look out for the race.

We come into Number One about four o'clock, and Pa tied up right there and went on shore with his box in his pocket and Red Peril inside the box. There must have been ten men crowded into the shanty, and as many more again outside looking in the windows and door. The lock tender was a skinny bezabor from Stittville, who thought he knew a lot about racing caterpillars; and, come to think of it, maybe he did. His name was Henry Buscerck, and he had a bad tooth in front he used to suck alot.

Well, him and Pa set their caterpillars on the table for the crowd to see, and I must say Buscerck's caterpillar was as handsome a brute as you could wish to look at, bright bay with black points and a short fine coat. He had a way of looking right and left, too, that made him handsome. But Pa didn't bother to look at him. Red Peril was a natural marvel, and he knew it.

Buscerck was a sly, twirpish man, and he must've heard about Red Peril—right from the beginning, as it turned out; for he laid out the course in yeller chalk. They used Pa's ring, a big silver one he'd bought secondhand just for Red Peril. They laid out a lot of money, and Dennison Smith lifted the ring. The way Red Peril histed himself out from under would raise a man's blood pressure twenty notches. I swear you could see the hair lay down on his back. Why, that black-pointed bay was left nowhere! It didn't seem like he moved. But Red Peril was just gathering himself for a fast finish over the line when he seen it was yeller. He reared right up; he must've thought it was butter, by Jeepers, the way he whirled on his hind legs and went the way he'd come. Pa begun to get scared, and he shook his needle behind Red Peril, but that caterpillar was more scared of butter than he ever was of cold steel. He passed the other insect afore he'd got halfway to the line. By Cripus, you'd ought to 've heard the cheering from the Forestport crews. The Rome men was green. But when he got to the line, danged if that caterpillar didn't shy agin and run around the circle twicet, and then it seemed like his heart had gone in on him, and he crept right back to the middle of the circle and lay there hiding his head. It was the pitifulest sight a man ever looked at. You could almost hear him moaning, and he shook all over.

I've never seen a man so riled as Pa was. The water was running out of his eyes. He picked up Red Peril and he says, "This here's no race." He picked up his money and he says, "The course was illegal, with that yeller chalk." Then he squashed the other caterpillar, which was just getting ready to cross the line, and he looks at Buscerck and says, "What're you going to do about that?"

Buscerck says, "I'm going to collect my money. My caterpillar would have beat."

"If you want to call that a finish you can," says Pa, pointing to the squashed bay one, "but a baby could see he's still got to reach the line. Red Peril got to wire and come back and got to it again afore your hayseed worm got half his feet on the ground. If it was any other man owned him," Pa says, "I'd feel sorry I squashed him."

He stepped out of the house, but Buscerck laid a-hold of his pants and says, "You got to pay, Hemstreet. A man can't get away with no such excuses in the city of Rome."

Pa didn't say nothing. He just hauled off and sunk his fist, and Buscerck come to inside the lock, which was at low level right then. He waded out the lower end and he says, "I'll have you arrested for this." Pa says, "All right; but if I ever catch you around this lock again I'll let you have a feel with your other eye."

Nobody else wanted to collect money from Pa, on account of his build, mostly, so we went back to the boat. Pa put Red Peril to bed for two days. It took him all of that to get over his fright at the yeller circle. Pa even made us go without butter for a spell, thinking Red Peril might know the smell of it. He was such an intelligent, thinking animal, a man couldn't tell nothing about him.

But next morning the sheriff comes aboard and arrests Pa with a warrant and takes him afore a justice of the peace. That was old Oscar Snipe. He'd heard all about the race, and I think he was feeling pleasant with Pa, because right off they commenced talking breeds. It would have gone off good only Pa'd been having a round with the sheriff. They come on arm in arm, singing a Hallelujah meeting song; but Pa was polite, and when Oscar says, "What's this?" he only says, "Well, well."

"I hear you've got a good caterpillar," says the judge.

"Well, well," says Pa. It was all he could think of to say.

"What breed is he?" says Oscar, taking a chew.

"Well," says Pa, "well, well."

Ned Kilbourne says he was a red one.

"That's a good breed." says Oscar, folding his hands on his stummick and spitting over his thumbs and between his knees and into the sandbox all in one spit. "I kind of fancy the yeller ones myself. You're a connesewer," he says to Pa, "and so'm I, and between connesewers I'd like to show you one. He's as neat a stepper as there is in this county."

"Well, well," says Pa, kind of cold around the eyes and looking at the lithograph of Mrs. Snipe done in a hair frame over the sink.

Oscar slews around and fetches a box out of his back pocket and shows us a sweet little yeller one.

"There she is," he says, and waits for praise.

"She was a good woman," Pa said after a while, looking at the picture, "if any woman that's four times a widow can be called such."

"Not her," says Oscar. "It's this yeller caterpillar."

Pa slung his eyes on the insect which Oscar was holding, and it seemed like he'd just got an idee.

"Fast?" he says, deep down. "That thing run! Why a snail with the stringhalt could spit in his eye."

Old Oscar come to a boil quick.

"Evidence. Bring me the evidence."

He spit, and he was that mad he let his whole chew get away from him without noticing. Buscerck says, "Here," and takes his hand off'n his right eye.

Pa never took no notice of nothing after that but the eye. It was the shiniest black onion I ever see on a man. Oscar says, "Forty dollars!" and Pa pays and says, "It's worth it."

But it don't never pay to make an enemy in horse racing or caterpillars, as you will see, after I've got around to telling you.

Well, we raced Red Peril nine times after that, all along the Big Ditch,[2] and you can hear to this day—yes, sir—that there never was a caterpillar alive could run like Red Peril. Pa got rich onto him. He allowed to buy a new team in the spring. If he could only've started a breed from that bug, his fortune would've been made and Henry Ford would've looked like a bent nickel alongside of me today. But caterpillars aren't built like Ford cars. We beat all the great caterpillars of the year, and it being a time for a late winter, there was some fast running. We raced the Buffalo Big Blue and Fenwick's Night Mail and Wilson's Joe of Barneveld. There wasn't one could touch Red Peril. It was close into October when a crowd got together and brought up the Black Arrer of Ava to race us, but Red Peril beat him by an inch. And after that there wasn't a caterpillar in the state

would race Pa's.

He was mighty chesty them days and had come to be quite a figger down the canawl. People come aboard to talk with him and admire Red Peril; and Pa got the idea of charging five cents a sight, and that made for more money even if there wasn't no more running for the animile. He commenced to get fat.

And then come the time that comes to all caterpillars. And it goes to show that a man ought to be as careful of his enemies as he is lending money to friends.

We was hauling down the Lansing Kill again and we'd just crossed the aqueduct over Stringer Brook when the lock keeper, that minded it and the lock just below, come out and says there was quite a lot of money being put up on a caterpillar they'd collected down in Rome.

Well, Pa went in and he got Red Peril and tried him out. He was fat and his stifles acted kind of stiff, but you could see with half an eye that he was still fast. His start was a mite slower, but he made great speed once he got going.

"He's not in the best shape in the world," Pa says, "and if it was any other bug I wouldn't want to run him. But I'll trust the old brute," and he commenced brushing him up with a toothbrush he'd bought a-purpose.

---

2 *Big Ditch:* the Erie Canal.

"Yeanh," says Ned. "It may not be right, but we've got to consider the public."

By what happened after, we might have known that we'd meet up with that caterpillar at Number One Lock; but there wasn't no sign of Buscerck, and Pa was so excited at racing Red Peril again that I doubt if he noticed where he was at all. He was all rigged out for the occasion. He had on a black hat and a new red boating waistcoat, and when he busted loose with his horn for the lock you'd have thought he wanted to wake up all the deef-and-dumbers in seven counties. We tied by the upper gates and left the team to graze; and there was quite a crowd on hand. About nine morning boats was tied along the towpath, and all the afternoon boats waited. People was hanging around, and when they heard Pa whanging his horn they let out a great cheer. He took off his hat to some of the ladies, and then he took Red Peril out of his pocket and everybody cheered some more.

"Who owns this here caterpillar I've been hearing about?" Pa asks. "Where is he? Why don't he bring out his pore contraption?"

A feller says he's in the shanty.

"What's his name?" says Pa.

"Martin Henry's running him. He's called the Horned Demon of Rome."

"Dinged if I ever thought to see him at my time of life," says Pa. And he goes in. Inside there was a lot of men talking and smoking and drinking and laying money faster than leghorns can lay eggs, and when Pa comes in they let out a great howdy, and when Pa put down the Brandreth box on the table they crowded round; and you'd ought to've heard the mammoth shout they give when Red Peril climbed out of his box. And well they might. Yes, sir!

You can tell that caterpillar's a thoroughbred. He's shining right down to the root of each hair. He's round, but he ain't too fat. He don't look as supple as he used to, but the folks can't tell that. He's got the winner's look, and he prances into the center of the ring with a kind of delicate canter that was as near single footing as I ever see a caterpillar get to. By Jeepers Cripus! I felt proud to be in the same family as him, and I wasn't only a little lad.

Pa waits for the admiration to die down, and he lays out his money, and he says to Martin Henry, "Let's see your ring-boned swivel-hocked imitation of a bug."

Martin answers, "Well, he ain't much to look at, maybe, but you'll be surprised to see how he can push along."

And he lays down the dangedest lump of worm you ever set your eyes on. It's the kind of insect a man might expect to see in France or one of them furrin lands. It's about two and a half inches long and stands only half a thumbnail at the shoulder. It's green and as hairless as a newborn egg, and it crouches down squinting around at Red Peril like a man with sweat in his eye. It ain't natural nor refined to look at such a bug, let alone race it.

When Pa seen it, he let out a shout and laughed. He couldn't talk from laughing.

But the crowd didn't say a lot, having more money on the race than ever was before or since on a similar occasion. It was so much that even Pa commenced to be serious. Well, they put 'em in the ring together and Red Peril kept over on his side with a sort of intelligent dislike. He was the brainiest article in the caterpillar line I ever knowed. The other one just hunkered down with a mean look in his eye.

Millard Thompson held the ring. He counted, "One—two—three—and off." Some folks said it was the highest he knew how to count, but he always got that far anyhow, even if it took quite a while for him to remember what figger to commence with.

The ring come off and Pa and Martin Henry sunk their needles—at least they almost sunk them, for just then them standing close to the course seen that Horned Demon sink his horns into the back end of Red Peril. He was always a sensitive animal, Red Peril was, and if a needle made him start you can think for yourself what them two horns did for him. He cleared twelve inches in one jump—but then he sot right down on his belly, trembling.

"Foul!" bellers Pa. "My 'pillar's fouled."

"It ain't in the rule book," Millard says.

"It's a foul!" yells Pa; and all the Forestport men yell, "Foul! Foul!"

But it wasn't allowed. The Horned Demon commenced walking to the circle—he couldn't move much faster than a barrel can roll uphill, but he was getting there. We all seen two things, then. Red Peril was dying, and he was losing the race. Pa stood there kind of foamy in his beard, and the water running right out of both eyes. It's an awful thing to see a big man cry in public. But Ned saved us. He seen Red Peril was dying, the way he wiggled, and he figgered, with the money he had on him, he'd make him win if he could.

He leans over and puts his nose into Red Peril's ear, and he shouts, "My Cripus, you've gone and dropped the butter!"

Something got into that caterpillar's brain, dying as he was, and he let out the smallest squeak of a hollering fright I ever listened to a caterpillar make. There was a convulsion got into him. He looked like a three-dollar mule with the wind colic, and then he gave a bound. My holy! How that caterpillar did rise up. When he come down again, he was stone dead, but he lay with his chin across the line. He'd won the race. The Horned Demon was blowing bad and only halfway to the line . . .

Well, we won. But I think Pa's heart was busted by the squeal he heard Red Peril make when he died. He couldn't abide Ned's face after that, though he knowed Ned had saved the day for him. But he put Red Peril's carcase in his pocket with the money and walks out.

And there he seen Buscerck standing at the sluices. Pa stood looking at him. The sheriff was alongside Buscerck and Oscar Snipe on the other side, and Buscerck guessed he had the law behind him.

"Who owns that Horned Demon?" says Pa.

"Me," says Buscerck with a sneer. "He may have lost, but he done a good job doing it."

Pa walks right up to him.

"I've got another forty dollars in my pocket," he says, and he connected sizably.

Buscerck's boots showed a minute. Pretty soon they let down the water and pulled him out. They had to roll a couple of gallons out of him afore they got a grunt. It served him right. He'd played foul. But the sheriff was worried, and he says to Oscar, "Had I ought to arrest Will?" (Meaning Pa.)

Oscar was a sporting man. He couldn't abide low dealing. He looks at Buscerck there, shaping his belly over the barrel, and he says, "Water never hurt a man. It keeps his hide from cracking." So they let Pa alone. I guess they didn't think it was safe to have a man in jail that would cry about a caterpillar. But then they hadn't lived alongside of Red Peril like us.

Understanding What You Read

1. Where did Pa find Red Peril?
   a. in a pet shop
   b. in his backyard
   c. along the road as the family was riding home from church

2. What did Red Peril dislike most?
   a. too much heat
   b. butter
   c. noise

3. How does Red Peril meet his end?

Writer's Workshop

1. This story is told in dialect—a regional variety of a language. Find at least five examples of spelling, grammar, or vocabulary that distinguish this dialect from the one you speak. For example, in the fourth paragraph, Edmonds describes the caterpillar as hitching itself up "like a man lifting on his galluses." **Galluses,** which are suspenders, is probably not a word in your working vocabulary.

2. Discuss whether dialect adds flavor and authenticity to a story or whether it simply makes for hard reading.

3. Would this story have been as effective if Pa had told it? Why or why not? Is there an advantage to showing the events through the eyes of the boy? If so, what is that advantage?

4. When people get caught up in a sport like horseracing or football, their unreasonable behavior often passes unnoticed. But when the sport is caterpillar racing, their bizarre behavior stands out. Walter D. Edmonds uses caterpillar racing to highlight the behavior of sports fans. (Remember, the word **fan** is a shortened form of the word **fanatic.**) You could use this same device to write a story in which you poke fun at the behavior of overly intense spectators. You might, for example, create a story around a Super Bowl for Scrabble players or the World Series of watermelon-seed spitting. Try to give your story, as Edmonds did, a regional flavor.

A Public Nuisance

Some people just won't be hurried.

You know the fellow,
I have no doubt,
Who stands and waggles
His club about.

Empires crumble   5
And crowns decay;
Kings and Communists
Pass away.

Dictators rise
And dictators fall—   10
But *still* he stands
Addressing his ball.

Understanding What You Read

1. Who is the target of this poem?

2. Is there a player like this in every sport? In other areas of life? Give examples.

Writer's Workshop

Finally, although the end of the world may be at hand, this golfer must swing. What happens then, after all the preparation? Using the rhythm and rhyme patterns of Arkell's poem, write four lines showing what you think happened next.

Ode to a Used Optic Yellow Wilson

Even a tennis ball has feelings.

From within pressurized can you came,
emblazoned with your famous name.
Fresh yellow fuzz, so firm of bounce,
compressed with power in every ounce.
Show the world that you've got class   5
upon all-weather, clay and grass.
Longing for distinguished honors
of playing a match with Jimmy Connors.
You're reconciled to weekend hackers,
tennis tyros, crazed ball whackers.   10
You've survived volleys at the net,
been slammed with joy at winning set.
Tossed up high and served the ace
or doublefaulted in disgrace.
You've made the rounds of country clubs,   15
were trounced by pros 6–love, 6–love.
And while not winning any cash,
you certainly had made a splash.
(A backhand sent you landing in
a half-full glass of someone's gin.)   20
But now your nap's begun to wear,
and balding felt commenced to tear.
You've felt the sting of many a racquet.
Too bad, it seems you just can't hack it.
Your cover's gone, your seams have split,   25
and so, I'm sorry, this is it.
Though once you thrilled to serve and smash,
today you go out with the trash.

Understanding What You Read

1. Is this a serious poem or a funny poem? How do you know?

2. Consider the effect of the rhymes. Do they add a solemn note or a humorous note? Explain.

Writer's Workshop

The writer of this poem addresses a tennis ball as though it were a person. List some of the personality traits this tennis ball has. Then, write a brief poem of your own in which you address an object connected with sports. It could be a hockey puck or a football jersey, a catcher's mitt or a soccer shoe. Be sure to endow the object with human personality traits.

One Down

The poet has the last word.

Weight distributed,
Free from strain,
Divot replaced,
Familiar terrain,
Straight left arm,   5
Unmoving head—
Here lies the golfer,
Cold and dead.

Understanding What You Read

1. Besides in a book, where else would you expect to find the lines of this poem? Explain.

2. The success of this poem depends on surprise. Only when you have reached the last line do you realize what the poem is about. Then the earlier lines take on a new meaning. Explain how the lines of this poem work on one level, describing a golfer at play, and at the same time on another level, describing a golfer who has putted his last.

Writer's Workshop

The epitaph represents a minor literary form. One of the most famous was written by John Keats:

Here lies one whose name was writ in water.

Here's another by William Butler Yeats:

Cast a cold eye
On life, on death.
Horseman, pass by!

Still another adds a humorous touch:

Here lie I, Martin Elginbrodde:
Hae mercy o' my soul, Lord God:
As I wad do, were I Lord God,
And ye were Martin Elginbrodde.

Look up the word **epitaph** in a dictionary to make sure you know what it means. Then write an epitaph for yourself. It doesn't have to be serious.

Pass, Punt, and Talk

For some, it's as thrilling as watching paint dry.

I went to a professional football game in Washington. It was remarkably restful, and the game was good and interesting to the very end. The visiting players, working for a company licensed in Cleveland, won by the football equivalent of a hair in the final minute.

Interesting curiosity: A minute in football bears no relationship to a minute in real life. A football minute lasts from 10 minutes up. Football's creation of the almost infinite minute makes the game longer that any game ought to be, except cricket. I allow the exception for cricket because the accompanying beverage for cricket is tea.

Football, however, apparently cannot be enjoyed without beer, and three to three and a half hours of beer is—well, a lot of beer unless you're a fiend for gassy-bloat. It's the rare game these days that doesn't go three hours.

The Washington game was such a rarity, ending slightly under three hours, but I put that down to the fact that I was in the stadium rather than by my parlor TV where the length of the average game makes Wagnerian opera feel like a preview of coming attractions.

What was striking about seeing a game in the arena, rather than on television, was its restful quality. After watching football on television, I always feel wrung out, irascible,[1] and guilty.

The guilt arises from a Calvinist[2] conscience reacting to the discovery that it is hanging out with a man who can waste a whole afternoon staring at a box when he could have been composing limericks, bagging leaves for mulch, or listening to Bach.

The wrung-out, irascible feeling results from television abuses aimed at keeping everybody's nerves stretched to the screaming point; to wit,

Batterings by beer and car commercials. Constant interruptions to

---

1 *irascible:* hot tempered.

2 *Calvinist:* loosely, a puritan; someone who feels guilty about having fun.

see a spectacular play in the far-away and utterly irrelevant and preposterously boring Seattle-Miami game. Cuts back to Football Headquarters for bulletins on the status of Big Running Back Buck Backbreaker's three crushed rotator cuffs. Endless "instant replays." Inexhaustibly uninformative chatterings of broadcasters chosen for their power to deny the viewer a moment's peace. (Unless you're lucky enough to catch a game broadcast by the incomparable John Madden–Pat Summerall team.)

At the stadium you enter another world. There is the calming beauty of the field, an expanse of brilliant green grass under a great vault of sky, which in Washington Sunday was full of furious black and gray clouds. Nature is present, as it never is on television. (Nor in stadiums encased under domes with fake-grass carpets for fields.)

Even in a good seat you are far away from action, and action seems surprisingly infrequent. From a seat high over the field, the players become small armored figures who periodically engage in brief bursts of violent activity. Most of the time, though, is passed in hundreds of conferences and consultations, as though some immensely complex negotiation were in progress.

The players assemble for confer-ences on the field. A half-dozen authority figures—"the officials"—confer constantly with one another, often with the players, occasionally with the battalions of coaches clustered at either side of the field.

These coaches confer incessantly among themselves, or with players who have come off the field, or by telephone headsets with unseen consultants posted at remote points around the arena.

Because television, working to create nervous breakdown, harps on metaphors of football as combat, it is startling to discover that, instead of a battlefield, the arena is actually like a more disorderly Geneva,[3] with dozens of talks almost constantly in progress.

The long talky pauses between bursts of action become restful after awhile. How lovely it is not having an instant replay of that key block. How peaceful not having to see the incredibly portentous[4] field goal that tied the absolutely vital clash in faraway Nevada between the Las Vegas High Rollers and the Akron Steel Belteds.

How sweet it is to see the players standing idly on the field with

---

3 *Geneva:* city in Switzerland, the site of many international conferences.

4 *portentous:* of exaggerated importance.

nothing to do but scratch themselves, and know that this is a "TV timeout," and that somewhere—but not here—millions are being psychologically jump-started to get out and buy beer, fast cars, snow tires, batteries . . .

What is this? The Washington team has lost? Ah well. They were probably out-talked in the conferences. Free from TV, one can find philosophical calm and recall what the philosopher Red Smith observed: It's only a game that boys can play.

Understanding What You Read

1. Is Russell Baker critical only of televised football or of stadium football as well? Explain your answer.

2. Instead of referring to the members of the Cleveland Browns football team, Baker calls them "players working for a company licensed in Cleveland." What is the difference? Instead of calling it **Astro-turf,** Baker refers to it as "fake-grass carpets." Again, what is the difference?

Writer's Workshop

Football is supposed to be an exciting game to watch. Yet Baker praises it as "remarkably restful." Select a sport that you feel is overrated—for its interest or level of skill—and write a humorous essay praising the sport for a characteristic not normally associated with it. You might even consider comparing the spectators at different sports events. For example, do baseball fans do a better job of singing the national anthem than hockey fans? The idea is to play up a feature of a sport not usually mentioned.

That's What Happened to Me

Even the wildest dream is better than loneliness and scorn.

I have done things and had things happen to me and nobody knows about it. So I am writing about it so that people will know. Although there are a lot of things I could tell about, I will just tell about the jumping because that is the most important. It gave me the biggest thrill. I mean high jumping, standing and running. You probably never heard of a standing high jumper but that's what I was. I was the greatest jumper ever was.

I was going to high school and I wasn't on any team. I couldn't be because I had to work for a drugstore and wash bottles and deliver medicine and sweep the floor. So I couldn't go out for any of the teams because the job started soon's school was over. I used to crab to the fellows about how old man Patch made me wash so many bottles and so they got to calling me Bottles Barton and I didn't like it. They'd call me Bottles in front of the girls and the girls'd giggle.

Once I poked one of the fellows for calling me Bottles. He was a big fellow and he played on the football team and I wouldn't have hit him because I was little and couldn't fight very well. But he called me Bottles before Anna Louise Daniels and she laughed and I was so mad I didn't know whether I wanted to hit her or the football player but finally I hit him. He caught my arm and threw me down and sat on me and pulled my nose.

"Look, Anna Louise," he said, "it stretches."

He pulled my nose again and Anna Louis put her arms around herself and jumped up and down and laughed and then I knew that it was her I should have taken the first poke at. I was more mad at her than the football player although it was him pulling my nose and sitting on me.

The next day I met Anna Louise in the hall going to ancient history class and she was with a couple of other girls and I tried to go past without them noticing me. I don't know why but I had a funny feeling like as if somebody was going to throw a rock at me or something. Anna Louise looked at me and giggled.

"Hello, old rubbernose," she said.

The girls giggled and I hurried down the hall and felt sick and mad and kind of like I was running away from a fight, although nobody'd expect me to fight a girl. And so they called me Bottles sometimes and Rubbernose other times and always whoever was near would laugh. They didn't think it was funny because Jimmy Wilkins was called Scrubby or Jack Harris was called Doodles. But they thought it was funny I was called Rubbernose and Bottles and they never got tired of laughing. It was a new joke every time.

Scrubby pitched for the baseball team and Doodles was quarterback of the football team.

I could have pitched for the baseball team or played quarterback on the football team. I could have pitched no-hit games and I could have made touchdowns from my own ten-yard line. I know I could. I had it all figured out. I went over how I'd throw the ball and how the batter'd miss and it was easy. I figured out how to run and dodge and straight-arm and that was easy too. But I didn't get

the chance because I had to go right to Patch's Drugstore after school was out.

Old man Patch was a pretty good guy but his wife, she was nothing but a crab. I'd wash bottles and old man Patch he would look at them and not say anything. But Mrs. Patch, old lady Patch, she would look at the bottles and wrinkle her nose and make me wash half of them over again. When I swept up at night she'd always find some corner I'd missed and she'd bawl me out. She was fat and her hair was all straggly and I wondered why in the deuce old man Patch ever married her, although I guess maybe she didn't look so awful when she was a girl. She couldn't have been very pretty though.

They lived in back of the drugstore and when people came in at noon or at six o'clock either old man or old lady Patch'd come out still chewing their food and look at the customer and swallow and then ask him what he wanted.

I studied salesmanship at high school and I figured this wasn't very good for business and I wanted to tell them but I never did.

One of the fellows at school was in waiting for a prescription and he saw me working at some of the things I did at the drugstore. So when another fellow asked me what I did this fellow he laughed and said, "Old Bottles! Why, he rates at that store. Yes he does! He rates like an Armenian's helper."

That's about the way I did rate but I was planning on how I'd someday own a real, modern drugstore and run the Patches out of business so I didn't mind so much.

What I did mind was Anna Louise at school. She was the daughter of a doctor and she thought she was big people and maybe she was but she wasn't any better'n me. Maybe my clothes weren't too good but that was only temporary. I planned on having twenty suits some day.

I wanted to go up to her and say, "Look here, Anna Louise, you're not so much. Your father isn't a millionaire and someday I'm going to be one. I'm going to have a million dollars and twenty suits of clothes." But I never did.

After she laughed at me and started calling me Rubbernose, I began planning on doing things to make her realize I wasn't what she thought I was. That's how the jumping came about.

It was the day before the track meet and everybody was talking about whether or not our school could win. They figured we'd have to win the high jump and pole vault to do it.

"Lord, if we only had old Heck Hansen back!" said Goobers Mac-Martin. "He'd outjump those Fairfield birds two inches in the high and a foot in the pole vault."

"Yeah," somebody else said, "but we haven't got Heck Hansen. What we got is pretty good but not good enough. Wish we had a jumper."

"We sure need one," I said.

There was a group of them all talking, boys and girls, and I was sort of on the outside listening.

"Who let you in?" Goobers asked me.

Frank Shay grabbed me by the arm and dragged me into the center of the circle.

"The very man we've been looking for," he said. "Yessir. Old Bottles Rubbernose Barton. He can win the jumping events for us."

"Come on, Bottles," they said. "Save the day for us. Be a good old Rubbernose."

Anna Louise was one who laughed the most and it was the third time I'd wanted to pop her on the nose.

I went away from there and didn't turn back when they laughed and called and whistled at me.

"She'd be surprised if I did," I said.

I kept thinking this over and pretty soon I said, "Well, maybe you could."

Then when I was sweeping the drugstore floor I all of a sudden said, "I can!"

"You can what?" Mrs. Patch asked me.

"Nothing," I said.

"You can hurry about sweeping the floor, that's what you can do," she said.

There was a big crowd out for the track meet and we were tied when I went up to our coach. It was just time for the jumping to start.

"What are you doing in a track suit?" he asked me.

"I'm going to save the day for Brinkley," I said. "I'm going to jump."

"No, you aren't," he said. "You run along and start a marble game with some other kid."

I looked him in the eye and I spoke in a cold, level tone of voice.

"Mr. Smith," I said, "the track meet depends on the high jump and the pole vault and unless I am entered, we will lose those two events and the meet. I can win and I am willing to do it for Brink-ley. Do you want to win the meet?"

He looked amazed.

"Where have you been all the time?" he asked. "You talk like you've got something on the ball."

I didn't say anything, I just smiled.

The crowd all rushed over to the jumping pits and I took my time going over. When everybody had jumped but me the coach turned and said, "Come on now, Barton, let's see what you can do."

"Not yet," I said.

"What do you mean?" he asked.

"I'll wait until the last man has been eliminated," I said. "Then I'll jump."

The crowd laughed but I just stared coldly at them. The coach tried to persuade me to jump but I wouldn't change my mind.

"I stake everything on one jump," I said. "Have faith in me."

He looked at me and shook his head and said, "Have it your own way."

They started the bar a little over four feet and pretty soon it was creeping up toward five feet and a half. That's always been a pretty good distance for high school jumpers. When the bar reached five feet seven inches all our men except one was eliminated. Two from Fairfield were still in the event. They put the bar at five feet nine inches and one man from Fairfield made it. Our man tried hard but he scraped the bar and knocked it off.

The crowd started yelling, thinking Fairfield had won the event.

"Wait a minute," I yelled. "I haven't jumped yet."

The judges looked at their lists and saw it was so. Maybe you think it was against the rules for them to allow me to skip my turn but anyway that's the way it was.

"You can't make that mark," one of the judges said. "Why try? You're not warmed up."

"Never mind," I said.

I walked up close to the jumping standard and stood there.

"Go ahead and jump," one of the judges said.

"I will," I said.

"Well, don't stand there," he said. "Come on back here so's you can get a run at it."

"I don't want any run at the bar," I said. "I'll jump from here."

The judge yelled at the coach and told him to take me out on account of I was crazy.

I swung my arms in back of me and sprung up and down a second and then I jumped over the bar with inches to spare. When I came down it was so silent I could hear my footsteps as I walked across the sawdust pit. The judge that'd crabbed at me just stood and looked. His eyes were bugged out and his mouth hung open.

"Good Lord!" he said. "Almighty most loving Lord!"

Our coach came up and he stood beside the judge and they both looked the same, bug-eyed.

"Did you see that?" the coach asked. "Tell me you didn't. Please do. I'd rather lose this track meet than my mind."

The judge turned slowly and looked at him.

"Good Lord!" he said, "there's two of us."

All of a sudden everybody started yelling and the fellows near me pounded me on the back and tried to shake my hand. I smiled and brushed them aside and walked over to the judge.

"What's the high school record for this state?" I asked.

"Five feet, eleven inches," he said.

"Put her at six," I said.

They put the bar at six and I gathered myself together and gave a heave and went over the bar like I was floating. It was easy. Well, that just knocked the wind out of everybody. They'd thought I couldn't do anything and there I'd broken the state record for the high jump without a running start.

The crowd surrounded me and tried to shake my hand and the coach and judge got off to one side and reached out and pinched each other's cheeks and looked at the bar and shook their heads. Frank Shay grabbed my hand and wrung it and said, "Gosh, Bottles, I was just kidding the other day. I didn't know you were such a ring-tailed wonder. Say, Bottles, we're having a dance tonight. Will you come?"

"You know what you can do with your frat," I said. "I don't

approve of them. They're undemo-cratic."

A lot of fellows that'd made fun of me before crowded around and acted as if I'd been their friend all along.

When Anna Louise crowded through the gang and said, "Oh, you're marvelous!" I just smiled at her and said, "Do you think so?" and walked away. She tagged around after me but I talked mostly with two other girls.

They didn't usually have a pub-lic address system at our track meets but they started using one then.

"Ladies and gentleman," the announcer said, "you have just wit-nessed a record-breaking perfor-mance by Bottles Barton————."

He went on like that telling them what an astonishing thing I'd done and it came to me I didn't mind being called Bottles any more. In fact, I kind of liked it.

Mr. and Mrs. Patch came up and Mrs. Patch tried to kiss me but I wouldn't let her. Old man Patch shook my hand.

"You've made our drugstore famous," he said. "From now on you're a clerk. No more bottle washing."

"We'll make him a partner," old lady Patch said.

"No, you won't," I said. "I think I'll go over to the McManus Phar-macy."

Then they called the pole vault and I did like I'd done before. I wouldn't jump until our men'd been eliminated. The bar was at eleven feet.

"It's your turn," our coach told me. "Ever use a pole before?"

"Oh, sure," I told him.

He gave me a pole and the crowd cleared away and grew silent. Everyone was watching me.

I threw the pole down and smiled at the crowd. The coach yelled for me to pick up the pole and jump. I picked it up and threw it ten feet away from me. Every-body gasped. Then I took a short run and went over the bar at eleven feet. It was simple.

This time the coach and the judge took pins and poked them in one another's cheeks. The coach grabbed me and said, "When I wake up I'm going to be so mad at you I'm gonna give you the beat-ing of your life."

Anna Louise came up and held my arm and said, "Oh, Bottles, you're so wonderful! I've always thought so. Please forgive me for calling you Rubbernose. I want you to come to our party tonight."

"All right," I said. "I'll forgive you but don't you call me Rubber-nose again."

They moved the bar up again and the fellow from Fairfield couldn't make it. I took a short run and went over. I did it so easy it came to me I could fly if I wanted to but I decided not to try it on account of people wouldn't think it so wonderful if a fellow that could fly jumped eleven feet without a pole. I'd won the track meet for Brinkley High and the students all came down out of the stand and put me on their shoulders and paraded me around and around the track. A lot of fellows were waving papers at me asking me to sign them and get $1,000 a week as a professional jumper. I signed one which threw in an automobile.

That's what I did once and nobody knows about it, so I am writing about it so people will know.

Understanding What You Read

1. Is this an accurate account of a young man's sports exploits in high school? What makes you think so?

2. Are there realistic touches—events, responses—in this story? Find one and explain what makes it true-to-life.

3. Is there a point to this story? If you think so, what is it?

. . . .

Writer's Workshop

Some say that most creative writing is simply wish fulfillment—that is, the writer converts his or her daydreams into a kind of reality by putting them down on paper. Clearly, Michael Fessier, the writer of this story, seems aware of this tendency. But Fessier pokes fun at writers who do this.

Use a daydream of your own to create a story. Imagine yourself as the hero. Add some realistic touches, as Fessier has done, but exaggerate in a humorous way. Before you begin, you might like to read James Thurber's famous story, "The Secret Life of Walter Mitty."

CHAPTER SIX

A Valedictory: To Those in the Arena

A final question comes down to this—What is the purpose of sports? Is it to train physically talented people to excel? Is it to provide entertainment for mass audiences? Is it to make money for team owners and promoters? Is it to offer programs of physical development for the young?

Obviously, all of these purposes are active in both professional and amateur sports. But which is most important? And which, least important? In a 1961 speech at the annual banquet of the National Football Hall of Fame, President John F. Kennedy outlined the answers as he saw them. As you read his speech, think about these questions yourself. Think about what you have read in this book. See whether you agree with President Kennedy or whether you have a different idea of the role of sports in American society.

The Importance of Participation

Even if you never made the first team, you can still be President of the United States

Mr. LaRoche, Ladies, and Gentlemen:

I want to express my thanks to you for this award. Politics is an astonishing profession—it has permitted me to go from being an obscure lieutenant serving under General MacArthur to Commander in Chief in fourteen years, without any technical competence whatsoever; and it's also enabled me to go from being an obscure member of the junior varsity at Harvard to being an honorary member of the Football Hall of Fame.

Actually, there are not so many differences between politics and football. Some Republicans have been unkind enough to suggest that my election, which was somewhat close, was somewhat similar to the Notre Dame-Syracuse game. But I'm like Notre Dame; we just take it as it comes and we're not giving it back.

I'm proud to be here tonight. I think General MacArthur, when he was Superintendent, really spoke about football in the classic way, because on so many occasions, in war and peace, I have seen so many men who participated in this sport—some celebrated and some obscure—who did demonstrate that the seeds had been well sown.

I am delighted to be here tonight and participating with you. This is a great American game. It has given me, personally, some of the most pleasant moments of my life—from last Saturday when I had a chance to see the Army-Navy game to a Harvard-Yale game I saw forty years before.

And I'm also glad to be here tonight with some men who also gave me some of the most exciting moments of my life. Clint Frank, who I understand is sitting down there, whom I saw score five touchdowns against Princeton. Tom Harmon who scored 21 points on my twenty-first birthday in the first half of a game against California. Cliff Battles who made George Marshall look good at Boston way back in the thirties.

And Jay Berwanger who's here tonight, who, when Chicago was tenth in the Big Ten, was on everyone's All-American. And Sam Huff, who campaigned with me through the coal mines of West Virginia—and he's even better at that than he is on Sunday.

So I'm like a good many other Americans who never quite made it—but love it.

I do see a close relationship between sports and our national life and I sometimes wonder whether those of us who love sports have done as much as we should in maintaining sports as a constructive part of this country's existence.

I will not enter into a debate about whether football or baseball is our national sport. The sad fact is that it looks more and more as if our national sport is not playing at all—but watching. We have become more and more not a nation of athletes but a nation of spectators.

Professional athletes—professional athletics—I believe has a great place in our national life, but I must confess that I view the growing emphasis on professionalism and specialization in amateur sports without great enthusiasm. Gibbon[1] wrote two centuries ago that professionalism in amateur sports was one of the early evidences of the decline and fall of the Roman Empire.

Football today is far too much a sport for the few who can play it well. The rest of us—and too many of our children—get our exercise from climbing up to seats in stadiums, or from walking across the room to turn on our television sets. And this is true for one sport after another, all across the board.

The result of this shift from participation to, if I may use the word "spectation," is all too visible in the physical condition of our population.

Despite our much-publicized emphasis on school athletics, our own children lag behind European children in physical fitness. And astonishingly enough, when Dr. Kraus and Dr. Weber recently went back, after ten years, to Europe they found a sharp decline in the physical fitness of European children, because in the last decade mechanization had begun to get at them too.

It's no wonder that we have such a high proportion of rejections for physical reasons in our Selective Service.[2] A short time ago

---

1 *Gibbon:* Edward Gibbon (1737–1794), English historian and the author of *The History of the Decline and Fall of the Roman Empire.*

2 *Selective Service:* U.S. government agency responsible for drafting men into military service.

General Hershey told me that since October of 1948, of some six million young men examined for military duty, more than a million were rejected as physically unfit for military service. A good many of these men would not have been rejected if they had had an opportunity, when younger, to take part in an adequate physical development program.

To get two men today, the United States Army must call seven men. Of the five rejected, three are turned down for physical reasons and two for mental disabilities. To get the 196,000 additional men that we needed for Berlin, the government had to call up, therefore, 750,000 men—and the rejection rate is increasing each year.

I find this situation disturbing. We are underexercised as a nation. We look, instead of play. We ride, instead of walk. Our existence deprives us of the minimum of physical activity essential for healthy living. And the remedy, in my judgment, lies in one direction; that is, in developing programs for broad participation in exercise by all of our young men and women—all of our boys and girls.

I do not say this in order to decry excellence in sports or anywhere else. But excellence emerges from mass participation. This is shown by the fact that in some areas of our Olympic Games, we have steadily fallen behind those nations who have stressed broad participation in a great variety of sports.

I believe that as a nation we should give our full support, for example, to our Olympic development program. We will not subsidize our athletes as some nations do, but we should as a country set a goal, not in the way the Soviet Union or the Chinese do, but in the kind of way that Australia and other countries do—perhaps in our own way, to emphasize this most important part of life, the opportunity to exercise, to participate in physical activity, and generally to produce a standard of excellence for our country which will enable our athletes to win the Olympics—but more importantly than that, which will give us a nation of vigorous men and women.

There are more important goals than winning contests, and that is to improve on a broad level the health and vitality of all of our people.

We have begun this year to make progress toward this goal with the new President's Council on Youth Fitness. The idea behind our youth fitness program is to give as many American boys and girls as possible a chance for a healthy physical development.

Coach Bud Wilkinson and the

council staff, in cooperation with the nation's leading educators and medical organizations, have worked out a basic physical fitness program for our elementary and secondary schools. Pilot projects have been set up in a number of cities.

The results so far show the effectiveness of what can be done and the extent of the need. In Muskogee, Oklahoma, for example, a city which prides itself on athletic achievement, which has had seven All-Americans in recent years, forty-seven percent of the students failed a minimum physical fitness test. Only a fraction of those who qualified could pass the more comprehensive test of physical capability. Yet only six weeks of participation in a daily fifteen-minute program of vigorous exercise brought about a twenty-four percent improvement among those who failed the first test.

Throughout the country we have found equally discouraging examples of deficiencies—and equally encouraging examples of progress. I hope that every school district in this country will adopt our minimum program. I urge every parent to support the program and his own children's participation in it. I urge our colleges and universities to lay down basic standards of physical fitness. I urge the nation's community recreation centers to provide more opportunity for those who are no longer attending school. And finally, I urge organizations such as this, with all of the prestige and influence which you bring to American life, to help establish more programs for participation by American boys and girls—by Americans young and old. In short, what we must do is literally change the physical habits of millions of Americans—and that is far more difficult than changing their tastes, their fashions, or even their politics.

I do not suggest that physical development is the central object of life, or that we should permit cultural and intellectual values to be diminished, but I do suggest that physical health and vitality constitute an essential element of a vigorous American community.

No one knew this better that the men of Greece, to whom our civilization owes so much. The Greeks sought excellence not only in philosophy and drama and sculpture and architecture, but in athletics. The same people who produced the poetry of Homer, the wisdom of Plato and Aristotle—they also produced the Olympic Games. The Greeks understood that mind and body must develop in harmonious proportion to produce a creative intelligence. And so did the most brilliant intelligence of our earliest days, Thomas Jefferson, when he said, "Not less than two hours a day should be devoted to exercise." If a man who wrote the Declaration of Indepen-dence, was secretary of state, and twice president could give it two hours, our children can give it ten or fifteen minutes.

There's no reason in the world—and we've seen it tonight—why Americans should not be fine students and fine athletes. When I was young, Barry Wood used to play with Ben Ticknor football for Harvard—and hockey and baseball and tennis. He was a ten-letter man—and also the First Marshal of Phi Beta Kappa. And since then he has combined a life of leadership in the medical profession.

I have in Washington, as you know—and he is a friend of many of you—the Deputy Attorney General, Byron White, who was simultaneously a Rhodes scholar and a halfback for the Detroit Lions, and the year that he led the league in ground gained rushing, was also number one man in his class at the Yale Law School. We can combine and must combine intellectual energy and physical vitality.

Theodore Roosevelt once said, "The credit belongs to the man who is actually in the arena—whose face is marred by dust and sweat and blood . . . who knows the great enthusiasms, the great devotions—and spends himself in a worthy cause—who at best if he wins knows the thrills of high achievement—and if he fails at least fails while daring greatly—so that his place shall never be with those cold and timid souls who know neither victory nor defeat."

The athletes in this room—you gentlemen—and your colleagues across the country have known victory and defeat, and have accepted both. I salute you.

Understanding What You Read

1. Which of the following statements best sums up the meaning of John Kennedy's speech?
   a. Sports belongs exclusively to those who have outstanding physical abilities.
   b. Sports is a waste of time compared to developing the mind.
   c. Participation in sports is essential for the healthy development of everyone in society.
   d. Americans are way ahead of the rest of the world in subsidizing athletic teams.

2. John Kennedy says that too many young Americans get their only exercise "from walking across the room to turn on our television sets." How do you think John Kennedy would feel about remote control devices?

3. Some athletes have been rejected for military service because of the injuries they have sustained playing sports. How does this square with John Kennedy's assertion that participation in sports promotes the physical well-being of citizens?

Writer's Workshop

Since President Kennedy's time, sports have grown even more competitive. Young people trying out for teams frequently have samples of their muscle tissue analyzed to determine whether they have sufficient potential. And some athletes have used steroids to enhance their abilities.

Write an essay of 200 to 400 words describing some of the changes that have taken place in sports since 1961. Tell whether you feel this nation is closer to or farther away from John Kennedy's ideal of "programs for broad participation in exercise by all of our young men and women."

Index of Authors and Titles